TRANSFORMATION & TROUBLE

Transformation & Trouble

CRIME, JUSTICE, AND PARTICIPATION IN DEMOCRATIC SOUTH AFRICA

Diana R. Gordon

The University of Michigan Press
Ann Arbor

Copyright © by the University of Michigan 2006
All rights reserved
Published in the United States of America by
The University of Michigan Press
Manufactured in the United States of America
♾ Printed on acid-free paper

2011 2010 2009 2008   5 4 3 2

No part of this publication may be reproduced, stored in a retrieval system, or transmitted in any form or by any means, electronic, mechanical, or otherwise, without the written permission of the publisher.

A CIP catalog record for this book is available from the British Library.

Library of Congress Cataloging-in-Publication Data

Gordon, Diana R.
    Transformation and trouble : crime, justice, and participation in democratic South Africa / Diana R. Gordon.
      p.   cm.
    Includes bibliographical references and index.
    ISBN-13: 978-0-472-09914-6 (cloth : alk. paper)
    ISBN-10: 0-472-09914-0 (cloth : alk. paper)
    ISBN-13: 978-0-472-06914-9 (pbk. : alk. paper)
    ISBN-10: 0-472-06914-4 (pbk. : alk. paper)
    1. Criminal justice, Administration of—South Africa.   2. South Africa—Ethnic relations.   3. Democracy—South Africa.   I. Title.

HV9960.S6G67   2006
364.968—dc22   2005024416

To Gail Gerhart & Tom Karis

Contents

	Preface	ix
	List of Abbreviations	xv
1.	Introduction: Two Paradigms and a Program	1

I. FROM RACIAL ENFORCEMENT TO POST-APARTHEID CRIME

2.	Pre-apartheid Justice: Versatile Instrument of Repression	23
3.	Apartheid Justice: A Contradiction in Terms	50
4.	Bitter Fruit from Poison Seeds	83

II. SHIFTING THE CONSTITUENCY: THEORY AND PRACTICE

5.	Elements of Liberal Justice in a New Democracy	113
6.	Protection, Integrity, and Rights: South Africa's Achievements	137

III. DEEPENING DEMOCRACY THROUGH SOCIAL ORDERING: THEORY AND PRACTICE

7.	Public-Empowering Justice: Resource for a New Democracy	179
8.	Participation Thwarted: South African Failures	214

IV. POST-POST-APARTHEID CHALLENGES

9.	Wielding the Big Stick	249
10.	Democratic Justice and the Competent Citizen	273
	Notes	287
	Bibliography	327
	Index	351

Preface

How much can be expected of criminal justice systems in countries making the transition from authoritarian rule to democracy? What credence can be given to vows of accountability, transparency, participation, and equal representation in criminal justice as free and fair elections usher in determinedly democratic regimes? How are obstacles to realizing these aspirations—resource constraints, political differences, habits of the past—overcome; or do they defeat even the best intentions of reformers? Given that democratization is a continuing process, what does a democratized justice system look like, anyway? Are there some universal features; or are cultural divides—of East and West, North and South, traditional and modern—and the economic chasms between postindustrial countries and developing ones unbridgeable? These are questions that drew me to study South African efforts to transform the country's police and courts after apartheid.

For a quarter of a century I have written about the politics of criminal justice in the United States, always with a nagging concern that my reformist critiques of domestic policy lacked a bedrock understanding of how and whether criminal justice could live up to *any* realistic set of democratic ideals. Neither political scientists nor criminologists have successfully adumbrated, in my view, how the state can further the human dignity and emancipation that is the largest aim of a democratic system through its criminal justice practices. Although liberal democracies profess to protect their citizens against arbitrary surveillance, arrest, prosecution, and confinement—and some live up to this ideal with commendable consistency—no country that I knew of when I started thinking about this problem in the 1970s had fashioned its political system with the affirmative object of building criminal justice institutions that reflected democratic aims. So when dawn broke over the new era in South Africa—when President F. W. de Klerk unbanned the African National Congress in February 1990 (it had been an illegal organization for the previous thirty years); when Nelson Mandela walked free of twenty-seven years of confinement a few days later; when South Africa's whites voted in a 1992 referendum to continue negotiations that would lead to majority rule; when it was finally possible to believe that the blood of the those who had resisted apartheid had not been shed in vain—I thought the country's planned reforms of criminal justice presented a natural experiment from which I could learn. For South Africa the present was truly the beginning of the future, with a set of democratic ambitions that detached it decisively from the past.

Conditions for thoroughgoing reform seemed auspicious. The rhetoric was heartfelt, and the world was watching to see if it was matched with action. As a police official—one of the "clean" middle-management Afrikaners who welcomed democratic transition—said to me on my first research trip in early 1994, "We don't have any choice but to get it right." I set out to see how police and courts would approach that challenge and whether the new government would support a program that protected its citizens—all of them, not just the affluent minority—and encouraged equitable resolution of their social conflicts.

My book presents a mixed picture of progress a decade later. Despite occasional painful lapses, liberal institutions that respect the citizenry, foster integrity, and protect rights operate with reasonable consistency and seem likely to endure. The Western ideal of a rule of law that constrains police, courts, and executive zeal is intact. The early vision of a more open, participatory, pluralistic justice system has, however, been scrapped, and the formalities of constitutional protection reach far too few people. Furthermore, the new regime has heeded the siren song of punitive policy directions adopted in the United States (and, to a lesser extent, in some other Western countries), retreating to a distressing degree from the rights orientation it initially embraced.

I think I have concluded, with Michel Foucault, that truly popular justice—the grassroots initiative that can right wrongs, monitor police and courts, and foster consensus and reconciliation—is inevitably compromised by state intervention that imposes forms and practices necessary for modern (and crime-ridden) countries. (Foucault thought that the court, with its contending parties and an umpire, was a "particularly disastrous model for the clarification and political development of popular justice.")[1] However, I continue to believe in deliberative democracy and in its potential to make modest inroads into relations of power in both fledgling and mature democracies. Participatory, public-empowering mechanisms tolerated (and even funded) by the state but independent of it in most respects can and should flourish—along with fair and competent professionals—in democratizing countries; and civil society must prick the state's conscience with challenges to its policies and to its overall domination in the maintenance of order. Whether any pressure exerted by responsible citizens and professionals on government can significantly address the structural causes of crime is open to question.

During the period covered by this book there have been important efforts to remedy prison conditions. The corrections bureaucracy was demilitarized, and its employees became civil servants. The South African constitution provides for "conditions of detention that are consistent with human dignity," and the courts have fleshed out that principle by finding a prisoner's right to vote and to be treated for HIV and AIDS.[2] A judicial inspectorate monitors prison conditions, and citizens will have input into future parole decisions. But democratizing the prisons has proved at least as great a challenge as democratizing police and courts; a current analysis concludes that delay in implementing the progressive Correctional Services Act of 1998 "suggests that neither prisoners' rights nor public participation are high priorities."[3] I decided early in this project that I could not do justice to the special issues that prison reform in South Africa presents. I also think that corrections is to some extent the tail of the dog; if police and courts were democratized in ways envisioned by the early reformers, reform of some aspects of prison life and administration would follow.

I sometimes agonize over how long it has taken me to write this book—perhaps five years of thinking about it and another three to write it. Dirk van Zyl Smit, a thoughtful and distinguished South African criminologist, has, however, explained the struggle to my satisfaction: of the promise of criminal justice reform in democratic South Africa he writes, "Working out the logical implications of these primarily individual and defensive rights in the wider context of a constitution that also seeks to guarantee some social and economic rights, as well as rights of democratic participation, is a major and fascinating intellectual task."[4] I say amen to that.

Many people have helped beyond any reasonable expectation. Some were correspondents, who advised me from all corners of the world, often by the magical (if often pesky) medium of e-mail. Alice Hills helped me think about how police in South Africa might be different from those in other democratizing countries in sub-Saharan Africa; Steven Gelb helped me understand the government's shifting perspectives on criminal justice in the context of South Africa's post-apartheid foreign policy. Adrian Louw gave me the perspective of the thoughtful but frustrated white citizen confronted with high crime levels in post-apartheid society. Ineke van Kessel and Monique Marks sent me papers on the difficulties of transformation for the police that fill a real lacuna in the literature. Neil Boister shared his knowledge of the importation of U.S. policies abroad. Patrick Bond exposed me to the dark side of some of South Africa's economic choices. Ted Leggett and Anton du Plessis answered innumerable data questions. Francois Botha's wit and wisdom has given me much more than just his impressive expertise on the magistracy. John Cartwright supplied me with an insider's view of the Community Peace Programme operating in Western Cape and Eastern Cape. Keith Gottschalk patiently answered never-ending e-mail inquiries about what was going on in South Africa when I was nine thousand miles away.

Colleagues in South Africa and New York have shared information and given me invaluable advice along the way, among them Wilfried Schärf, Dirk van Zyl Smit, Janine Rauch, Jonny Steinberg, Louise Stack, Jeremy Seekings, Cheryl Frank, David Greenberg, Jim Levine, Todd Clear, John Harbeson, Ned Schneier, and Steve Ellmann. Penny Andrews, Gail Gerhart, Richard Goldstone, Andrew Lawrence, Velile Notshulwana, Jeremy Seekings, Nicoli Nattrass, Martin Schönteich, and Steve Kahanovitz read chapters and gave me useful comments. Michael Keating was my kindly but critical editor at home and told me when to stop. Barbara Swartz was the invaluable friend who put up with my hand-wringing and assured me that I would finish the book. Sinead Coleman and Sandrine Dikambi provided invaluable research and administrative assistance. I have been lucky to have financial support from the Research Foundation of the City University of New York and to be welcomed with office space at various times by the Centre for Policy Studies in Johannesburg, the Institute of Criminology of the University of Cape Town, and the Human Sciences Research Council in Pretoria.

Working in a foreign country becomes much easier when you have friends there. I must thank Lael Bethlehem, Emilia Podesta, David Unterhalter, Helet and Chris Merkling, Nicoli Nattrass, Jeremy Seekings, Michael Osborne, Verna and Bev Gower, Mynda and Tony Mansfield, Morley and Joanna Nkosi—and especially Gail Gerhart and the late John Gerhart, as well as Myrna Kaplan—for providing hospitality and encouragement on many South African visits. I am most grateful to Tuntufye Mwamwenda for welcoming me to Umtata and to Given Mkhari for giving me a glimpse of the struggles of young Africans to assume positions of significance in post-apartheid South Africa. David A. Gordon, a South African advocate (the term for a senior trial lawyer), stirred my initial interest in South Africa forty years ago and made it politically and financially possible for me to make my first trip in 1991 to see how the country was changing.

Finally, my interviewees—too numerous to mention individually—were uniformly thoughtful and ready to share their experiences. Very busy people paused in building their new society to guide me—judges and magistrates, local and national police officials, people in research institutes or grassroots groups, community activists and lay assessors. I especially learned from the staff of the Centre for the Study of Violence and Reconciliation and the Institute for Security Studies. And I must mention with sadness one person who gave me three lengthy interviews of uncommon intelligence and usefulness—Mduduzi Mashiyane, a talented organizer who died much too soon in July 2002.

My greatest debt is expressed in the dedication. Gail Gerhart and Tom Karis have contributed immeasurably to the English-speaking world's understanding of South African struggles for freedom and equality through their multivolume documentary history of African politics in South Africa, *From Protest to Challenge.* To me they gave generously of their knowledge and served as exemplars of the observer who sheds light on a country not his or her own.

Terminology when referring to the various racial and ethnic groups that have created South Africa's history can be confusing, even to residents of the country. *Black,* for example, is sometimes used to refer to Africans and sometimes to all those who are not white, that is, Africans, coloureds (mixed-race people), and Indians. The problem is compounded when discussing the past, as a number of terms used for centuries are no longer appropriate or accurate *(Hottentots,* for example, when referring to people whom anthropologists more correctly call *Khoikhoi).*

In this book the indigenous people found by white settlers in the Cape, who later mixed with whites and Asians, will be called *Khoikhoi* in historical discussions and *Coloured* in modern ones. Nguni-speaking people (also called Bantu-speaking in much of the historical literature) will either be identified by their particular ethnicity (e.g., Xhosa, Zulu, Swazi) or, more generally, as Africans. I will use *black* as a collective identification for all groups who are not of European origin. *Dutch* will refer to the original white settlers and the Dutch East India Company officials who led them; their descendants will be called *Boers* in the days when they were striking out on their own, leaving the Cape Colony to develop the territory to the north and east, and *Afrikaners* as they came into the towns and formed their own governments. *British* will refer to the immediate colonizers—the Parliament in England that set policy and the officials who came to South Africa to carry it out—while *English* will designate South Africans whose ancestors came from the United Kingdom and whose primary language is English.

Finally, when referring to contemporary white residents of South Africa, I will follow the lead of G. H. L. Le May, who says in a preface to *The Afrikaners,* "I have tried to avoid the word 'European' which has often been used to distinguish between whites and nonwhites. It has always seemed to be inappropriate as a description of those who have left their European origins far in the past." And, of course, *nonwhite* suggests that the standard for all racial designations is whiteness, so I don't use that either. *Native* is used only in reference to particular laws or—in quotes—as designations of policy (e.g., "native problem"). *Tribe* is not used because it is not relevant after colonialism altered the sovereign status of traditional groups.

Abbreviations

ANC	African National Congress
CPF	Community Police Forum
CPP	Community Peace Programme
ICD	Independent Complaints Directorate
IMF	International Monetary Fund
JSC	Judicial Service Commission
PAC	Pan Africanist Congress
SADF	South African Defence Force
SANDF	South African National Defence Force (renamed SADF after apartheid ended)
SAP	South African Police
SAPS	South African Police Service (renamed SAP after apartheid ended)
TRC	Truth and Reconciliation Commission
UDF	United Democratic Front

1 Introduction
Two Paradigms and a Program

> The Constitution demands . . . that our society be transformed from the closed, repressive, racial oligarchy of the past, to an open and democratic society based on human dignity, equality and freedom.
> —Arthur Chaskalson, chief justice of South Africa[1]

THE TRIUMPH OF South Africa's rejection of apartheid and embrace of nonracial democracy is often described—by both South Africans and outsiders—as a miracle. The titles of an explosion of post-apartheid celebrations say it all: *Anatomy of a Miracle, Beyond the Miracle, Small Miracle.*[2] This view casts the repeal of unjust laws, the avoidance of war, the negotiated settlement (by no means inevitable), and the free and fair election of April 27, 1994, as events without history and unexplainable by means other than divine intervention. On the surface, that is not surprising. Accomplishing such a definitive transition without outright revolution or foreign occupation or peacekeeping forces is rare in the violent annals of twentieth-century coups and collapses in sub-Saharan Africa. And the political results seem in some ways blessed: the new regime enjoys broad legitimacy; opposition parties are tolerated and represented in national and local government; and the constitution, with its embrace of rights that have been denied to most of the country's people for most of its history, enjoys great respect around the world.

But draping the mantle of the miraculous over the democratic transition neglects both the struggles that brought it about and the dilemmas it still confronts. A haze of beatification obscures the commitment and the agony of those who fought to bring about the transition (and often sacrificed their lives or their livelihoods to do so) in the Defiance Campaign of 1952, the Soweto revolt of 1976, the urban strikes of the 1980s, and the resistance of township residents to the government's repeated efforts at military occupation. It also overlooks the labor of those who began, in South Africa's churches and prisons and universities and civic associations (and in exile in other lands), to dream of and plan for a democratic South Africa decades before it was born.

Finally, the mutual congratulations of winners and losers in a war that never happened disguise the limits to what political liberation alone can do. Casting off the carapace of apartheid did not usher in a new world of freedom from want and pain. Nadine Gordimer, reflecting on the triumphant voting day in 1994, noted, "The law places the ground of equality underfoot; it did not feed the hungry or put up a roof over the head of the homeless, today, but it changed the base on which South African society was for so long built."[3] The base has indeed changed, and the changes are profound and permanent. But in the decade since Gordimer and Nelson Mandela, along with 19.5 million other South Africans, dropped their vote into the ballot box the promise of full citizenship, with the means to exercise and enjoy the hard-won political freedoms, has seemed elusive. For many South Africans—certainly a majority of the population—the shift from one kind of government to another has meant very little material betterment. Fewer than half of South Africans surveyed in 2002 said that the democratic government was better at delivering services than the apartheid government.[4] AIDS and violence have cut down too many of the country's new citizens and substituted new conflicts for the repressions of apartheid. A fragmented society with persistent poverty, inequality, crime, ignorance, and disease needs more than the momentary relief provided by a miracle.

Transformation is the preferred and overarching word that South Africans use for what is needed to make their country the vibrant, nonracial democracy they yearn for. Interpreted narrowly, transformation is merely the shifting of political and economic power from the white minority (9.3 percent of the population as of a May 2005 estimate) to the black majority.[5] Frustrated whites often complain that "transformation" is merely affirmative action, which is in turn a justification for substituting unqualified blacks for competent whites in jobs, legislative bodies, or university classrooms. And blacks—police, teachers, journalists—argue that because racial representation in their occupations still doesn't reflect the demographics of the society, transformation is lagging. But the broader and deeper meaning of transformation emerges in the constitutional context—not that the word is part of the text but that it embodies the spirit of that document's provisions for rights and powers, especially as they elevate the protection of dignity and equality.

This kind of transformation is a tall order. It presupposes that the hearts and minds of a deeply divided country can be united in a common purpose that will require enormous initiative from some and enormous sacrifice from others. It necessitates the development of a culture of rights through education and dialogue in a population where individual liberties are often either inimical or unknown. It demands commitment to definitions of equality that respect diverse cultural traditions without allowing them to impinge on individual autonomy. It assumes that the imperatives of participation in global markets and forums can be accommodated without neglect of local needs. It requires that political change and redistribution of the country's resources benefit not just an elite slice of the black majority. Transformation means universal access to jobs and education as well as the provision of adequate housing to the approximately 20 percent still living in shacks. It means access to flush or chemical toilets for all, a luxury to millions of South Africans. And, I will argue, the enterprise requires that a commitment to the reform of institutions providing social order—both formal criminal justice agencies and community efforts—cannot be deflected by obstacles of fiscal and social turmoil.

In Pursuit of Transformation

It could be said that planning for transformation long preceded apartheid, the ideology and practices of racial segregation and repression imposed by the National Party government starting in 1948.[6] Early resistance to colonial rule was aimed at recognition of Africans' interests and improvement in the conditions of their lives, although that challenge aimed at reform within the segregated system, rather than bringing about racial equality through its abolition. Demands for an expanded franchise and for legislative representation began as early as the 1880s; in the Cape Colony property-owning blacks with substantial incomes could vote by the mid–nineteenth century.[7] Fledgling African political organizations, emboldened by the defeat of the Boer republics in the South African War (1899–1902, previously called the Anglo-Boer War), pressed for protection under British law in 1902. The constitution of the African National Congress (ANC), founded in 1912, sought to bring together all tribes and clans to "defend their freedom, rights and privileges" through such actions as demands for an end to the color bar in education and industry.[8]

But it was the 1955 Freedom Charter, the document endorsed by a multiethnic Congress of the People (sponsored by the ANC and several other black organizations), that first articulated a vision of the South Africa that the country now reaches for. The bold preamble announced that "our people have been robbed of their birthright to land, liberty and peace" and called for "a democratic state, based on the will of the people."[9] Specific provisions embraced both Enlightenment ideals of liberal democracy—equal protection of the law, free speech and press, privacy, freedom to travel and to practice a chosen religion—and substantive rights to education, housing, land, and the fruits of labor. As Allister Sparks, a prominent South African journalist, has said of the Freedom Charter, "It is like a combination of [Martin Luther] King's dream and a political program."[10]

The National Party government saw that document as treasonous, Communist-inspired. Its promulgation, along with campaigns of passive resistance to unjust laws, led to the prosecution of many of the leaders of the liberation movement, including Nelson Mandela. Thirty years later, however, with the country in the grip of a national emergency imposed to quash resistance to apartheid, the Freedom Charter had become a kind of ghostly blueprint for the political system that progressive activists, scholars, and lawyers planned to erect in place of the increasingly despised and desperate state. Even as the government was detaining tens of thousands of people without benefit of court appearance, interrogating and torturing many of them, the banned ANC developed rights-oriented guidelines for a future constitution. South African academics and activists made study trips to other democracies to discuss their constitutional designs, gathering ideas and testing language in Germany, Canada, the United Kingdom, and the United States. By 1996—after the apartheid government's foot-dragging in negotiating the country's nonracial future, after the violence that divided the black parties and ethnic groups and threatened to derail full participation in the first democratic election, after public hearings on the final constitution held across the country and receipt of testimony and suggestions submitted by two million people—Thabo Mbeki, then ANC deputy president, could remind the world of the staying power of dreams of transformation. He hailed the adoption of the new constitution by the Constitutional Assembly on May 8, 1996, with the clarion call of the Freedom Charter: "South Africa belongs to all who live in it, black and white."[11]

Transformation and Criminal Justice

The long liberation struggle that mobilized the victims of apartheid inside the country and sympathizers around the world sought much more than procedural political change. As the activists recognized, democratization is not merely a matter of transferring political power, instituting formal requirements for broad participation in free and fair elections, and then living by those commitments. It is also a much larger modernist (and mostly Western) project of expanding moral and political communities by taking steps to enhance the dignity of various groups and acknowledging the legitimacy of their participation in the public sphere. So slaves were freed, women got the right to vote, and criminal defendants were no longer completely at the mercy of police and prosecutors.

The beacon of South African democracy identified particular institutions for immediate reform. Police and courts were among them, for many reasons. Criminal justice institutions are more than reflections of the state; they are emanations of its basic character. The core authority of the state—central power to guide and command—rests on its enforcement capabilities.¹² The regulation and defense of a modern society depends in part on policing and judging, whether they are carried out primarily through the state's highly structured and centralized legal proceedings or diffused with cooperative efforts of state and citizen and supplemented by private—sometimes very intimate and informal—rituals. At their most basic, these functions include the maintenance of order, however conceived, and representation of the regime. The legitimacy of a transition from authoritarian to democratic government is therefore measured in part by the extent to which police and courts, now infused to a significant degree with values of liberty and dignity, operate in service to the people rather than to the state.

At the practical level police had to be reformed simply because, along with the army and the prisons, they had been visible and brutal instruments of state repression. For forty years they were the face of apartheid encountered on a daily basis. (Planners of the new government were initially also worried that without major reform the police might join the military in a coup.)¹³ They maintained white domination by removing people from their land, controlling their movements, and quelling resistance with the extralegal brutality of beatings, killings, and torture. (During the Truth and Reconciliation hearings in the late 1990s witnesses revealed that police had bragged of saving as souvenirs the fingers of people they had killed.) The police were frontline enforcers of apartheid.¹⁴

The picture of apartheid courts is more complex. While some journalists and ANC leaders—and even the pacific Nelson Mandela—insisted that the legal system faced a fundamental legitimacy crisis, a 1990 poll suggested that almost as large a proportion of Africans as whites—a substantial majority—had a good deal of confidence in the legal system, despite the fact that magistrates and judges were overwhelmingly white and male.¹⁵ It is hard to know how to interpret these data since they do not disaggregate attitudes toward the judiciary specifically and because confidence was lower both before and after 1990; perhaps that year was a watershed attributable to the release of Mandela and the unbanning of the ANC. It may be that blacks did believe that courts were, to some extent, a bulwark against apartheid laws; the same poll showed greater confidence in the legal system than in parliament or the police.

But public attitudes are not the whole story. During the 1980s, internal security legislation gave police and judges expanded powers to arrest without warrant and to detain indefinitely (and often in solitary confinement) anyone who, in their view, threatened "the safety of the public or the maintenance of public order."¹⁶ As one former judge put it, "[H]uman rights do not flourish, but rather wither and die, when, on pain of criminal and other sanctions, a government enforces extraordinary rules at variance with a country's common law and in conflict with fundamental western norms, in order to regulate the lives and behavior of its citizens."[17] Despite doctrinal traditions that would have permitted judicial evasion of some repressive regulations issued pursuant to the states of emergency in the 1980s, South Africa's highest court never directly supported a single challenge to their validity.[18]

The task of reforming the administration of justice is not only particularly pressing; it is also particularly difficult. To begin with, police and courts are inherently repressive institutions—regimes create them, after all, to articulate and enforce rules—and are prized for their coercive powers.[19] In authoritarian countries these powers serve the political interests of the state rather than more neutral ideals of community protection. (Even in democracies the tendency to enact and enforce rules that benefit favored classes crops up with troubling frequency.) Altering this pattern is not a simple matter of sending out new directives, particularly where it is not practical to staff law enforcement and the judiciary with new recruits, as was the case in South Africa.[20] Additional forces of resistance to change include the general police culture, which is deeply entrenched all over the world, and judicial arrogance, which often takes the form of declarations of independence from the ideologies and identities of political leaders, whether they are persistently authoritarian or newly democratic. Furthermore, organizational traditions run deep. David Bayley points out that the history of state formation in a society is a particularly powerful and durable determinant of how police will be structured and operate, even following subsequent change in the political system.[21] And political change in the rest of sub-Saharan Africa in the 1990s did not provide a model to be emulated; in general the core organization and functions of police and courts changed very little.

Another influence that militates against democratizing the operations of criminal justice is the complexity of the concept of liberal, constitutional democracy—and its limits. The processes that yielded this form of government for South Africa were broadly participatory and were led by elites who nonetheless had great popular legitimacy. But many South Africans knew little about the constitutional deliberations or about their results, whether from ignorance, indifference, or lack of access to information. And for those who yearned for protection from the crime and violence of the previous decades the introduction of restraints on the state's coercive power as it was directed toward providing that protection would seem both incomprehensible and contradictory. Citizens of a new democracy, once they are convinced that the repressive qualities of criminal justice institutions will not be visited on themselves for political reasons, may not wish their core operations to be substantially modified; South Africans, like the citizens of many Western countries, tend to think that courts are not tough enough on wrongdoers. A purely majoritarian definition of democracy—often expressed by South Africans unaccustomed to having political power—would support the idea that these views should prevail if policymakers are to represent their constituents responsibly. Individual and group rights as a brake on the authority of the state in criminal matters are frequently alien ideas.

Reforming police and courts involves not only rejecting the repressive apparatus of the old authoritarian state but also shaping new institutions that fit the pluralism of the new democratic one. South Africa is a country of multiple and diverse cultures, with far-reaching implications for criminal justice. Traditions of self-help and restorative justice in some African communities clash with Western practices that vest control of social disorder in the state; the social conservatism of those same communities rejects modern notions of individual autonomy, especially for the young. Vigilante groups claim—and sometimes get—legitimacy when democracy fails at physical protection. To vanquish spirits and witches with force is honorable to some groups but criminal to the state. Conflicts erupt out of the assertion of hierarchies with long histories: the white farmer over black workers, the township youth over his girlfriend, the clan elders over restless youth. Ethnic rivalries like those that threatened to derail the process of negotiations to end apartheid still simmer in more than one province, occasionally with violent results.

Despite social and political cleavages, as South Africans held their first democratic election a decade ago a strong sense of national identity prevailed—not nationalism, which rests on excluding those not part of the elect, but the pride that comes from the choice by disparate peoples of a conjoined future. It might be argued that the overwhelming mandate for change evidenced by the massive turnout of voters and the large majority (62 percent) that voted for the ANC, the party of liberation, did not directly reflect a desire for criminal justice reform. But most ANC voters would have understood that outcome—especially as applied to the police—to be an important corollary of voting for the party that had brought them not only the promise of participating in political decisions that would shape their future but also a constitution founded on values of "human dignity, the achievement of equality and the advancement of human rights and freedoms."[22] If they had learned nothing else from the brutalities of apartheid, they understood that police and courts define the state's relationship with its people and that daily interactions with them reveal the priorities of the regime.

So change in the political system had to mean changes in the justice system. Planning for that change, aided by consultation and funding from several more mature democracies, began several years before the first democratic election in April 1994. Discussion, both internal and international, about the provisions of a new constitution and the composition of a new court to interpret it was ongoing from the late 1980s. The National Peace Accord, which brought together political parties, interest groups, and government bodies to try to stem the political violence of the early 1990s, provided a setting in which the South African Police (SAP) and the ANC could work together toward a common goal—a novel experience for all concerned. Although resistance to change was inevitable, there was also a reservoir of goodwill and good intentions in the institutions to be reformed. Many police supervisors, particularly younger ones, were relieved not to have to use deadly force to uphold the political system. Judges who had strained to interpret apartheid laws as narrowly as possible had a champion in the new chief justice of the highest court—Michael Corbett, appointed in 1989 when the hardliner Pieter Rabie retired—and they welcomed the opportunity to use the law to reassert fundamental rights.

During the early 1990s people concerned with criminal justice reform—representatives of civic and human rights organizations, researchers, ANC members ready to take up positions in the new dispensation, and lawyers—met to design a new system. The conversion of apartheid police and judges to guarantors of public accountability and constitutional rights was an ambitious goal with which all were in accord. Some of the planners of post-apartheid justice, however, wanted more. They saw in the themes of their political transition the opportunity to acknowledge the great variety of cultures in the country and to honor that diversity by encouraging wide participation in the exercise of state authority by police and courts. They thought the democratic ideals of accountability, transparency, representation, and participation could best be realized with a communitarian form of community policing and by encouraging lay participation in criminal trials and in other kinds of dispute resolution. They had enough access to powerful political figures—one of the planners later became principal legal advisor to Nelson Mandela when he was president—to command attention for their ideas; their design for community police forums became part of the 1993 interim constitution.

The first decade of South African democracy has reformed race-based institutions of criminal justice in important respects, reflecting the paradigm of a liberal, constitutional democracy. Despite inheriting many of the civil servants of apartheid—a condition of the negotiated settlement—the new government managed to find uncorrupted midlevel managers to send new messages to the rank and file in the South African Police (now renamed the South African Police Service—the SAPS). The legal profession—during apartheid virtually closed in its upper reaches to people of color (and, to a lesser extent, women)—redefined itself to create opportunities for judgeships that were previously barred. The brand-new Constitutional Court demonstrated its commitment to the human rights emphasis of the constitution even before it was finalized by rejecting capital punishment. In the first case it considered the court ruled that the death penalty violated the constitutional right to life and to human dignity.[23] Despite public enthusiasm for a return of capital punishment in the face of astronomical rates of criminal violence, the government has not supported a constitutional change.

There are still gaps in the record of achievement, of course. Commissioned officers in the police are still disproportionately white, and it will be a long time before training, working conditions, and pay are adequate to deter the rank and file from corruption. Racial bias or indifference on the bench still occurs occasionally in the higher courts, more often in the magistracy; integrating the Supreme Court of Appeal has lagged. When police set dogs on a group of Mozambican immigrants in 1998—an incident captured on video—South Africans and viewers around the world were reminded that habits of brutality die hard. The lack of adequate resources for training existing personnel and hiring a cohort of fresh and reform-minded justice professionals has limited the diffusion of the new rights orientation. But overall the post-apartheid government has successfully established core institutions of criminal justice that reflect the procedural requirements of liberal democracy—police and courts subject to the oversight of citizens' representatives put in place by competitive elections in which most adults were eligible to vote. Substantive values of democracy—human dignity and equality—have shaped the reform of these institutions, reflecting the constitutional aspirations of the new society.

This conclusion is not the same as saying that police and courts perform their tasks with consistent competence. The post-apartheid planners quickly discovered that the repressive machine that was so good at quelling resistance to apartheid was not competent to put down ordinary crime. South Africans of all races and classes complain that police do not arrive on a crime scene fast enough, that they are poorly trained and often lazy or corrupt, that criminal investigation is often lacking, that crucial evidence for prosecution of crimes goes missing. The press rakes prosecutors and magistrates over the coals for long delays in processing criminal matters, and parliament has criticized higher-court judges for spending too little time on the bench. Although these criticisms are sometimes unfair, they reflect the reality that implementation can be a messier process than agenda-setting.

These shortcomings are troubling, especially in light of the tide of violent crime that has swept away some of the glow of the relatively peaceful political transition. But the fact that critics focus now on conventional performance measures of criminal justice institutions is itself a sign of democratic health. The fundamental issue is no longer the legitimacy of police and courts. The rule of law has replaced apartheid's rule of force, and ordinary citizens may now sound off on the inevitable flaws of normalcy.

Beyond the liberal reforms of enhanced rights and accountability, however, the directions of criminal justice policy do not display the same democratic commitment. The healing process that was conceived as a vital part of transformation—and that was reflected in the country's choice to confront the sins of apartheid with the Truth and Reconciliation Commission—has not included the development of forums and activities that involve citizens in preventing and managing the violent crime that has made democratic South Africa a dangerous place. Many post-apartheid planners saw in the transformation of criminal justice a different paradigm—a community-oriented project that would involve citizens as monitors and participants in efforts to maintain social order and broaden access to justice. The more ambitious reforms they envisioned have either not materialized or have changed character and become far less progressive. The community policing model and the program for lay participation in criminal trials discussed in the chapters that follow are either in decline or have been abandoned, and I contend that these failures cannot be explained away as inevitable in a country with very limited resources for justice and very high rates of violent crime. The government has also failed to harness the creativity and energy of ordering mechanisms—so-called popular justice—that previously operated outside the aegis of the state and that, through support and regulation, could have become responsible contributors to public peace and safety.

Finally, the post-apartheid state has embraced the punitive, ineffective, symbolically driven get-tough program of some Western societies, particularly the United States and the United Kingdom. As the euphoria of 1994 waned and problems of many kinds assumed center stage, policymakers and administrators turned in a direction very different from that which the post-apartheid planners had prized. Admiration for the zero-tolerance approach of former New York City mayor Rudolph Giuliani reflected an unrealistic yearning for police and courts to put an end to the violent crime that plagued both affluent suburbs and poor urban townships. Hard-line measures from the West were hastily enacted with little evidence that they would provide relief from crime. The result is a clutch of policies associated more with authoritarian regimes than with either the procedural values—accountability, transparency, participation—or the substantive principles of human dignity and equality that had been trumpeted as emblems of a protective criminal justice system. And in most parts of the country the punitive trajectory has overshadowed the plans for participatory innovations that might have helped heal the wounds that three hundred years of repression have inflicted on communities.

But the story is hardly ended. As President Thabo Mbeki said in his first State of the Nation speech to the South African parliament in 1999, "The continuing process of social and national emancipation, to which we are all subject, constitutes an evolving act of self-definition."[24] Perhaps what can be instructive about the South African experience is not an outcome but a process—the extremely complex dynamic whereby a criminal justice system is called upon to carry out shifting mandates imposed from within and without on a democratizing regime in an atmosphere polluted with the detritus of old inequities. It is not only the legacies of routine brutality from colonialism and apartheid, however, that impede the movement for a South African criminal justice system that can further the country's democratic commitments. It is also a "criminology of intolerance" that parallels the country's yearning for acceptance in a global community of neoliberalism.[25]

Two Paths to Democratic Justice

This book tells the story of South Africa's efforts to conform its justice system to the requirements of its democratic transition. It examines particular reforms—their programmatic contours, the influences that have shaped them—and the values and dynamics that they reflect. It tries to put the developments of the past decade in historical and political contexts. It examines particular measures in light of two policy shifts initially embraced by post-apartheid planners as essential to the movement from authoritarian to democratic justice. Each shift, if negotiated successfully, yields a pattern of institutions and activities that constitute a paradigm of criminal justice in a twenty-first-century democracy. The paradigms can be both complementary and conflicting and represent different directions in criminal justice that are widely debated beyond the borders of South Africa. Crudely generalized, they are liberal and communitarian; they honor, respectively, procedural and substantive traditions of democracy.

Shifting constituencies. The first policy change shifts the institutional focus of police and courts as they make and enforce the criminal law. It includes reforms—initiated by elites but sustained by popular legitimacy—that flow directly from the rejection of the old order and the embrace of electoral democracy—competitive elections with broad suffrage resulting in majority rule. It is essentially a tectonic movement replacing criminal justice that primarily serves state interests with criminal justice focused on the protection of the population. Priority for enforcing the regime—coercing compliance with its ideology and keeping its rulers in power—gives way to relatively neutral management of social conflict for the benefit of whatever community is threatened. Police and courts are subject to civilian authority and become carriers of constitutional mandates to protect the public from government as well as from each other. Commitments to the values and policies of the new dispensation bar corruption, clientelism, and secrecy that is not essential to the investigation of a felony. To be sure, practice will rarely conform to the ideal; police brutality and judicial bias are common in far more mature democracies than South Africa. But a continuing elite and popular consensus that citizens have the right to be protected by criminal justice institutions—whether as potential or actual victims of crime, suspects, or perpetrators—indicates that the divide has been crossed.

Empowering the public. Borrowing a term from the scholars of democratization, we might think of the second shift as deepening democracy.[26] It builds on what has become a broad consensus that democratic expectations for criminal justice are desirable, even essential.[27] In the panoply of principles behind those expectations—accountability, transparency, participation, representation, respect for human rights—it highlights participation through democratic deliberation, and it gives priority to citizens' determinations of how to prevent and confront crime and conflict with respect for the values of human dignity and equality. Democracy becomes more substantive—a spirit that animates collective life, rather than merely a scheme for choosing leaders and policies—as citizens are involved in both routine and innovative programs and in policy advocacy. Detaching police from the military is no longer enough, for example; mechanisms of civilian oversight enhance police accountability. An end to punishments that degrade—flogging, for example, in the case of South Africa—is succeeded by the development of least brutal and least restrictive alternatives for offenders—perhaps pretrial release programs. A concern with citizen involvement spurs community policing and lay participation in criminal trials and receives material and moral support from the state. Sensitivity to varying local conditions and acknowledgment that only a plurality of approaches will bring justice to everyone suggests decentralizing some state authority and actively supporting alternative visions of dispute resolution. Responsible forms of popular policing and judging—community order maintenance that bypasses state interventions but cooperates with them—supplement the official institutions of justice. Public forums at the local level encourage definitions of security that go beyond individual protection from interpersonal violence to collective protection from workplace injury and environmental degradation. Commitment to constitutional norms of liberty and equality is honored as much through the development of preventive, communitarian initiatives that seek to repair relationships—often called restorative justice in contemporary parlance—as through the state's protection of individual rights. Local governance is shared by state and citizenry. The pervasive theme is empowering the public in the search for social peace.

The first of these policy shifts is probably the easier to attain, though in many countries the divide has proved difficult to cross. Nigerian police continue to beat and torture participants in peaceful demonstrations, and detention without trial is still routine in some democratizing countries of Latin America. Shifting the constituency of police and courts is obviously linked to the electoral essence of regime change; meaningful democracy cannot exist if crime control is primarily an activity of political enforcement. The components of the paradigm that results are familiar attributes of political liberalism. They include a rights orientation likely to earn the approval of powerful Western democracies—and on occasion their material support—supplemented by the corollary that democratic citizens have responsibilities to the state and to each other.

Deepening democracy in criminal justice, where a focus on social harmony within a neighborhood is as important a goal as the punishment of an offender or the redress of a victim's loss or injury, makes greater demands and strikes out in directions not easily compatible with those of most mature liberal democracies in the new millennium. Top-down governance is the norm in the era of globalization, and public-empowering justice challenges that. And expectations about the quality of life to be delivered by democracy will define popular attitudes toward criminal justice and frame demands for regime performance that may make the goal of deepened democracy in this area seem risky to political elites.

But public empowerment in this area can be part of the larger democratization project, a prospect that I discuss in greater detail in chapter 7. In recent years scholars in several disciplines have noted (and promoted) the contributions that active, participatory citizenship can make to the economic, social, and political health of a democratic country. A Nobel Prize–winning economist who sees the "removal of substantial unfreedoms" as the essence of development argues that public discussion and debate not only force political leaders to attend to the needs of the people but shape the understanding of those needs.[28] A prominent political theorist conceives a model of modern democracy based on the "principle of democratic autonomy," envisioning its embodiment in individuals who are "free and equal in the determination of their own lives," a status that enables them "to participate in a process of debate and deliberation, open to all on a free and equal basis, about matters of pressing public concern."[29] Another extends this idea to endorse "the principle of governance through voluntary associations," a model of democracy in which the state cedes its primacy as service provider and instead supports and regulates the initiatives of civil society and protects individual rights.[30] And social scientists of many political stripes—journalists, too—have observed the extent to which twentieth-century social movements altered the political landscape to bring the influence of women and workers and racial minorities to bear on public policy, broadening democratic institutions and pluralizing Western culture.[31]

Democratization as a process that goes beyond guaranteeing the franchise to developing other mechanisms for holding governments accountable may be a particularly strong imperative in a country like South Africa, for a number of reasons. For one, the variety of cultural traditions in the country and its ugly political history have brought about mistrust and animosity. Taking counsel from several scholars who imagine democracy where popular deliberation over public issues and action is a supreme value, I argue that public-empowering reforms for dealing with some varieties of South African crime and disorder can strengthen the moral claims of democracy for citizens who are newly acquainted with it.[32] In fact, they are particularly appropriate in a country where conflict often stems from misunderstandings—cultural divisions or family tensions that might be bridged by the development of institutional space where discussion and mediation, rather than accusation and punishment, could more easily occur. In addition, they may recall forms of social ordering undertaken in traditional African groups or during the liberation struggle and thus have greater immediate relevance than Western crime control practices.[33]

South Africa also seems a likely locus for the public-empowering paradigm because of choices made in the development of its constitution. In addition to an orientation toward individual rights that resembles that of a number of Western countries—the so-called negative rights that protect citizens from unwarranted governmental interference with their liberties—the South African constitution imposes positive obligations on government to protect a person's dignity, equality, and freedom and, more specifically, guarantees a range of socioeconomic rights—to access to adequate housing and health care, among others.[34] For these provisions to be meaningful opportunities for citizens to hold their government accountable, people must understand these constitutional values—the concrete benefits they promise and the sacrifices they demand. Public-empowering forms of justice can provide opportunities for complementing the formal rights conveyed in the constitution with local understandings of how they play out in maintaining social order.

Finally, there seems no logical contradiction between this policy paradigm and the currently fashionable ideals of decentralization and privatization in the neoliberal world. The orientation that views security as a commodity to be bought and sold, accountable to the market as well as the state, has generally benefited (and isolated) affluent people. But pluralizing responsibility and authority for social ordering can also have meaning for poorer citizens. Accountability to their interests in community security and harmony furthers the operational assumption—also relevant in the private sector—that those closest to potential disruptions of social peace will know how best to prevent and treat them. The trick is to disprove the conclusion that "pluralizing increases safety at the cost of equity."[35] In a society as committed to the primacy of human rights as democratic South Africa, this should be a manageable challenge.

The two policy shifts in the democratization of criminal justice, taken together, cannot properly be considered a model because no country that I can think of has even approximately conformed to its contours. The stages of democratization in criminal justice may overlap and include events and elements not mentioned. Furthermore, problems arise that sprawl across the stages and appear to contradict the general democratic movement. On the other hand, in many democratizing countries, including South Africa, there are preauthoritarian traditions that would support many of the features of public-empowering criminal justice. And in many mature liberal democracies policy impulses to regard participatory social protection as a goal equivalent to state sanctioning have begun to alter the crime control program. Restorative justice, an approach imported from premodern societies that puts reconciliation in a community ahead of the infliction of pain on the offender, is taking hold in many parts of the world. That spirit gave life to South Africa's Truth and Reconciliation Commission.

The strains of adapting to democratic ideals for justice are apparent in South Africa. The country is coping, for example, with the difficulty of balancing the need to restrain vigilantism with the desire to encourage citizen participation in maintaining order at the neighborhood level. In addition, affluent urban neighborhoods rely more on private security than on public policing, creating the impression that the state condones a system that protects its citizens unequally. Finally, in a classically dialectical development, the promise of material betterment that is part of the appeal of democracy has raised unrealistic expectations of what police and courts can do about crime, fueling demands for repressive and antidemocratic policies. In criminal justice as in other areas South Africans are continually confronted with the question of how the state can be strengthened to function efficiently in a competitive world and at the same time encourage the pluralism, equality, and participation that sustains democracy.

A principal theme of this book is the impossibility of considering crime policy formation and implementation in isolation, divorced from a country's history and the political, social, and economic forces that are shaping the national future. So a number of chapters, in whole or in part, focus on context. (South African readers may find these chapters old hat, and I wouldn't be insulted if they skipped to the theoretical material and policy analysis of subsequent sections.) Part 1 paints background pictures in chapters 2 and 3 of colonial and apartheid justice, both their priority for political enforcement and the institutions and policies that characterized their approach to ordinary crime and delinquency. While it is impossible to analyze this history in depth, attention must be paid to it for its contribution to both the liberal and communitarian themes that emerged as post-apartheid planners undertook the task of criminal justice reform. Following the historical chapters I turn to crime in South Africa today, which I consider in light of two separate but related legacies of apartheid—the model of the violent state and the legitimacy of violence conveyed and assumed by those fighting to liberate themselves from that state.

Although this is a book about policy, not a theoretical exegesis, parts 2 and 3 develop the paradigms I've just described—in each case starting with a more abstract chapter dealing with the underpinnings of the particular approach followed by a chapter about the concrete realities in post-apartheid South Africa. Chapter 5 discusses the first policy shift—crossing the divide between a justice system primarily responsible to the state and one that finds its principal constituency in the public while chapter 6 relates its features to South African initiatives for post-apartheid police and courts. That section of the book concludes that South Africa has been moderately successful in shifting the constituency of police and courts from the regime to its democratic citizens. Chapter 7 discusses the nature of the public-empowering approach to justice, my conceptual contribution to the crime policy literature. It reviews some of the innovations in community-oriented justice that are springing up around the world. It attempts to justify the paradigm in terms of recent theorizing on the need for deliberative democracy in a world where widely divergent values and cultures must coexist if liberal democracies are to thrive. It suggests that implementation of efforts to control crime with informal mechanisms are doomed in countries that are responding to the clarion call of the punitive approach favored by neoliberal globalizers. In chapter 8 I consider as case studies South Africa's experiments with this type of reform—a particularly communitarian form of community policing and the introduction of lay participation in criminal trials through the use of lay assessors. In documenting how these innovations were neglected or abandoned as pressures in other directions rendered them ineffective—at least in the short term—I try also to explain that development. There is also a brief discussion of an aborted interest in the development of nonstate structures, community courts that would have recalled the achievements of township residents in maintaining order during the liberation struggle.

Chapter 9, which introduces part 4, describes the punitive direction crime policy has taken in place of the participatory idealism of the early post-apartheid period. While institutional reform has moved South African criminal justice into general compliance with its progressive new constitution, a "get-tough" policy direction has superseded democratic idealism as a palliative for both internal and foreign concerns about the country's security and stability. The concluding chapter presents lessons learned from the experience of South Africa about the limits of democratic reform in this area, dilemmas and contradictions of the tasks of democratizing police and courts. How these lessons might be relevant for other democratizing countries with their own unique histories and contemporary economic and cultural pressures remains an open question. But South Africa, I maintain, must take another look at the public-empowering possibilities of justice if its new democracy is to be not only nonracial but truly inclusive.

Introduction 17

Toward the Carceral Society?

Lapses in the democratization of criminal justice in South Africa must be seen in the larger context of a country's moving from the triumph of electoral democracy to the harder tasks of economic development and institutional reform in many other areas. It is not only in criminal justice that the record to date is studded with accomplishment tempered by setbacks. The postapartheid government has subsidized the construction of almost two million houses to address the housing crisis, but they are widely criticized as flimsy and poorly equipped.[36] It has brought primary health care to most people in rural areas, but infant mortality and the frequency of low birth-weights have increased. The state provides for ten years of compulsory (though not free) education, and universities that were closed to most blacks have become far more inclusive; black students at the University of the Witwatersrand, one of the most prestigious of predominantly white institutions in the past, now comprise a majority in most disciplines. But it is taking more than a decade to reorient and bring substantial improvement to the "historically disadvantaged tertiary institutions"—the black colleges that were the culmination of Bantu education in the twentieth century but are still often the only opportunity for higher education for many poor black students.

AIDS and unemployment present special challenges, separately and together. AIDS has galloped through the land—United Nations estimates suggest that approximately one-quarter of South African adults aged fifteen to forty-nine are HIV-positive—and the government has appalled international observers by its failure to respond quickly and adequately with preventive strategies and proven treatments. The transfer of political power and the virtual end of employment discrimination (including uncompromising affirmative action programs) has created opportunity for middle-class, educated blacks, but a widening intraracial income gap has left many Africans poorer than in 1994.[37] A million jobs were lost during the 1990s, most of them unskilled or semiskilled jobs in mining or manufacturing that had been available to the poor. Economist Nicoli Nattrass estimates that almost five million people were out of work at the turn of the century and points out that "the South African growth path has become increasingly skill- and capital-intensive and has delivered benefits to both capital and labour. In this postapartheid 'distributional regime,' the unemployed have been the biggest losers."[38] Although the government has recently agreed in theory to provide antiretroviral treatment to those who are now without it—most employed people have access to it through their employers—universal availability cannot become a reality without a major tax increase, which is likely to meet with resistance. Without labor market reform that would include job creation and expand the pool of taxpayers, Nattrass says, treatment will remain out of reach for millions of South Africans who are infected with HIV and are out of work. (At the level of realpolitik the government's credibility is at stake in its handling of unemployment and AIDS. As one political commentator notes, "If [the ANC] cannot reduce [these problems] to manageable proportions, if it is perceived to pander to the rich black elite rather than alleviate the plight of black proletarians, or if it stumbles indecisively in implementing its new commitment to provide anti-retroviral drugs to people living with Aids, it may alienate a significant component of its black constituency.")[39]

Some of the shortcomings of transformation are attributable to the country's failure to prosper economically. While often described as the economic engine of Africa, South Africa at the end of apartheid was nearly bankrupt, and the economy has not grown since the end of apartheid in the manner that was hoped. The increase in GDP for 2003 was 1.9 percent, less than in 1994, the tumultuous year of the first democratic election, although that figure rose to 4 percent for the last quarter of 2004. The value of the rand fell in the early years of the democratic decade, making basic necessities like fuel and some foods more expensive. Despite economic policies that have reduced budget deficits, national debt and inflation, foreign direct investment in the hoped-for amounts has not materialized. The official national unemployment rate, 26.2 percent as of September 2004, does not reflect discouraged workers or provincial variations; in the Western Cape the rate is lower, in Limpopo and the Eastern Cape it is higher.[40] Nattrass notes that in 2003 nonagricultural employment was lower than twenty years earlier and describes the implications of the jobs crisis:

> The failure of the South African economy to expand the number of formal jobs (let alone provide enough employment growth to absorb new entrants into the labour market) is clearly worthy of being classed as a "fundamental" and "structural" problem. Without job creation, South Africa's already high levels of inequality will continue to worsen.[41]

To address the country's economic problems South African leaders settled on a conservative macroeconomic strategy (called GEAR, for growth, employment, and redistribution) that included the privatization of state assets, deficit reduction, and market liberalization. Although a certain amount of belt-tightening was necessary to rescue the bankrupt state that the ANC inherited in 1994 and organized labor successfully beat back some efforts at privatization, the policy tendency reflects a contradiction that characterizes the post-Soviet triumph of democratic capitalism in a number of countries. On the one hand the government has embraced an egalitarian, rights-oriented ideology with guarantees of dignity, self-determination, and even opportunity (through the political and socioeconomic rights promised in the constitution). On the other hand it has been committed to a particularly competitive economic system in which inequalities of access, influence, energy, and capital will determine winners and losers in society as well as in the marketplace. The egalitarian and participatory values of democracy are challenged by the demands of free trade and balanced budgets. Or, as Robert Dahl has noted, "[T]he outcome of a system of competitive markets may be excessively harmful to the processes and institutions of democratic government."[42]

Foreign observers and the media cite, along with unemployment and AIDS, violent crime as one of the new democracy's most serious problems. South Africans agree. Over and over public opinion polls cite crime reduction as first or second—alternating with jobs—in their national priorities.[43] While political leaders worry about crime's effect on investment and tourism, ordinary people feel unsafe as they go about their daily lives. How the government deals with the reality of high rates of murder, rape, and robbery—as well as the growth of organized crime gangs that operate internationally—has become an important challenge in the ANC's stewardship of the country. It tests the feasibility of the state's dual commitment to liberal democracy and a competitive market economy. The choice of a get-tough criminal justice program mirrors its emphasis on economic restructuring and fiscal discipline and substitutes for more progressive approaches that might be equally effective at controlling crime and much more in keeping with the rights culture that South Africans are trying to develop.

To conclude that for the time being the post-apartheid government has only partially embraced democracy in criminal justice is not to say that it will regress in the overall process of consolidating its democracy. South Africa has not descended into the pit of collapse and corruption that many sub-Saharan states have fallen into, nor is it likely to. Though the country is plagued with crime, AIDS, and unemployment, its leaders are not a secret cartel that gives away precious resources to bourgeois clients; it does not depend on crime as a principal source of productivity; and it does not routinely repress opposition parties or viewpoints. Although its economic restructuring program has increased deprivation for many, it has not progressed, as an important essay characterized Nigeria in the 1980s, "from nurture capitalism to . . . pirate capitalism."[44] On a continent where many countries are afflicted with negative growth in GDP, South Africa looks relatively healthy. It is not engaged in endless, draining civil wars, and its military budget, at 1.7 percent of government expenditure (as of 2002), does not overwhelm the need to invest in domestic development. It has not developed an edifice complex, erecting presidential palaces and grandiose conference centers as in many countries. Although there have been scandals of individual government ministers living rent-free and getting discounts on their Mercedes as part of a questionable arms deal, the state is not robbing the peasants to fatten the bureaucrats.

But South Africa is contributing to a worldwide intensification of punishment that shows very little effect on crime, contributes to a widening of the gap between rich and poor, and primarily serves to express the anxieties of late-modern citizens—by and large, the comfortable middle classes who influence policy—yearning for order in an increasingly insecure world.[45] For South Africa to follow this pattern would be to contribute to the development of what Michel Foucault called carceral societies, where pervasive surveillance and supervision are products of centralized power that constrain freedom in crucial ways—inhibiting creativity, repressing political expression and choice, deterring the exercise of rights, maintaining race and class divisions. Such a society would fall short of a transformed South Africa.

From Racial Enforcement to Post-Apartheid Crime

2 Pre-apartheid Justice
Versatile Instrument of Repression

> [The natives] are a savage set, living without conscience. . . . we should, therefore, act cautiously with them and not put much trust in them.
> —Jan van Riebeeck, 1651[1]

> I have made up my mind that there must be class legislation, that there must be Pass Laws and Peace Preservation Acts, and that we have to treat Natives where they are in a state of barbarism, in a different way to ourselves. We are to be the lords over them. These are my politics and these are the politics of South Africa.
> —Cecil John Rhodes, 1882[2]

POLICE AND COURTS, as they interpret the will of the state, manifest its character. But the relationship between the state's interests and the operations of its coercive institutions is seldom tidy or constant. The same government can be punitive in some arenas, lenient in others, as witnessed by American lapses in the prosecution of corporate malfeasance. And regime change can alter the roles and responsibilities of those who deliver justice—or not, as continuing reports of torture in Brazil and spying on citizens in Russia attest. In a democratizing country with a turbulent past and an ethnically diverse population, the politics of the moment will have only a limited influence on how the state realizes its aims through the performance of its police and courts. Equally important will be patterns of the past, deeply embedded in complex political and social history.

It is much too easy to conclude that South African criminal justice during the apartheid era provided the policy antagonist for the reformers of the 1990s to rout. Although, as in Nazi Germany, the justice system was the regime's very cruel and visible instrument, it did not spring, fully formed and theoretically consistent, from the heads of the strategists of apartheid. It was a logical culmination and intensification of previous centuries of law enforcement (and extralegal violence, both state and nonstate) in service to the racial repression that began with seventeenth-century slavery.[3]

Comprehensive analysis of the roots of apartheid is not possible here. But some of the forces and events that led up to the National Party's narrow victory in 1948 and to the subsequent political strength of South Africa's "peculiar institution"—to use the nineteenth-century term for American slavery—shed light on criminal justice policymaking and on the behavior of police and courts as they implemented the regime's cruelty and virulence. Particularly important were the British imposition and adaptation of colonial institutions as well as the development of Afrikaner nationalism to form a white consensus around the necessity of systematic separation of the races and the enforcement of black subservience.

A history of criminal justice in South Africa before 1994 is really a three-hundred-year screed of oppression under two interlocking justifications. One was the need of the dominant whites for cheap and compliant workers, first for the farms and later for the mines. Lord Alfred Milner, British high commissioner for South Africa, expressed a common attitude when he wrote, in a report to the head of the British Colonial Office in 1900, "[T]he more natives that are engaged in mining and other industrial pursuits the better for them and for the country."[4] The other was the assumption that those "natives" were inferior, a conviction that sprouted with the introduction of slavery in the original Dutch settlement and found support in the religious and scientific mythologies of Afrikaner nationalism and British imperialism. The two rationales fused in the effort to construct whites as perpetual and omnipotent masters and blacks as perpetual and submissive servants. Even in days when the Cape was merely a restocking station for Dutch ships, legal authority reinforced the hierarchy. "Economically they [the local indigenous people] had their place in the field and the kitchen; socially and politically they stood outside the circle of the rights and privileges of white men; even legally they existed in an ambiguous region between law and the arbitrary will of their masters."[5]

Throughout most of South Africa's history, and in most of its communities, the relationship between the themes of labor exploitation and racial domination in the general culture and criminal justice policy and practice was transparent. Using criminal law and enforcement to control ordinary crime like the theft of livestock was almost incidental to its value in regulating race relations for the benefit of white enterprise on the farms or in the mines.[6] Sometimes the effort to combine segregation with coerced labor bred contradictions, as when the exclusion of blacks from the growing towns created labor shortages in fledgling industry. The criminal law had utility for such situations; it could try to deter prohibited migrations by criminalizing unemployment through measures like vagrancy laws and Masters and Servants Acts. Perhaps the most enduring and important of these kinds of measures were the pass laws, which laid the foundation for the apartheid system of influx control.

Until 1910, when the two former Boer republics (the Orange Free State and the Transvaal) and the two British colonies (the Cape and Natal) came together as a self-governing state within the British Empire, South African criminal justice was fragmented and capricious. It reflected internal conflicts between white populations—the Boers (or Afrikaners, as the urban descendants of Dutch settlers increasingly called themselves) and the British—as well as tensions between blacks and whites. While the principles of servitude and inferiority for blacks were assumed from the time the Dutch East India Company officials sent for slaves to perform the manual labor of the new community, their application as social control, whether through procedures that were arbitrary and informal or bureaucratic and state-centered, varied from place to place and with the provenance of those in charge. In nineteenth-century British-run Cape Town, for instance, a spirit of liberalism and legalism prevailed, while isolated inland communities of poor Boer farmers applied summary and informal justice to the criminality and social unrest that often expressed resistance to oppression. It meant little that law enforcement was an instrument for conveying state legitimacy when there was not much of a state to validate.

To understand the diverse and decentralized influences that coalesced in the development of apartheid justice it is useful to view them as products of three phases in South African history: the period from initial settlement of the Dutch refueling station in 1652 until British occupation at the turn of the nineteenth century, the period of inland expansion and colonization from the early nineteenth century until the end of the South African War, and the period from the time of the British creation of the Union of South Africa until the electoral victory of the National Party in 1948 that ushered in the apartheid era. Although from time to time and at various locations the British government or individual magistrates and Boer landowners attempted to apply enlightened criminal justice policies, they inevitably yielded to repressive and lawless demands for cheap labor supplied by subjugated peoples. Even a British strategy for using traditional African law to effect social control in black communities was devised for dominating their leaders and ensuring that their members would participate in the developing society only as serfs. Although behavior could be criminalized without regard to race, it was usually done with the express purpose of repressing blacks. Contradictions abounded also in the white groups' treatment of each other, particularly in the tensions, from the early nineteenth century on, between Afrikaners and English-speakers. Five participants in the abortive Boer rebellion of 1815 were executed (an event that later became a symbol of martyrdom to the aggrieved Afrikaners), while the leaders of the infamous and unsuccessful 1895 Jameson raid on the Transvaal were allowed to buy their way out of their death sentences.[7]

Both the superficially rights-oriented British governments and the more blatantly repressive Afrikaner administrations made clear that the fundamental task of police and courts was to establish and maintain the racial subjugation that was at the heart of all South African political communities from the time slaves were first imported in 1658. The role included putting down resistance to the humiliations suffered by blacks and sending an unyielding symbolic message of invincible white authority. Perceived deviations from that assignment were generally met with (white) public scorn. An undated memo (probably written in 1839) to the Cape governor from a group of emigrants to Natal explaining why they left the Cape Colony perfectly expresses the twin assumptions underlying the racial order and the association between blackness and criminality that justified them. It noted with indignation the freeing of the slaves (a British initiative consonant with the libertarian winds of the age in Europe) and the subsequent liberties allowed them "whereby our slaves have been spoiled and we have been ruined." It goes on to say, "The emigration was also greatly influenced by the vagabondizing of the Hottentots and free blacks, to whom this and also other offensive acts of drunkenness,—cursing, swearing, and profanation of the Sabbath, was allowed with connivance and impunity."[8]

Settler Justice, 1652–1795

The history of the first white South African settlement—the Cape Colony—indicates the continuity of South African oppression. Its origins as a slave society; its growing appetite for land, livestock, and cheap labor; and the colonists' assumptions of the racial inferiority of the indigenous people are all reflected in later events and in locations beyond the colony's original boundaries. And the forces of slavery, colonialism, and armed conquest gave rise to institutions and processes of social control that laid the foundation for the cruelties of apartheid police and courts.

When the first group of whites arrived in the Cape in 1652, they had no intention of forming a permanent community. The Dutch East India Company had sent them to Table Bay to establish a post with provisions for Dutch merchant ships plying the route between Europe and the eastern outpost of the Dutch empire in Java. The company employees who were stationed there were expected merely to supply exhausted, scurvy-ridden crews of the enormous Dutch fleet with fresh water, meat, and vegetables. But infrastructure was needed even for such a modest enterprise, and the company was eager to minimize costs. Slaves were soon imported from other parts of Africa and from southern Asia to build a fort, a hospital, and roads. The company then found it could conduct its business more efficiently by reducing its staff and giving land to those who had been discharged in return for an agreement to buy their produce at fixed prices.[9] For this it needed to displace indigenous people, starting the process of colonial acquisition. Within a generation a substantial settlement that showed all the signs of becoming a permanent community had supplemented the refreshment station; by the end of the seventeenth century there were about a thousand "free burghers," adding yet another population group with its own economic and political interests to the company employees, slaves, and indigenous blacks.

It may seem that to begin the account of criminal justice in South Africa with the arrival of Europeans carries with it the assumption that there was effectively no social control among indigenous people before the Dutch. That was certainly not the case. The intrusion of the Europeans into African communities, however, disrupted settled traditions of social control among black South Africans, and the resulting power relations began to form the backdrop for apartheid justice.

The indigenous people the Europeans found when they arrived were small and olive-skinned—the nomadic and peaceful Khoikhoi pastoralists, who had traded with Portuguese mariners long before settlement of the Cape Colony, and the San hunters (collectively referred to as the Khoisan). The settlers called them Hottentots and Bushmen and profited from the Khoi experience in herding cattle, for which they traded copper, beads, tobacco, and brandy.[10] The Khoisan were nonliterate and nomadic, so our knowledge of much of their social and legal relations is very limited. Accounts by visitors to the Cape Colony in the late seventeenth and early eighteenth centuries and literate observers from the eighteenth century forward are all we have to go on.

From these accounts—and from later observations of similar behavior that confirm them—it appears that peacemaking within a clan or chiefdom was at least as important as punishment. Writing from the Cape Colony in 1707, Peter Kolb noted, "The Hottentots run to the suppression of strife that has seized a family as we do to putting out of a fire that has seized a house; and allow themselves no rest until every matter in difference is adjusted."[11] Well into the twentieth century hunting groups thought to have similar origins had recourse to mediation as a primary means of social control. This orientation to dispute resolution may have contributed to later forms of white adjudication; a late-seventeenth-century account describes the Cape Council mediating between two indigenous groups, a form of the "indirect administration" that became a major strategy of control in later periods.[12]

Kolb, whose account has been considered the most reliable of the early chronicles, tells us much more about the Khoikhoi (a word meaning "men of men") and how they dealt with social disorder. Assigned by a Prussian nobleman to conduct astronomical and meteorological research at the Cape Colony, his fascination with the "Hottentots" took him in another direction (which eventually got him fired). He found them "lazy" but intelligent, honest, and loyal—"They make excellent servants, and perhaps the faithfullest in the world"—and writes sympathetically of their institutions as well as their character.[13] He confirms the later conclusion of trained anthropologists that the tight hierarchies of the clans provided effective social control. He describes hereditary chiefs as the final authority in maintaining order and waging war and local headmen as arbiters of most disputes in the kraal. The headmen use their authority sparingly, he says, "unless it comes to a Murder or a General Commotion, for then they will interpose, and exert their Authority. And the People have generally so much Remorse when their Strifes issue in such a Catastrophe or general Confusion, that at those Times, the Captain of the Kraal no sooner appears than they return to their Duty."[14]

Apparently this restraint did not extend to mountain-dwelling cattle-rustlers, who seem to have been the principal external threat to the peace of the kraal. When one was caught, he was "instantly put to Death, not a Soul daring to say one Word for him."[15] In other situations elements of due process prevailed. Sitting as a court, the men of the kraal gathered in a circle; "[t]he Center of the Circle is always the Place of a Criminal, because, say the Hottentots, the Matter touching his Life, he ought to have the best Situation for Hearing and being heard."[16] Death and damages were imposed only after the presentation of evidence on both sides and consultation by the headman with the other men. Adultery was, in some cases, punishable by death, as were robbery and murder. Deserters in the tribal wars that arose over cattle theft and trespass on valuable pasturage were also executed, usually immediately upon conviction.[17]

Other accounts confirm that traditional law, despite the tradition of mediation, could be brutal and arbitrary. It presumed guilt and decreed punishments from fines (paid in livestock) to death for the usual offenses against property and person and for behavior that angered the ancestors or for witchcraft. One nineteenth-century chronicle asserts that among the Khoikhoi theft of small items was punished by a beating from the headman; whipping was also used on occasion to punish premarital sex.[18]

The Dutch settlers, too, were punitive, and less accountable than the Khoikhoi for their sanctions. Justice in the early days of the colony bore little relation to modern Western notions of the rule of law as a neutral force protecting individuals from arbitrary authority. The commander (later called governor) and other officers wore many hats in the governance of the company town. Historian Eric Walker characterizes the Council of Policy as leviathan, with executive and legislative functions (though the commander could simply say, "I take it upon myself . . ." and overrule all group decisions), as well as being "the nucleus of the High Court of Justice."[19] The council could operate in secret and had complete discretion in the imposition of punishments, including banishment and death. While petty offenses were settled out of court, whipping and branding were common, and even whites were occasionally executed for violent crimes. Sachs notes that the company's directors in Holland provided only the vaguest directives as to how court proceedings should be conducted and cites the admonition in 1685 that the governor should be "severe and terrible to the wicked."[20] Policing was erratic and fragmented, undertaken in the roles of night watchmen or assistant to the prosecutor. It was only ambiguously allied with the racial politics of the colony; police were expected to control trade between the colonists and the Khoikhoi, but slaves did some of the policing.

During the period when the settlement was still run by company officials, the administration was sometimes tougher on its employees than on the indigenous people it relied on for meat and later for labor. Jan van Riebeeck, who led the settlement for its first decade, was under strict instructions to treat the natives kindly. Despite his initial view that they were "dull, stupid, lazy and stinking" he sought to prevent conflict with the Khoikhoi by prescribing whippings for white workers who lost their tools (creating a temptation to steal) or assaulted the natives.[21] He seems to have been willing to presume a settler's guilt in a confrontation with a "savage."[22]

The treatment of slaves was another matter. As their numbers increased—by the late eighteenth century slaves outnumbered white settlers—attitudes toward their control hardened.[23] They were subjected not only to the harsh and haphazard legal system set up by company officials but also to their masters' private "discipline," which could be brutal indeed and was seldom punished unless it resulted in serious injury or death. Roman-Dutch law was applied in a manner that gave preference to company employees and white farmers, and access to the courts for the slaves was limited. Though slave complaints of violence could be entertained in the colony court, they were rarely upheld, and an adverse ruling could bring retribution from the employer and penalties imposed by the court, ostensibly to deter frivolous charges.[24] Escaped slaves were shot, though not frequently, as their labor was too valuable. Torture was not uncommon for serious crimes; in 1732 a slave was broken on the wheel and hanged for stealing a violin.[25] Though organized slave insurrections were rare, punishment for violent rebellion against the individual master was merciless and dramatic. A 1773 observer described the beheading of a slave who had murdered his master: "The delinquent being laid on the cross and tied fast to it, first his arms and legs were burned in eight different parts with jagged tongs, made red hot; afterwards his arms and legs were broken on the wheel, and lastly, his head was cut off and fixed on a pole."[26] Death by mutilation was reserved for slaves.

As for the indigenous Khoikhoi (the ethnically similar San were less numerous and much less involved with the Europeans because they had no livestock), they were less likely to run afoul of the colonial legal system, at least initially. Kolb notes that, with regard to early relations with the Khoikhoi, "the Dutch never intermeddl[ed] in private Quarrels among the Natives."[27] Violence by the Khoikhoi in and around the colony was punished only when it involved settlers as victims. They suffered extralegal punishments, however, usually for theft of stock or tools, the most common offenses. The Dutch also sent vigilante posses to raid Khoikhoi encampments, ostensibly to protect the colony—justified as defense in war rather than as punishment by the state— but also to enforce land grabs and sometimes to commit their own stock thefts. And as the seventeenth century gave way to the eighteenth, court records of the Cape Colony show increasing prosecution and punishment of the Khoi, though slaves still appear more frequently as convicted of offenses including "desertion," assault, and murder.[28]

So the patterns of informal and brutal proceedings and punishments in a society highly stratified along both class and race lines were set very early. Their dynamics prevailed even beyond the advent of democracy more than three hundred years later. John Brewer notes the connection in his study of South African police in the twentieth century: "The Afrikaner police lineage is . . . one of paramilitary policing by *ad hoc* commando-type units made up of armed local citizens controlling the Black population by displays of superior force and brutality."[29] And the flogging tradition of the colonial courts lingered into the post-apartheid era; the magistrates' courts were permitted to impose a sentence of not more than seven lashes until 1995, when whipping was declared unconstitutional.[30]

In addition to the subjugation of blacks to white domination, racial repression increased social insecurity and conflict within the black groups, both in the form of resistance to cruelty and also in ordinary crime. Among the slaves and the indigenous people collaborations with the oppressors were punished, jealousies inflamed violence, and access to consumer goods brought by the Europeans heightened social competition. The slaves responded to their treatment by whites both actively and passively, sometimes setting their masters' property on fire and sometimes running away. The Khoikhoi, who had initially had relatively peaceful relations with the Dutch, fought the colony's encroachment on their grazing lands unsuccessfully with border skirmishes, but the colonists' superior weaponry and strategy of divide and conquer prevailed. Losing control over pasturage meant losing independence, and many became suppliers or servants of the Dutch and later of the British, who occupied the Cape in 1795 and imposed their own colonial regime. "By 1828, Whites were the legal owners of nearly all the productive land in the colony, and the emancipated Khoikhoi—and, later on, the emancipated slaves—had few alternatives but to continue to work for white people."[31] Dependence can lead to deviance, and this was no exception. Some blacks rejected subservience and, lacking their traditional occupations, became vagrants and thieves. Robben Island, where Nelson Mandela was later imprisoned for eighteen years, was first used to confine Khoikhoi suspected of theft.

Colonial Justice, 1795–1902

British occupation of the Cape, initially to protect it from seizure by the French and then simply to add it to the empire, brought both order and disorder to the society that had taken root there: order in the administrative practices that regularized what had often been chaotic and corrupt governance, and disorder arising from the political threat felt by the Afrikaners who had to conform to new policies. Initially, the changes were few but significant and often opposed with vehemence. Disputes over the application of criminal sanctions expressed the political tension. High Court judges imbued with Boer traditions strongly objected to the first British governor's abolition of the practice of torturing black suspects and keenly resented the interference of British missionaries, who brought cases against brutal masters in the newly established circuit courts.[32] Although a succession of early British governors continued the autocratic Dutch practices—requiring passes and service contracts from the Khoikhoi, exercising legislative functions as well as executive ones, and hearing appeals in criminal cases—new administrators and a Commission of Inquiry brought winds of liberalizing change to the Cape Colony.[33]

The British arrivals saw the political issues of the Cape in light of the larger Enlightenment movement to improve conditions for subject peoples of the empire. Their view of the place of subjected people in colonial society and of how their behavior should be regulated was very different from that of the Afrikaners. They abhorred the servile status of most blacks, though morality was not the only basis for their views; it was joined with an immediate material concern that forced labor was economically inefficient.[34] Guided by the British Parliament, the new colonial order forbade the more gruesome forms of capital punishment. In 1828 it enacted Ordinance 50, which entitled "Hottentots and other free persons of colour" to all the legal rights of British subjects, including ownership of land; prohibited the "obnoxious usages" of "compulsory service" of the Khoikhoi; and abolished vagrancy laws that had restricted the movements of nonslave blacks.[35] As part of empire-wide policy, the British colonists ended slavery in stages during the 1830s.[36]

The British also imported their institutions, procedures, and people, instilling institutional forms that have persisted to this day. Police functions were separated from the military, and efforts were made to discipline and professionalize the ragtag Cape Town watchmen and constables, though the model of British "bobbies" was only adopted in 1840.[37] English divisions in the legal profession—between barristers and solicitors, judges and lower-court magistrates—were adopted. Lawyers came from England to serve as judges. They staffed the Supreme Court, which decided serious cases and reviewed magistrates' decisions in minor ones, and passed on the legality of laws and administrative actions; they rode circuit twice a year to bring courts to outlying districts.[38] Local magistrates were appointed to resolve disputes—they also collected debts and taxes—replacing the Dutch *landdrosts* who had held both administrative and judicial authority. Juries of six or nine (depending on how many "good men and true" could be found in a community) advised the judges. Though Roman-Dutch law was retained for civil proceedings, British criminal law was adopted, with its emphasis on open courts, rules of evidence, and a modicum of due process.

The new legal standards reinforced British social attitudes.[39] The British abolished vagrancy laws that required passes for people of color—again a development that promoted equality and also fostered the mobility that they believed would stimulate enterprise among black workers—and guaranteed equal access to white courts. A newly independent judiciary, prodded by missionaries, entertained charges of brutal treatment of the Khoikhoi by their employers and proved unwilling to impose on blacks the harsh punishments for minor offenses that had become routine with the Dutch.[40] Both slaves and the Khoikhoi began to take advantage of the right to sue their masters, a serious threat to the coerced labor on which the colonists had come to depend.

To the Boers these developments added insult to occupation. Both the British (especially the missionaries with their humanitarian crusades) and the blacks—Khoisan and slaves—were blamed for disrupting the peace of the colony. On one level the Boers feared that formal equality would destroy the social hierarchy and force miscegenation—a particularly absurd contention, since interracial sexual relations and occasional marriage had existed since the days of the original white settlement. They also claimed serious material losses with the end of slavery, even though its consequence was to substitute mandatory apprenticeships that closely resembled peonage. The British had betrayed them, they felt. Instead of ending slavery gradually, as had been promised, and restraining the newly freed people, the British had shown "undue partiality for persons with black skins and savage habits."[41] Furthermore, they did not compensate the slave-owners, arguing that the fund set aside for this purpose had been depleted by a border war with the Xhosas. In vain the Boers tried to reestablish their dominance over black laborers by pressing for vagrancy laws that would force them to work.[42]

Expressions of anxiety over economic and ideological change took the form of "antivagrancy hysteria" and fear of black crime, though there was no evidence that blacks were disproportionately criminal.[43] Keppel-Jones likens the frenzy to the rumors of uncontrolled banditry that accompanied the French

Revolution; "the lawless Hottentots were believed to be everywhere, expected to arrive everywhere, but never seen in the flesh."⁴⁴ A related issue was the Boer view that punishment for cattle raids by black groups on what they regarded as white territories was insufficiently severe; the British apparently regarded the attacks as acts of war to be dealt with through negotiation, rather than as criminality to be brought to court.

Expansion of the Cape Colony to the east during the first half of the nineteenth century was the direct outcome of these tensions. By this time more than a century had passed since some of the original settlers and their descendants had left the employ of the Dutch East India Company and drifted eastward from Table Bay. They worked hardscrabble farms, sometimes living in huts or their wagons or becoming as nomadic as the indigenous people they displaced. The migration increased as Boer trekkers voted with their feet against English rule of the Cape. A manifesto signed by Piet Retief, the most prominent leader of what was later called the Great Trek, suggests the victimization the settlers felt at the hands of the British and their association of crime with resistance by oppressed people to their oppression. His first of several "sufficient reasons" for leaving the colony cites "evils which threaten it by the turbulent and dishonest conduct of vagrants," and his second decries the "severe losses" occasioned by the "emancipation of our slaves." He complains of "plunder which we have ever endured from the Caffres and other coloured classes" and asserts that, in future settlements, the trekking Afrikaners, while not supporting the reinstitution of slavery, will "maintain such regulations as may suppress crime, and preserve proper relations between master and servant."⁴⁵ A sympathetic historian of the late nineteenth century synthesizes the views of the trekkers: "How is it possible, said the farmers, for us to cultivate the ground or breed cattle with all these savages and semi-savages constantly watching for opportunities to plunder us, with no police, and no law under which suspicious characters can be arrested and made to account for their manner of living?"⁴⁶

The "Caffres" to whom Retief referred were an African racial group whom the Boers encountered when they first moved into the interior. (As settlers migrated eastward in the Cape Colony some married the Khoisan, who gradually either became assimilated—forming part of the genetic mix of today's coloured population—or died out, often victims of smallpox.) They were mixed farmers who cultivated land as well as herding cows and sheep, mostly speaking Nguni languages—Xhosa, Zulu, and Swazi—who migrated south and west and eventually made up the largest proportion of South Africans. They were larger, healthier, darker-skinned people than the Khoikhoi and had more developed economies. They established villages, engaged in specialized activities like mining and smithing, and had local and long-distance trade relationships—for tools and weapons as well as livestock and metals like copper and iron. The largest group, the cattle-breeding Xhosa, were also fierce in war, almost as eager for land to establish new chiefdoms as the British were keen on imperial expansion.

What we know about the social organization of these people comes mostly from anthropologists' accounts beginning in the early twentieth century. Although their origins are very different from those of the Khoisan, they handled conflict in ways that were similar but with more formality and a startling degree of consonance with the British principles and procedures that characterized nineteenth-century courts. While the tribal law was unwritten, its provisions were detailed and known to most adult males, who were all permitted to attend a court proceeding and were, in fact, legally responsible for knowing the business and behavior of other members of the clan.[47] Traditional law was based on precedent and prized continuity and community. Criminal acts were presumed to be offenses against the society (as represented by the chief), as they are considered offenses against the state in Western legal systems. Remorse and a showing that an accused was a first offender were mitigations in determining penalties as in Western courts, and principles like the right of an accused to confront accusers and the desirability of a speedy trial were similarly valued.[48]

Even as late as the mid-1930s, when colonial justice had subsumed many African traditions, ethnographic studies found that, as with the Khoikhoi two centuries earlier, tight bonds of clan and lineage exercised primary social control and headmen and chiefs presided over African courts.[49] Isaac Schapera, a South African anthropologist responsible for organizing and conducting much research among these groups, found even the twentieth-century chief to be virtually omnipotent within the clan. As the "supreme judge" hearing both new cases and appeals "Nothing of any importance can be done without his knowledge and authority," though he continued to consult with his councilors.[50] Only the chief could decree death or banishment, punishments that could be imposed for revolt against his authority as well as for offenses against person and property. But in at least some situations he too could be punished. Visitors to the Xhosa in the eastern part of the Cape Colony in the seventeenth century later commented on the importance of the rule of law in their society and the subjection of the chief to it.[51]

Unlike the San and the Khoikhoi, most Africans fought fiercely against white domination. Through repeated and intense conflicts—the so-called nine "Kaffir wars" (1779–1878) with whites (both English and Boer) and intergroup conflicts on the eastern frontier of the Cape Colony and in the interior—they were able to retain at least some of their social control traditions throughout most of the nineteenth century. To a surprising degree they preserved chiefdoms and cultures even as their lands were appropriated and their resistance brutally punished. Their military and political defeat—with the aid of mounted police (often including Africans) in both British colonies—was inevitable, but even as they were forced to submit to the white man's technological and economic advantage, "[t]hey adapted their culture and their social, economic, and political institutions to the new order."[52] Perhaps the ability of African groups to preserve group identity in the face of unrelenting invasion helps explain why were able to mount a liberation movement that ultimately triumphed.

But in the meantime they could not escape institutional repression of many kinds. In white-dominated South Africa the nineteenth century was a time of chaotic and contradictory political developments; by its end police and courts had become the bedrock of a system that put down any resistance to it.

Although the British government found the maintenance of the Cape Colony an expense that it wished to contain, local colonial administrators continued to pillage Xhosa land to the east, claiming jurisdiction over "British Kaffraria" (now part of the Eastern Cape) and, in 1843, annexing the territory of Natal on the Indian Ocean.[53] Although Parliament wanted the colonists to fight their own battles, it financed "Kaffir wars" that cost British taxpayers millions of pounds. In the interests of economy and self-determination it allowed the Afrikaner trekkers to form two autonomous republics but later annexed the Transvaal with ultimately bloody results. While the Cape was a freer place—blacks and whites mingled more easily there, the franchise was open to males of all races if they met the property qualifications, and blacks served on some Cape Town juries—the Afrikaners who migrated to the north and east built their new states on the nationalistic dreams and religious values that had sustained them as trekkers.[54] The original constitution of the Transvaal asserted, "The people desire to permit no equality between coloured people and the white inhabitants, either in Church or State."[55]

Adding to the chaos in the interior during the first third of the nineteenth century were forces that decimated African chiefdoms: persistent droughts and Zulu incursions to the north, known as the *mfekane* (the crushing). Anarchy prevailed as other chieftains fought back and people fled from one group to another. Missionary teachings persuaded many Xhosas that they must abandon their old beliefs and customs to thrive. The militaristic Zulu nation, whose kings—especially the famous Shaka and his successor Dingane, who was also his assassin—ruled with brutality, plundered large areas of southeastern Africa and destroyed much community life. (Historian Leonard Thompson likened the rule of Shaka, the earliest and most famous chieftain, to the "reign of terror" of such leaders as Robespierre and Stalin.)[56] In the short term, violent encounters between the Zulus and the migrating—or, more properly, invading—Boers and English resulted in crippling defeats for both; but ultimately the Africans capitulated to the superior technology and organization of white military power. As a result of both tribal and interracial conflict, by midcentury the territory was a bloody and decimated frontier without any semblance of law and order. Nothing better illustrates the futility of British dreams of "civilizing" both the Africans and unruly Boers in the outposts beyond the Cape Colony than the irrelevance of the pass laws for lack of local police and magistrates to enforce them.

The British commitment to legal equality for black South Africans did not last. The retreat from protection of their interests was directly related to the eastward migration of the Boers and the difficulties it posed for maintaining sovereignty. In 1835 the British government passed the Cape of Good Hope Punishment Act, conveying what one historian calls "shadowy powers" over white settlers east of the Cape preying on the Xhosa (who were also raiding their settlements, stealing cattle and burning wagons).[57] Henceforth British subjects would be as criminally liable for offenses committed against indigenous people as they would have been within the colony—assuming they could be brought back within reach of Cape courts. But this project was halfhearted to begin with and was soon eclipsed by more pressing concerns. Successive colonial governors in the 1830s and 1840s tried to forestall Afrikaner expansion by encouraging the formation of client states run by chiefs in the interior, an even more expensive and complicated approach to acquiring what many in Britain saw as a worthless addition to the empire. By the 1850s the British were ready to cede sovereignty in much of the interior to the Afrikaners. They withdrew from the highveld and entered into agreements of independence that included no protection of blacks other than commitments not to permit slavery. State-building in the new Boer republics (the Orange Free State and the South African Republic—commonly called the Transvaal) was left to defensive, puritanical emigrants who needed labor for their farms and were surrounded by desperately poor Africans. The British surely knew that in such a society exploitation and brutality would trump the more liberal values they had championed. "The pendulum had swung hard over since the early 1840s, from a declared policy of protecting black South Africans from disruption by turbulent British subjects, to a policy that amounted to an alliance with independent white communities against their black neighbors."[58]

In Natal, the second British colony, the capitulation to racial repression was more blatant. During the late nineteenth century the Natal police were primarily a military force with the primary task of suppressing African unrest, and magistrates often imposed brutal and arbitrary punishments on blacks.[59] Believing that Africans and whites should be kept separate for the good of both races (which meant preserving the subservience of one race and the supremacy of the other), Theophilus Shepstone, secretary of native affairs for over thirty years, had earlier developed and implemented a "native policy" that was adopted officially throughout the country (except for the Orange Free State) in 1927 and emulated in slightly different form informally in other regions. It segregated native populations geographically and gave the chiefs—subject to the "Supreme Chief," the British governor—limited authority to apply customary law in local governance. Draconian and comprehensive, the Natal Code of Native Law that evolved out of Shepstone's directives closely resembled the system of "indirect rule" that Britain and other colonial powers employed elsewhere in Africa until the middle of the twentieth century.[60] It can be considered the precursor of the segregation policy of the early twentieth century and the subsequent forty years of apartheid. This strategy reflected the demographic reality that at the time of annexation (1843) blacks outnumbered whites in Natal by about fifty to one. Containing one hundred thousand Africans (belonging to dozens of aboriginal groups who had been dispersed by Zulu expansionism and were in a state of flux) was essential to prevent resistance to white domination. The colonists justified it with assumptions of racial superiority and the convenient myth that the Africans were "intruders," immigrants without rights.[61] Blacks were also thought to be living in a lawless—and therefore dangerous—state that would have to be controlled.

Colonial manipulation took many forms. During the late 1840s the colonial Natal legislature set aside "locations" (later also called "reserves") for Africans; the spaces each family received were too small and barren to cultivate successfully and ensured that the residents could not be self-sufficient and would therefore have to depend on colonial employers.[62] Africans were also excluded by ordinance from the protections of British and Roman-Dutch law that operated in colonial courts. Except when charged with crimes "repugnant to the general principles of humanity, recognized throughout the whole civilized world" (a state to be determined by the "civilized" colonial masters, of course), they were subject to the colonists' conception of their customary law.[63] The institutional hierarchy was clear; in the late nineteenth century efforts were made to codify customary law in such a way that it would become assimilated into the "uses and practices of civilized nations."[64] Far from deferring to tribal authority, the divided legal order colonized it.

Over time what was originally rationalized as a beneficent nod to communal autonomy became its clenched fist. The colonial governor, acting as supreme chief, paid local chiefs and village headmen to impose and enforce order in their communities; courts staffed by white magistrates would apply his interpretation (often distorted) of traditional law, undermining the institutional power of the chief. Although Shepstone purported to be managing the adjudication of conflicts between Africans according to their law, his justice reflected the view he expressed in 1883: "The main object of keeping the natives under their own law is to ensure control of them."[65] Historian David Welsh contrasts the "flexible and consultative" nature of Zulu rule with the "harsh and arbitrary bureaucratic despotism" that characterized Shepstone's judgments and weakened the chiefs' relations with their subjects.[66] By a kind of legerdemain the colonists took control of African law while appearing to respect it, superseding traditional leadership by co-opting it in service to subservience and pacification. A version of this "indirect rule" became a cornerstone of the edifice of apartheid.

Inevitably, the values of the colonizers colored both their recognition and interpretation of traditional law (which, as the creation of preliterate people, was uncodified and therefore easily manipulated). They were much more committed to capital punishment than the Africans; on the other hand, they were unwilling to tolerate harsh traditional African punishments for witchcraft. At the slightest indication of political motives behind deviant behavior they were prepared to impose harsh penalties. In the 1874 prosecution of a chief convicted of rebellion for refusing to appear in court to explain why he had not ensured that the guns of his followers were registered—the notorious Langalibalele affair—the supreme chief, Sir Benjamin Pine, opened the proceedings by announcing that the accused was being tried for "the greatest crime a human being can commit against society—for rebellion against the authority of the Queen."[67] The colonists were also prepared to adapt customary law to their own ends with means that would have been impermissible under their own legal rules. Langalibalele was tried in a specially created "Supreme Chief's Court" headed by the colonial lieutenant-governor, who, as representative of the state against which the chief had supposedly offended, was a party to the case. The only legal representation the accused was permitted was that appointed by prosecutors; the advocate he requested (without success) later wrote of the trial:

> [Langalibalele] had not the chance nor the intelligence to prepare any defense; and I believe that until the morning of the trial he had never heard of the long written indictment against him, and that he had no notice of it. At the trial itself the strangest anomalies prevailed. It was stated to be by native law. There was not a single element of trial by native law in it. . . . Native law not only permits, but constantly employs in its trials, not one, but twenty Advocates. Here there was no Advocate allowed. In a native trial everyone that the audience will listen to may speak for or against the accused. . . . But in the face of the red jackets and the fixed bayonets, no one spoke or dared to speak for this man. All the disadvantages of both systems, English and Kafir, were against him.[68]

It is during this period—in the fledgling Afrikaner republics and the original Cape Colony as well as the newly annexed Natal—that the use of statutory offenses enforced almost exclusively against blacks (as distinguished from common-law crimes like assault and theft that applied to all) became a club wielded by police and courts. Until then informal restraints imposed on black labor by bosses and landowners had been the norm, especially in the Boer republics, where law enforcement was cumbersome and rudimentary. "More and more the legal machine which affected the whole population was hitched to the administrative machine which affected Africans only. The established police, court and prison system was used to penalize Africans who broke the special laws aimed at their control."[69] By the late 1930s, one historian estimates, 90 percent of the convictions of Africans were pass and liquor law violations, Masters and Servants Acts, or failure to pay the poll tax.[70]

The intertwined policy threads that dominate South African history—exploited (and often coerced) labor and racial repression—shaped the prosecution of these crimes. Perhaps most important—at least until racial unrest spurred the creation of all-encompassing and often bizarre political crimes and enforcement methods—were the Masters and Servants Acts that came into being in every district ruled by whites and the pass laws that controlled the mobility of blacks in cities and towns. These laws, generally applied to farm and domestic workers, were among the forms of subjugation that succeeded and mimicked slavery. (Another was the capture of African children to use as "apprentices" to whites—begun with Cape Colony commandos, continued with trekker raids, and institutionalized by law that permitted the white farmer to apprentice children born to black tenants on his land. As late as the early twentieth century, this peonage was given a veneer of respectability by the practice of taking children from orphanages to serve as house servants.) As with the policy of forcing Africans onto barren and unfamiliar land set aside for them, masters and servants legislation was a British creation that conveyed benefits with one hand and snatched away freedoms with the other and then developed into an all-encompassing attribute of serfdom. A Cape colonial ordinance enacted in 1841 provided the model; it was expanded in the laws of Natal (1851), the Cape (1856), the Transvaal (1880), and the Orange Free State (1904). After the 1910 unification of the country the principle became a national law that not only held a sword over the head of the individual worker but deterred efforts to organize.

While the acts required explicit understandings as to wages and the work to be performed and limited the punishments employers could inflict on workers, they also criminalized breach of contract, which included such sins as the refusal to perform a particular job and the failure to exercise adequate care in tending to livestock. The laws were quite ineffective at forcing workers to work, many commentators allege, partly because many blacks were unfamiliar with and unsympathetic to the basic notion of a contract. But they were vigorously applied. Magistrates—colonial employees with little training and less judicial independence—often did the bidding of local landowners by imposing harsh punishments on reluctant workers.[71] Violators in the Cape faced mandatory imprisonment, and flogging was a common sentence in Natal, the "lashing colony."[72] The laws had greater reach and more restrictions as the growth in the economies of the various territories demanded more labor. In 1926 the national Masters and Servants Act, which had previously covered only short-term wage laborers, was extended to "labour tenants," residents on white farms who, in a quasi-feudal relationship, were expected to work for their right to remain on the land they had often occupied since long before the whites arrived.[73]

Pass laws were also crucial to white control over labor, with crime control a very secondary objective.[74] The pass was a form of bondage for both Khoikhoi and slaves in the Cape Colony. A slave going in or out of town had to show that he was on his owner's errand. When the British abolished the slave trade in 1807, the colonists looked increasingly to the labor of the Khoikhoi for their farms. The Dutch had annexed their grazing lands and depleted their herds, so the Khoikhoi, whose sheep and cattle were their only capital, were forced to work for the whites, who controlled their movements with mandatory labor contracts and passes.[75] Without a pass to leave the farm—required by a Cape ordinance—they ran the risk of being arrested as vagrants and punished by being assigned to a contract with a farmer.[76] Ordinance 50, the equality provision that the British imposed and the white Dutch colonists despised, essentially repealed pass laws as part of a charter of formal racial equality in the Cape Colony, but the device of the pass continued for other people in other forms. Xhosas, considered "native foreigners," were required to carry a passport in the colony, and "by degrees the passport grew into a pass."[77] By the late nineteenth century any Cape Colony landowner or official could require any African to produce a pass. Similarly, in the first republic settled by the Voortrekkers (Natal) in the 1830s blacks were not allowed to be in settled areas without a pass signed by a white employer. The South African Republic (Transvaal) simply adopted Natal's restrictions on Africans. The extent to which they were enforced depended on the demand for black labor, the need to regulate the proportions of blacks and whites in the towns, the amount of social conflict in the territory, and the predilections of local administrators. Keppel-Jones summarizes the reach of pass laws at the end of the South African War (1902) as follows:

> [E]very Native man (but not woman) in the two colonies [the Transvaal and the Orange River Colony] traveling from his home or place of employment had to carry a pass signed by his employer, his chief or an official. No railway ticket could be issued to him unless he produced this pass. In the Orange River Colony he required a residential pass, showing that he was entitled to live and work where he did, even when not traveling. In the Transvaal a Native entering a town to look for work was given a temporary pass allowing him to do so, and when work was found his contract was registered on another pass. In the Transvaal, too, no Native man in an

urban area could be abroad at night without a night pass signed by his employer, In Natal the system was simpler. Every Native employee who was not working on the farm where he resided had a permanent identification pass, and another was needed for entering or leaving Natal.[78]

By the early years of apartheid, before local passes were coordinated in the comprehensive "reference book," many people had to carry as many as six at all times.

After diamonds and gold were discovered (in 1867 and 1886, respectively, though Africans had previously mined gold), pass laws balanced the need for unskilled labor in mining and in the new industries that sprang up around it with the continuing need to keep the natives down on the farm. Increasing numbers of blacks, lured by the cash wage offered in mining, migrated to the frontier towns of Kimberley and Johannesburg, where their movements were controlled by pass laws, curfews, and requirements that they live in crowded, all-male worker housing, the precursor of the twentieth-century hostels that separated families and fomented violence, political and otherwise. Blacks could be imprisoned for being without a pass in a mining camp, where they were prohibited from digging or trading in diamonds, which effectively "divided ownership and production of diamonds by color."[79] As with earlier racially oppressive policies, these controls over Africans were justified with appeals to the need for crime control—in this case, the potential theft of diamonds. Vagrancy was the charge if blacks were caught digging for gold in the Transvaal.[80] Despite efforts to disarm them, African laborers often had guns, and whites worried about armed revolt.[81]

The brutality of pass laws can be understood, in part, as the product of a gross miscalculation. The policy of creating reserves and keeping "unneeded" blacks on them without plans for their development completely disregarded the inevitability of migration to the cities if opportunities were not available in the country. The collapse of rural economies and rapid industrial growth early in the twentieth century propelled a mass migration such that by 1936, when an official census was taken, there were more blacks than whites in urban areas (about 1.3 million whites, with the blacks divided between Africans (1.1 million), coloureds (400,000), and Asians (200,000).[82] The failure to develop the reserves or adapt to the reality of shared urban space and opportunities created an enforcement demand that could be met only with repression of the most aggressive kind. In 1930 in the Transvaal alone, 42,000 Africans were convicted of violating the pass law.[83]

Early incidents of resistance to racial oppression often involved the pass laws. Gandhi led one of the first—the refusal by Indians in 1906 to accept restrictions on their rights as traders. It was followed by a women's antipass campaign in the Orange Free State in 1913 and protest demonstrations on the

Witwatersrand in 1919. The first anti-pass campaigns rested on both economic and political arguments; the Witwatersrand activists argued that "passes prevent money," referring to the suppression of wages that tight control made possible. The inaugural address in 1912 of the president of the newly formed South African Races Congress inveighed against "the most exasperating regulations ever devised to vex and worry a people," a reference, among other things, to the omnipresent pass laws.[84] As isolated resistance metamorphosed into the liberation struggle, the pass became more than a hated mechanism of control. Ironically, as a symbol of racial humiliation it helped to mobilize mass resistance and further liberation.

Segregation Justice, 1910–1948

Segregation as routine practice can be said to have started in the Cape Colony with slavery, pass laws, and separated institutions like the Cape Mounted Rifles (white) and the Native Affairs Police (black). Throughout the eighteenth century white governments discouraged (mostly ineffectively) trade between the colonists and Africans. And the establishment of African reserves in Natal in the 1840s set a precedent for residential segregation, though blacks and whites continued to live in close proximity on farms and in some sections of some towns. Racial discrimination and exploitation in employment—often not very different from slavery—was the norm in the Boer republics of the nineteenth century; within a decade of the discovery of diamonds in 1867 Africans were shut out of the opportunity to register claims in Kimberley to dig for them.

But practice is not the same as policy, at least not explicitly. Spatial segregation became a countrywide political commitment only at the beginning of the twentieth century, partly as a consequence of the industrialization that intensified the need for a highly controlled labor force. The Natives Urban Areas Act of 1923 was a perfect expression of the utility of criminal law to ossify a fusion of ideology and self-interest, reinforcing racial separation but also ensuring the exploitation of black labor. The evils the law was designed to correct were summarized by a 1921 Native Affairs Commission report: "It should be understood that the town is a European area in which there is no place for the redundant Native, who neither works nor serves his or her people but forms the class from which the professional agitators, the slum landlords, the liquor sellers, the prostitutes and other undesirable classes spring."[85] Passed at a time when blacks were migrating to the towns in great numbers, the act restricted them to "locations" on the periphery (the precursors of modern townships) and extended pass requirements to cover limited permission to live and work in a white area. Amendments enacted over the next fifteen years gave local authorities virtually complete control over the movements of Africans. The law could be invoked to remove unneeded workers permanently from town or to force them to get back to work.[86] Despite the often brutal implementation of these policies, Africans continued to pour into urban areas, living in slums and squatter camps.

As political power coalesced under the British after the South African War, so did the separatist ideology that found expression in sweeping policies—and, therefore, criminal justice practices—to constrict the opportunities and movements of black South Africans. (From this time forward there was not much difference in the racial attitudes of the supposedly enlightened English-speakers and the openly conservative Afrikaners.) First, a commission appointed in 1903 by Lord Alfred Milner, the British high commissioner who believed that "[t]he white man must rule because he is elevated by many, many steps above the black man," recommended separate, permanent "locations" for Africans.[87] Then the new constitution for the Union of South Africa (1909), the national entity officially uniting the two former British colonies and the two former Boer republics, contained a political color bar, limiting membership in parliament to white males and limiting voting rights for blacks to the Cape (and, nominally, to Natal), where only those who met the steep property qualifications were still eligible to vote.[88] The 1913 Natives Land Act was landmark legislation prohibiting Africans from owning or leasing rural land except in that small fraction designated for Africans and turning thousands of families into squatters or driving them off land they had occupied for generations. A decade later the Natives Urban Areas Act effectively declared the African to be a foreigner in urban areas and made it a national priority to control his every movement. African men were required to have passes to work and live in the white towns, to travel or be out after curfew. In 1930 the law was amended to cover women and in 1937 to allow local authorities to remove unneeded African workers to another area.[89] An industrial color bar also outlawed strikes by African miners and consigned them to the most menial mining jobs, prohibiting their advancement to managerial positions. And in 1936 the Representation of Natives Act removed African voters to a separate voters' roll in the Cape and Natal, eliminating the threat that their numbers might one day multiply to swamp the votes of whites. (Until the 1950s Africans continued to elect white "native representatives" to parliament. Coloureds remained on the regular voters' roll until 1956.) While it was largely General J. B. M. Hertzog, prime minister of the Union from 1924 to 1939, who oversaw the enactment of this web of restrictions, it also realized the segregationist dreams of his predecessor (and successor) General Jan Smuts. In 1917 Smuts had told a London audience: "Instead of mixing up black and white in the old haphazard way, which instead of lifting up the black degraded the white, we are now trying to lay down a policy of keeping them apart as much as possible in our institutions. In land ownership, settlement and forms of government, we are trying to keep them apart."[90]

The separation of the races and the relegation of blacks to subservient status was crucial to capitalist development that required a large proletarian class that would work the farms and mines. While whites invoked the traditional master-servant relationship to support segregationist policies, another common justification was the threat of black crime. A Transvaal commission report that informed the political debate over the Natives Urban Areas Act of 1923 warned that "[t]he masterless native in urban areas is a source of danger and a cause of degradation of both black and white."[91] Crime by blacks was the white man's burden, to be controlled with legal provisions that applied only to "natives" and enforcement methods that expressed white disdain for blacks. Pass laws and liquor prohibitions were crime prevention devices; baseless crusades against black rape of white women were pursued with zeal as weapons in the fight against the "black peril." White concern about "law and order" warranted police brutality in suppressing black political protest and labor unrest, where both black and white strikers were sometimes gunned down.

The segregation policy required consolidation and centralization of the power of the institutions that were to enforce it. Police and courts, from the early days of the Cape Colony, had been charged with maintaining race relations, but that often meant keeping peace between the Boers and the British. Now the mandate was more explicit, announced by white political leaders and endorsed by the actions of the white parliament; black and white were to be relegated to their separate spheres.[92] It was a tall order, especially since black South Africans—that "vast engine of labour," as the writer Olive Schreiner described them in 1909—were the bedrock of the new industrial economy.[93]

Creating a national police force, which took place officially in 1913, was beset with problems.[94] Most Afrikaners detested the white South African Constabulary, which had overseen the reconstruction effort after the war and was associated with the scorched-earth policy of the British military.[95] The black force assigned to police the reserves of the Transvaal and the Orange Free State after the war was tiny, and the organizational strains inherent in knitting together the decentralized units of the four provinces with more than ten thousand men were formidable. Colonial police forces had been varied and fragmented; some were mounted, some were assigned to civil tasks as well as the maintenance of law and order, and some operated under the aegis of magistrates rather than the colonial or municipal administration. Police styles and functions varied somewhat between town and country. The rural Boer forces were swashbuckling and paramilitary, defending the interests and territory the settlers claimed; in the towns the British model of civilian policing prevailed, where police collected taxes and child support, checked passes, and were trained to think of themselves (inaccurately, for the most part) as apolitical.

Then as now, police-community relations were poor. Whites felt insufficiently protected against black crime, while blacks complained of police harassment and surveillance. Blacks formed a significant portion of the constabulary everywhere, about 39 percent nationwide in 1910, at the time of Union.[96] They lent legitimacy to the force that would control their brethren, and the pay was so poor that whites were unlikely recruits. But their behavior appears not to have deviated from the general policing style, "reserving for blacks methods of extreme cruelty and brutality."[97]

The South African Police (SAP) emerged as an institution that "bore the stamp of bureaucratic rationale, a new disciplinarian ideology of efficiency and, perhaps most significantly, a distinct militarisation of drill and organisational hierarchy."[98] Along with the political will of those who created it, the SAP reflected the social and economic forces of a turbulent time. The rush of country folk and immigrants—white and black—to the towns and mines gave rise to new demands on the police. Although the migrating whites were more prone than the blacks to the usual vices of mining communities—drunkenness, theft, prostitution, housebreaking—black crime commanded special attention as evidence of resistance to white rule. Labor protests spurred a rise in public order policing in which the police often took direction from the mine owners.

The depression that followed World War I necessitated cuts in the police budget—reducing low pay still further—and the 160 deaths from the flu epidemic of 1918 depleted the force. In combination (and because officials were reluctant to solve the manpower problem by hiring large numbers of blacks) these developments led to what Brewer calls "the Afrikanerization of the rank and file"—staffing the SAP with rubes whose English was rudimentary and heightening tensions between English-speakers and Boers as well as between blacks and whites.[99] Brewer portrays a law enforcement establishment trying mightily to modernize and rationalize—or at least conveying that impression in the rhetoric of its publications—but in fact remaining a colonial force, both externally and internally. Seen in this light, black and Afrikaner constables were poorly paid "subjects" carrying out the orders of a largely English-speaking officer corps whose primary emphasis was on demonstrating the coercive authority of the state, rather than on controlling and preventing ordinary crime.[100] Only in Cape Town was enforcement of segregation policies often halfhearted. Police there resisted the mandate of the Natives Urban Areas Act for evicting Africans from the city.[101]

The white courts, too, showed little reluctance to enforcement of the growing commitment of the English victors in the Boer War to segregation, though some distinction should be made between the trial courts and the appellate courts. The magistrates' courts took direction from the Native Affairs Department and followed examples from the higher courts, imposing stiff penalties—often with relish—for violations of the Natives Urban Areas Act and the antibrewing laws. When the Native Administration Act of 1927 formalized and nationalized segregation, decreeing separate and unequal treatment for blacks in many realms, the magistrates' courts were principally responsible for enforcing it.

By the beginning of the twentieth century, many of the African traditions of crime control had become casualties of European influence or fiat. The authority of the chief was much reduced as the result of British rule, which included his supervision and often co-optation by colonial administrators. The British government refused to allow ritual killings and punishment for witchcraft (which, however, still occurs), and the authority of the state superseded the jurisdiction of tribal courts for most serious crimes. The chiefs' courts were irrelevant as sources of racial justice, acting effectively as deputies for white governments and rarely dealing with racial matters. They dispensed customary law, ruling on customary marriages, succession, and conflicts between Africans, but could be overruled by white magistrates and judges. Appeals from the chiefs' courts were sometimes taken to the higher courts of general jurisdiction, with results that often demonstrated the impossibility of reconciling widely disparate judicial traditions. The real authority for resolving disputes lay with white police and magistrates, while chiefs and headmen did their bidding in return for government stipends.

It is a point of honor with many white South Africans (especially lawyers) that the judiciary (primarily appellate in criminal matters) maintained a benign neutrality in applying oppressive laws, doing what it could to interpret them narrowly when to do otherwise would have oppressive consequences. The image and reality of high-minded and dispassionate judges predates the segregation era. Even before Union the Cape Colony judiciary had developed an international reputation for competence and courage—Sachs describes its most distinguished chief justice as "learned, grave, courteous and prepared to stand up to the government"—and the Boer republics, too, had attracted competent judges who, in some kinds of cases, demonstrated their independence.[102] The Transvaal bench became a source of institutional stability in the context of postwar turbulence and the need for economic growth. Union brought the enactment of uniform national laws and the creation of a national court system—a Supreme Court with provincial branches and an Appellate Division in Bloemfontein, the dusty capital of the country's farmlands.[103] The reputation of this court for fairness and competence is perhaps explained as a penumbra of the liberal legal traditions—inherited from both Britain and the Cape Colony—that preceded and shaped its creation.

The South Africa Act (1909—also called the Act of Union) created a political system that was to hobble the courts in restraining apartheid in later years. Its dominant feature was parliamentary sovereignty, the familiar mode of governance for the former colonies of the Cape and Natal but not for the Boer republics (Orange Free State and Transvaal). Based on the British tradition of a flexible constitution that embraced the principle of equality before the law but lacked a bill of rights, it permitted no judicial review of legislation but did not explicitly limit judicial power. Although the integrity and objectivity of the white judiciary for the first half of the twentieth century was much celebrated—by themselves as well as by national and international observers—it proved inadequate to the task of curbing the excesses of the government.[104] During the turbulent period following the massacre of children and adults in the Soweto uprising of 1976 John Dugard, one of South Africa's most distinguished legal scholars, wrote, "In South Africa few holds are barred as far as parliament is concerned: parliamentary sovereignty has been taken to its logical and brutal conclusion at the expense of human rights."[105]

Hugh Corder, in his study of the role and attitudes of appellate judges in the forty years before apartheid, points out that the tradition of South African judicial decision-making in that era was cautious but not rigid, an approach that acknowledged judges' role in developing the law even as it renounced involvement in the partisan conflicts of the day.[106] The Appellate Division, despite an "aura of infallibility" and a reputation for being "color-blind," was not a source of racial empowerment, righting the wrongs of the legislative branch. (Although it was not until much later that the courts were specifically prohibited from reviewing acts of parliament, they probably, as a matter of practical politics, could not have set aside, for example, segregation in public accommodations or beaches or post offices even if they had been so inclined.) And it certainly upheld many instances of differential treatment by the legal system, benefits withheld or harsh punishments imposed on blacks that would have been considered unjust for whites. Corder concludes that, for the elite, white judges who sat from the time of Union until 1950, when apartheid was taking hold, there was

> no apparent attempt by the court to mitigate the harsh effects of oppressive laws, or to criticize their substance and application. Whether it be in respect of segregation of public amenities, the exercise of discriminatory liquor or sex laws, or crass prejudice, nowhere is there a sign of an endeavour to adhere scrupulously to the doctrine of equality of all people before the law, or even to remind the law-giver, ever so gently, of this principle.[107]

Nonetheless, there were occasions where pre-apartheid judges respected individual rights without regard to race, in contrast to the behavior of many apartheid-era judges and magistrates. Cape chief justice (and, after Union, the first chief justice of South Africa) J. H. de Villiers was an energetic proponent of equal justice and an opponent of indiscriminate flogging, which was disproportionately imposed upon blacks. Corder illustrates the extent to which appellate judges in the first half of the twentieth century respected the importance of a fair criminal process for both blacks and whites with the account of a 1933 case in which Appellate Division judges unanimously denied a policeman leave to appeal a judgment against him for shooting an African who ran away when asked for his pass. The judges based their decision on disapproval of the use of excessive force in making an arrest; "a policeman cannot shoot at a person arrested merely because he ran away," wrote Chief Justice Johannes Wilhelmus Wessels. Corder ruefully notes the contrast between this attitude and the acceptance of police violence displayed in statistics showing that during 1976 and 1977, 842 adults and fifty-five juveniles were shot and either killed or wounded by police when "escaping from custody."[108]

Conclusion

During the three hundred years between the first Dutch settlement and the 1948 National Party victory that ushered in the apartheid era, whites employed a variety of instruments of subjugation against blacks. They imported slaves and abandoned the institution of slavery only when forced to do so by British imperial decree. They fostered the dependence of the indigenous Khoikhoi and San, once they no longer were prime suppliers of livestock and produce needed by the refreshment station, and forced them into domestic service. They sent out commandos to deplete the herds of the Khoikhoi, and they ultimately exterminated the San. In their eastward migration they appropriated land and turned its previous occupants into either displaced persons or quasi-feudal tenants and servants. Except in the Cape, in limited circumstances, they denied blacks the vote. Military disruption and the co-optation of chiefs and headmen destroyed much tribal and communal life, including both authoritarian and consensual social control traditions. Vanquished by white military and technological superiority, Africans had no effective defense against white exploitation of their labor, first for the farms and then for the mines. Denied mobility and opportunity in an increasingly urban and industrial land, by the middle of the twentieth century they were an oppressed and fragmented proletariat in an expanding capitalist economy.

The long, anguished process of subjugation often relied on sanctions—whether officially imposed or carried out as acts of private retribution—that were justified as crime control. Commando raids and extrajudicial punishments—even the mass killings of three to four thousand Africans in the wake of the Bambatha rebellion in Natal in 1906—could be seen as legitimate reprisals.[109] Flogging punished the insubordination that was regarded as criminal because the role of blacks was to serve whites; enforcement of pass laws was felt necessary for crime prevention in the towns. As black labor became a more important element in the economic development of the country, criminal law became an essential disciplinary tool. Legislative definitions of criminality relegated blacks to the inferior status they were believed to deserve—and which, not coincidentally, would keep them in the unskilled labor pool. Police and courts were instruments of white domination. In addition to vigorous enforcement of race-based offenses, they identified blacks as primary targets of patrol and prosecution for ordinary crimes and inflicted disproportionately severe penalties on them. In the long run, neither the equal-rights rhetoric of the colonizing British nor the more liberal social atmosphere of nineteenth-century Cape Town broke the trajectory of increasing repression.[110] By the time the National Party assumed its forty-five-year rule the long and tight-fisted arm of criminal law was both the symbol and the weapon of that repression.

3 Apartheid Justice
A Contradiction in Terms

> Our motto is to maintain white supremacy for all time to come over our own people and our own country, by force if necessary.
> —Hendrik Verwoerd, 1965[1]

> [I]t can be stated with conviction that the administration of justice in South Africa conforms to the highest standards traditional in the Western world.
> —H. R. Hahlo and I. A. Maisels, 1966[2]

> [T]o be born into an apartheid society is to be born on a battlefield.
> —F. Chikane, 1986[3]

LONG BEFORE THE National Party's electoral victory in 1948 ushered in four decades of apartheid justice—a contradiction in terms—crime control policy and practice had underscored the power of whites over blacks. Dutch and British rule had relied on racial restrictions and the use of criminal penalties and extralegal violence over the previous three centuries to maintain white dominance. And the social attitudes of isolated and embattled Afrikaner communities had supplemented official policy to endorse a generally punitive stance toward black South Africans; a common remedy for insubordination or other deviance on white farms was private and summary justice by means of a thrashing—for whites as well as blacks. So in some respects the implication for criminal justice policy and practice of apartheid was merely a tightening of the noose, more of the same.

But the evolution of segregation policies into systematic separation of the races also brought with it qualitative changes in official social control. As it developed after 1948—many scholars note that intensified Afrikaner nationalism was a result of the election of the National Party government, rather than its cause—apartheid became an all-encompassing system of racial regulation and repression, what has been called a "civil religion."[4] It required a more overt role for law enforcement than did colonialism—and a militarized one. It was a formidable task, for example, to maintain order while forcing more than half of the country's majority African population into ten artificially designated "homelands" that covered less than 15 percent of the land. And the growing urbanization of the country, with blacks joining whites in both work (often) and play (occasionally), challenged the vision of "separate development" embraced in the early 1960s and called for the constant and forceful exercise of the machinery of criminal justice. Finally, perceived threats to internal security—from "communists" and other troublemakers who wished to disrupt the racial order—could be met only with the suppression of individual liberties that police and courts were called upon to impose. What had been a buttress of white domination became its bearing wall.

The use of criminal law and its enforcement to establish or maintain relations of power occurs in all contemporary societies. With respect to this function of social control, though they will embrace different philosophies, democracies and authoritarian states may in practice be separated primarily by matters of degree. Autocracies differ from more liberal states in their use of police and courts to subordinate even trivial challenges to the state and in their indifference to limits—basic procedural fairness—on the exercise of their power.

While police and courts were instruments of labor control and racial repression in pre-apartheid South Africa, they were not the monolithic source of unbridled state power that they were to become after 1948. And as resistance grew, so did repression: the Sharpeville massacre begat the riot police and the banning of organizations and individuals; the blacks' armed struggle gave rise to counterinsurgency forces in the police and the military; the Soweto uprising brought about police use of black vigilante groups to attack antiapartheid activists. Polite requests for better treatment became demands for rights—more threatening and more likely to be met with force, particularly in the early 1960s and then again from the midseventies until the apartheid system began to break up a decade later. Under the National Party government the police (aided by the military) protected the white state; the judiciary (including the lower-court magistrates) lost its reputation for equity and independence; and security laws swept aside many procedural protections that had been part of the British legal tradition adopted more than two centuries before and refined early in the twentieth century. Gradually, most white South Africans came to support the National Party worldview and to accept the necessity of enforcing it with harsh measures. As John Dugard, a prominent legal scholar, put it in 1978, "Many white South Africans who value the status quo above all else have come to equate the Rule of Law with the rule of law and order and have invoked it to support repression of those who seek to disturb the comfortable (for whites) prevailing social order."[5]

The two interlocking justifications for discrimination and segregation noted in the previous chapter prevailed throughout the apartheid years: the need of the white economy for black workers—in Marxist terms, a reserve army of labor—and the need to reassert the myth of white superiority.[6] Reforms instituted by state president P. W. Botha in the 1980s did not alter that. As Piet Koornhof, the minister of plural relations (in charge of administering apartheid), described it: "The policy of influx control is being scientifically applied, with the chief vision of placing blacks in service, organizing the provision of labor, and consolidating it with supply and demand."[7] To realize this "vision" the state needed to carry a very big stick. By the emergency era of the mid-1980s state-citizen relations all over the country were tainted by "the security forces' movement towards wholly extra-legal 'law enforcement.'"[8]

The Coming of Apartheid

The 1948 victory that ushered in the apartheid regime had a number of immediate sources.[9] The election came at a time when many whites felt besieged both domestically and internationally. Blacks were gaining demographically and getting restless; the spread of trade unionism among Africans had led to industrial strikes in the 1940s, culminating in the mineworkers' strike of 1946, in which seventy thousand men refused to work and joined in protests that left twelve dead and twelve hundred injured.[10] The mass migration of blacks to the cities—the result of economic collapse in the reserves—defied efforts at control. Many Afrikaners resented the British influence in government and felt that the ruling United Party and the prime minister had not been sufficiently vigilant in stamping out what they saw as a growing Communist threat in labor and government. They also felt threatened by a policy encouraging British immigration of skilled workers; sixty thousand entered the country in 1947–48 alone.[11]

The National Party responded to these concerns with strategy and rhetoric that spoke to Afrikaner voters' underlying resentments of English-speakers as well as of blacks. Afrikaner nationalists felt little in common with the British beyond their shared whiteness. The British had not only humiliated Afrikaners in one nasty war—razing villages and farms, slaughtering livestock, and imposing on them the English language after it was all over—but then had made them unwilling combatants in two larger ones. Their sons had gone to fight the Germans, with whom they often felt a greater affinity than with the British. (While there are conflicting views about the degree of Afrikaner support for Hitler, it is incontrovertible that pro-Nazi organizations sprang up in South Africa—one of them, the Ossewabrandweg, boasted a membership of

250,000 early in World War II—and that there were links between them and the Broederbond, the Afrikaner secret society founded in 1918 that dominated important government appointments during much of the apartheid era. With some success the National Party worked hard to convince the general public that it renounced these associations.) In the Nationalist leaders' quest to unify Afrikaners—who constituted a majority of the voters—and to achieve national political supremacy an appeal to antipathy to Britain was, therefore, almost as powerful as the appeal to defend whites against the risk of racial contamination.

The latter threat gained credibility from the specter of rampant black criminality that could only be contained by a firm white hand. As the 1947 Landsdowne Commission put it: "Means must be found to ensure that the natives in town become decent members of society, and obey European standards of morality in order to lessen crime."[12] The contemporary mythology that black criminality could infect whites was a powerful political resource for the National Party, which pledged to serve and promote Afrikanerdom and "to ensure the safety of the white race and of Christian civilization," as the first apartheid prime minister, D. F. Malan, put it in an address to parliament four years before his party took power.[13]

The campaign slogan of *apartheid* was a relatively new term for the central idea of all-encompassing separation of the races that had been debated by Afrikaner intellectuals since the thirties. It appealed to white people's racial fears by eliding the political agenda with the religious notion of the Afrikaners as an elect people whose blood could not be diluted without defying the will of God. (The Dutch Reformed Church has been described as "the National Party at prayer.")[14] This association gave rise to an absolutist view of preserving a secure, white Afrikaner nation and suggested the inevitability of repressive criminal justice policies to follow.[15] Apartheid was "based on the Christian principle of right and justice," said the report commissioned by the National Party for release before the 1948 election.[16] For the National Party to live up to its campaign promises—which it did—it would have to meet any threat to the Afrikaner state—racial or otherwise—with a firm hand, demonstrating the congruence of state power and God's law. The link between legal and religious righteousness prevailed for many decades. Brogden and Shearing quote a reminder from the 1985 police yearbook that policemen on the front lines of apartheid enforcement were serving "the King of Law and Order—Jesus Christ."[17]

Despite its narrow electoral victory, the new government acted as though it had a popular mandate. Prime Minister D. F. Malan proceeded from an assumption that the state existed to serve Afrikanerdom; any pretense of neutrality in government that the British had espoused was quickly jettisoned. The state's embrace of the role of protector and sponsor of the cultural, political, and economic interests of Afrikaners was blatant. Political appointments went to Afrikaner applicants; government contracts went to Afrikaner businesses. Purges of English-speaking employees in the civil service transformed the Department of Native Affairs, where many apartheid regulations were implemented, as well as the police and the military.[18] Afrikaner policemen increased at a rate nearly three times that of English-speakers between 1946 and 1960, and virtually all police supervisors were Afrikaner by the end of the apartheid era. The judiciary, which, for the pre-apartheid period, was described by a prominent scholar as "not drawn from one tightly-knit cultural, geographical, or political grouping," became more densely Afrikaner, with most appellate judges Afrikaans-speaking.[19] The government released Afrikaner prisoners serving sentences for wartime offenses, including treason, sending a powerful message that it would thumb its nose at the rule of law in order to redress perceived inequities of the past.

The Law of Apartheid

Apartheid laws controlled every aspect of life. Black South Africans could not live, work, or travel freely. They could neither advance professionally nor protect the working conditions they had. The laws prevented them from taking steps to improve their children's education, from demanding better health care and other services, from voting, from protesting against forced removal from lands they had occupied for generations and displacement to unfamiliar and dilapidated townships. Resistance to these laws, or violations of them, brought criminal penalties.

Reflecting on apartheid as legal repression, toward the end of the era, Dullah Omar, who later became the first post-apartheid minister of justice, wrote that "state lawlessness *is* the law."[20] By this he meant that the law functioned principally to maintain the economic exploitation and political exclusion of blacks that were the priorities of the state. The ideal of law in a constitutional system as constraint on government was turned on its head; unconstrained by an independent judiciary, law became an enabler of tyranny. A quick review of a few important apartheid statutes and regulations reveals the apparent paradox of a legal system that was nonetheless, in this sense, lawless.[21]

The laws that were most onerous on a daily basis were those that limited mobility and opportunity, gradually trapping most Africans in the impoverished worlds of township or "ethnic homeland" except when their labor was needed by whites. The 1950 Population Registration Act mandated that people be classified by race and that adults carry identification that documented their classification; Dugard noted in 1978 that "[t]his classification is not left to social determination because this might allow a person to climb from a less privileged racial group to a more privileged group if his physical appearance or social acceptance permits such a change."[22] Section 10, a 1952 amendment of the Bantu (Urban Areas) Consolidation Act, sought to limit the urbanization of Africans by providing that they could not remain in an urban area for more than seventy-two hours without a permit. (Exceptions were made for people born in town or who had lived there continuously for fifteen years or were employed there by the same employer for ten, but police enforcing Section 10 with a nightstick did not always abide by these legal niceties.) Enacted in 1953, the Reservation of Separate Amenities Act authorized the setting aside of separate sections for members of a particular race; theaters, beaches, even witness boxes in court separated blacks and whites. "The 'separate but equal' approach has been repudiated and in its stead South Africa approves the 'separate but unequal' philosophy," noted Dugard.[23] Particularly confining and humiliating was the Group Areas Act of 1950—"the essence of apartheid," as Prime Minister Malan acknowledged without apology. It provided for the allocation of residential areas along racial lines and the gradual removal of people not members of the designated racial group—though few whites were forced to move. In 1961 the Appellate Division (the country's highest appellate court) rejected the contention that the act was discriminatory, ruling that, by implication, parliament had authorized the "substantial inequalities" that would result from the forced removals.[24]

Apartheid laws were comprehensive enough to effectively exclude most of the South African population from opportunities to participate meaningfully in the shaping of their own and the country's future. The 1953 Bantu Education Act imposed on the segregated schools a curriculum intended to prepare African children only to work at low-level jobs in the white economy—an "education for inferiority" based on lawmakers' assumptions of intellectual inferiority—and replaced university-educated white teachers with blacks who sometimes had not gone beyond Standard Six (the equivalent of the American eighth grade).[25] By 1968 the per pupil expenditures for white children were ten times that of expenditures for Africans.[26] The 1959 Extension of University Education Act effectively ended integrated higher education by prohibiting enrollment at the English-speaking "open universities." The University of Cape Town and the University of the Witwatersrand were prestigious but also relatively liberal, so the law provided that black students could attend them only with a permit from the education minister. The act also created colleges (usually in remote locations) for coloureds, Indians, and Africans.[27] Supervisory positions in key industries like mining had long been denied to Africans. Male Africans and coloureds in the Cape who qualified by education and property ownership had exercised a limited franchise; they could vote but not hold office in white assemblies like the parliament. That right was revoked in 1960 for Africans and in 1968 for coloureds. By then other forms of political participation had been criminalized. Protest "against a law or in support of any campaign against any law" had been prohibited in 1953, punishable by whipping and imprisonment of up to three years.[28] Interracial political parties were outlawed in 1968.

The pass laws became a cornerstone of apartheid, a direct result of concern that the wartime migration of Africans to the cities had caused a labor crisis on the white farms and a surfeit of unruly blacks in the cities. The promise to separate the races could be kept only if blacks were seen as "temporary sojourners"—the phrase of apartheid's chief architect, Prime Minister Hendrik Verwoerd—in urban areas, tolerated for their utility as wage laborers but carefully tracked and controlled.[29] The government centralized the many local pass laws (with the deceptively titled Abolition of Passes and Coordination of Documents Act) in 1952 to require every African to carry a "reference book" containing detailed personal information and the signature of his or her employer. Failure to carry and display the pass was a criminal offense (from 1958 for males, from 1960 for females). The system controlled employment as well as movement. The worker had to get a new signature from his employer each month to legalize his presence in town and could not change jobs without a discharge signature in the passbook from the previous employer, which made it impossible to look for a job while still employed.[30]

The expanded pass laws had both practical economic consequences and symbolic meaning. They spoke to the core of the National Party's concern with controlling black labor and enforcing the strictest racial segregation. They were also a daily reminder to Africans of their servile and alien status. The party's Sauer Commission report, which came out shortly before the 1948 election and set forth the new apartheid government's policy for reversing African urbanization, was explicit: "Natives in the urban areas should be regarded as migratory citizens not entitled to political and social rights equal to those of whites.... The entire migration of Natives into and from the cities should be controlled by the state, which will enlist the cooperation of municipal bodies."[31]

These controls caused great suffering and spurred widespread defiance. Although passes had long been a daily burden for urban Africans—during the years 1939, 1940, and 1941 almost three hundred thousand Africans were convicted of pass law violations in the Transvaal alone, according to one critical official—their function as the emblem of official racial control intensified.[32] Influx control policies separated families, as one parent was permitted to work in town and the other refused a permit. Night raids in houses and shebeens (bars) to check passbooks were not uncommon; police interpreted the laws as a license to harass. In a 1959 article Lewis Nkosi wrote:

> I do not live apart from my reference book anymore. In fact I have decided
> I AM THE REFERENCE BOOK.

It stands for my personality. It delineates my character. It defines the extent of my freedom. Where I can live, work and eat.

Whenever I see a police constable looking at me, the lifting of his eyes is at once adequate to make me understand that my right to walk the streets, to be about in a White area, even to confront my White fellow being with the sheer physical fact of my existence is now being called into question.[33]

Not surprisingly, the pass laws gave rise to enormous numbers of arrests and imprisonments. Between 1951 and 1952 alone pass law convictions rose from 217,389 to 252,470, an increase of more than 16 percent.[34] Convictions increased throughout the next decades. Sachs estimates that by the late 1960s a million people were being prosecuted annually under the race statutes.[35] Pass law cases jammed the Bantu commissioners' courts, where defendants without counsel were at the mercy of the virtually unlimited discretion of the prosecutor and magistrate.[36] In many cases the penalty was a fine, but incarceration was also common; during the fiscal year 1978–79 (July 1–June 31) 89,059 people were imprisoned for pass law offenses.[37] Many went to jail farms, where they were dispatched to local farmers as free labor.

The pass laws were the irritant that brought about the most notorious mass violence of the apartheid era. The Sharpeville massacre manifested the frustrations of blacks and the relentlessness with which the state was prepared to quash them. Responding on March 21, 1960, to a demonstration in a township south of Johannesburg—part of an antipass campaign called by the Pan Africanist Congress (PAC)—the police fired on thousands of Africans, killing sixty-nine and wounding hundreds more. Other black communities erupted too, with thousands of people burning their passbooks and staying away from their jobs. In the weeks that followed, thousands of dissidents—members of the ANC and the PAC—were rounded up; people were dragged from their houses and whipped and then summarily imprisoned.[38] Nelson Mandela was detained along with many others on the authority of the state of emergency that was declared. The disaster ushered in a new era of repression as Prime Minister Hendrik Verwoerd committed his government to "separate development" and rejected indictments of apartheid at home and abroad. Almost immediately additional security laws sprouted in parliament, rationalized as defensive measures necessary to ensure the country's survival.

The new laws were a blatant and pitiless reminder that no form of organized resistance to apartheid would be countenanced. The Suppression of Communism Act of 1950 was used to convict and ban leaders of the ANC; the defendants were convicted of furthering the aims of Communism by advocating the end to laws of racial separation, specifically the pass laws. After Sharpeville the perception that the ANC and the PAC were committed to revolution led to the passage of the Unlawful Organizations Act, which outlawed both organizations and laid the foundation for banning other groups and the individuals that supported their aims or activities. (Restrictions on the lives of banned persons could include prohibitions on writing or speaking in public, communicating with other banned persons, participating in political or labor organizations, teaching, and meeting with more than one person at a time—including social gatherings. Many of those who were banned were also required to report regularly to the police.) The 90-day detention law passed in 1963 (later amended to 180 days) enabled warrantless arrests and detention in solitary confinement not only for suspected saboteurs and Communists but also for anyone deemed by the state to have information about violations of the "Sabotage Act" or other security laws.[39] In the Rivonia trial of 1963–64 Nelson Mandela was charged as an accomplice with over two hundred acts of sabotage. By this time the pattern of resistance and repression was clear; it was, in the words of Albie Sachs, "an era of sabotage, insurrectionary activity and guerilla warfare, on the one hand, met with progressive suspension of habeas corpus, large-scale imprisonment and allegations of torture and brutality on the other."[40]

The security laws did not distinguish between dissent and delinquency. Their orbit included both people directly involved in insurrection and those who merely expressed political concern around the dinner table. The 1967 Terrorism Act gave senior police officials authority to detain without trial or legal counsel, secretly and indefinitely, anyone who they had "reason to believe" had committed an act defined as terrorism by the law. The law brought "virtually every criminal act within the statutory scope of terrorism," and just for good measure it included any conduct likely to embarrass the national administration.[41] National sweeps during the late 1960s and 1970s, authorized by the limitless police powers of the Terrorism Act, subjected thousands of people to abuse and interrogation for activities that would have been constitutionally protected expressions of opinion in liberal democracies. Winnie Mandela was arrested and held in solitary confinement without access to a lawyer for two hundred days in 1969 for distributing ANC pamphlets.[42] States of emergency that became a permanent condition in the 1980s gave police virtually unlimited discretion to arrest and detain without trial, declare curfews, control public spaces, and silence the media.[43] By then the ninety-day detention law of early apartheid had metamorphosed into the infamous "Section 29," which extended to the national police commissioner the power to hold anyone in solitary confinement for "interrogation" until "no useful purpose will be served by his further detention."[44] In subjecting children as well as adults to detention under these conditions the state was effectively committing a form of child abuse.[45]

The states of emergency in the 1980s—one in 1985 and another in 1986, which was continuously renewed—put the final bricks in the edifice of the lawless legal system. The 1953 Public Safety Act, passed in response to the ANC's Defiance Campaign, had authorized a declaration of emergency by the state president whenever he was of the opinion that the "ordinary law" was "inadequate to ensure the safety of the public, or to maintain public order."[46] The risks of capital flight and international censure, however, inhibited the exercise of this discretionary power of dictators, which was not invoked in the two decades after the first state of emergency in 1960. Stephen Ellmann notes that the National Party government had accomplished almost the same thing by tightening the noose of "ordinary law."

But emergency regulations in the mid-1980s amounted to a "second internal security regime."[47] Brewer describes new offenses punishable by a prison sentence of up to ten years:

> They included such innocuous acts as: verbally threatening harm to another person; preparing, printing, publishing, or possessing a threatening document; hindering officers in the course of their duty; destroying or defacing any notice of the emergency regulations; disclosing the name or identity of anybody arrested under the regulations before their name had been officially confirmed; causing fear, panic and alarm or weakening public confidence; and advising people to stay away from work or to dislocate industry.[48]

In addition, the law expanded state power to arrest and detain without trial, ban organizations and gatherings as well as people, and muzzle the media. News accounts of government repression and resistance to it were prohibited, as well as publication of the words of dissenters or photographs of antigovernment unrest. Seeking to silence the judiciary, the state immunized public officials from most civil and criminal liability attributable to the emergency and prohibited any legal effort to set aside the regulations.

Enforcing Apartheid: Policing Unbound

Scholars of police behavior sometimes distinguish between "high" and "low" policing. "High" policing has been defined as the policing of political activities—policing of demonstrations and the surveillance of dissenting organizations, but also, more broadly, policing that "reaches out for potential threats in a systematic attempt to preserve the distribution of power in a given society."[49] "Low" policing is routine order maintenance and the control of common crime. Both are normal aspects of state policing in all societies; the balance between them reflects the state's political commitments. In order to understand the administration of criminal law in apartheid South Africa it seems, on the surface, important to observe this distinction. The South African Police (SAP), after all, separated its dreaded Internal Stability Unit (and previously the Special Branch) organizationally from ordinary law enforcement in a bureaucratic acknowledgment that the maintenance of internal security was different from common-law crime enforcement.[50] And annual police reports separated common-law crimes from race-statute and political offenses; in 1967 the record showed that 715,000 prosecutions out of a total of 2,300,000 were for such crimes as assault, motor vehicle theft, and drunkenness.[51]

But it is not easy to discern where political enforcement left off and public protection from theft and interpersonal violence began. One might even conclude that by midcentury high policing had largely subsumed low policing. Regime priorities for racial control (from the days of the Cape Colony) and separation (from the time of Union) necessitated high policing and contaminated low policing as well. The race statutes—dealing with curfews, passes, liquor, and so on—had more in common with overtly political enforcement than with the order maintenance they purported to be. Influx control laws were enforced with particular brutality against those suspected of political activity, and dawn pass raids were conducted as retribution for political protests. The tensions occasioned by high policing separated families, increased poverty, and undoubtedly increased ordinary crime, necessitating low policing. The racial ideology that propelled high policing carried over to assumptions about appropriate standards for low policing; Minister of Justice Jimmy Kruger, commenting on the use of live ammunition during the Soweto uprising of 1976, said that blacks need to be made "tame to the gun."[52] Low policing was used as a screen for high policing when an activist was arrested for a common crime because no basis for violation of apartheid laws existed.

The concentration of resources on high policing determined both the general neglect of low policing and its distribution. In 1951 the government adopted the "own areas" policy, policing by blacks in black areas (supervised by whites, of course) and by whites in white areas. (By this time almost half of police manpower was black.)[53] Although the national commissioner piously hoped that with this change in the townships "the police may come to be regarded, as they should be, as friends and protectors of law-abiding citizens," this was an unlikely outcome.[54] The fundamentally authoritarian style of the SAP, coupled with the proliferation of administrative regulations for control of where blacks could live and work, cast police-resident encounters, particularly in African townships, in the mold of confrontation rather than protection. Brewer characterizes the police role as still essentially colonial, having failed to adopt the modern, Western role of civil policing in servicing the townships with respect to ordinary crime.[55] And in urban areas the enforcement of curfews and other exclusions from white neighborhoods drew manpower away from regular law enforcement in black ones. Increasingly in the

1950s police deployment was determined by the ideological commitment to maintaining the boundaries between black and white, not by the need for increased protection from violence. "Passes and documents were checked, raids for illicit liquor conducted, and illegal squatters evicted, all while murder, rape, and gangsterism flourished in the townships."[56]

As the end of apartheid neared in the early 1990s, interviews with township residents emphasized the neglect of police response to theft and assault as well as the brutalities inflicted by the enforcement of apartheid. At community meetings and in individual conversations people noted that it was futile (and sometimes dangerous) to go to the charge office in local police stations to report a crime. One of the few African advocates (South Africa's term for lawyers who appear before the higher courts, the equivalent of British barristers) in Natal told me in 1991 that when his home in the Umlazi township was burglarized, it took many hours for the police to arrive, by which time they could do nothing. "If they treat me this way, imagine how unresponsive they are to ordinary people," he said. Corruption was also rampant, particularly among police assigned to control gambling, prostitution, and liquor, where the opportunities for fraud and vice were plentiful.[57]

It is hardly surprising that high policing was taken to the extreme. Between 1950, when the Suppression of Communism Act was passed, and the embattled late 1980s, internal security legislation and the regulations promulgated by it became more and more inclusive, granting to the minister of justice and the state president great discretion to ban individuals and organizations and detain dissidents of many kinds. Implementation of these orders fell to the police, where intense Afrikaner nationalism held sway and interpretations of the authority given them were extremely broad. Legislation passed in 1963 made it a criminal offense even to advocate a policy or practice that seemed *similar* to the aims or activities of the banned Communist Party, the ANC, or the PAC.[58] The SAP could be confident that it played a key role in political enforcement, as arrests of members or supporters of these groups frequently led to prosecution. Early in the apartheid era it saw itself as defending the country against subversion and racial mixing; by the late 1980s the challenge was to vanquish a Communist-inspired "revolutionary onslaught."[59]

The obsession of a police state with internal security gives the green light to boundless police surveillance and harassment, to casual violence and routine torture. The very scope of South Africa's apartheid laws sent a message that the assignments of the security police came with a license to kill. That license extended in practice if not in theory to regular police work, partly because political motives were often attributed to ordinary criminals—the gangs that increasingly disrupted the townships, for instance. Even when that was not the case, police violence against blacks was very common, including torture with electric shock. In addition, the view that police operated in black areas to maintain the subservience of blacks to whites justified raids—often for liquor or passbook violations—that led to assaults or to shooting people who resisted or protested; warrantless searches were legal after 1955.[60] The law also allowed the use of lethal force when arresting a suspect, and, if the force was "reasonably necessary to overcome the resistance or prevent the person concerned from fleeing," killing someone suspected of a serious crime would be "deemed to be justifiable homicide."[61] Even the hastily recruited black guards of government property in townships during the 1980s acted violently toward residents, often as a result of drunkenness or personal vendettas.[62]

But the principal tasks of the SAP were policing the country's racial divide and defending the apartheid state. They were undertaken with barely a thought for conventional crime control; even a sympathetic police historian had little to say about its place in institutional priorities.[63] The centrality of police in repressing mass protest, antiapartheid campaigns, and individual acts of "terrorism" increased after 1960, when the Sharpeville massacre led to the criminalization of virtually all black political activity. Also at that time, apartheid's "separate development" policy led to the creation of so-called self-governing homelands. (They were neither self-governing nor homelands, in fact. The bits of barren land set aside for blacks—13.7 percent of the land area for 68 percent of the population in 1960—were really ruled by white commissioners and were areas where many "citizens" had never set foot.) More consistent use of influx control laws was needed to push people into them.[64]

Sharpeville & Beyond

The vigor of police enforcement of the pervasive racial restrictions of apartheid was increasingly unconstrained. In 1959 a London paper reported that businessmen in Cape Town complained that their secretaries could not work because of the screams of people being beaten at the central stationhouse nearby.[65] In the ensuing decades the stories of people being thrown out of precinct windows or tortured in detention became so common that even an accurate report of suicide while in police custody would never have been believed. Most notorious was the 1977 death from head injuries of Steve Biko, leader of the black consciousness movement. He was beaten, tortured, and kept naked and comatose in chains for three days in a cell in Port Elizabeth and then transported without medical attention in the back of a van (still naked) to a prison hospital in Pretoria twelve hundred kilometers away.

After the ANC and the PAC were banned in 1960, many liberation movement leaders went underground or into exile. Armed resistance and other explicitly political activity declined sharply in what one commentator has called "the silent decade of the 1960s."[66] Ordinary crimes, however, increased, especially in the depressed townships; in Soweto alone in 1966, according to the South African Institute of Race Relations, there were 891 murders, 1,156 rapes, 7,747 aggravated assaults, 8,075 regular assaults, and 33,489 thefts.[67] (Any population number for Soweto at this time would be a guess, but it was surely less than 300,000.) The SAP, however, was not interested in refocusing on ordinary crime and attempting to provide some protection to beleaguered township residents. Instead, it intensified the enforcement of racial separation, in furtherance of the aim of driving the black population out of the cities and into the "homelands." Arrests for pass law offenses increased dramatically, and police stepped up social enforcement, bursting into bedrooms where whites and blacks might be sleeping together and raiding racially integrated parties. The government banned more and more individuals and infiltrated more and more organizations, preparatory to outlawing them on the slightest pretext.

Counterinsurgency also became a priority for the SAP, with units of police sent off to fight the "terrorists" who threatened South African occupation of Namibia (formerly South West Africa) and British control over Rhodesia (now Zimbabwe). Gavin Cawthra notes that these assignments, which pitted the police against African nationalists, reinforced the suspicions police had about the Africans at home and that "a culture of counter-insurgency" followed them when they returned to South Africa.[68] In the townships the residents seemed more like enemies than candidates for protection, and later, in the black "homelands" during the violent 1980s, the police used what they had learned in Rhodesia and Namibia to arm and train black auxiliary forces for the dangerous work of keeping order and repressing resistance. Brewer argues that the recruitment of African and coloured police for guerilla warfare bolstered the police image: If blacks were now killing blacks in the name of apartheid, how strong could their opposition really be?[69]

This counterinsurgency experience, added to the general tendency of national police forces to conform to larger developments in state strategy, made it easy for the SAP to embrace without hesitation the increasingly militaristic perspectives of the apartheid regime. From the late 1960s police commissioners had stressed the role police should play in the defense of the nation against "subversives" and "communists." In the 1970s they justified their infiltration of groups hostile to apartheid as protection against "militant leftist subversion against the Republic."[70] Joining the South African Defence Force (SADF) in putting down both township rebellions and the growing armed struggle of the ANC during the latter part of the decade, the police felt vindicated in their perception that militant African nationalism and the threat of Communist revolution were one and the same.

State police had always been supplemented by private forces hired by the railroads and the mines and by the Reserve Police—mostly white volunteers protecting white communities. The Native Affairs Department (later renamed the Department of Bantu Administration and Development) had long employed police for the "locations." Less official tactics included the deputizing of conservative black vigilantes to put down political resistance as early as the 1950s. But policing became far more pluralized as the "separate development" ideology took hold in the 1960s and the "homelands" established their own police forces. (As Brewer sees it, "This fitted the ethos of the second phase of apartheid, which emphasized 'self-development.' In effect, the 'own areas' strategy asked Africans to police their own subordination.")[71] In addition, the 1970s brought a resurgence of mass action that was more violent and more threatening to apartheid. By the early 1980s policing blanketed the townships and "homelands," an occupying force not limited to the SAP. Police auxiliaries included *kitskonstabels*—literally, "instant constables," blacks hastily employed and trained for duty in the townships and often regarded by the black majority as traitors—municipal "guards," and, in an informal and usually secret capacity, vigilantes and ANC members (called *askaris*) who had been "turned" by the police.[72] The addition of these recruits reinforced the police perception that the country was in a state of war and that they were worthy warriors.

Hostilities in this war escalated after more than a decade of relative quiescence. In 1976 Soweto schoolchildren rebelled at the proposal for teaching half of their classes in Afrikaans, widely perceived as the language of the oppressor. Firing into a crowd headed for a demonstration in the Orlando Soccer Stadium, the police killed a twelve-year-old boy, precipitating riots all over the country. Within eighteen months at least seven hundred people had been killed. Steve Biko had been murdered and his black consciousness movement outlawed, school boycotts had prompted mass resignations of teachers all around the country, and tens of thousands of activists had been jailed or forced into exile. But the spirit of resistance was still very much alive. The defiance of the Soweto youth and the death of one of them, Hector Peterson, served somewhat the same function as the 1955 lynching of the black American teenager Emmett Till, who had whistled at a white woman and been murdered by her husband. As that event spurred the civil rights movement in the United States, the Soweto uprising fed a new kind of political energy during a period of coalition building that was crucial to the maturation of the liberation struggle in the next fifteen years. As one activist remembered it,

> [There was] a lot of introspection going on, a lot of thinking, a lot of discussion groups, little corners critiquing the Black Consciousness movement. People were reading *What Is to Be Done?* by Lenin. Others were reading Trotsky, *1905,* trying to find answers, trying to find out where do we go from here? What do we do?[73]

The Botha Era of Reform & Repression

The late 1970s brought another development, which was key to the bloody conflicts of the following decade. P. W. Botha, who had been defense minister at the time of the Soweto uprising, became prime minister (and later state president) in 1978 and immediately gave notice that he intended to centralize military and police power in the State Security Council. (The SADF was by now expected to supplement the SAP at all times, whether putting down internal unrest or suppressing the guerilla activity by ANC cadres outside the country.) He also set about trying to realize his plan for defending the country from the "total onslaught" of creeping Communism with a "total strategy" that would loosen some of the strictures of apartheid. Essentially a form of pacification, the plan was to bring about change through reform measures like permitting racially mixed marriages and integrated movie theaters, softening the influx control laws, investing in improved infrastructure for selected townships, and encouraging the development of a small black middle class. The strategy relied on winning hearts and minds in the long run, but it did so by advancing the interests of some while marginalizing others; many saw it as a strategy of divide and rule.

In the short run the total strategy decreed that the state would ensure law and order. Reforms could occur only after the security forces stamped out resistance, and for that Botha's inner circle of generals and ministers (including the minister of law and order, who supervised the police) endorsed "maximum force." As one commentator puts it, "When total strategy was first implemented. . . . repression was its cornerstone."[74] It was an approach that resonated with the views of many senior police officials. The officer who had ordered his men to fire on Soweto demonstrators in 1976 told Alister Sparks several years later that he wished he had been able to shoot them immediately. "When things get to that stage you have no option but to tell your men, 'Open fire on the evil-doers.' Law and order must be restored irrespective of what it's going to cost."[75]

Repression was swift and brutal. Some was done to effect population resettlement. There is disagreement about the numbers of people who were moved to confine blacks within the "homelands" or to vacate areas, like Cape Town's District Six, considered desirable for whites. One study estimated that between 1960 and 1982, 3.5 million people were removed from their homes, but in 1984 the government disputed this figure and asserted that it was 1,971,908—and there were more after that.[76] (The term *forced removals* for this practice is literally accurate; police conducted nighttime raids to arrest people resident in illegal squatter settlements.) The application of existing apartheid laws intensified. Arrests for pass law offenses rose; in 1984 there were 238,894 countrywide.[77] The Internal Security Act was used to ban meetings where school boycotts or strikes were to be discussed.

Such unjust laws invite extralegal abuse. In 1982 a group of parents of political detainees sent to the minister of law and order statements from seventy people alleging widespread torture—sleep deprivation, electric shock, suffocation, midair suspension, assault to the genitals, and so on.[78] Apartheid victims who later testified before the Truth and Reconciliation Commission (TRC) told of similar atrocities and worse. Violence in responding to unrest of any kind was the norm. Riot control became civil war; even at what would otherwise have been peaceful funerals the security forces opened fire. Equipment for public-order policing was buckshot instead of tear gas, and police often shot to kill when they encountered real or imagined resistance. The State Security Council's National Security Management System and its local committees spied on student organizations, church groups, trade unions, and even private social gatherings. Although leaders of the liberation movement were particular targets, dragnets swept up children and people with no political connections.

The reinvigoration of the resistance struggle in the early 1980s owed a good deal to Botha's reform program. It was the government's proposal for a new constitution, creating a tricameral legislature with houses for coloureds and Asians—but no political representation for Africans—that spurred the development of a united front bringing together hundreds of organizations—white and black, mainstream and radical—to fight apartheid. From their initial opposition to the insulting notion that political participation and "separate development" could coexist, the United Democratic Front (UDF) moved on to support rent strikes, school boycotts, rallies, and work stoppages.[79] Local unions, youth groups, and civic organizations pursued a strategy of making the townships ungovernable. They sought to take over local governance by shutting down the town councils that had not only been imposed by the national government but were often the source of the vigilantes that attacked opponents of apartheid. The liberation movement would no longer be driven primarily by intellectuals at the helm of dissident groups or by guerilla forces outside the country or operating underground. A broadly based, decentralized mass movement would meet "total onslaught" with "total resistance" and give notice to the security forces that they faced combatants, not subjects. Furthermore, "people's power" would regulate social order, challenging the state's monopoly.

By this time the police were hardly credible as agents of order maintenance or crime control. Catholic bishops, reviewing the violence of 1984, asserted that police were "now regarded by many black people in the townships as disturbers of the peace and perpetrators of violent crime."[80] Brewer notes their failings, starkly revealed by the slaughter of Soweto and its aftermath:

> [T]he police were managerially incompetent and professionally undeveloped, understaffed in terms of regular manpower, lacking in legitimacy, and crude and brutal in their strategy of relying on violence as a first resort, as well as outmodedly colonial in believing that Black demands could be met only with suppression and force.[81]

The loss of legitimacy was well deserved. The police had failed to respond to reports of theft or assault in the townships, but had manufactured offenses where none existed in order to realize political and economic aims of the state. The continuous raids conducted to intimidate residents and force them out of the urban areas were billed as "crime prevention" measures. Local security forces harassed people who were involved with organizations seeking change, accusing them of hiding terrorists and weapons. Crime was used as a justification for delaying or curtailing promised improvements in living conditions. In 1979 in Crossroads, a squatter community on the Cape Peninsula, the newly appointed apartheid minister had negotiated a settlement with the residents that involved giving them permits to allow them to remain there until alternative housing could be provided. When the permits didn't arrive, the delay was justified by the "impending investigation" of a local leader said to be selling fraudulent permits, and some families were denied the right to move to a new township being built to house the squatters.[82]

Crossroads was also the site of particularly brutal efforts to remove families forcibly from one place to another—in this case from a township near Cape Town, where many people worked, to one much farther away. The police co-opted civilians to act as their surrogates, and over three days in February 1985 the police and vigilantes killed eighteen people—many of them shot in the back—as the result of militant and widespread resistance to being removed to Khayelitsha. The following year the recently appointed local police, aided by vigilantes seeking territorial control, raided the satellite squatter camps of Crossroads and burned down most of the shacks where people were living. Although initially the justification given was the search for arms and "terrorists," an alternative motive seemed clear: "As far as the state was concerned the destruction of the satellite camps had provided it with an opportunity to carry out its policy of 'orderly urbanization,' and it would allow nothing and nobody to turn it from this course."[83] An estimated one hundred people died in fighting and seventy thousand were left homeless.

The squatter struggles illustrated the internal tensions that now split many black communities. Africanist radicals who spurned alliances with whites—primarily the PAC and its adherents—clashed with black activists who made common cause with antiapartheid groups of whatever hue. The "comrades"—usually young—who embraced the ANC's armed struggle and assisted in its bombings and sabotage defied the cooler heads—usually older—who still believed that change could be negotiated. Antiapartheid activists and their sympathizers regarded municipal law enforcement officers and local town councilors—black residents co-opted by the white government as part of an "own areas" strategy of black-on-black repression—as traitors. The pro-ANC UDF battled with supporters of Inkatha, a more conservative Zulu-based movement in Natal, in the southeastern region of the country. Retributive attacks on perceived collaborators were as brutal as assaults by the security forces. The "comrades" (and sometimes ordinary residents) frequently stoned them, and "necklacing"—putting a gasoline-soaked rubber tire around the neck of an offender and settling it on fire—became a highly publicized informal sanction. (The legitimation of violence as part of political struggle also served as a screen for ordinary crime; some of the young people who participated were thugs or gang members who found new justification for their crimes in liberation circles.)

Whether a township was divided or united, the state had tactics to deal with it. The security police and the regional administrative boards exploited internal power struggles, co-opting residents to spy on activists and deploying vigilantes to maim and kill them. On the other hand, when the community mobilized in solidarity, the violence of the police and military was more overt and conducted with impunity. The Vaal uprising of 1984, where protesters in townships near Johannesburg attacked police and people they perceived to be collaborators, mobilized a combined force of seven thousand to raid hundreds of homes and arrest their occupants without ever bringing political charges against them. Considered by the UDF to be a declaration of war, this response spurred countrywide unrest—what one commentator calls "another Soweto"—which in turn led to the government's declaration of states of emergency, starting in July 1985.[84] The state and much of its population were locked in an undeclared war. The ANC attacks on public buildings and power stations escalated, and police became victims as well as perpetrators of violence. Between mid-1984 and early 1985 alone it was estimated that one thousand people died in violent incidents related to political unrest.[85]

Under the declaration of the states of emergency the security police had what one prominent commentator calls "a license to kill."[86] They already had the power to use any level of force to disperse gatherings of people suspected of opposing apartheid and to detain those people indefinitely and without access to legal counsel. They were immune from liability for their violence by tacit institutional understanding as well as by the Indemnity Act of 1977, which shielded them from lawsuits or criminal charges based on what they did while preserving order or maintaining internal security. Now the Internal Security Act of 1982 and the emergency regulations promulgated under the Public Safety Act of 1953 effectively permitted uncontrolled violence; lethal force could be used if people failed to heed police instructions given "in a loud voice," and children under fourteen years old who were in detention could be flogged (and were often, in fact, tortured).[87] Furthermore, the law now gave magistrates and law enforcement officials rule-making power. They could bar the press from entering areas of unrest, and they could ban a wider range of people, organizations, and gatherings—to commemorate the Sharpeville shootings or the anniversary of the issuance of the ANC's Freedom Charter, for example. Meetings of the UDF and its affiliates were banned for specific periods; in late 1985 SAP divisional officials for the Cape province banned all meetings of 102 organizations.[88] Even some outdoor funerals—of which there were many—were banned.

It is not surprising that secret death squads arose within the SAP. Nico Steytler presents a convincing analysis of the fusion of political and organizational interests that led police officers to become torturers and assassins.[89] The overtly political role of the police as a primary instrument of apartheid colored the sense of professional mission within the organization. It gave the counter-revolutionary mind-set of the South African government an unassailable logic. The anti-Communism that emanated from their prime ministers and police commanders and, in some cases, their families merged with the culture of apartheid. "On every level—in the homes, churches, schools and civil society in general—they [the apartheid assassins] were indoctrinated to embrace the National Party dogma of 'a Christian lifestyle based on Western Civilization and values.'"[90] Even the black policemen—exposed to the military and ideological indoctrination inherent in police training and the threat of retribution from antiapartheid activists—absorbed this institutional thinking. In addition, the obsession with internal security meant that the best and brightest were recruited for the units responsible for it, which were sometimes the route to national office; General Johan Coetzee, commissioner of the SAP during the mid-1980s, had previously been the head of the security branch of the SAP. Organizational reward combined with the dominant political discourse to turn out officers fanatically committed to eliminating the enemy by whatever means necessary.

Of course this analysis did not apply to all officers or even to all security policemen. But the trend was pervasive enough that death squads came into being in all regional police divisions. Endorsement of these units—or at least the willed ignorance of their existence—seems to have come from the highest levels of government, where officials received police and military memos using the word "eliminate" to refer to what should be done with antiapartheid activists. Despite this evidence, apartheid executives have vigorously denied participating in decisions to permit assassination as opposed to detention for the purpose of curbing security threats. In the TRC hearings in 1996, as death squad killers pleaded for amnesty, State President F. W. de Klerk asserted that he never knew that the "unconventional strategies" used by top former officials of the government "included the authorization of assassination, murder, torture, rape assault or the like."[91]

Imbued with counterrevolutionary zeal, the apartheid assassins found the technology to act on it within their institution and the norms to support it among their fellows. While the numbers of people who were "disappeared" and disposed of in the late 1970s and 1980s were not as great as in Argentina,

Guatemala, or El Salvador, the methods of the death squads were equally barbaric.[92] It would be hard to exaggerate the savagery with which the policemen in these squads set the bombs and struck the matches and pulled the triggers that killed their victims. They electrocuted and poisoned and torched young ANC activists; they shot mothers holding babies; they put electrodes on their victims' genitals and rammed cattle prods up their anuses. Jacques Pauw, a journalist who interviewed many of them, writes of the various ways the assassins got rid of the corpses, "Each security police death squad had to find a way of making people disappear. De Kock blew bodies to smithereens with explosives, while Coetzee burnt the bodies to ashes on a fire of wood and tires."[93] Their relationships with one another were bizarre. At Vlakplaas, the best known of the camps from which the death squads operated, they egged each other on and celebrated their murders with drunken orgies and barbecues. They stuck closely together, but occasionally they also tried to murder each other.[94]

The failure of police to act on death squad activity suggested not only indifference to the crimes of their colleagues but also complicity in them. A summary of a 1989 report of the Independent Board of Inquiry into Informal Repression states:

> It is alleged that since 1985, 165 houses, offices, clinics, churches, and vehicles have been destroyed by fire that has been started by various incendiary devices. There have been seventeen alleged incidents of petty vandalism, including the slashing of tires, the placing of dead animals on door steps, and the firing of gunshots though the windows of parked cars. Six incidents of teargas being fired into homes have been alleged, as well as two grenade attacks on homes, thirteen cases of homes being stoned, thirty-seven burglaries, fifteen bombings of offices and homes, plus a host of incidents of obscene phone calls, bomb threats, death threats, and, more recently, the use of poisonous substances to deter left-wing activists.[95]

None of these offenses were prosecuted.

The Turbulent Transition

By 1991 negotiations leading to the end of apartheid were well under way; accords between the government and the ANC agreed to the suspension of armed conflict and to a code of conduct that would prevent excessive force by the police and military. Yet death squad activity continued. It had taken on a momentum of its own, and the prospect of being held to account still seemed dim. Justice system indifference to police crime continued, with criminal convictions of the killers (police in the Ciskei, one of the "homelands") of only one of the fifty government opponents identified by Amnesty International as having been assassinated between 1977 and 1989.[96] The commission of inquiry

(Harms Commission) that was appointed in 1990 to investigate the involvement of police and military in the killings absolved the police, a conclusion that might have been predicted from the fact that the investigators were police officers. Early that year the new state president, F. W. de Klerk, put police on notice that they were no longer to engage in political enforcement, but housecleaning in the SAP did not immediately follow.[97] The squad at Vlakplaas was still in operation in early 1991 when a court found that the head of the forensic division—still in office a year after de Klerk's speech—had lied when he denied supplying its chief with poison to kill antiapartheid activists.[98]

During this period the atrocities of public-order policing declined in most parts of South Africa, but the "homelands" police, seeking to retain the authority that they were to lose with the demise of apartheid, were as brutal as ever. At an observance of "Sharpeville Day" in Bophuthatswana in 1991 they fired without warning into a crowd, killing a young teacher and wounding several other people. The 160 demonstrators arrested reported to Amnesty International that in detention

> they were tortured in local police cells by having electric shocks applied to their genitals, and by having sacks placed over their heads and tied tightly around their necks. Some were hit on their toes with building bricks, or beaten with truncheons and sjamboks, or kicked. Many were coerced into signing statements implicating themselves and others in stone-throwing or arson incidents. Prisoners and their relatives complained that those tortured or wounded were denied proper access to medical treatment.[99]

"Homelands" police also fomented violence by assisting conservative black elements to prey upon political rivals, particularly ANC supporters; one historian regarded the police of KwaZulu (a "homeland" in the then-province of Natal) as "little more than Inkatha's private army."[100]

Police involvement in political violence was not limited to the "homelands." In several areas of the country in the early 1990s police constituted a "third force" providing money, weapons, tactics, and manpower to black groups battling each other.[101] Over the first four years of the decade more than ten thousand people died in clashes between ANC and Inkatha supporters, much of it in Natal. A commission of inquiry into the violence (popularly known as the "Goldstone Commission," for its chair, Judge Richard Goldstone) found that senior police officials had supported the conflicts and noted that a lengthy history of state criminality also contributed to the violence. (To many this conclusion was hardly surprising. The association of members of the South African Police with right-wing extremists, in the words of one scholar, took on "life-and-death importance" during apartheid.)[102] The government, however, preferred to put the blame entirely on the warring parties, and the investigation of police involvement was desultory.

In addition, the police seemed indifferent to the terrible toll of violence in the black areas and on the commuter trains, where murderous and random attacks that seemed to coincide with advances in the national peace talks left hundreds of people dead or injured. The ANC briefly withdrew from the negotiations over transition when Zulus, assisted by police, massacred forty people in June 1992 in Boipatong, a township south of Johannesburg. Rather than destabilizing the country in its hour of change, however, the conflicts underscored the need for democratic process that might prevent or resolve them, and negotiations continued.

The political violence among African groups diminished sharply after the first democratic election in April 1994. On the one hand, the falloff is not surprising in the context of the resolution of intense political differences through the ballot box. (KwaZulu-Natal, the province where most of the killings occurred, was one of only two that voted for representation by a party other than the ANC. Inkatha, the Zulu party led by conservative leader Mangosuthu Buthelezi, prevailed. Battles between its followers and those of the ANC had been most violent.) On the other hand, the indication that by that time police were pulling back from their violent effort to resist change is perhaps surprising. It suggests that the autonomy of apartheid police may have been quickly curbed by the necessity for accountability to leaders with new politics and new directives. The new regime did not have as much authority as it might have had because of the accommodation made in the negotiated settlement to retain civil service employees, including police, for the five years between the first election and the second. Nonetheless, the democratic vote heralded a sea change in institutional messages about how policing was to be done—and the SAP heard them.

Apartheid Judging

It would be a mistake to assume that all judging occurring during apartheid was done by tribunals of the white state. Chiefs' courts in the rural areas continued to dispense judgments in limited areas and were, in fact, supported by a regime eager to keep Africans allied with the conservative, premodern culture that did not encourage political challenge. And nonstate dispute resolution centers sprang up in the urban townships in the 1980s as an indigenous response to the neglect by police and courts of community protection. But it is in the higher courts where the state reveals its ideology.[103] And in South Africa the courts of the white government—in some cases forced by legislative mandate—largely defined the legal relationships between state and individual; they retained the monopoly on coercion for most people embroiled in serious conflict. In these roles they assisted the police, the military, and the apartheid ministries in delivering the violence of the regime.

The Supreme Court of South Africa, as it existed during the apartheid era, was made up of provincial and local divisions and an Appellate Division (also called the Appeal Court), the country's highest appeals court. The provincial and local divisions of the Supreme Court served primarily as trial courts, though the provincial divisions also heard appeals from the magistrates' courts, which dealt with minor civil matters and criminal cases where the penalty was ten years' imprisonment (or ten thousand rand) or less. While magistrates' courts tried the vast majority of ordinary crimes, Bantu commissioners' courts handled both civil and criminal matters involving Africans, including pass law and other race statute violations. The elite judges of the Supreme Court set legal standards for the magistrates, who were civil servants with a good deal of authority but relatively little prestige. The first black magistrates were not appointed until the late 1960s and then only in the Transkei, where the white government, eager for a model of "separate development," had ceded some local legislative power.

The Supreme Court and Human Rights

The behavior of the higher courts in the forty years of the National Party regime can best be understood in the context of the consolidation of the apartheid state. Some commentators see apartheid as a "grand plan" essentially conceived and delivered from the start of the forty-year reign of the National Party. Others see it as developing in fits and starts with setbacks and revisions forced by political struggles and catalyzing events.[104] This latter view, to which I subscribe, sees conflict and compromise shaping the development of apartheid: factional party disagreements, internal struggles among and within state departments, external pressures and resistance of various kinds. So the vigorous protests in 1950 of the proposed requirement of passes for women led to delays and compromises in the imposition of influx control, a core policy for apartheid. "Separate development," with its fiction of establishing self-governing homelands for Africans, was not a planned and articulated feature of the original apartheid design. It was an idea harbored by Hendrik Verwoerd when he was still the head of the Native Affairs Division. Faced with international condemnation of apartheid and the opinion of the all-powerful Department of Bantu Administration and Development (BAD), among others, that it was undesirable to have large numbers of Africans in the cities, Verwoerd turned the establishment of the "homelands" into a concrete proposal only after he became prime minister.

The uneven development of apartheid rules and institutions is also evident in the struggles between the government and the higher courts, principally in the first fifteen years of the apartheid era. Judicial resistance to the government's program was never very widespread or very effective but the Supreme Court at both trial and appellate levels mounted some opposition to the rigidity of segregation and the broad application of security laws. It won a few minor skirmishes but no major battles. And the judges were by no means unified in their efforts to interpret oppressive laws narrowly or to apply them parsimoniously. Support for the National Party and disdain for racial equality—or perhaps fear of black rule—shaped judicial attitudes not only in apartheid rulings but also when it came to adjudicating criminal matters and sentencing ordinary criminals.

Resisting Repression

Despite the obvious cruelties of the apartheid regime, until the 1960s the South African judiciary—that is, the higher courts—retained the image, both at home and abroad, of a beacon of equity and equality in an ocean of repression. (The same was not true of the magistrates' courts, although some magistrates attempted to mitigate the cruelties of segregation and apartheid.) Exploiting the gaps or ambiguities of harsh legislation, the judges often softened its blows or imposed restraints on its application. Even a botanist prosecuted in 1935 for publishing an article in the Communist newspaper urging Africans to boycott the segregated festivities for the silver jubilee of King George V praised the judges of the higher courts, calling them "usually men of experience and culture. They have been to universities overseas and have a wider outlook than the average South African magistrate, policeman or Member of Parliament."[105] A leading critic of the highest appellate court (then called the Appellate Division, now the Supreme Court of Appeal) in the immediate pre-apartheid period could still refer to the "aura of infallibility" of the South African judiciary in the mid-1980s, one of the darkest periods of apartheid.[106]

But by that time the reputation of fairness and judicial protection from governmental tyranny was stained. Some early cases foreshadowed the higher courts' capitulation to apartheid; even in the early years of Union the Appeal Court had endorsed the government's theme of racial exclusion. Initially it rejected as unreasonable discrimination some local requirements of separate facilities for public travel and recreation—"petty apartheid," as it was called. (Although judicial review of laws passed by parliament was not permitted, the Supreme Court could rule on laws enacted at lower governmental levels.) But other cases justified segregation as culturally appropriate and administratively convenient. The court's willingness to accede to the racial standards of the day was apparent in cases where the judges supported segregation on the basis of presumed legislative intent, rather than on the words of the law. In a 1911 case the court interpreted a Cape statute providing for separate schools for children of white "extraction" to permit the exclusion of children with three white grandparents and one black one. In the decision the chief justice opined that it was "inconceivable" that a legislator "would be a consenting party to an Act by which European parents could be compelled to send their children to a school which children of mixed origin can also be compelled to attend."[107] In a 1923 case a regulation prohibiting nonwhite Asian immigration was upheld, although the immigration statute specified that exclusions were to be based on economic grounds.[108]

During the 1950s what ability and interest the judiciary had in curbing the inequities of apartheid diminished significantly. The government found several ways to tighten the noose around court decisions that might subvert racial repression in general and apartheid policies in particular. Through the appointment process it ensured that most magistrates and judges were Afrikaners, who were generally sympathetic with the regime, though the basically English judicial structure and organization were retained and English continued to be the language generally used in the higher courts. The dense welter of apartheid laws and regulations was a forceful reminder of legislative supremacy. And in 1951 parliament reinforced its power by riding roughshod over the core principle of "entrenched clauses" in the South Africa Constitution Act that could be repealed only with a two-thirds vote of both houses of parliament sitting together.

What became a constitutional crisis began with an effort by the Appellate Division to preserve the last remnant of the franchise for black South Africans. The five-man court ruled in favor of plaintiffs who challenged the government's attempt to negate the "entrenched clause" that prohibited removing coloured voters in the Cape from the common voters' roll. It held that the Statute of Westminster, which had ended the legislative supremacy of the British Parliament over South African courts, had not affected the South Africa Constitution Act and that therefore the constitutional provision of "entrenched clauses" still applied. The Separate Representation of Voters Act, therefore, violated the constitutionally mandated process for repealing the guarantee of voting rights for qualified coloureds in the Cape.[109] The decision enraged the government, which tried to constitute the parliament as a high court that could overrule the Appellate Division; but the court blocked this end run around its authority by holding that such a court was not a court at all but a thinly disguised legislative body.[110] In response the government enlarged the Senate and packed the Appellate Division. Parliament fell into line with the supermajority needed to remove the voters, and the new court—now with eleven members—acquiesced with only a single dissent. With the separation of nonwhites from the common voters' roll the pigmentocracy was complete.[111]

Defending Apartheid

The courts apparently learned from this failed exercise in judicial independence; from that time, with some exceptions, they generally capitulated to government power. In many instances they were sympathetic with the reigning ideology anyway and would have been unlikely to attempt the "testing right" even if it had been available. In a famous case interpreting the scope of the Group Areas Act the Appellate Division found that an order reserving an area of Durban for whites constituted discrimination against the Indian plaintiffs—"partial and unequal treatment to a substantial degree"—but that the discrimination was valid. The opinion reasoned that parliament, in fashioning "a colossal social experiment," clearly knew that "compulsory population shifts of persons occupying certain areas would inevitably cause disruption and . . . substantial inequalities."[112] The decision went beyond the imperative of deference to the legislative body in its willingness to infer discriminatory intent even when it was not clearly indicated by the language of the statute. Parliament's "colossal social experiment" as a justification for apartheid laws reverberated through later decisions and lent legal authority to inequalities of the most blatant and pernicious kind.

The constitutional crisis precipitated by the vote case made clear that parliament had become not just supreme but absolute. A provision of the South African Act Amendment Act of 1956, reflecting lessons learned by the government in the vote case, decreed that "[n]o court of law shall be competent to enquire into or to pronounce upon the validity of any law passed by Parliament" other than the laws that established the equal and official status of English and Afrikaans.[113] Such "ouster clauses" became increasingly common and hobbled the judges' ability to thwart the apartheid parliaments curbs on human rights, even where they were so inclined.

It is a truism that courts must apply the law as written, and if the writing is clear, the judiciary is constrained from rectifying injustice. The Appellate Division had little choice but to approve the 1952 conviction of the ANC leaders of the Defiance Campaign, for example, because they had been charged under a definition of "communism" in the relevant legislation that included efforts to instigate "any political, industrial, social or economic change within the Republic by the promotion of disturbance or disorder, by unlawful acts or omissions."[114] This language was so broad as to admit of little leeway even for judges who might have wished to restrict the application of the statute.

But often the security laws allowed for interpretation that would have mitigated some aspects of their harshness, and often the Appellate Division sidestepped those opportunities. In one case it ruled that a political detainee in solitary confinement (Albie Sachs, now a member of the Constitutional Court) could be denied reading and writing material under the ninety-day detention law, although the statute contained no mention of this deprivation. Left to infer legislative intent, the opinion speculated that parliament had enacted the law to facilitate questioning of suspects and that providing them with opportunity to read and write might make them less amenable to interrogation.[115] The following year the Appellate Division relied on the same law (and on the precedent set by the Sachs case) to rule that the Supreme Court had no jurisdiction to order the testimony of another detainee regarding the conditions of his detention, despite the assertion of his wife that he had been interrogated continuously for twenty-eight hours.[116] It might be argued that, beyond the benefits they would have provided to the litigants, more liberal results in these cases would have been pointless in the long run, since the parliament would merely have acted to fill in the holes left in the legislation. But it responded to the cases in any event; the mere fact that the court had been given the opportunity to involve itself in the conditions under which people were detained gave rise to new legislation endorsing police interrogation in solitary confinement and indefinite detention without trial.[117]

The courts even yielded to executive power when it took the form of atrocities committed by the security police. Sachs comments:

> The holding of accused persons and witnesses for months and even years in solitary confinement prior to their being brought to court led to no expressions of judicial concern, nor was there any vigorous judicial reaction to allegations by State witnesses that they had been subjected by the police to violence and sleep derivation, There were some rulings against the police, but they were so cautiously expressed that they did little to protect detainees in general from irregular treatment. The security police, accustomed to losing most of their cases in the 1950s, became used to winning nearly all their cases in the 1960s.[118]

Almost as constraining as the detention laws were banning orders, which could restrict the freedom of a political defendant for many years and could serve as a continuation of detention, often being imposed after release. The Appellate Division reinforced this extension of political punishment, supporting executive decisions to deprive released detainees of the most basic rights. During the 1970s a released detainee under a banning order was refused a passport to leave the country to accept a teaching offer in the United States. He requested that the minister of justice provide the court with information as to the reasons for the denial, and the court upheld the minister's refusal to do so, arguing that it lacked the power to question a decision the minister made in the public interest.[119] It also interpreted the prohibition against a banned person participating in a "gathering" to include meetings of only two people—the banned person and one other.[120] The ruling went beyond what was necessary to determine whether the defendant had violated the banning order, as the charge was based on being found with three others playing bridge. This deference to executive decisions and the perceived needs of the security forces lasted even into the late 1980s, when apartheid was collapsing of its own weight. After the 1986 state of emergency had failed to contain the mass movement challenging the government, the minister of law and order, in a desperate act of self-preservation, curbed the activities of seventeen organizations, including the United Democratic Front, whose success in supporting the mass movement had made it the bête noir of the government.

The period of the states of emergency in the 1980s brought with it the most arbitrary deprivations of freedom and the most craven capitulation to apartheid on the part of the highest court in the land. South Africa was and is a common-law country, with court-made law following precedent cases where no statute exists. The legacy of both English and Roman-Dutch law also includes the right to legal representation, the writ of habeas corpus, and the right to a hearing *(audi alterem partem)* where a deprivation of liberty is threatened. These traditions could have been invoked to find ways around many of the greatest assaults on human rights of that period. But as the alliance of parliament, the security forces, and the apartheid bureaucrats did whatever it could to curtail these rights—the emergency legislation of the 1960s made habeas corpus a largely illusory remedy—the Appellate Division put up little resistance. Stephen Ellmann has identified an "emergency team" of judges on that court who consistently interpreted the regulations of the 1980s states of emergency very broadly. Without being forced by doctrinal imperative, they accepted warrantless arrests based on the subjective judgment of the officer, they permitted the extension of the prescribed period of detention without notice or hearing, and they accepted the refusal of the state to grant detainees the right of access to counsel.[121] Ellmann concludes: "We are left with the sense that the court was loath to abridge what it took to be the State President's judgment that sweeping power was necessary for the emergency."[122]

It might be said that these judges believed it was their professional task to follow the lead of parliament, to defer to the elected representatives of the polity in their role as the principal policymaking body of the political system. But parliament had become the rubber stamp of the executive—the state president and his State Security Council, the inner circle that carried out the core function of security strategy for a highly centralized and repressive government. In allowing the executive free rein under a loosely worded emergency authorization given to it by parliament, the judges effectively acquiesced in both the aims and the tactics of apartheid.

Judges of the local and provincial divisions of the Supreme Court were also expected to defer to the security forces, even though it was widely known by the mid-1980s that they often tortured detainees. (A 1985 study by the Institute of Criminology of the University of Cape Town found that 93 percent of

Africans interviewed reported being tortured while in detention.)[123] A rumor circulating in the legal community that judges protected the apartheid police was confirmed in 1997 when a judge told the Judicial Service Commission, the body that screens applicants for advancement to the Appellate Division, that he had been reprimanded by his judge president in the 1980s when he had criticized the police in court.[124] He was never again assigned a case with political implications.

This bleak picture should not obscure cases in which the "junior divisions" of the Supreme Court struck a blow for human rights. Occasionally the Supreme Court curbed the security forces by simply acquitting a victim of an apartheid law. And several decisions challenged the actions of police by ruling that arrests under the security law must be based on reasonable grounds and that the arresting authority had the burden of proving that those grounds existed.[125] Others held that the government must give people detained under the emergency regulations a chance to be heard when their detention was extended.[126] In 1985 a Durban judge released a detainee on the grounds that the police could show no reasonable basis for believing that he had committed or intended to commit a violation of the Internal Security Act. Despite an "ouster clause" in the legislation that, on its face, prohibited the courts from ruling on the validity of detention under the law, as well as statutory language that seemed to allow a police officer to base his decision to detain on subjective grounds, the Appellate Division assumed jurisdiction and affirmed the lower court judgment. The opinion reasoned that it was "inconceivable that the Legislature could have intended that a belief based on grounds which cannot pass the test of reasonableness would be sufficient to provide justification for such arrest and detention."[127]

The *Hurley* decision was theoretically a substantial victory for progressive forces, and it was hailed as a signal from the courts that police power was neither boundless nor unreviewable. But within a year it was succeeded by the *Omar* case, which read the regulations of the state of emergency to deny to detainees the right to be heard (the *audi alteram partem* rule) and the right of access to lawyers—and upheld their validity.[128] The "emergency team" of the Appellate Division was now at work, operating under the supposition that the state president had virtually limitless power to make rulings that were not only necessary but "expedient."[129]

Penalizing Ordinary & Political Crimes

Until the early 1960s procedural protections for criminal defendants resembled those of British and American courts—the presumption of innocence, a right to bail that was not excessive, a guarantee of due process in a trial, a right against self-incrimination, the requirement that prosecutors must prove defendants guilty beyond a reasonable doubt. The security laws changed that for political offenses but not, for the most part, for ordinary criminal charges. In addition, however, criminal procedure law was revised, which affected both political cases and ordinary criminal matters. It extended the authority of a judge to convict on a plea of guilty, without taking any evidence, to the magistrates' court.[130] The police were thus emboldened to force the defendant to plead guilty, a task made easier by the fact that most defendants were black and poor and without legal counsel. Another section of the law provided that a written confession was presumed to be valid and the burden of proof to show that it was not voluntary was on the defendant.[131] As a positive incentive for police assault and torture to obtain a confession from an unrepresented defendant, this provision could hardly be improved upon.

Both the race of the offender and the race of the victim influenced criminal sentencing; the disposition of interracial crimes displays the apartheid ideology. Penalties for blacks assaulting whites were more severe than for the same crimes committed by whites against blacks. Sachs notes a 1966 case in which a judge found the fact that the black defendant had raped a white woman grounds for an enhanced sentence since the shock of the crime would have been greater for her than for a black woman. The defendant was executed. Whites were rarely executed for the rape of white women and never for the rape of blacks, while blacks were often executed for raping whites. Police data show that between early 1961 and mid-1966 the interracial murder rate was six times as high for whites as for blacks.[132] While it is not known how many of each group were actually put to death, it is possible to get a rough indication from data for the period 1911–68, when only six of the approximately two thousand people executed for murder were whites who had killed blacks. No reports are available for how many of the 1900 blacks put to death for murder had killed across the color line, but Sachs reports that "such information as is available suggests that the number runs into hundreds at least."[133] White judges commonly assumed that execution as punishment would not have the same disruptive effect on a black community as on a white one.

In general, judges were not reluctant to impose the death penalty, which, from 1958, covered an increasing range of offenses. Robbery and aggravated housebreaking, sabotage, receiving training that could further the aims of communism, kidnapping, and terrorism were added to preexisting capital crimes of murder, rape, and treason, though most capital convictions were for murder.[134] As social and political tensions surged under the yoke of apartheid, death sentences increased and commutations declined. The result was a rising tide of executions—up from 21 per year between the time of Union (1910) and the advent of apartheid, to 70 per year in the first two decades of apartheid, to 1,477 between 1977 and 1989, approximately 1 every three days.[135] Criticism of this pattern was not tolerated. A law professor was prosecuted in 1970 for contempt of court when he published an article reporting on a survey that found that many advocates saw racial bias in the imposition of the death penalty and calling for its abolition; he was sued for defamation five years later when he assailed the minister of justice for granting a reprieve from execution to a white defendant but not to his black accomplice.[136]

Other penalties imposed during the 1980s also reflected the harshness of apartheid and the unrest it caused. Magistrates, who dealt with most noncapital offenses—a recent chief justice called the magistrates' courts "the engine rooms of justice"—were mostly Afrikaners, often National Party loyalists and often closely allied with prosecutors in a system where few of the accused had legal representation.[137] Long sentences imposed for drug offenses, auto theft, and housebreaking were justified as responses to "the abuse of the unrest situation by criminal elements" and led to some of the highest rates of incarceration—four hundred per one hundred thousand in population in 1986—in the world.[138] Even children were sentenced to lengthy terms and were sent to Robben Island, the maximum security prison where Nelson Mandela spent eighteen years. Each year magistrates sentenced tens of thousands of Africans for pass law violations.[139] Remaining in an urban area for more than seventy-two hours was a common basis for these charges. The reason was immaterial; the law applied equally if you were visiting a relative in the hospital or drinking in a shebeen.

Most pass law charges were brought to the Bantu commissioners' courts, the bottom-feeders of the apartheid judicial system, which operated under the aegis of the Bantu Administration and Development Department and were generally staffed with inexperienced (and often poorly trained) magistrates and prosecutors. On top of the obvious substantive injustice of the laws enforced there, the proceedings in these courts were cursory, dehumanizing, and even fraudulent. The guilt of the accused was presumed, they were given no chance to defend themselves, and the fines imposed were farcical, since most defendants could not possibly pay. A lawyer who practiced before these courts in Port Elizabeth for more than a decade described the process:

> Every day, police vans, crowded beyond capacity, deliver their human cargo to the cells at the Bantu Affairs buildings. Mondays are particularly busy as a result of the weekend swoop. Armed with a list of names the prosecutor will initiate the proceedings by arranging the accused in rows according to his list. With the magistrate in position on the bench, the names are called in rapid succession. The accused are led to the dock and through an interpreter are asked to plead to the charge and state whether they have anything to say. A lengthy reply in Xhosa is usually forthcoming, wherein the accused explains his reason for being within a prohibited area and the circumstances surrounding his arrest. The interpretation of the reply is standard: "The accused pleads guilty with nothing to say, your

worship." The rubber stamp descends. "R30 or thirty days." "Yes Mr. Prosecutor. Next one, please." The accused is led to the cells to begin his sentence.[140]

Conclusion

With a long history of white conquest and domination, South Africa under the Nationalist government was well equipped with enforcement measures to sustain apartheid for forty years. It is easy to lay the blame for carrying out the program primarily with the security forces; the physicality of police violence made it the more blatant abuse of human dignity. But the edifice of apartheid was held together by both police and courts; they were its tools—the hammer and the vise. It is sometimes said that South African courts provided a buffer during the apartheid years between the state and the police. On occasion this was true. But the indifference and bias of magistrates and judges—their gradual co-optation by executive power and their willingness to use the law for such virulent racial domination—constituted a different form of violence. The Appellate Division of the 1980s also expanded on apartheid policies—filling in gaps left by the legislative process and thereby furthering the repressive aims of the law. And courts often allowed broad license for police discretion, reinforcing extreme brutality. It is easy to see why, when the edifice began to crumble, these same instruments of repression—needed in a new form to build a democratic society—were primary targets for reform.

The state violence carried out by apartheid laws and their enforcement helps to explain the crime that characterizes the post-apartheid society. Graeme Simpson points out that a consequence of political conflict in that period was the criminalization of much of the poor black population. "The social history of the apartheid era is in fact an account of the massive and widespread dislocation in which human beings were forced to endure lives in the most precarious and depraved of settings, punctuated by daily violence and violation."[141] It is hardly surprising that such a criminogenic past cannot usher in a peaceful present.

4 Bitter Fruit from Poison Seeds

> The day after [the] Sharpeville [massacre in 1960] I behaved in a very reckless fashion. I was so angry that I got very drunk that evening and started a terrible fracas, threatening to kill people with a tiny penknife. It had that effect. We were all pushed willy-nilly across this great divide. It marked a turning point to violence in a very systematic way.
> —Neville Alexander[1]

> In South Africa, at present [1988], the normalization of violence and atrocity threatens to blunt our human sensibilities.
> —J. Cock[2]

> Of course the boys here [in 2003] dream of being gangsters. It's their only hope for becoming somebody.
> —Jeffrey Arendse[3]

CARS ARE HIJACKED in the black townships and white suburbs of Gauteng, sometimes with bloody outcomes. Heavily armed gangs rob middle-class citizens in their living rooms. Irate farmers shoot trespassers and beat workers. Neighbors rape small girls. Police assist feuding groups in assassinations. It is all lumped together as rampant and violent crime in post-apartheid South Africa, reports that cast a pall, locally and internationally, on the triumph of transition from apartheid to nonracial democracy. The world is surprised—even South Africans have been surprised—that, having vanquished the evils of colonialism and apartheid, the country seems incapable of addressing an enemy within.

Some of the sources of violent crime in South Africa today—like the access to markets for stolen goods in other African countries, the increased demand for illegal drugs, and the increased availability of guns of all kinds—are recent. But criminal violence there is hardly a new phenomenon, and patterns of some kinds of criminal behavior were established even before the forty years of apartheid. Understanding current violence and the challenges it presents requires poking below the surface to see the violence of colonialism and apartheid—structural as well as physical—that shaped the habits of the present. The context is psychological and cultural as well as economic and political, and the deprivation and humiliation that characterize it reach different population groups in different ways. Perhaps the best metaphor for the influences of the past on present crime is an octopus, simultaneously dense and various, whose tentacles grip and sting both rural and urban communities.

The Clamor over Crime

In 1998 the widow of Alan Paton, whose novels *Cry the Beloved Country* and *Too Late the Phalarope* exposed millions of people worldwide to the horrors of South African racism and oppression, announced that she planned to return to England, where she was born. She was leaving, she said, because she had been carjacked at gunpoint and robbed in her own home, and because she could not bear the "general lawlessness" of post-apartheid South Africa.[4] Her decision prompted a predictable outcry—against the criminals who had victimized Anne Paton, against white liberals who had failed to deliver the country from apartheid before it made blacks desperate and delinquent, against the ANC leadership that was held to be corrupt and incompetent. Violent crime had become the deepest wound on the new body politic. As one contributor to the *Electronic Mail & Guardian* chat room railed at another, "Crime is high; that is why people are fleeing this country. Your policies aren't working. Your government is a failure; that is the issue here."[5]

The salience of crime, especially violent crime, in South Africa is evident in many quarters. Lurid media accounts, anticrime political tirades, and data from public opinion surveys and government agencies keep it alive. Political opponents of the ANC government rail against a "culture of violence," and there seems to be general acceptance of the idea that South Africa is "a society which endorses and accepts violence as an acceptable means to resolve problems and achieve goals."[6] Cartoons make fun of cowed citizens and inept robbers. Crime awareness campaigns may reduce citizens' vulnerability but also heighten fears, though one novel approach—a one-man trek across the country undertaken in 1999—stressed the need for unity in fighting crime. Many thousands who have left South Africa—during 1998 a researcher put the number emigrating at ten thousand per year, though the exodus has slowed since then—have, like Mrs. Paton, cited crime as the main reason.[7] Business people engage in a great deal of handwringing over reports of violence that inhibit tourism and investment, both domestic and foreign.

Interaction of public concern and political exploitation adds to the frenzy. Public opinion polls show that concern about crime alternates with unemployment as number one in surveys of citizens' views of the greatest problems in South Africa.⁸ While these findings varied only slightly between 1994 and 2001, the perception of crime as an important problem has receded somewhat in recent years relative to the yearning for job creation. This pattern presumably reflects the massive job losses during the 1990s. South African Reserve Bank figures show that nonagricultural formal employment declined by more than 20 percent, and that figure wildly understates the problem if informal employment is considered; the official unemployment rate was 26.5 percent, as of March 2005, but many observers estimate it as closer to 40 percent.⁹ It may also be related to an increase in the numbers of people who have more faith in the efforts of the justice system; in a survey conducted by the Human Sciences Research Council (HSRC) in early 2000 almost 60 percent of respondents thought that the government had some control over crime as compared with slightly less than half in a survey two years earlier.¹⁰ On the other hand, even as some kinds of crime are declining somewhat, people do not seem to feel any safer; a victimization study conducted in 2003 found that the percentage of respondents who felt very safe in their area during the day had dropped by more than half since the previous survey, five years earlier.¹¹

The apparent contradiction between greater confidence in criminal justice and increasing anxiety about crime may be in part explainable by heightened political spin. Crime was a hot issue in the second democratic national election in 1999. The New National Party, the Democratic Party, and Inkatha all attacked the ANC for its inability to stem the increase in violence; even Mandela was criticized for indifference to crime, when he did not stress it in his 1999 speech for the opening of parliament. Keenly aware of this vulnerability, Thabo Mbeki began his presidency with a much tougher stance on crime than his predecessor, taking aim at visible (if minor) disorder like squatting and street hawking as well as vowing new initiatives against violence. Shortly after the election he appointed Steve Tshwete, formerly minister of sport and a hero of the armed liberation struggle, as minister of safety and security. Tshwete's tough talk delighted many citizens beleaguered by crime. He called criminal offenders "rogues" and "sub-humans" and embraced the "noble mission" of the police "to make life miserable for them," a goal he would pursue by "all means, constitutional or unconstitutional."¹² With great fanfare he announced Operation Crackdown, his program of police sweeps; he favored lengthening the period when suspects could be legally detained without trial.¹³ The minister of justice who came into office in 1999 also talked tough; he chided judges for not working hard enough and vowed that new resources for magistrates would eliminate delays and backlogs.

The symbolic power of crime in political life leads desperate political leaders to demonstrate how hard they are trying to control criminal violence with strategies that sometimes backfire. After a number of bombings and assassinations in Cape Town, including the 1998 bombing of a popular bar that killed ten people and wounded twenty-five, officials and citizens alike saw the urban violence as a deliberate attempt to create a climate of fear.[14] Parliamentary discussion labeled it terrorism and prompted parliamentary consideration of drastic measures. The ANC national executive committee debated the use of a brief state of emergency, a proposal that harkened back to repression of the previous decade. Instead, the South African Law Commission (since 2002 the South African Law Reform Commission) proposed an antiterrorism bill that was immediately attacked by human rights groups as draconian and unconstitutional with its provisions for long mandatory sentences and fourteen-day detention of those withholding information about terrorism. The legislation was then revised to conform with international conventions and charters, substituting fact-finding hearings for detention without trial for persons thought to have information on terrorist acts. It went into effect in May 2005.

Perceptions of the seriousness of crime vary along both race and class lines. Africans are less likely than whites, coloureds, or Indians to see it as the most important problem facing the country. In a comprehensive survey taken to assess the population's views on major issues before the second democratic national election, whites were almost twice as likely as Africans to cite "fighting crime" as the desired top priority for the country over the next ten years, and whites were less than half as likely to cite job creation, presumably reflecting the high unemployment rate among blacks.[15] The picture was more complicated for respondents in different income groups. The likelihood that respondents with the highest living standard would see crime control as the top priority (41 percent) was greater than for those at the levels somewhat below them, but more than half (59 percent) of the people with the lowest standard of living also gave it top priority, suggesting the perception of criminogenic living conditions among the poor.[16]

The cold data do not, of course, reflect individual fears or anger, and it is safe to say that all groups decry the vast amounts of crime and that everyone in South Africa has a tale to tell of either personal victimization or that of a friend, relative, or coworker. Affluent suburban whites tell of being hijacked (and sometimes shot) as they wait for automated security gates to open in the driveways of their homes, poor blacks tell of being seized and raped on the way home from school or work, farmers recount terrible stories of assaults or murders on their land, and businesspeople condemn extensive employee fraud. Although perceptions of government corruption have diminished in recent years, a national survey taken in late 2002 suggests the extent to which the general public believes its law enforcers are also criminal; 87 percent of respondents said that at least some police were corrupt, and 59 percent shared these views of judges and magistrates.[17]

Crime is a salient feature for portrayals of post-apartheid South Africa internationally. It is routine to see Johannesburg described in the foreign press as "reputedly the most dangerous city in the world outside of a war zone."[18] What terrifies foreigners and provides fuel for sensational media reports is not, however, the most common kind of violence, which occurs in the homes and communities of poor South Africans—though coverage of child abuse and rape is plentiful. Hijacking an expensive car out of a suburban driveway, robberies of Brinks trucks (called cash-in-transit heists in South Africa), and bank robberies get most of the international attention. They are, of course, the crimes more likely to affect affluent people, but not exclusive to them; auto theft and commercial burglary afflict poor areas as well. The view of South Africa as dangerous and, to a lesser extent, corrupt has been cited as a deterrent to foreign direct investment almost since the days of post-apartheid euphoria in 1994 and 1995. Whether it really is or not remains an open question; other factors, like the availability of skilled (and healthy) workers, are also important. But in 1996 German business leaders—representing South Africa's top trading partner—issued a statement noting that sixteen out of thirty chief executives of German companies had recently been victims of violent crime and warning that investment would dry up if the government could not guarantee the safety of expatriate managers.[19] A delegation of members of the European Parliament visiting the country in 2001 publicly berated the government for not addressing either AIDS or crime aggressively enough. European and American news reports of assaults, robberies, and murders of foreign businesspeople have proliferated. As the *Independent* (London) noted in 1999:

> "The statistics show that there has been a reduction or stabilisation in most serious crimes," said President Nelson Mandela on Friday when he addressed parliament in Cape Town. But the gallery seat reserved for James Bartleman, the Canadian high commissioner, was empty. He was in hospital with bruises and a broken nose after being mugged in his hotel. South Africa is once again grappling with what sometimes seems like an awful punishment for its peaceful transition from apartheid state to multi-ethnic "Rainbow Nation." Just when the young democracy most needs the world's tourists and investors, it is labelled crime centre of the world.[20]

While there is no denying that crime is a very serious problem, some caveats to the picture of unbridled violence and corruption are appropriate.

The crime of present-day South Africa is often portrayed as a recent phenomenon, a scourge of the post-apartheid era with a variety of sources. In 1999 Mbeki bemoaned the "disastrous collapse of social values" that he attributed to the aftereffects of a system that encouraged self-enrichment.[21] Whites in chat rooms and coffeehouses associate criminal violence with the liberation of primitive peoples. Victims of suburban robberies and carjackings blame the gangs that now steal luxury cars at gunpoint and send them north to other African countries. Policy analysts debate whether the causes of crime can be found in the social and economic conditions of the past—the legacy of colonialism and apartheid—or the poverty and inequality that most South Africans live with today. People of all colors and classes berate the police for being incompetent or corrupt, incapable of either containing or preventing the violence that threatens nearly everybody. Judges and magistrates are excoriated for being either too easy on criminals in general or biased against defendants who are poor or black.

Mbeki, as well as others less sympathetic to the new dispensation, finds the source of the crime problem in declining moral fiber; in an address to parliament in 2002 he called for a Moral Regeneration Summit to "address the issue of the responsibility that each and all of us should take for our lives."[22] But attributing crime to the moral failings of South Africans since 1994 does not account for patterns of crime in the generations preceding the end of apartheid. If individual immorality is increasing, how to explain the gang violence of the 1950s, the township crime of the 1960s reported anecdotally by domestic workers in every white kitchen but rarely in the white press, the brutalization of black farmworkers and miners by white bosses, the "culture of violence" engendered in the 1980s by state brutality and responses to it? It was, after all, 1948 when Alan Paton wrote, "For what can men do when so many have grown lawless? Who can enjoy the lovely land, who can enjoy seventy years, and the sun that pours down on the earth, when there is fear in the heart?"[23]

Particular kinds of offenses and their distribution among the population have changed since the early 1990s, to be sure. But today's crime problem has precedents that long predate the end of apartheid. Centuries ago, as noted in chapter 2, the tensions of racism and colonialism, and the efforts to maintain the social stratification that followed from those forces, gave rise to a society where theft and violence were common. The early white settlers and the indigenous people that lived among them stole livestock from one another regularly. Slaveholders and employers inflicted brutal punishments on subordinates, who occasionally fought back. Later, the "tot system" on wine farms, where the worker received part of his meager pay in wine, contributed to a culture of uncontrolled drinking; alcohol-lubricated violence was common in the home as well as in the streets. Urbanization and labor market demands separated families and heightened poverty and insecurity; gangs formed in the early decades of the twentieth century provided both succor and criminal opportunity for displaced country boys.

Then came apartheid. It was "a generator of criminal victimization and violence in South Africa through policies which have resulted in massive social dislocation."[24] The forced removal of more than three million people deposited poor blacks in overcrowded slums, often in tin shacks with no protection from predators. Social and economic conditions in the "homeland" and the township bred theft and violence; unemployment was high, and when adults were working, they had little control over their children. Murders and assaults reported to the police increased sharply in the 1960s and 1970s; the gangs multiplied. The townships outside Cape Town were murderous communities in the 1980s; a massive flow of drugs into the country began in that decade while the government was preoccupied with stamping out dissent. Many believe that the apartheid government turned a blind eye to violence deliberately, dismissing it as the result of political agitation and evidence of the venality of primitive peoples who were to be contained.

Indeed, the line between political and criminal violence was blurry in the 1980s. Young men marginalized by apartheid and its dislocations—and already credentialed as common criminals—responded to the liberation struggle along with their more privileged fellows, and their involvement fueled its violence. Their need for inclusion and power did not end with the collapse of apartheid. What Graeme Simpson calls "the easy slide across the boundaries between political and criminal violence" led some of them into the post-apartheid world of gangs and violence.[25] Simpson notes that it is naive to assume a clear demarcation between violence that is socially approved as part of political resistance and that which is merely antisocial. If the criminal violence of today threatens the rights orientation of the new democracy, he concludes, it "ha[s] its roots in the sometimes seamless interface of youth involvement in criminal and political violence of the preceding era."[26]

In recent years violent crime has been identified as a serious problem not only because its incidence has risen but also because it has spread to people and places previously protected by apartheid policies. When South Africa was a security state, it would have been inconceivable that the most prominent judge in the land and his wife would be accessible enough to be robbed in their home, as happened to Arthur Chaskalson, president of the Constitutional Court, in 1998.[27] In addition, crimes that were previously overlooked are now taken seriously; wrenching accounts of little African girls raped by their neighbors or schoolmates are standard journalistic fare since blacks gained political power. Once influx control laws were repealed neighborhoods formerly off-limits to any African without a pass presented tempting targets for newly liberated burglars and robbers. As Willie Hofmeyr, then a member of parliament, put it in 1999, "With the coming of democratic society, crime democratized along with it. It started affecting middle class and more prominent people, not only blacks."[28] Crimes in affluent neighborhoods—homes with fancy cars and valuable objects—were (and are) often terrifying. Carjacking and midnight holdups, hitherto unknown to comfortable whites in South Africa, became commonplace, although still not as routine as crimes of equivalent violence in townships.

The information on crime issued by the government must be viewed with caution. Crime data, which are notoriously unreliable everywhere, are no less misleading in South Africa, and in some respects more so. The turbulence of the apartheid era and the change in methods of data collection and analysis make historical comparisons almost impossible. South African criminologists generally assert that national crime statistics are nearly worthless before 1994.[29] Many people during the apartheid years were fearful of indifference from the police or reprisals from their neighbors if they reported crime. During the apartheid years crime records in black areas were doubtful at best, duplicitous at worst; victims were sometimes beaten when they reported crime to the police, who were either unsympathetic or in league with the criminals. Police might simply beat the suspects too and leave it at that, unconcerned about keeping records of ordinary—that is, nonpolitical—law enforcement. The function of police and courts as enforcers of apartheid superseded their importance as agents of crime control. Detectives often had little or no training in investigation and little or no interest in it (and those that did tended to leave the police after 1994). The South African Police Service had no research capacity; its reports could not explain the raw data. Statisticians in the current government say that the surge in violent crime began not after the democratic elections, as the official data suggest, but during the political chaos of the 1980s when people in every sector of society were under extreme stress and the apartheid government had lost all semblance of the authority needed to maintain social peace. Since the end of apartheid an attempt by the professionalized research office to collect data more systematically and perform more sophisticated analyses of crime patterns has been limited by a lack of resources and indifference among senior police officials to the importance of providing better information. In 2000 the minister of safety and security imposed a one-year moratorium on the issuance of crime data because he said they were so unreliable (though many charged that he wished to hide the bad news from the public). While the moratorium was lifted after a year, the quarterly reports that were formerly made public were not widely available, and annual summaries have only been published recently, since they have begun to show decreases in some of the crimes that generate headlines and public fear.

The data collected on violent crime since 1994 do indeed paint an alarming picture of very high rates of offending and an increase in a few important categories. Consider the astronomical incidence of robbery. In 2001, just between January and September, 153,376 robberies were officially recorded, a rate of 351 per 100,000 population.[30] This compares with 422,921 (for the whole year) robberies in the United States—a relatively violent country—where the *rate* of robberies per hundred thousand is less than half that of South Africa, at 148.5.[31] The 2001 figure for South Africa reflects a 39 percent rise in aggravated robbery—which includes carjacking—since 1994, and the rate continues to rise, though more slowly.[32] (One indicator of the relationship between this crime and the opening of South Africa to the rest of the continent at the end of apartheid is the fact that in Pretoria, the large city closest to the northern border of the country, it increased by 96 *percent* between 1994 and 1999.)[33] Reports of rape, too, increased after 1994, but have declined since 1997; nonetheless, in 2003 incidence was more than three and a half times that of the United States (113 per 100,000 population, as compared with 32 in the United States).[34] Particularly troubling are reports of sexual assaults against children, which more than doubled between 1993 and 1996.[35] Overall, violent crime constituted one-third of all reported crime in 2001–2, a proportion far higher than in the United States and unthinkable in most other Western countries.[36] As for *un*reported crime, we know from victimization studies that there is a great deal of it, though the most recent national survey found that reporting was on the increase for crimes of theft and assault (but not robbery).[37]

While there is no doubt that rates of criminal violence are high, we cannot know the extent to which the increases of the 1990s really reflect a crime wave as opposed to a crime-*reporting* wave.[38] If one measure of a legitimate criminal justice system in a democracy is whether citizens turn to it when help is needed, the official data might signal a new willingness to report crime when it occurs. South African police are now more responsive to crime victims in many neighborhoods, particularly in urban areas, and better access to phones makes reporting easier. The possibility of a reporting artifact that distorts the picture of actual offending may be particularly significant when it comes to the rape data. Sharp increases in reported incidence in the early post-apartheid years could reflect growing confidence that police will take the crime seriously; the real story may be the steady state reflected in the reports after 1996. (Women's groups have also tried to heighten awareness of rape as a crime and reduce the shame associated with reporting it, and the new Domestic Violence Act now mandates reporting of sexual assault charges.)

For most countries the most reliable crime data are assumed to be the reports of murder, since it is difficult to hide a body. Looking at the trend in murder should induce skepticism about the accuracy of reports of other crime increases. While the rate of reported murders remains very high indeed—roughly seven and a half times that of the United States in 2003—it declined, according to SAPS data, by 36 percent between 1994 and 2003.[39] And murders noted by respondents dropped by more than half between the 1998 and 2003 national victimization surveys.[40] Other data suggest that the reports of a crime wave since the end of apartheid may be overstated. Commercial burglary and auto theft are crimes that, like murder, are likely to be reported, principally because insurance claims rely on police reports—and they too have gone down.[41] The SAPS reported in 2002 that the rate of increase in reported crime had slowed, from about 7 percent between 1999 and 2000 to about 1 percent between 2001 and 2002.⁴² And figures for 2002–3 showed actual decreases in assault, rape, housebreaking, and hijacking, as well as murder. Leggett comments on surprising trends in the data:

> The number of non-firearm assaults that resulted in death has decreased dramatically, at the same time that non-lethal assaults have allegedly increased. A similar paradox is seen with the divergent trends in residential (up by a third since 1994) and business (stable) burglary. This incongruity suggests that much of South Africa's post-democracy crime wave is simply the recording of crimes that had been hidden in the past.⁴³

Admittedly, the evidence that the incidence of some crimes is decreasing does not go far toward reassuring the general public when the numbers of crimes remain so high. One 1995 media report on murder noted that, according to official data, someone was murdered every twenty-nine minutes, twelve seconds; it would not have been much more comforting to hear, in 2001—reflecting the 24 percent drop in incidence—that the interval had been reduced to one murder every thirty-six minutes, forty-seven seconds!⁴⁴ And concern about the high level of many crimes must include taking note of the large numbers of crimes that are not reported to the police. What is called the "dark figure" of crime has been brought into the light in recent years—at least to some extent; people may not always be candid about crime experiences or may forget some incidents—by surveys of victims. A 1997 victimization survey that asked South Africans who had been robbed during the previous year whether they had reported it to the police found that only 41 percent had done so, meaning that there may have been more than 215,000 actual robberies, not the 88,247 reported to police.⁴⁵

Even here, however, reality may not be as grim as the statistical picture makes it seem, at least if one views it in an international context. Crime is grossly underreported in most societies; one can expect only a relatively small portion of many crimes to be reported. In the United States the percentages of robbery and assault reported to the police are only slightly higher than in South Africa, a country where, until recently, police have been, to many people, enemies rather than protectors. According to South Africa's 1997 victimization study both burglary and car theft—and, most surprisingly, sexual offenses—were *more* likely to be reported than in the United States.⁴⁶ So, with the exception of the reporting of robbery and assault, it may be that the South African picture of police reporting reflects a degree of confidence in police similar to that found in America. On the other hand, the victimization study of 1997, which asked people whether they reported crimes to the police, may understate the "dark figure." As one researcher commented to me, "If you aren't going to report a rape to the police, why would you report it to some stranger at your door?"

It is important to note that the focus on crime is, in some respects, a very skewed perspective in that the attention given to personal violence post-apartheid reflects, to some extent, a labeling shift. Crime is the creation of states—deviance or morally repugnant behavior is not crime until it is officially prohibited—and by definition, therefore, it changes with political change. The pass laws, the Land Act, the Master and Servants Act all created crimes—being in the wrong place at the wrong time, being unemployed, walking off the job—that vanished when the laws were repealed. In a technical sense, then, the end of apartheid brought with it a huge decrease in crime. Yet presumably some of the behavior that had been criminalized by the policies to enforce the political system could now be sanctioned as ordinary crime—breaking and entering, assault, and so on—and has contributed to the perception of an increase in disorder. In addition, some of the violence attributed to angry participants in the liberation struggle—assaults and arson and even execution of suspected informers—was undoubtedly committed for personal reasons by *tsotsis* (youthful hoodlums). And some deep-seated frustrations that found expression in political violence directed at the old regime were channeled in different directions when it collapsed. Once apartheid ended, interpersonal violence of whatever kind could be redefined as ordinary crime.

Post-apartheid Crime: A Problem with a Past

Notwithstanding serious problems with the collection of crime data and the likelihood that some of what is perceived as a crime wave is actually a reporting wave—that is, many people are more willing to report crimes than they were in the bad old days—one cannot escape very troubling conclusions about post-apartheid crime. One is that violent crime is rampant—with women and children victimized in appalling numbers—and in some categories has almost certainly increased since the end of apartheid. New types of crimes have emerged, and populations that were previously protected from much of the violence of past decades—mainly affluent whites and blacks—are newly affected. Much acquisitive crime and the violence that is associated with it can be laid at the door of organized crime groups that have proliferated and become more sophisticated since the opening of national borders after 1990.

Most of these problems could have been predicted (though South African criminologists sometimes say they and the police were taken by surprise). The transitions to democracy worldwide in the final decades of the twentieth century have not diminished crime and have probably increased it, particularly violent crime. Explanations vary from country to country, and data that would enable definitive conclusions are lacking, but some patterns emerge. Countries undergoing political transition—Poland, Hungary, Brazil—have often discovered that the costs of liberation may include the availability of new criminal opportunities and the weakening of social controls that might previously have operated to resist them. Democratizing countries are usually poor, and many have adopted economic policies that have increased unemployment and inequality.[47] Countries that are emerging from conflict are particularly likely to have high levels of violence as former insurgents take up ordinary crime. Rachel Neild comments, "Some analyses posit a continuum of violence from authoritarianism through the transition to democracy, with state violence replaced by private violence. State impunity for political crimes undergoes a perverse metamorphosis into criminal impunity."[48] Furthermore, chaotic law enforcement in postauthoritarian situations—as police are pushed to alter their primary allegiance from protection of the state to protection of the populace—is the norm.[49] With official order maintenance out of reach, vigilantism—often taking violent forms—thrives. Finally, in countries like South Africa and Brazil some analysts find that the criminal pathology of past regimes has endowed the current democratic state with a culture of violence—an assumption in many quarters that violence is the natural solution to daily problems.[50]

The end of South Africa's authoritarian regime has provided many criminal opportunities, and taking full advantage of them often necessitates violence. Merely ending the country's physical and political isolation—opening borders and trade—has expanded the possibilities for both legitimate and illegal commerce. Less tangible, but no less real, is the license that some feel as the blanket of repression has lifted. The constraints of apartheid imposed a certain amount of social discipline, at least with regard to relations between the races. The freedom that came with the regime's collapse is both social and political; loosening external controls can loosen personal inhibitions. Finally, the implicit promise of a better life after apartheid has not materialized for many people, and the resulting desperation and disillusionment may add a dimension of violence to what would otherwise be ordinary property crimes.

Inadequate official crime reports add to the problems of identifying trends in the incidence of particular crimes and violent crime in general. Nonetheless, piecing together what records exist and synthesizing the analyses of South African criminologists enables a broad-brush picture of South African crime since the end of apartheid and a focus on particular offenses—the violent ones—that give the country a reputation (in some ways unfair) for being "the crime capital of the world."

I have already noted the very high incidence of murder, rape, and robbery. Violent crime—as opposed to property crime—made up 34.6 percent of all reported crime in 2003–4, a significantly higher share of overall crime than in the United States, where violent crime—relatively high compared with most European countries—constituted 11.6 percent of the total.[51] A Johannesburg survey found that between 1993 and July 1997 about two-thirds of the residents of that metropolitan area were victims of crime, about equally divided between property and violent crimes. Burglary was the most common offense (24 percent of respondents), but robbery and assault totaled a greater number (32 percent of respondents), and 84 percent of assaults involved the use of a weapon.[52] Property crime for the country as a whole is not significantly out of line with many Western countries, and it seems likely that overall the "dark figure" is not higher than for, say, the United States and the United Kingdom.

What is striking about crime patterns in post-apartheid South Africa is that a careful observer can find in most categories of present-day violent crime a link—often direct, sometimes indirect—to the apartheid and colonial regimes that spawned past violence or the transition to democracy.[53] Taken together, those links make a powerful case for the importance of social and political context as explanation for crime trends and suggest the superficiality of the state president's attribution of declining moral fiber in individuals. Overwhelmingly, the types of crime that get the most media attention and are most apt to evoke political expressions of concern reflect structural inequality and insecurity. And, despite the thrilling democratization of South Africa, those conditions still exist and will continue to breed crime and violence in the foreseeable future.

Organized Crime

The proliferation and power of international crime syndicates is an aspect of globalization, as loosened borders and markets create both legitimate and criminal business opportunities. In 1999 a United Nations report estimated that these syndicates gross $1.5 trillion per year and named South Africa as one of nine countries with particularly powerful syndicates.[54] They and the local gangs with whom they develop allegiances operate with impunity in the urban areas of South Africa. This kind of crime affects foreigners as well as South African suburbanites and township residents; in February 1999 alone gangs were blamed for the death of a South Korean businessman and the robberies of a Canadian diplomat and a group of nineteen American tourists visiting a township preschool. Gangs that formerly operated primarily from the townships have moved into cities, most notably Cape Town, where their control of some bars and nightclubs has led to murder and mayhem. International syndicates originating in West Africa (particularly Nigeria), eastern Europe, Latin America, and China have identified South Africa as an "emerging market" for drugs, guns, and prostitutes; they also conduct elaborate e-mail scams and commercial crimes.[55] They employ professional money-launderers who—notwithstanding their disguises as respectable businesspeople with fancy offices and cars—are the supergangsters who grease the wheels of substantial illegal enterprises. The groups that deliver drugs and other contraband to communities are often offshoots of prison gangs; they work with wholesale operations—a famous one in the Western Cape is the Firm, a cartel that laundered and invested money in local real estate—and recruit "freelance" workers, including children, who act as couriers.[56]

The manufacture and trafficking of drugs has become a major industry in the past decade. The United Nations Office on Drugs and Crime has identified South Africa as an international drug capital, a regional hub for the transporting of drugs to other parts of the world and a manufacturing center.[57] The drug trade is a source of revenue for fighting civil wars in other parts of Africa.[58] An estimated 80 percent of worldwide sales of Mandrax (methaqualone) takes place in South Africa, where the sedative is often combined with dagga—the local name for marijuana—to produce the high of choice (the "white pipe") in many poor communities, particularly the Cape Flats townships. In July 2002 South African officials seized more than a hundred tons of chemicals hidden in Johannesburg warehouses that could have been used to make ninety million tablets of the drug. Labs for manufacturing methamphetamine, crack cocaine, and MDMA (Ecstasy) have also sprung up in recent years, and thousands of small rural plots in several provinces are devoted to the cultivation of marijuana, the country's most common drug. Two drug seizures in 2002 indicate the importance of South Africa as a transportation hub: thirty-six thousand tablets of MDMA en route in to New Zealand and $10 million worth of cocaine on its way to Togo. Seizure of marijuana has fallen off in recent years as law enforcement priorities have shifted to heavier drugs.

The groups often engage in more than one kind of illegal activity. The modus operandi for cash-in-transit heists, for instance, is that the gang steals cars that are used to force the vehicle carrying the money off the road. The thieves make off with the spoils, sometimes leaving behind the stolen automobiles, now battered beyond repair because they have been used to ram the targeted vehicle. Car theft syndicates dabble in the trafficking of Mandrax. And, just as legitimate businesses provide support for collateral enterprises, so do organized crime groups—chop shops that repaint stolen cars and trucks, fences who buy stolen jewelry, police that look the other way for a cut in the proceeds.

Crime in Communities

Organized crime takes its toll on the marginalized people who lose themselves in the drugs it makes available. It also exerts criminal control over communities; gang rivalries in schools, burgled homes and cars, and thefts from stores and warehouses are common. A study conducted in 2002 by the *Mail and Guardian* reported 137 gangs in the Cape Peninsula with one hundred thousand members—groups that have been around for decades, like the Americans and the Hard Livings and those that have sprung up in recent years, like the Taliban and the Fancy Boys.[59] The report estimated that gang-related crime constituted 40 to 60 percent of the violence in the area. Police statistics showed that forty-four people were killed and ninety-two wounded in gang-related violence in the first four months of 2000. In March 2002 alone five children were killed in one week, bystanders to gang wars. Adults are strong-armed to cooperate with the gangs, and young people are recruited to sell drugs or commit burglaries for them. Gun battles attributed to gang conflicts have become so frequent that one area has been dubbed "Klein Bosnia."

While dagga (marijuana) and Mandrax are the most frequently used drugs, crack cocaine has taken hold also.[60] (Heroin is generally too expensive for poor people to buy.) But health workers and police both say that among mind-altering substances the primary source of crime in communities is alcohol. Family violence is widespread in poor communities—perhaps in more affluent ones, too, but probably less likely to be reported to the authorities. More than half of the homicides occur in the home or in other residential settings, like the hostels where many workers stay when separated from their families.[61] Domestic abuse is often traceable to the frustrated man who deadens the pains of unemployment or loneliness or disease at the local shebeen (informal bars in townships) and then beats or otherwise abuses the women and children at home. Alcohol-related crime—rape and assault—is reputed to be particularly prevalent in Venda (in the northern province of Limpopo, near the border with Zimbabwe) and in the Northern Cape. In the latter area the apartheid-era "tot" system, though now illegal, still exists on some wine farms, and the number of liquor licenses issued is much higher than in South Africa in general.[62] Researchers working in several parts of the country suspect that rape is often the outcome of alcohol abuse (by both victim and perpetrator), though the causal relationship has not been definitively established.[63]

Rape has received a great deal of attention in recent years from both criminal justice and public health officials. It is alarming partly because it is so widespread; a quick examination of Interpol international crime statistics for several other African and European countries suggests that the rate may be the highest in the world.[64] Particularly alarming is the high incidence of child rape; the victims in about 40 percent of the fifty-two thousand rape cases reported in 2000 were under eighteen, and many were little girls.[65] Whether or not the explanation for this pattern—widely believed by the public and some health workers—lies in the myth that having sex with a virgin will cure you of AIDS, the disease plays an important role. The chance of HIV transmission to a rape victim is high, since so many young male rapists are HIV positive and gang rape is common.[66] Parliament decided against requiring antiretroviral treatment for rape victims in 2003, so a woman or girl in most parts of the country who is raped by someone with HIV or AIDS may well feel that her attacker has committed a gradual kind of homicide.

The prevalence of serious crimes varies significantly from one area to another. Rape is highest in the rural Northern Cape, murder in the urban Western Cape; aggravated assault is astronomical in the Northern Cape, and Johannesburg outdoes the rest of the country in armed robbery, burglary, and car theft.[67] But the violence of community life, at home and on the street, is a daily reality for most South Africans. The toll is greatest in poor and black areas, where violent crime is most prevalent; a 1990 study found that Africans were twenty times more likely to be murdered than whites.[68] A survey conducted in 1995 by the Human Sciences Research Council found that half of the respondents in the lowest income group named assault as "the most important crime" committed against them or a member of their household, as opposed to only 10 percent of the respondents in the highest income group.[69] Even in more affluent and protected neighborhoods, however, children live in fear. At a 2001 drama festival for 850 teenagers—most from expensive private schools—half raised their hands when asked how many had witnessed a robbery. Most had experienced a burglary, and about a third had a relative who had been murdered.[70]

Children have also suffered a horrific amount of abuse, often sexual. In 2001 the minister of safety and security testified before parliament that during the previous year the domestic violence and child protection units of the SAPS had received 65,017 reports of child abuse, about a third of them cases of rape.[71] Police reported in 2001 that 41 percent of rape victims were under eighteen.[72] As in other countries, the perpetrators are often relatives or neighbors, but girls are often not safe at school either; in fact, sexual assaults by male students and teachers are common.[73] Shooting and stabbing are leading causes of death for teenagers ages fifteen to nineteen, and a recent survey of children in early adolescence in low-income areas found that almost half had been victims of assault.[74]

A contributing factor to the violence in poor communities is conflict among vigilante groups, gangs, and the police. Vigilantism, as conceived in this discussion, is self-help intended to remedy the perceived failures of the police and courts to curb crime.[75] (During the 1980s another kind of vigilantism destabilized many black communities—attacks by right-wing African gangs, sometimes aided by police, on antiapartheid activists and supporters of the ANC.)[76] During the late 1990s the best known of contemporary vigilante groups was People Against Gangs and Drugs (known as Pagad), originally a loosely organized, largely Muslim organization in the Western Cape whose appeal lay in its call to ordinary citizens to empower themselves in fighting the drug dealing that plagued them.[77] Initial demonstrations against gangsters at their homes and ultimatums to drug dealers led to violent retaliation, widespread negative media coverage, and police allegations that Pagad had become part of the crime problem. The murders of a number of gang leaders and bombings on the Cape Town waterfront and in the Cape Flats townships have been attributed to the organization, though criminal trials have not led to convictions for these crimes. Alleged police complicity in violent clashes between gangs and Pagad and the tampering of evidence in criminal cases brought against both Pagad and gang members complicated the picture. Over a period of several years the campaign by Pagad and the law enforcement response claimed the lives of police, magistrates, and innocent civilians—as well as twenty-eight drug dealers, according to Wilfried Schärf.[78]

Other vigilante organizations abound elsewhere. One—Mapogo a Mathamaga ("the colors of the leopard"), originally organized by black businessmen in the Northern Province (now Limpopo) to deal with property crime—now has branches around the country and operates as a security company with protection services provided to clients—Schärf calls it "abusive commercial security."[79] It is known for brutal retaliation against criminal suspects—torture, lynching, and assault—and its leaders are proud of their methods. Mapogo's claim to prowess in vanquishing criminals rests primarily on *sethlare* ("medicine")—whipping suspects with a *sjambok* or a whip dipped in salt and herbs.[80] Violent responses to crime may also be spontaneous and unorganized—residents who resist drug dealers by burning down their houses, neighbors of a thief who become enraged and beat him to death. As with gang violence, innocent bystanders may be victims, and young people become involved as both victims and perpetrators.

Farm Crime

As a general rule around the world serious property and violent crime is greater in urban than in rural areas. In South Africa, however, the large cities have high rates of murder and robbery, but the countryside is often very violent, too. A 1998 survey in rural areas found that 59.6 percent of residents had been victims of crime in the previous five years, and, while stock theft headed the list of offenses, more serious property crimes and violent crime were not far behind.[81] Gangs battle each other in rural areas as well as in the townships, especially in KwaZulu-Natal. Murder, rape, and assault among intimates—often fueled by alcohol—are disproportionately high in the Northern Cape, the least populated province. While robbery and rape are relatively low in the Eastern Cape, a poor and largely rural province, serious assault and murder—often related to stock theft and residents' efforts to combat it—are high.[82] The commercial farms of South Africa, many of them large and isolated, have been the locus of a great deal of robbery, assault, and murder since the end of apartheid. (Minor crop theft and poaching by tenants, historically tolerated as a kind of compensation for white control of the land, continues.) Gruesome murders and robberies by blacks of white farmers and their families—sometimes even pets are killed—increased alarmingly in the late 1990s and have been the subject of much media and government attention.[83]

But the problem of farm crime is more complicated than is commonly reported, and the focus on farmers as victims reflects once again the disproportionate attention paid to crimes against whites. Farm owners and managers are themselves sources of violence, sometimes very extreme.[84] Casual physical discipline of workers and residents of the farms (the families of workers often live on the farms) is routine, and in recent years there have been murders of trespassers and torture of tenants, sometimes by guards hired by the farmers or army reservists (the "commandos" of the past) who are supposed to provide security. Much of this crime goes unreported because its victims either assume law enforcement indifference or fear retaliation from the farmers on whom they are dependent. The Institute for Security Studies reported 361 murders in more than two thousand attacks on farms between January 1997 and December 1999; no comparable data exist for murders or assaults by farmers or their surrogates.[85]

Police Crime

Cutting across all the categories of violent crime noted above is the crime of police. In 1998 the minister of safety and security released data to a parliamentary committee on charges brought over a seventeen-month period against police—for almost every imaginable offense, from poaching (16), fraud (291), and shoplifting (25) to assault (7,263), armed robbery (195), rape (149), and murder (332).[86] The minister asserted that police were three times more likely to commit a crime than ordinary citizens, though it remains unclear whether this conclusion was supported by presumptions of the guilt of officers who were charged or by actual convictions. The following year 1,551 members of the SAPS were convicted of crimes, about a quarter of which were for some form of assault; on average between 1995 and 1999 thirty-four officers annually were convicted of murder.[87] These data could not have come as a surprise to many people. Much police crime is committed off-duty in private relationships, but a great deal also victimizes the public police are supposed to protect. Reports of extreme police brutality—kicking and beating suspects, attaching electrodes to their genitals, using tear gas to flush people from their houses—complement complaints that police help detainees escape and supply gang members with weapons. Harassment of citizens has been also common. In the countryside women have been especially vulnerable to police violence, with occasional gang rapes in precincts reported. In one particularly violent township citizen members of the community police forum hid a young boy who had given them information about gang and police violence, whereupon the police arrested them for murder.⁸⁸ Violent treatment of suspects drew international attention in 1999 when the BBC televised two South African policemen beating four African and coloured men whom they suspected of carjacking and setting dogs on handcuffed suspects, while ten of their colleagues stood by and did nothing.

If one accepts the view of Paul Chevigny that police reflect the social and political worlds in which they operate, some of this crime is understandable, though hardly forgivable.⁸⁹ In both past and present South Africa's social order has been criminogenic, as violence—both individual and institutional— has begotten more violence. It is worth noting, however, that South African police researchers, in a report on police shootings known to the SAPS from 1996 to 1998, concluded, "The information provided indicated that the level of fatalities 'as a result of police action' recorded by the SAPS is not necessarily exceptional in relation to that recorded in many US cities, if one takes into account general levels of societal violence."⁹⁰ And post-apartheid South Africa, unlike many South American countries, is not a culture of impunity where crimes of police and military define the political climate.⁹¹ The blossoming of democracy may well crowd out much police crime committed on the job.

Rounding the Corner?

The grim picture of the preceding paragraphs should not overshadow the apparent drop in recent years of some kinds of violent crime. The political clashes of the early 1990s, which were often fatal, have been steadily declining since 1994.⁹² As noted, the rate of reported murders dropped by more than a third between 1994 and 2003.⁹³ While the overall number of crimes reported to the police continues to increase each year, the rate of increase for 2001–2 was the smallest (1 percent) since 1994.⁹⁴ Over the two-year period between 1999 and 2001 the Independent Complaints Directorate, the constitutionally mandated agency that investigates complaints of police misconduct and reports on deaths attributable to police, found that "deaths in custody and as the result of police action" fell by about 20 percent.⁹⁵ And the most recent national victimization survey found that crime overall declined slightly between 1998 and 2003, with housebreaking the only crime that had increased.⁹⁶

There is no way to know at this point what has caused this drop. Some of the reductions may indicate increased efficiency in policing, prosecution, or crime prevention; the 14.3 percent drop in the rate of business burglaries may reflect crime watches mounted by both the SAPS and private security. But other social factors may be more important; the fact that the 2003 victimization study reported a drop of almost 50 percent in assaults suggests that people may be feeling less aggressive and desperate than five years earlier.[97] If so, it is not because the material prospects for most people have improved. Nonagricultural formal employment fell throughout the 1990s, and intraracial inequality is growing, rather than declining.[98]

Particularly interesting as evidence that some kinds of conflicts can be mediated are developments in the large and violent taxi industry, which was for many years one of the few avenues for private enterprise (with the exception of running illegal shebeens) open to Africans. Now, however, concern with improving transportation for the poor and those who live far from workplaces and urban centers has replaced the authoritarian state's indifference to the needs of black workers and its exclusion of black entrepreneurs from the formal economy. New law has established municipal transportation authorities that plan routes and let contracts for taxi companies; the government sets standards for the service provided and, in 2000, made it possible for the owners of antiquated and dangerous taxis to trade them in for sturdy new buses, free of charge. Regulating and regularizing the industry has drastically reduced the bloodshed, though pockets of violence remain, particularly in KwaZulu-Natal. In October 2002 two rival taxi companies operating out of Soweto merged into the Meadowlands-Diepkloof Taxi Association, which will own one thousand minibus-taxis.[99] In theory at least, the merger represents the end of eight years of murderous competition. But taxi violence has not completely abated; taxi "warlords" shot at each other in Cape Town in mid-2004.

Criminal Violence in Context: Ideology and Structure

In decrying the violent crime of today, the South African public (black as well as white) makes only limited connections to the violence of yesterday. If they acknowledge the influence of the past upon the present at all, it is with the "culture of violence" argument: that violence is assumed by many to be an appropriate first recourse for solving problems. The source of that attitude is presumed to be the period of revolutionary struggle, when violence in the pursuit of liberation was no crime. It is certainly true that resistance to apartheid took a turn to violence in the 1960s and accelerated in the 1980s. But resistance to white domination was largely nonviolent throughout the twentieth century. Decades of coercion and violence perpetrated by the colonial and apartheid regimes spawned the shift—violence responding to violence. The cultural habits that resulted could not be altered simply by the transformation of the political system, the ascendance of the racial majority, or the reconciliation process initiated by the new government and its revered and charismatic leader. Perhaps political violence did not end but was merely transformed—into the social violence that may prove as damaging and as intractable.

During the Rivonia trial in 1964 Nelson Mandela testified at length that he and ANC colleagues had determined very explicitly after the Sharpeville massacre that the ANC's commitment to nonviolence should be abandoned, that the time had come to embrace "properly controlled violence" in the political struggle. By this he meant actions undertaken by a separate organization Umkonto We Sizwe (Spear of the Nation) that would, however, be subject to the political guidance of the ANC leadership.[100] The strategy they chose was sabotage, rather than guerilla warfare or terrorism. It was a decision that was both practical and ethical. The ANC policy of peaceful protest throughout the first fifty years of its existence was becoming less effective, as violence had already erupted at demonstrations during the 1950s and younger Africans were impatient with the lack of progress in bringing about political change. Mandela also felt that, in the tense and repressive atmosphere of the time, Africans might turn on one another if they did not have the outlet of violent forms of resistance; "I felt morally obliged to do what I did," he said of his decision to push for a change in ANC policy.[101]

While other liberation groups did not follow suit in such an explicit manner, they did not reject violence either. The PAC, founded in 1959 and representing the Africanist movement, aimed ultimately for total revolution, an outcome that would presumably entail violent acts of many kinds; but its leaders counseled nonviolence when they mobilized their followers for the antipass campaign of 1960. The black consciousness movement of the 1970s implicitly endorsed violence, though its goal was "not to trigger a spontaneous Fanonesque eruption of the masses into violent action, but rather to rebuild and recondition the mind of the oppressed in such a way that eventually they would be ready forcefully to demand what was rightfully theirs."[102] Steve Biko, the black consciousness leader who was tortured by the police and left to die in 1977, believed that "some type of agitation" was necessary to rouse the African masses from their torpor, but he was speaking generally of activism that would bolster the confidence and resolve of those who engaged in it, not violent action for the sake of conveying a direct and immediate threat to the state.[103]

It is the apartheid bureaucrats and the colonial governments before that—not the groups that struggled against them—that turned homes, communities, and workplaces into sites of violent struggle.[104] At the height of the revolts against the institutions of apartheid that shook the late 1970s Gail Gerhart described apartheid as "an ideology of violence in that it sanctions the full use of the coercive powers of the state to preserve racial domination."[105] It is impossible to prove a direct causal relationship between the license conveyed by that ideology and the violence of today's South African society, and the connections are complex. But if, as some allege, the habit of violence has been ingrained in many South Africans, it is unlikely that the source of the habit is the liberation struggle, in which only a small minority participated actively and an even smaller number violently. A more credible influence is the message conveyed by the apartheid state that violence is the preferred strategy for maintaining or acquiring power and control. As abusing adults often reflect experience as abused children, those who are violent in South Africa have lived in the shadow of an abusive regime, even if they have not themselves experienced its violence directly and physically. The "easy slide" has made criminal violence as functional in the new South Africa as political violence was in the old.[106]

The atrocities carried out in the name of apartheid are legion and have been well documented by testimony given in the Truth and Reconciliation hearings and a plethora of literature, scholarly and personal, from victims, observers, and perpetrators. The beatings, tortures, and arrests were arbitrary as well as brutal. The sources of violence were fluid. State agencies were violent in themselves, but they also found allies to do their dirty work, collaborators who could be as cruel as the official assassins. Carrying on the colonial tradition of indirect rule, that is, co-opting traditional chiefs to revive disintegrating tribalism in order to control the natives, apartheid administrators anointed (and paid) conservative chiefs who did not hesitate to put down resistance with violence. Closer to the central home of apartheid, the Civil Cooperation Bureau, a secret death squad of criminals, soldiers, and police cobbled together in the South African Defence Force, engaged in "actions [that] ranged from shootings, bombings and poisoning to intimidation, breaking windows, stealing heart pills and hanging a monkey foetus in a tree at the residence of a Nobel Peace Prize laureate [Archbishop Desmond Tutu]."[107]

Whether clandestine or overt, operating under official supervision or with independent impunity, the death squads carried on up to the very end of the regime. Although Vlakplaas, the police counterinsurgency unit responsible for hundreds of deaths and mutilations, was exposed in 1991, it was reconstituted as "Section C10" in the Crime Intelligence Service and given a mandate to trace illegal weapons and infiltrate organized crime. But in shifting the unit's focus to "ordinary" crime the state merely provided a wider kind of license to its pathological murderers. In March 1992, on the road between Nelspruit and White River, they ambushed a minivan and killed its five occupants, hoping to be paid for the recovery of weapons that had, in fact, been planted on the victims. (One of the murderers later falsely testified in court that the slaughter was justified "to prevent a tragedy . . . and arrest the suspects before they could rob a bank.")[108] Vlakplaas also made common cause with smugglers they were assigned to arrest, getting kickbacks from their operations. And, along with other units, they stoked conflict in the deadly political civil war between Inkatha, the Zulu-based party, and the ANC; during the early 1990s they provided weapons—AK-47s as well as rocket launchers, hand grenades, and pistols—to Inkatha's hired guns.

Communities besieged with apartheid violence turned on each other in ways that seem in some respects to mirror or imitate the oppressor's tactics. The death squads dismembered their victims; liberation fighters put rubber tires around the necks of collaborators and set them afire. Police beat people in detention; township residents beat the *impipis* (police informers). The apartheid state forced workers into crowded hostels, away from their families and from social contact with whites; those hostels became hotbeds of violent party competition, with Inkatha supporters gunning down ANC loyalists and sometimes vice versa. The deadly tit-for-tat between the oppressors and the oppressed was often a kind of violent policy conversation. During the campaign against Bantu education in 1977, when police forced students back to school to crush the boycott, defiant parents burned down the schools.[109] When the government initiated the rural Bantustan program, PAC supporters murdered chiefs and headmen who were designated as local administrators. By the time negotiations to end apartheid began in the early 1990s the violence was out of control, generated from within communities and visited upon them.

Those negotiations did not stem the violent tide, an indication that the racial ideology of apartheid was not its only determinant and assault or torture not its only expression. Tracing the development of patterns of violence that persist into the new millennium also requires looking at the effects of long decades of inequality, deprivation, and denial of opportunity. The violence of apartheid went beyond the forced removals of millions of people from their homes, the punishments for violations of the pass laws, or the torture and murder of dissidents, to assume an institutional form. Apartheid policies—Bantu education, "separate development," employment discrimination, the barriers to social and sexual relations between the races—resonated throughout the culture. Although force was at times required to effectuate them, their violence was not primarily physical. The added influence of particular forms of capitalist development cannot be ignored either. Apartheid institutional violence built on pre-apartheid structural developments of farming (nineteenth century) and mining (twentieth century), which drove the processes of urbanization, segregation, and migratory labor to shape a deeply divided society with criminogenic consequences.

The persistence and transformation of gang activity illustrate both the effects of institutional violence before and during apartheid and links to the criminal behavior of today. As blacks became permanent residents of urban areas in the early decades of the twentieth century, fettered by lack of education and opportunity, a young male gang subculture developed that scorned the work ethic—an understandable position when jobs available to blacks were so limited—and sought excitement and material gain in thefts, con games, and robberies. Gangs fought each other, raided each other's lairs, and raped each other's women (though they often banded together against intruders from other territories). Clive Glaser, whose work on the *tsotsis* of Soweto provides a rich history of the evolution of gang culture, notes that youth gangs "emerged almost organically out of the social and economic dead ends that township youths faced throughout the 1930s, 1940s and 1950s."[110] By the late 1940s and 1950s, concern over young gangsters was shared by the government and the African elite. The state, however, was not prepared to address the overcrowded housing, the poor-quality education, and the lack of jobs that had driven young males to make a living in the streets. It responded to "the youth problem" instead by tightening the noose of law enforcement and—using the influx control laws that allowed only employed persons with passes to remain in urban areas—sending unruly youth back to the countryside. Enforcing the pass laws against them to force them into jobs that would give them passes turned out to be counterproductive, however. Glaser notes:

> Influx control backfired tragically as a strategy for combating juvenile delinquency. Instead of allowing the administration to concentrate its energy and resources on a limited number of strictly legal urban youths, the pass laws created a massive population of influx-control refugees who lived a shadowy illegal existence in the townships. Hounded by police and without any chance of finding legal employment, their best chance for urban survival lay in joining criminal street gangs.[111]

During the 1960s the government's forced removals severed family and community ties and may have increased the appeal of gang membership as a substitute.

It would be a mistake to see the youth gangs of the apartheid era as committing crimes for political reasons, as an explicit challenge to the regime. (It was initially school-going adolescents and young adults, rather than the unlettered hoodlums of the streets, who signed on to the liberation struggle through the defiance of Bantu education in the 1970s.) Members of youth gangs were trapped in a society that valued what they could not have, and their response was not to fight it directly but to subvert its institutions through crime. In this respect they fit sociologist Robert Merton's characterization of the criminal as innovator—the person who adapts to the strain of living such a contradiction by embracing the consumerism of the larger (white) culture while simultaneously rejecting the legal pursuit of whatever crumbs might fall from that culture.[112]

A decade later politicized youth congresses reached out to mobilize gang members, and they responded. They became "comrades" who helped to make the townships ungovernable—a key strategy in the resistance of the 1980s—

and led to violent confrontations with security forces. Some continued to commit ordinary crimes, however, and the distinction between criminal and political activity was blurred; whatever the motivation, violence was seen as legitimate. As apartheid collapsed and the new dispensation came into being, political activism lost its appeal and the criminal gangs flourished once again.[113] "Viewed historically, the revolutionary resourcefulness of the youth in the forefront of the struggle in the 1980s has become a deviant resourcefulness in the 1990s and the structure of gang life and the criminal underworld has replaced political organization."[114] Simpson's analysis of post-apartheid criminal violence in relation to the violence of the political struggle is instructive. He points out that in countries coming out of a period of political and economic turmoil "conflict may change its shape, but it will not go away."[115] In South Africa young men marginalized by a brutally racist society found a home in the political organizations fighting apartheid that "allowed them a central role as the 'shock troops' of liberation." But when the struggle moved from the streets to the negotiating table, they were once again excluded from the world that determined their fate, and they took refuge elsewhere. "The Party had given people a new uniform, a new language, new songs of liberation, but now the criminal gangs offered ready-made alternatives. Membership of these gangs provides an identity, social clothing, a language of its own, and the added advantage of providing some alternative forms of wealth creation."[116]

Those alternative opportunities became increasingly important as living conditions for many people worsened after apartheid ended. The township gangs now have easy access to weapons and drugs and smuggling routes into many other African countries. Their acquisitive crime—with its attendant violence—has become so normal that those engaged in it—and their families, who rely on its proceeds—regard it as employment. The democratic state has proved no more relevant than the apartheid regime for socializing young people into law-abiding lives.

The taxi wars also reflect the structural violence of apartheid and the consequent, desperate measures to turn disaster into opportunity. When blacks streamed into the cities and needed transportation that the apartheid government did not provide, poor but crafty entrepreneurs stepped into the breach and built fleets of minibuses, making themselves rich through the provision of an essential service. Competition for routes, however, often became violent, and the taxi wars carried over to the post-apartheid years. (It has been estimated that between 1994 and 1999 in Gauteng alone between fifteen hundred and three thousand people were killed in the turf conflicts of the minibus industry.)[117] In the Western Cape people in the townships turned to the armed and dangerous enforcers hired by taxi owners to carry out vigilante vengeance, and a 2000 report on taxi violence in Gauteng found that police had supplied the assailants with weapons and uniforms.[118] As apartheid capitalism neglected the transportation needs of its urbanizing black population, bandit capitalism took over and has thrived despite the end of the oppressive regime.

Crimes against women and children are also heavily influenced by the structural violence of apartheid as it affected power relations in the home. Removed from their families for long periods as the result of policies requiring them to live far from their jobs, black men asserted their authority brutally when they returned. If they were poorly paid or unemployed, they were frustrated by their marginality and took it out on their partners and, less often, on children.[119] Also relevant are psychological explanations of some kinds of violence as responses to challenges to group identity. African men are increasingly unable to command the kind of respect and power prized by the patriarchal cultures in which they were raised. A 1990 study undertaken in the Durban townships of the attitudes of men and women toward family relationships found a complex association between gender identity and violence in the home. First, capitalism and apartheid took their toll on the class and race status of African men, causing a "crisis of masculinity" inside the home as well as outside. Then the political struggle during the 1980s became an outlet for the reassertion of masculinity, and violence became a permissible solution to social conflict as well. A recent study has estimated that 1,349 women were murdered by an intimate partner—boyfriend or husband (current or former) or rejected would-be lover or same-sex partner—in 1999 and that these murders comprised 41 percent of all female homicides that year.[120] As Catherine Campbell sees it,

> The undermining of masculinity is one of the intricately interlocking contextual factors that cannot be ignored in attempting to understand the upsurge of violence in working class black communities. In a community where the opportunities for assertion of masculine power are limited, violence is a manifestation of the structural forces of patriarchy reasserting themselves at a time when race and class oppression has dealt the status of adult men a particularly severe blow.[121]

Conclusion

The violence perpetrated and encouraged by the apartheid government is gone now; but it is naive to assume that the transformation of the superordinate political authority will automatically defuse the tensions of race, class, and gender that it spawned. Violence in one form or another has been a continuous presence since whites first settled on the Cape peninsula 350 years ago, and it has been so pervasive over such a long period that some commentators assume it is endemic and intractable, a central feature of national life that cuts across multiple South African cultures. The increased availability of lethal weapons and markets for stolen goods provides new incentives for the commission of crimes that can become violent. (Other countries have had similar experiences—new criminal problems associated with the instability that accompanies political change.)[122] Furthermore, it might be argued that structural violence—defined by one scholar as "violence in the metaphorical sense as a denial of human rights or life chances"—has not been lessened significantly by the advent of democracy.[123]

Democracy itself generates a certain amount of the crime people fear. Intangible but real is the license that some feel—especially young males left behind in the educational vacuum of the turbulent 1970s and 1980s—as the blanket of authoritarian repression has lifted. The constraints of apartheid imposed a certain amount of social discipline, at least with regard to relations between the races. The freedom that has resulted is both social and political—and spatial, as Nelson Mandela noted when he remarked in 1998, "What's happening now with liberation is that criminals have also been liberated to move into white areas."

Questions of legitimacy arise here, as people adjust to the liberating principles and practices of a new regime, which, however, has assigned the old operatives to new tasks. On the one hand, police and courts are expected to serve the public with a different set of laws, values, and constitutional mandates that now comprise the standards that the national polity has chosen to live by. On the other hand, under the new order criminal justice institutions may simply be perceived as less authoritative than they previously were, defanged sanctioners whose status and pronouncements are not to be taken seriously as deterrence. In ceding the opportunity to overhaul the entire apparatus of criminal justice—perhaps an impossible enterprise, given the available human resources—the negotiated settlement may not have adequately protected the new democracy's capacity to exercise its core function of regulating social order.

It is hard to assess the overall impacts of so much brutal and uncontrolled crime. Some observers worry that it threatens to destabilize the hard-won and precious political democracy. Others say that formal democracy is secure—surveys show widespread support for it in the abstract—but that the sense of civic nationhood, so evident in the immediate aftermath of the 1994 election, is not. The reconciliation process, widely hailed at its initiation, has been discredited as giving license to criminals who see that apartheid thugs have been given amnesty. (This analysis is surely wrong; the gang members with guns looking for a Mercedes to steal and the neighbor lying in wait for the teenage girl he intends to rape are not thinking that because the political criminals of apartheid are not serving prison terms, they will get off scot-free.) Victimization of both the poor (especially) and the affluent—and the measures that all groups have taken to protect themselves—have reinforced the social divisions that colonialism and apartheid imposed. Behind the pain and injury and anger of such social harm lies the despair that accompanies a broken promise, the sense that the aims of Nelson Mandela and others who dedicated their lives to a peaceful nonracial democracy are now a distant chimera. One critic asserts that "most South Africans have merely traded danger at the hands of an oppressive government for danger unchecked by a representative one."[124] If he is right and if the dangers do not recede, many in the beleaguered majority may conclude that the achievement of constitutional democracy is irrelevant.

II Shifting the Constituency
Theory and Practice

5 Elements of Liberal Justice in a New Democracy

> Democracy appears to legitimate modern political life: rule-making
> and law enforcement seem justified and appropriate when
> they are "democratic."
> —David Held[1]

Yearning for Justice

THE CRIMINAL JUSTICE system in all state societies—criminal law and the institutions that apply it—is essentially repressive. It regulates by prohibition, patrol, surveillance, judgment, and punishment. Its primary function is to exercise the most fundamental domestic power of the state—the ordering of society—through the sanction.[2] Like law more generally, it generally operates, omniscient and often oppressive, to provide a structure on which people rely to conduct their daily lives. When recourse to prisons or courts is necessary, the rewards for those who turn to them—victims of crime, people who feel threatened by disorder around them—are fundamentally negative: the capture and containment of the wrongdoers, the invocation of state power to settle scores, the eviction of an intruder. When the president of the United States speaks of bringing terrorists "to justice," he promises a remedy of force, taking from the wrongdoers their freedom of movement, their human relationships, their access to earth and sky, perhaps even their lives. Although a country's courts and police may restrain and penalize legitimately through a popularly approved process, that process is our acknowledgment of human failure—to keep order and to sanction bad behavior relying on informal social controls. Acquittals and pardons are reprieves from a collective agreement that coercion must sometimes prevail over socialization.

Reinforcing the inherent coerciveness of police and courts is their deployment in many parts of the world as regime enforcers. The world's history suggests that maintaining social order more often than not is secondary to maintaining political order. Law, as an expression of the state's priorities, has often, as in South Africa, promoted injustice or has proved to be the idealistic mask for real repression. Recent examples abound. In Sierra Leone between 1991 and 1996, despite a constitution that prohibited torture and mandated judicial independence as well as laws that provided rights to counsel and due process, police and the military entered and looted homes, detained opponents of the regime illegally, and tortured supporters of free elections, chopping off limbs and carving slogans—"No Elections"—on people's backs.[3] An effort to depoliticize criminal law and law enforcement following a free and fair presidential election in February 1996 stalled two years later as the new government's fragility made it defensive. Demonstrating the malleability of law in a hostile political environment, rules of evidence and criminal procedure were altered after a momentarily successful military coup to ensure conviction of reporters accused of collaborating with the perpetrators and to demonstrate the authority of the restored regime.[4] At the other end of Africa Robert Mugabe, regarded in the 1980s as the progressive liberator of Zimbabwe, had little difficulty twenty years later in rewriting the law to criminalize dissent; those who "used abusive language on the person of the president" could now receive a sentence of up to a year.[5] And in May 2001 an Egyptian court, enforcing increasingly restrictive laws that limit the funding and activities of NGOs, sentenced a prominent scholar to seven years' imprisonment for tarnishing the country's image through his advocacy of human rights.[6]

Selective enforcement by abusive police and harsh penalties imposed by a biased or corrupt judiciary may also be less the product of authoritarian laws than the result of styles of political leaders, patterns of class domination, prosecutorial and judicial indifference, or a pervasive culture of repression. Nominally democratic countries may use police to brutalize labor protesters, as in Bolivia in the mid-1990s. In both Brazil and Argentina, despite repudiation of their military regimes and the adoption of human-rights-oriented constitutions, police brutality and torture continue with only tepid and inefficient responses from courts.[7] Widespread belief that the police and courts are corrupt and ineffective has spawned the use of private security companies, often staffed with former lieutenants of past dictatorships who merely substitute for the political enforcement of the past the maintenance of public order, with equally violent results. A population grown cynical about the government's ability to protect them often has recourse to vigilantism, and support for police violence—at least if it is directed against the apparently guilty—is strong.[8]

We should not assume that Western democracies are immune to the use of criminal justice to give priority to protecting the regime rather than the people. France recently passed a law that could impose a two-year sentence and a thirty-thousand-dollar fine on a person who curses a police officer or government official, and the United States routinely uses minor criminal charges to justify deportation of legal as well as illegal immigrants. For the time being at least, however, these measures appear to be temporary reactions to crisis—resorting to a resource that is simply too handy to resist—rather than patterned activities that suggest long-term rejection of the polity as the ultimate policymakers in a democracy. But considered worldwide, the criminal law as both theory and practice is a resource more often invoked for the benefit of the short-term political and economic interests of the state and its elites than for the protection of the citizenry. Politically neutral law enforcement reflecting democratic values is largely a chimera.

Despite the inherent coerciveness of police and courts and the abuses in which they can be enlisted, there remains a collective yearning, whether in a republic or a monarchy, a dictatorship or a democracy, for the state to provide policing and judging that protect people and their rights, however defined. Hopeful citizens of countries in turmoil repeatedly express the view that the institutions of official social control can enhance rather than humiliate, ennoble as well as punish. The conventional understanding that police, prosecutors, judges, and court officers have been granted a monopoly on violence as delegates of vengeful or potential victims leaves out a less tangible but no less important role, one that does not rely on retributive feelings and is quite independent of the effectiveness of law enforcement in reducing violence and disorder. People yearn for public mechanisms that keep order in many arenas—on the street, resolving disputes—to help define the moral and social community. And even when it is understood that criminal justice can play only a very limited role in controlling crime, people want to know that the effort is being made and made with a commitment to universal protection.

This chapter presumes that the yearning for justice is a part of the impulse for democratization and that it must be honored in significant ways if a constitutional democracy is to be consolidated. The pages that follow elaborate the connection between democratization and the reform of police and courts and suggest that the search for justice furthered by those institutions is crucial for a state that purports to both respect individual autonomy and protect individual rights. Anticipating the charge that specifying particular reforms—as I do—would force a Western-style liberal state on countries with other agendas, I concede that for some—particularly countries where Islamic law applies in some circumstances or areas—the policy direction does not fit. It should be noted, however, that in the late twentieth century an international political culture began to evolve—as often the result of popular revolt as of elite imposition by the United Nations and Western countries offering assistance—that values rights, democracy, and constitutions. Although embryonic and contingent, that culture has shaped political reconstruction all over the world.[9]

Nigeria—a country where the sharia law of Islam prevails in some northern states—professes to be as concerned about police reform and judicial independence as countries, like South Africa, that have explicitly taken the Western path of constitutional, liberal democracy. Accountability, transparency, and the protection of rights in criminal justice have become near-universal goals, though their manifestations will certainly vary from country to country—and in some may be, at least for the time being, primarily rhetorical gestures.

Linking Coercion and Democracy

As anyone who lives—and eats—in a large city in North America knows, globalization is not solely a matter of expanding markets and manipulating world trade. The migration of people and cultures enlarges the world in many ways for both participants and observers. Ideas about governance are among the exports being traded and consumed worldwide, and foremost among them is constitutional democracy. Even in countries where dictators are entrenched or the dominant religion discourages elections, people yearn to choose their own leaders and to be free to express themselves. The rule of law that undergirds constitutionalism has become a beacon for both the sanctity of contract and the liberation of oppressed peoples—objectives that clash as often as they complement.

That tension illustrates the inevitable slipperiness of democracy, both as a concept and as a political reality. The debate over how to define it will probably always be a lively one among political scientists and concerned publics alike. Some still cling to the rather narrow, procedural definition of democracy—"that institutional arrangement for arriving at political decisions in which individuals acquire the power to decide by means of a competitive struggle for the people's vote"—adopted by Joseph Schumpeter more than sixty years ago.[10] Rational choice theorists have embraced this definition with their presumption that democracy is nothing more than the public aggregation of private preferences and demands. Others broaden it with a general commitment to political equality or add elements that are corollary to the "institutional arrangement," like the right to free expression, the right to form organizations, and equal access to justice.[11] Still others do not consider a state to be fully democratic unless its standard of social justice includes economic benefits, "a social minimum providing for the basic needs of all citizens."[12] As the definition includes substantive attributes, the importance of democratic participation beyond pulling the lever in the ballot box increases. Some theorists assert that the legitimacy of morally contested public policies like abortion and capital punishment depends on active citizen deliberation.[13] And definitional problems prevail among activists as well as academics; even within a single country democratic standards may shift as economic and political realities impinge on the idealism of the liberation struggles that brought about regime change. Finally, there is the fact that democratization is not the same as democracy—the former a variable and often capricious process and the latter a state of being (though some will argue that democracy is always incomplete as well as imperfect and that therefore democratization is a relevant idea at all times and places).

For the purpose of this chapter I am adopting a definition of the process of democratic change that avoids the pitfalls of the most ambitious goal for democracy—self-government in matters of material benefit—but assumes that the promise of democracy has a moral dimension. Democratization as I see it does not stop with the narrow procedural requirement of adopting a system in which a broad spectrum of voters make political choices in multiparty elections. It recognizes human dignity as it extends to both peasant and prince the power of political participation not only through the vote but also in public debate, protest or editorial. It assumes that the individual benefit is an ethical one, that the new freedom extends to self-development, the maximizing of human powers.[14] It is quintessentially liberal in the sense that it concedes "the centrality, in principle, of an 'impersonal structure' of public power, of a constitution to help guarantee and protect rights, of a diversity of power centres within and outside the state, of mechanisms to promote competition and debate between alternative political platforms."[15] The democratizing state respects legitimate variation in the way people define their interests and welcomes the energies that are expended in the defense of those interests.

In choosing a definition that guarantees some benefits and rights that bear on the performance of police and courts I am, in part, reflecting on what democratization movements on several continents (Latin America, Africa, Asia, and eastern Europe) have demanded. The embrace of democracy since the 1960s—what Samuel Huntington has famously called "the third wave," referring to the latest in a series of emancipatory accomplishments among nations over a period of almost two centuries—has depth as well as breadth.[16] The leaders of democratizing countries of the past generation generally seek—sometimes without success—not only to transform the electoral system but also to reform government institutions so that they protect rights and privileges prized by people. The promise of regime change, then, includes the prospect that people's trips to the polling place will have positive outcomes for their lives.

The consent to be governed—and therefore to accept collective and individual constraints that result from our collective choices—is the other side of the power that democracy provides to choose the methods and leaders of governance. The relationship between criminal justice—policing and judging—and democracy is an aspect of that consent. Skeptics of democracy argue that popular choice will produce results that will injure those who made the choice; its adherents respond by asserting that people do not willingly tyrannize themselves. One must accept this answer to find a democratic basis for the inherently coercive functions of criminal justice and the obligation of democratic citizens to respect them. But vigilance is also necessary. If people are to make political choices in an open, competitive environment, they need to be able to do so without fearing either police brutality or judicial punishment for exercising their right to vote or taking part in public protest or associating with like-minded citizens. The common description of a repressive regime as a "police state" identifies the dominant source of its authority and suggests that, conversely, the democratic state will not need to assure allegiance through primary reliance on law enforcement.

The embrace of democracy is a leap of faith—not only an appeal for self-government but also an expression of confidence that citizens are competent to control the public ordering of their lives. Taking the leap, democratic citizens reveal their fears—vague or distinct, depending on past experience—of what the coercive agencies of the state will do to them in the absence of democracy. The license of police and courts in a dictatorship can be as energizing for those subject to it as for those exercising it. Experience of police brutality, secret tribunals, detention without trial, and the arbitrariness of internal security laws that come into play during an "emergency" may be more likely to propel people toward support for democracy than abstractions of future liberty, equality, and prosperity. If self-government will end the raids in the night and the confinement and torture of outspoken youth, most people will back it.

This analysis suggests that democratic transition must shift the constituency for institutions of criminal justice from the state to the citizenry, either directly or through broadly representative surrogates. The immediate connection to democratic governance is the idea that criminal justice is a process and an outcome that should be fundamentally acceptable and understandable to most of the population. While people may not wish to be in direct control of its operations, they want to know that occupational competence and respect for the general population can be enforced; a democratic political culture will encourage them to feel entitled to play a role in that enforcement. That the population will be able to hold officials' feet to the fire when performance falls below standards they have consented to—whether that performance consists in preventing crime, catching and punishing wrongdoers, or providing a fair process for defendants and victims alike—is the essence of the accountability promised by self-government. Citizens of a democracy may acknowledge that criminal justice institutions, even if they operate with both efficiency and respect for human dignity, cannot solve the problem of crime; "performance legitimacy" is less important than the democratic guarantee of what might be called "insistence legitimacy," the exercise by citizens of authority over police, courts, and criminal custody within broad, constitutionally approved limits.[17]

Perhaps the role of extracting the society's resources in the form of taxes is analogous. As taxation is expected (in theory) to raise revenues that benefit all and to redistribute, to some extent, material burdens that fall, for whatever reason, unevenly on people, so criminal justice ideally yields a quantum of general social security and redistributes rights to mitigate somewhat the pains of human conflict and predatory behavior. Also like taxation, it has a powerful symbolic function. It sends messages about the state's commitment to the daily security of its citizens—in its decisions about both how to identify and pursue wrongdoers and how to protect the general population against excesses in that enterprise. To the degree that a state promises both control and liberty, so does criminal justice.

Shifting the constituency for police and courts is part of democratic consolidation, moving from the procedural accomplishment of contested elections decided by a broad electorate to an effectively functioning democracy. Consolidation deepens the commitments made in the initial transition to democracy, makes democratic political activity routine, and provides a modicum of policy consistent with the wishes of the polity.[18] It is a mixture of the normative—conceptual support of democracy and its institutions—and the instrumental—support conditioned on performance. Its attributes of change from the old ways include commitment to a rule of law—autonomous and generally applicable standards applied by an independent judiciary in a "spirit of constitutionalism"—that enjoys wide and deep support.

Political scientists rarely examine the role of criminal justice reform in democratic consolidation, but it is crucial. It is a truism that there are some common conditions of authoritarian regimes that only thoroughgoing justice reform can correct. The Stasi of East Germany conducted surveillance of even the most innocuous situations if they seemed to suggest any interest in the corrupt and capitalist West. "Regime policing" in Asia, Africa, and Latin America rode roughshod over human rights during much of the twentieth century.[19] In Egypt it was the State Security Court, operating in a system parallel to that of the civil courts, that sought to punish Professor Saad Eddin Ibrahim for proposing to monitor parliamentary elections. And in South Africa an "emergency team" of appellate judges developed a cruel jurisprudence that consistently interpreted internal security and emergency law during the tumultuous 1980s to fit the apartheid ideology and favor security over rights.[20] So in order for democracy to become "the only game in town" these institutions and the laws that empowered them must be decisively repudiated. The tasks are organizational, legal, and behavioral. Restructuring criminal justice institutions and fostering a responsive culture within them must complement legal reform that fosters accountability, transparency, and participation.

For the purpose of this discussion I will assume that what people want from democratic governance falls into three categories that come up with great frequency in polls and interviews.[21] One is personal freedom and civil liberties, the sense that the yoke of authoritarianism has been lifted and individual autonomy has been increased by the regime change. ("During the military regime, soldiers would just come and arrest us and make us work for the army or on their farms," a Malian told the *New York Times* in 2002. Reflecting on a decade of democracy in 2002, he added, "Now that doesn't exist. We are free. We can go where we like.")[22] Closely related is the expectation of a self-governing future, a life in which political institutions are open, accountable, and accessible to a public that controls them.

What these conditions mean in practice varies tremendously according to the culture, politics, and level of economic development of the country undergoing change. We know, for example, that in some parts of the world benevolent authority and community consensus are more appealing than the Western emphasis on the individualistic assertion of rights. On the other hand, it is hard to imagine a situation in which the new regime's core respect for human rights and its adherence to constitutional limits on its power is not key to maintaining a consensus that will continue to support democracy.[23] For many countries, to be sure, the cost of supporting the legal infrastructure that demonstrates commitment to a rights orientation is simply too great.[24] As Samuel Huntington, often considered the father of modern democratization studies, points out, "Poverty is a principal, probably the principal obstacle, to democratic development."[25] But it should be noted that even some very poor countries, like Sierra Leone, embrace notions of rights and justice as part of the social renewal spurred by the experience of war and violence.

Despite the obstacles of poverty and democratic inexperience, the third primary expectation that citizens of democratizing states have is that democracy will reduce the misery of their material lives. They anticipate benefits from public goods like improved infrastructure—wells and roads—and education, the products of the regime as it directly delivers services to the citizen as client. Equally important are hopes for general improvement in the country's economic performance brought about by increased employment opportunity (not solely for a ruling elite), reduced inequality and poverty, as well as political stability. These expectations may well be unrealistic. Democracy may be inefficient both economically—as the elites who benefited from authoritarianism disinvest—and administratively, as consultation replaces diktat.[26] Furthermore, the close association of democracy and relatively unrestrained capitalism that has prevailed in recent years may leave behind many of those who initially supported democratic movements. Robert Dahl warned a generation ago that "[b]ecause of the powerful impact on government policies of such factors as a country's level of economic development, the characteristics of its social and economic systems, and its traditions, it may well be that the character of the regime has little independent effect on most government policies."[27] Larry Diamond points out, however, that the legitimacy of a regime depends greatly on its performance, that we can assume "densely reciprocal relations between legitimacy, effectiveness, and democratic stability."[28]

This conclusion is likely to be particularly valid for criminal justice. Its implications are not difficult to fathom. When respondents to a survey conducted between 1999 and 2001 in twelve African countries overwhelmingly cited civil liberties and personal freedoms as the most meaningful aspect of democracy, they were expressing the importance of consent to the way a government treats its citizens.[29] The delivery of conventional criminal justice services—arrest, prosecution, punishment, and crime prevention—provides an obvious indicator of whether that democratic condition is being met. And, other than the poll-watcher, it is hard to imagine the public functionary with greater responsibility for delivering democracy at its most visible and comprehensible level than the cop on the beat or the judge on the bench.

One measure of self-government in any society—even where citizens are reluctant to assert individual rights—is access to political institutions, which includes rule-making bodies that decree punishment levels and forums where disputes are resolved. Another is the opportunity for representation in perpetuating those institutions, whether directly through professional or lay participation or indirectly through having a voice in deciding who should be chosen for those posts and with what professional standards. Openness in most criminal justice proceedings demonstrates accountability to the public and enables the political choices at the heart of self-government. Finally, the promise of freedom in political choice is incomplete if police and judges do not see their role as including the protection of citizens expressing their preferences, whether at the ballot box or in the streets.

The regime performance that citizens may expect from criminal justice in a democracy is riddled with the contradictions that characterize its institutions. Domestic peace and security as an expectation of democracy is, to a considerable degree, beyond the powers of courts, prisons, and legislators even in countries with long-standing experience of stability and political legitimacy. American and British criminologists generally agree that, barring the garrison state that hovers over its citizens and punishes every infraction harshly, police and courts can only control crime at the margins. In countries where the advent of democracy follows a civil war or a lengthy period of conflict and widespread public deprivation, crime control is not likely to be very effective. And new criminal opportunities arise where individual liberty has replaced widespread repression, as is evident in the rise of drug and arms trafficking in eastern Europe since the fall of the Soviet Union. Strengthening the state to provide regime performance that realizes the aims of safety and security may have the ironic result of threatening the infant democracy, as when a state abandons a conciliatory reform in favor of aggressive police tactics and harsh sentences.[30]

On the other hand, if citizens and their leaders adopt more modest goals that acknowledge that social peace and security are more general responsibilities, to be addressed at the level of macroeconomic policy as well as through social policy that supports a broad range of public and private services, the criminal justice system may contribute significantly to democratic consolidation. David Bayley's study of police reform in many democracies concludes that a police force supportive of democracy must be oriented toward public service, abide by the rule of law, respect human rights, and expose its activities and personnel to public scrutiny.[31] To the extent that police and courts, through following these norms, support the activities that constitute liberal democracy, they contribute to its overall development. While this chapter addresses the aspects of criminal justice that generally operate after the fact—responding to crime or criminogenic conditions to protect victims, potential victims, and offenders—democratic justice that frames its task in terms of prevention is also possible. Within some countries in transition, including South Africa, there are resources that can be employed to deepen democracy through the potential of criminal justice to promote group and individual safety, empower communities, and redistribute some rights and benefits.

Criminal Justice in a Democracy: Accountable, Transparent, and Respectful of Rights?

What can be expected of criminal justice systems in countries making the transition from authoritarian rule to democracy is an open question. Vows of accountability, transparency, participation, and equal representation in criminal justice are difficult to honor even in countries with considerable experience in democracy. The realization of such aspirations encounters many obstacles—political, ethnic, and racial differences; habits of the past; and, usually, resource constraints. Can a democratized justice system include wildly fluctuating policy directions—lenient one decade, punitive the next—without losing its credibility as an cluster of institutions that help to preserve a democratic society? Keeping in mind the democratic citizen's general expectation of the rewards of the new regime as outlined above, we may now posit some standards by which to measure the fit of criminal justice with the democratizing state.

This chapter discusses the policy direction that I have called *constituency shifting*. Its core characteristic is the assumption that criminal justice institutions that have been primarily oriented to serving state interests must now—

as the result of political leadership, popular activism, or a new constitution (or all three)—become primarily oriented to protecting the population.[32] The normative prescription goes something like this: Serving the people, those institutions become instruments of self-government. Operationally they arrive at a balance between accountability and independence for courts and police that reflects responsibility to law enacted by the polity but does not capitulate to the interests of its most politically powerful members. A policy of transparency in general operations is the norm, with secrecy permitted for the tactical particulars of criminal investigations, justified by privacy interests. Individual rights are honored through the application of constitutional principles. Finally, criminal justice personnel must represent all demographic groups in the society, whether directly by sharing identifying social and ethnic characteristics or indirectly as champions of their needs and values.

The principles that drive this paradigm, to be sure, reflect the liberal traditions of the industrialized West.[33] In some respects this is problematic, since democratizing countries often have recent colonial histories, civil and tribal wars, or military dictatorships that may suggest problems of social ordering unknown in European or North American nations. On the other hand, ideals of police as community protector and judges as independent finders of fact are widely held all over the world—even in some Islamic countries—and are articulated in many of the more than one hundred new constitutions adopted in the last half of the twentieth century, including that of South Africa. My formulation of the policy direction is necessarily preliminary, awaiting evidence from other countries of developments that further democratic practice. It is also deliberately general, to avoid what Richard Joseph has called "the passive application to Africa of externally devised frameworks."[34]

The operatives of criminal justice in most countries are "organized to be responsive upward"; they do the bidding of the state unrestrained by popular scrutiny or review.[35] The fundamental ideal of democratizing criminal justice reverses this direction of accountability in two directions. Policing and judging are organized to be responsive outward to the general public interest—to officeholders the citizens elect and to the laws they have passed in a popularly approved process—and downward to the individual citizen affected or potentially affected by the actions of the justice system. Individual standards in this policy direction—initiated by elites but sustained by popular legitimacy—follow directly from the rejection of the old order and the embrace of electoral democracy. Evidence of accountability includes the protection by police and courts of elections, expressions of political views, and equal participation in public choices. Priority for enforcing the regime—coercing compliance with its ideology and keeping its rulers in power—gives way to relatively neutral management of social conflict for the benefit of the public. Judges comply with constitutional standards that include definitions of due process for suspects and convicts—whether brought before a single state court system or dealt with in a system of legal pluralism, where indigenous or customary law operates in tandem with state rules.

Of course this rosy picture is merely a construct, uncomplicated by the inevitable problems that afflict even mature and affluent democracies. Accountability to democratic political authority has the advantage of being closer to citizens but has significant risks, too. It can too easily compromise the police as handmaidens of politicians—beneficiaries of patronage and accomplices in corruption, as in American cities in the nineteenth century (and, less often, today). The bureaucratic alternative, however, has its costs. While it substitutes professional and legal standards for bonds of loyalty, it also distances law enforcement from ordinary citizens and induces a kind of arrogance toward the necessity of transparency; oversight of the American FBI by the congressional committee assigned to the task, for example, is notoriously difficult. As for the judiciary, the tension between accountability and independence is likely to arise whenever the state makes new and unfamiliar demands on courts or when politicians criticize judges' decisions and rationales. Independence took precedence over accountability when judges refused to testify before the South African Truth and Reconciliation Commission, leaving many citizens ignorant of the role played by the judiciary in sustaining apartheid.

As countries democratize, patterns of activities to assure general accountability occur. The drafting and interpretation of a constitution or other core documents is obviously one with primary significance for criminal justice. But constitutional standards and the ways in which they are interpreted do not tell us much about what should happen operationally as part of the democratization process. What follows is a brief presentation of principles that guide institutional changes that shift the constituency of police and courts from the state to the people. It is to be expected that policies that follow from acceptance of the principles will vary tremendously, according to the political history, stage of economic development, and general culture of the democratizing country.

Repoliticization & Demilitarization of Law Enforcement

Law enforcement will always have a political role by definition; its mandate is to enforce the choices the state has made with respect to how the society shall be ordered. So democratizing it is only a process of depoliticization to the extent that it consists of removing police from participation in overt political conflict.[36] Democratization, however, changes the state's choices, at least theoretically, to honor the commitment to self-government by imposing two basic requirements on law enforcement. One is that police and courts will support only generally applicable laws enacted by democratic means. This ideal also has a corollary: those laws that were not the product of democratic process must be rejected and their victims given at least symbolic compensation. Of course the theoretical formulation does not take into account the possibility that even laws that have withstood the test of proper procedure may be contaminated—by enactment influenced by clients of the old (or new) regime, for instance, or by executive and legislative pressure on police and courts to evade the law. (Many African states have a particularly poor record in this regard, making limited liberalization a far more common development than democratization.)[37]

This is where the second requirement comes in. The laws that are honored in the new democratic dispensation must reflect core values of democracy. This ideal departs from the purely procedural definition of democracy as a political system put in place by elections in which a broadly enfranchised electorate makes political choices through majority vote. It necessarily admits of great variation in its particulars if individual polities are presumed to have different visions of the good life. Greater and lesser degrees of personal liberty will be valued, greater and lesser access to sources of information about political choices will be tolerated. The diversity of interests in a democracy is best acknowledged by the variety of institutional arrangements that countries have found in practice to be consistent with democracy: police authority that is primarily national or primarily local authority, a judicial system that permits judicial review or doesn't, and so on.

Aiming for the duly democratic administration of justice, the democratizing state redirects its law enforcement agents (legislators, judges, and prosecutors as well as police) to dismantle internal security mechanisms that enabled the repressions of the regime and to free the political prisoners that were their product. In addition to rejecting the old tactics of hunting down dissenters and gassing demonstrators, the newly democratic state is expected to separate the functions of defense and community protection. (A practical consideration in this reform is that historically police are far less likely to rebel against the new dispensation than the military, and functional and organizational separation deprives the military of potential support in the event of resistance to the new democracy.) Police become part of civil service, do not receive military training, and are stripped of responsibility for military tasks except in emergencies. A superficial but symbolic element of demilitarization may also include efforts to alter the militaristic elements of the internal culture—dropping military titles, for example. The desired realistic goal of these organizational and legal shifts is perhaps best embodied by Robert Reiner's characterization of what he sees as the high watermark of police legitimacy: "By the 1950s, 'policing by consent' *was* achieved in Britain to the maximal degree that it is ever attainable—the wholehearted approval of the majority of the population who do not experience the coercive exercise of police powers to any significant extent, and *de facto* acceptance of the legitimacy of the institution by those who do."[38]

Shifting authority for the maintenance of civil order from the military to elected officials, who then delegate it to police and courts, is part of making the democratic connection. But the route to achieving it is often twisted and full of potholes. Continuing violence and corruption in states emerging from civil war often impede the separation. Sometimes the state determines that postauthoritarian chaos is so extensive that it must be met with military force, as in Nigeria. Sometimes past collaborations of police and military in secret political and economic ventures have become so entrenched that they cannot be dislodged without adding to the chaos. In Guatemala local police still report regularly to military officials, who are often themselves perpetrators of organized crime. The experience of Romania, however, suggests that demilitarization itself can curb corruption; a senior police official there concluded in 2002 that part of the demilitarization efforts under way in that country was a specialization of function that would enable police to ferret out corruption and financial crimes in their own ranks as well as in the general population.[39]

Specifying the boundary between police and military activity is often difficult and varies from state to state. Even some mature democracies continue to have police with military functions—the French gendarmerie, for example—and in some instances the police serve as adjuncts to the military (and vice versa) in emergencies that the state has determined to be threats to national security. The European Code of Police Ethics has recognized both the importance of the separation and the likelihood that it will continue in some form to be subject to extraordinary pressures by providing that "[t]he police, *when performing police duties in civil society,* shall be under the responsibility of civilian authorities."[40] Military involvement in drug enforcement is common around the world, even in countries that support a clear distinction between the tasks of the army and the police. Where drug trafficking is extensive, as in Bolivia, it is simply regarded as a warlike challenge appropriate for military action. Countries vary in the degree to which military law enforcement is expected to conform to procedural requirements applicable to civilian police and courts, though the United Nations Code of Conduct for Law Enforcement Officials applies the same standards to all officials exercising the powers of the police, especially arrest and detention.[41]

Balancing Judicial Accountability and Judicial Independence

Accountability matters as much for the judiciary as for any other institution in a liberal democracy. Judges wield the power of the state—to define rights and benefits, to distribute property and liberty, to confine and to execute. In the exercise of these powers they must submit to some forms of supervision; the administration of justice, like public education, is too important to be left entirely to the professionals. Most democratic societies reject the direct accountability to the electorate that some American states have adopted as too subject to popular whim and insufficiently respectful of the rule of law. But regulation of judges' status and conduct can come from many sources. It is built into the structure of government by the lawmaking function that creates and regulates courts and by the executive function that appoints (or at least nominates) judges. In most legal systems the availability of appellate review for lower-court decisions supplies another brake on an excess of judicial autonomy. Constitutions can provide for the impeachment of judges, and in societies where judges are part of civil service, they are subject to discipline and removal according to the rules of that structure. Professional bodies of lawyers can set standards for judicial conduct that enhance judges' overall standing and performance. Public evaluation of judges' integrity and professionalism—through some formal system for hearing complaints and informal assessments through polls or by pundits in the media—is a corollary to general public acceptance of the judicial process for the resolution of conflicts.[42] By definition, legitimacy is lost if people think judging is corrupt or unfair.

Vigilance over judicial behavior may be particularly appropriate in democratizing countries. New constitutions and statutes present challenges that are unfamiliar. New rights and increased demand for access to courts may present new opportunities for corruption.[43] And where judges from the bad old days have been retained to determine rights and duties in the new dispensation, accountability will seem particularly important to prevent backsliding into the application of values that have been rejected as undemocratic. Transparency need not necessarily accompany accountability in mature democracies; disciplinary proceedings for judges may be held behind closed doors, after all, and still function to hold them to account. But in a newly democratic country the population may need more than usual openness in government proceedings to counter skepticism, acquired from previous experience, about the regime's honesty. In countries with a recent past of secret proceedings the appointment of judges and the regulation of their behavior will gain democratic credibility if done in relatively open arenas.

Established liberal democracies—and not just those with Anglo-Saxon roots—also embrace the notion of judicial independence.[44] The concept includes a behavioral standard for individual judges—that they apply a duly enacted law on the basis of their own interpretation, without succumbing to extraneous pressures. But it is most importantly understood as dealing with a *relationship*—a restriction on individual or institutional pressures on the judge that threaten to compromise the fundamental fairness that democratic citizens have a right to expect when the courts undertake to resolve their disputes with each other or with the state.[45] Theories of separated powers and judicial review—the authority of judges to assess the constitutionality of laws and official conduct—support the ideal.[46] The two ideals—of the judge with the temperament and integrity to act independently and the institutional environment that will permit that independence—are related, of course. A supportive institutional environment should enable independent judgments that honor democratic rule-making and the values it embodies—the liberal grail of the rule of law.

> We want judges to enjoy a high degree of autonomy so that, when disputes arise about our legal rights and duties to one another and in relation to public authorities and these disputes cannot be settled informally, we can submit them for resolution to judges whose autonomy or independence gives us reason to believe they will resolve the issues fairly, according to their understanding of the law, and not out of fear of recrimination or hope of reward.[47]

Perhaps judicial independence is best understood with examples of its violation. While "telephone justice"—the direct and blatant interference with judicial decision-making by executive and legislative forces, as occurred in former Soviet states—is an obvious case, more common are curbs thinly veiled as policy shifts: stripping court jurisdiction over controversial issues or cases, narrowing judicial discretion over court procedures or sentences, suppressing the publication of judicial decisions. More blatant are threats of removal from the bench or reduction of judicial salaries for unpopular decisions and arrest of judges on trumped-up charges—witness the recent harassment of the judiciary and the expulsion of the chief justice in Zimbabwe. Parliamentary supremacy may be abused to prohibit challenges to judicial interference. The threat to independence may come from outside the governments, too, from influence-peddling (or bribery) by powerful individuals or interest groups, especially where the previous regime has been held together by the support of client governments or other interests.

While political scientists and legal scholars often assert that judicial independence is merely a myth or rhetorical device, both myth and rhetoric are important as carriers of aspiration.[48] Infant and mature democracies alike aspire to judicial decision-making that will adhere as closely as possible to their first principles—whether embodied in a constitution or other document or even in understandings that transcend written texts—and meddling from the other branches can intrude on that activity. (In the American context, Paul Bator has described the ideal that "at the end of the day, judges free of congressional and executive control will be in a position to determine whether the assertion of power against the citizen is consistent with law (including the Constitution).")[49]

Accountability and independence are often wrongly seen as concepts in perpetual tension. Instead, they interact to support judicial power in a complex, modern democracy; and the task is to find a balance between them that furthers the goals of the particular society.[50] Accountability should serve to honor fundamental political commitments, but independence is needed to avoid judicial entanglement in the politics of the day. Both are particularly important in criminal cases, where physical liberty is often at stake—accountability to restrain judicial arrogance or bias with respect to defendant or victim, independence to ensure that a judge will not be removed for making decisions unpopular with a public thirsty for revenge.

As with the depoliticization and demilitarization of law enforcement, definitions of judicial independence may be blurry and interpretations of appropriate practice will vary. Democratic policy shifts may legitimately alter judicial behavior, such as legislation that creates new crimes or increases penalties; executive power may change the professional demands on judges, such as calls for a longer day on the bench. Even in the absence of manifest interference, judicial integrity may be compromised by unspoken understandings about politically or culturally proper decision-making. On the other hand, it can be difficult to distinguish between the effects of such influences and the inevitably indeterminate aspect of the judicial process. Justice Benjamin Cardozo, after examining the influences of history, philosophy, and sociology on judicial decision-making, acknowledged that reasoning and ruling were also colored by "other forces, the likes and dislikes, the predilections and the prejudices, the complex of instincts and emotions and habits and convictions which make the man, whether he be litigant or judge."[51] He was not suggesting that these forces undercut the judicial independence that he would have understood as essential for a system that separates and regulates governmental power in order to minimize the possibility of tyranny.

The goal of retaining accountability while also maximizing judicial freedom may also be met in varying ways that reflect a country's faith in positive law as the expression of popular preference. While Americans assume that the power of judicial review of legislative and executive rules is the touchstone of independence, many democratic societies maintain some autonomy for the judiciary without giving it such a sweeping license to weigh in on core policymaking; they would rather rely on popularly elected legislators than on unelected judges for the last word. At the other end of the spectrum is the idea that constitutionalism gives the judiciary greater autonomy that may, in the end, best serve the core principles of the democratic legal system. Kim Lane Scheppele suggests that judges empowered to interpret a constitution have a "critical distance" from positive law and with it the opportunity, in passing on that law, to be more faithful to the underlying precepts of the constitutional document (or its equivalent, for example, Israel's twelve Basic Laws); "in order to be free of temporary politics in a satisfactory way, judges need to be *depen-*

dent at the level of principle."⁵² If constitutions can be seen as emanations of popular will—some are written, after all, by constituent assemblies that are widely representative—judges who feel free to make policy based on them are demonstrating the link between democracy and judicial independence.

It is important to note that balancing judicial accountability and independence does not assure a particular perspective on criminal sanctioning or even on proper criminal procedure; it assumes that variation in constitutional mandates, statutory interpretation, and judicial attitudes will lead to different processes and judicial outcomes that may either support or impede democratic initiatives. Impartiality is also not guaranteed, though its absence may undermine the fundamental fairness standard (see below) for democratic criminal justice systems.

Integrity of Criminal Justice Operatives

Each of the above standards relies on a public and professional understanding that police and judges are themselves generally law-abiding. More particularly, as keepers of the public trust their offices and resources must be put to public uses. Ridding police and courts of corruption is therefore important to democratization of criminal justice. While corruption may be rife in democratic as well as nondemocratic states, the experience of newly democratizing states in South America, eastern Europe, and Africa bears out the likelihood of a legacy of cronyism and clientelism from authoritarian regimes. Opportunities for the exploitation of the public are a routine feature of the social and political environment, not merely the occasional sins of a few bad apples. In both Nigeria and Brazil—to name recent examples—the future of democracy is threatened by widespread corruption. President Olusegun Obansanjo of Nigeria commented sadly of the recent past in his country, "Corruption was not only rife, it had eaten so deeply into the marrow of our existence that looters and fraudsters had become our heroes, and it seemed we could not longer place any faith in honesty and decency and hard work."⁵³ Yet his administration has been criticized for retaining ministers accused of corruption in the previous military regime.

Even as pressure must be put on police and judges to turn away from corruption, it is important to acknowledge that its definition varies widely and that cultural and economic realities in some countries reduce the stigma attached to it in others. Not surprisingly, corruption tends to be more prevalent in developing countries. Where public police are not paid a living wage by the state, private compensation for some services may be the norm and may compromise the integrity standard. Along with personal profit, group loyalties, and an interest in organizational gain—a favorable view of police from businesses that would prefer to have their sins ignored, for example—may be common motives.⁵⁴ To combat corruption in public services of poor countries is likely to require more than committed political leadership, legal sanctions, and strong internal management. Economic prosperity that renders corruption opportunities less tempting is likely to be the only remedy. One observer, in fact, worries that strict anticorruption laws, which lack credibility where rampant corruption is accepted as normal behavior, may actually worsen the situation in poverty-stricken Nigeria; "the effectiveness of law in the fight against corruption, already at an all-time low, will continue to diminish if the social and economic factors that cause the initial problematic behavior are not addressed."[55]

It would be inaccurate to suggest that democracy cannot flourish in an atmosphere where corruption has become normalized. Even in some mature democracies bribes are routine; a household survey of people seeking public services in five Asian countries recently found that 100 percent of respondents in India who had contacted police or court within the previous year had either encountered corruption or given bribes.[56] Nonetheless, corruption in criminal justice presents a major obstacle to the democratization process, where shifting authority from a dictator or oligarchy to the polity is the central value. The citizen of a still-consolidating democracy is unlikely to believe that the justice system is protecting the public interest—that reliance on and respect for it is warranted—if the integrity of police and judges is not assured. The old bromide that justice must not only be done but be seen to be done applies here.

Revelations of corruption—at least if large sums of public money are involved—can also spur demands for the accountability and transparency that democratization promises. The discovery that a senior labor judge in Brazil had participated in skimming off almost ninety million dollars from a courthouse construction project played a role in the rejection of the political leadership and the eventual election of a presidential candidate, Luiz Inacio Lula da Silva, who promised a campaign against corruption along with his agenda of social and economic reform. Thabo Mbeki underscored the link between reducing corruption and promoting democracy at the celebration of the birth of the African Union in 2002. That embryonic organization, faced with the daunting task of bringing African nations together to assist one another in assuring security, political stability, and economic development, has given priority to the adoption of a convention on combating corruption that will require each member country to report annually on the state of corruption within its borders.[57]

Oversight and Scrutiny

Transparency—that is, the openness in government that exposes its institutions and their personnel to public view—is always important in a democracy, nowhere more so than in the application of the criminal law, where individual liberty is at stake and the power of the operatives who dispense it is highly discretionary, located in the "twilight zone between law and morals."[58] In addition, how police and courts behave is generally of great public interest everywhere, with citizens feeling themselves competent to judge their actions and decisions. In a democratizing country, where suspicion of government will usually have deep roots, opportunities—formal and informal—for public examination of how authority is exercised over citizens are crucial mechanisms of accountability.

Transparency is perhaps most frequently invoked as a hedge against corruption—the almost exclusive focus of the organization Transparency International—but it has many other purposes as well. Internal investigative bodies and citizen complaint mechanisms are intended to deter police brutality; public hearings for important judicial appointments offer the public a chance to evaluate public decision-makers who are not removable by vote; press reports of crime and punishment may influence the outcomes of local elections; court proceedings that are usually open to the public and result in a public record are important to enable the press and the population to follow trends in judicial behavior and interpretation of the laws. Civic education is as important an aspect of transparency measures as monitoring performance of public servants.

An essential aid to public scrutiny of police and courts is press freedom. But while free expression as an ideal has gained ground all over the world in recent decades—it has been written into many of the new constitutions—it takes a variety of forms and is often honored in the breach. While that conclusion applies to mature democracies as well as to new ones, media restrictions can be particularly damaging in a country where habits of openness are not yet developed. Countries in transition are likely to be deeply ambivalent about press criticism of the government—including police officials and judges—and attacks on influential private citizens and groups. Suppressing stories, placing censors in newsrooms, and restricting reporters' access to leaders and institutions are common, weakening the public's right to information and the ability of journalists to hold officials' feet to the fire. In Brazil the censorship and privacy laws enabled political candidates to enjoin press criticism of them before the 2002 elections, and in 2003 the Rio de Janeiro chief of the civil police issued a gag order on his force prohibiting interviews with the media.[59] Sensitivity to exposure of police misconduct is hardly surprising; a São Paulo reporter was convicted of libel for publishing a story describing the abuse by military police of demonstrators for the homeless people's movement.

Impediments to a free press are not limited to government regulation. Violence against journalists is disturbingly common in some democratizing countries—notably in Latin America—and constitutes a deterrent to investigative reporting; its sources include the government as well as ordinary criminals. And there are countries where journalists are limited in what they can say by popular discontent with what the media disseminate. Rioting that killed two hundred people broke out when the 2002 Miss World beauty contest was to be held in Nigeria during Ramadan. The immediate trigger for the violence was a newspaper report written by a young woman whose suggestion that Mohammed would have endorsed the pageant and perhaps even wed one of the contestants offended many Muslims. The political flap that followed suggests a Nigerian commitment to free speech, however; President Obasanjo appealed for journalists to be sensitive and responsible but did not call for restrictions, and a subsequent effort to impose a code of conduct on reporters who work with the National Assembly failed. It is also significant that journalists from the new democracies are getting international recognition for their investigative work. In 2002 Mexican and Brazilian journalists won major awards from the Inter American Press Association, some for reports on crime and justice.[60]

It is unrealistic and counterproductive to specify transparency policies for police and courts in democratizing countries in general. Local culture and conditions will determine what is possible, as the Nigerian beauty contest riots indicate. Both law enforcement and dispute resolution are activities for which there is genuine need for both confidentiality and discretionary decision-making. In some areas the distinction between permissible and impermissible secrecy is clear—current police investigations would be seriously compromised and privacy norms violated if files were open to the press or to citizen monitors, for example—but in others it will be murky by whatever local standard is applied. Methods chosen for scrutinizing decisions and actions will also reflect widely varying capacities for disseminating the information obtained; a poor or rural country with low literacy that relies primarily on radio for its news will get very different information from one where better-educated citizens have easy access to television and newspapers. Requiring every law enforcement officer to wear an identification tag is relatively inexpensive and uncontroversial, but creating effective civilian complaint bodies is not.

Fundamental Fairness

This principle recognizes the constitutional element of what the democratic citizen has chosen. It presumes a moral tradition that respects certain near-universal norms: that there is no punishment without crime, that the state must treat citizens with respect and dignity, that only a person who is capable of moral responsibility can be held criminally liable and only for individual behavior. It tempers liberal democracy's respect for individual autonomy with the designation of police and courts as carriers of human rights to protect the public from government and from each other. Conditions of arrest and detention are humane and publicly known. Dispute resolution is carried out in a public forum where defendants are entitled to full information regarding the charges against them and the right to defend themselves with representation, if they wish.

Some will argue that all legal traditions do not necessarily embrace these standards and that as requirements for democratization they go beyond adherence to the rule of law. The Anglo-American concept of due process sees as fundamental the presumption of innocence and the prohibition against self-incrimination, for instance, but even mature democracies often do not give more than lip service to these protections. On the other hand, an international consensus around them has developed. The Universal Declaration of Human Rights, passed unanimously by the United Nations Security Council more than fifty years ago, reads in part, "Everyone charged with a penal offence has the right to be presumed innocent until proved guilty according to law in a public trial at which he has had all the guarantees necessary for his defence."[61] The 1966 International Covenant on Civil and Political Rights, which binds the signatory countries to honor a right to be free of arbitrary arrest or detention and due process for someone who is arrested or detained, may not be the harbinger of global constitutionalism, as some have predicted; but even China, a country not noted for its defense of individual rights, has signed it.[62] Signing (and ratifying) international treaties may signal only a shallow commitment to human rights, but it suggests that few countries want to be excluded from the dominant discourse of the day, which has a strong rights orientation.

To the charge that preventing and addressing social harm through legalistic protections against arbitrariness is solely an individualistic, Western commitment imposed on the rest of the world, political scientist Mahmood Mamdani has noted that a demand for rights is usually a response to oppression.[63] Proponents of all models of democracy—republicanism, liberalism, Marxism—are united in opposition to concentrated power, a force that can only be countered with rights.[64] And fighters for democracy the world over have called for such guarantees in the name of what they consider a higher duty than compliance with the law of an authoritarian state—human rights as transcendent law.

Conclusion

It is perhaps important to note what democratic criminal justice is not. With respect to democracy in general, Schmitter and Karl note that "democracy does not consist of a single unique set of institutions. There are many types of democracy, and their diverse practices produce a similarly varied set of effects. The specific form democracy takes is contingent upon a country's socioeconomic conditions as well as its entrenched state structures and policy practices."[65] Conceptualizing the criminal justice theory or practice that will best conform to democratic ideals cannot include specifying either the mix of public and private policing or the range of acceptable sanctions in the criminal law. The prohibition of the death penalty may be an exception. Since participation and consent are at the heart of democratic idealism, the penalty of death is too final; it brings to mind the refusal of the United States Supreme Court to allow the State Department to rescind a passport for any but the most drastic reasons; it removes the right to have rights.[66] Furthermore, it is the ultimate assault on human dignity, a democratic value.

It might be thought that to conclude that democratic criminal justice may embrace sanctions considered cruel in some societies is merely deference to majoritarianism, a willingness to accede, for instance, to a harsh penal code because it represents the political will of the greatest number. But other considerations are at work. Different cultures will have different authoritative sanctioning sources; to disrupt that aspect of a culture would be an imposition contrary to liberal democracy's embrace of liberty. In countries where informal sanctions are still powerful—the ostracism of the family or tribe—formal sanctions may be of less value. In Japan the arrest is often shameful in a way that it rarely is in the United States, for instance, which may account in part for why sentences tend to be shorter. Another consideration is the traditional use of particular punishments. How to deal with whipping and amputation and exile, which are taboo in most Western societies but widely accepted in many other cultures? Another reason not to dictate the range of severity of penal sanctions is that the state is not the sole source of sanctioning in any society and, in fact, is rarely the most crucial one. Families, neighbors, religious orders, schools, and employers apply sanctions on a daily basis; for the state to disrupt any but the demonstrably violent of these patterns of nonstate sanctions would be to counter the respect for choice that liberal democracy promises.

The democratic policy direction I have envisioned is not comprehensive, and no country that I can think of perfectly conforms to its contours. Stages of democratization in criminal justice may overlap and include events and elements not mentioned. Furthermore, problems arise continually that challenge one or more of the principles I have listed and appear to contradict the general democratic movement.

Finally, the primarily procedural and liberal formulation of justice that gives rise to these standards does not take into account the need for criminal justice to contribute to empowering the public. In most democratizing countries poverty and inequality are the norm, and a big sociological and political question is the extent to which criminal justice can further social justice as a part of fulfilling the promise that through greater freedom and equality the citizen of a new democracy will acquire the resources to enjoy participatory citizenship. A positive answer to that question may require what David Held calls "double democratization."[67] In his view modern democracy must combine the reform of the state and the reform of civil society. While the state's legal framework provides mechanisms for some kinds of social regulation, the liberal democratic tradition fails to articulate the role of voluntary associations and community institutions—religious, educational, occupational—in furthering democratic control of the political agenda. It may be that supplementing the state's role in enforcing fair laws and protecting rights with citizen initiatives and advocacy will be needed to bring the abstractions of democracy to bear on the concrete social problems of a country in transition.

6 Protection, Integrity, and Rights
South Africa's Achievements

> The law is no longer an instrument in the hands of a clique of racists. It is a tool for the preservation of a civilised and humane non-racial order.
> —Anthony Holiday[1]

LONG BEFORE THE 1994 elections post-apartheid planners of democratic South Africa—black and white—knew that their transition would entail much more than transferring electoral control of their leaders to a newly empowered citizenry. They saw the process of ensuring broad participation in free and fair elections as only the beginning. They supported the larger ideal of a state that conducts itself, in Nelson Mandela's words, "in a way that respects and enhances the freedom of others."[2] Democratization included the adoption of a constitution that stressed human dignity and equality and embraced not only the classic liberal protections of free expression, equality before the law, and due process, but also more substantive socioeconomic rights—to education and to access to health care and housing, for example. The result has been called "the world's leading example of a transformative constitution."[3]

With respect to criminal justice the planners knew that without accountability to a diverse public, transparent operations, and greater representation of blacks and women in senior positions in police and courts the state would have little authority either within the country or beyond its borders. The groups most oppressed by apartheid would have to take part in—and lead, sooner rather than later—the creation of a new legal order. And the government would have to deliver on promises of access to courts—or, in the words of the constitution, "another independent and impartial tribunal or forum" that would deal fairly with people who had often been neglected or mistreated by those same courts. Police would have to respect the public and apply the law with integrity and without bias. The courts would have to protect the rights of arrested, detained, and accused persons.[4]

The country's history made police and courts—emanations of the state's basic character—prominent candidates for immediate reform. Police had been the most visible and brutal instruments of oppression since the time of the early autocratic Dutch settlers, who required passes from the indigenous Khoikhoi in Cape Town and tortured rebellious slaves. But magistrates and judges also had contributed to South Africa's ugly political history. For more than forty years (1948–90) they had, in many situations, maintained white domination through the general enforcement of the laws of apartheid—removing people from their land, controlling their movements, imposing harsh punishments, restricting access to adequate education and health care and jobs. Police had supplemented the mandates of those laws with the extralegal brutality of beatings, killings, and torture. During the 1980s, "emergency" internal security legislation had given them expanded powers to arrest without warrant and to detain indefinitely (and often in solitary confinement) without judicial review anyone who, in their opinion, threatened "the safety of the public or the maintenance of public order."[5] Yet, less than a decade later, many of these same police (and some judges who had turned a blind eye to the fundamental lawlessness of the emergency regulations) were being called upon to maintain the order and implement processes through which South Africa would honor democratic ideals more ambitious than those of many countries with a long history of stronger participatory and egalitarian traditions.

Experience in much of the rest of sub-Saharan Africa did not bode well for post-apartheid democratization of criminal justice. Independence from colonial powers in many countries had brought limited reform at best and civil anarchy at worst. In some cases, efforts to maintain order bred more violence than they suppressed; in Nigeria, the police were a principal source of criminality, and in the Democratic Republic of Congo the police and military were considered more dangerous than the rebels. In South Africa both police and courts had the institutional capacity for resisting compliance with the new order. And, under the terms of the negotiated settlement that ended apartheid and brought the ANC to power, many of the civil servants—magistrates and police officials who had exercised broad discretionary powers during apartheid—would continue in office for the first five years of the new regime.

So the post-apartheid planners had significant challenges before them as they sought to conform their police and courts to the ideals of a liberal democracy. On the one hand they knew that commitment to controlling rampant and violent crime was necessary for legitimacy and stability. On the other hand, excessive reliance on police and courts to maintain order would undercut liberal principles and risk the perception and the reality that the new regime had reverted to the methods, if not the politics, of the old. Since South

Africa has thrown off its mantle of repression it has had difficulty enforcing compliance with even the most benign demands, like getting citizens to pay their utility charges and students their university fees. A weak state is not only incapable of maintaining the monopoly of violence that provides essential sanctions for wrongdoing; it also cannot make rules that will be followed without recourse to that monopoly. But strengthening the state with punitive policy and practice (especially when so much of the population is poor and can justly claim an inability to pay when state charges are due) risks distancing governance from the governed in ways that negate the most basic claims of democracy. As the planners considered this dilemma, perspectives inevitably varied, since they included ANC leaders who would set policy, apartheid bureaucrats retained to implement it, magistrates and judges struggling to adapt to new directives, and a gaggle of activists and academics equipped with the latest Western reform strategies.

Starting in the late 1980s, the prevailing view, supported by the South African Law Commission, a statutory creation of lawyers and judges mandated to study the law and make recommendations for its development and reform, was that apartheid laws should be repealed and that the new democratic state should embrace a bill of rights with enforceable protections of many kinds for criminal defendants.[6] Planning for the new constitution, aided by consultation and funding from several mature democracies, was well under way by the time Nelson Mandela was released from prison in 1990, and it resulted in an interim document even before the first democratic election in April 1994. Discussions of the demilitarization of police and the creation of a court dedicated to the interpretation of the new constitution had also begun in the early 1990s. Although resistance was inevitable, there was also a reservoir of goodwill and good intentions in the institutions to be reformed. Many police supervisors, particularly younger ones, were relieved not to be assigned to uphold apartheid, and judges who had strained to interpret its laws as narrowly as possible hailed their repeal.

Over the past decade South Africa has managed, with limited success, to conform the institutions of criminal justice to many of the expectations appropriate to a liberal democracy. While both judges and senior police officials have occasionally vented their frustration over continuing crime and violence with anticonstitutional calls for harsher measures in general and the death penalty in particular, the ANC government generally embraces ideals of public protection and individual rights. The accepted definition of police work has shifted from defense of the regime to protection of the population; while brutality still erupts and corruption is pervasive, the basic shift is evident in the increased willingness of residents of urban townships and rural settlements to turn to police when they are needed. Judges and magistrates—now far more representative in terms of race and gender than at any time in the country's history—are generally secure in trusting that neither the president nor the justice minister will dictate judicial perspectives or decisions in individual cases.

Most of the classic liberal protections for those at the receiving end of the state's coercive forces—due process as Western democracies understand it—have been adopted. Institutional habits die hard; while the general behavior of police and courts shows significant shifts toward honoring those protections, lapses still occur. But press reports of egregious behavior by magistrates and judges are vigorous, and official structures that can hold judges and magistrates to account are in operation. An Independent Complaints Directorate (ICD) investigates police misconduct with additional prodding from the private Centre for the Study of Violence and Reconciliation and the Human Rights Commission.[7] Public acceptance of the core authority of the state to regulate personal behavior testifies to the achievement of shifting the constituency for criminal justice from the state to the people.[8]

These achievements are, however, tempered by continuing conflicts of race and ethnicity; public and governmental ambivalence about some constitutional values; and institutional inability to deliver basic security. Not surprisingly, it has proved easier to create institutions and mechanisms to oversee the transformation of the repressive apartheid state than to realize their promise on the ground. Perhaps culture always lags behind policy in transitional contexts; South Africa has chosen a "top-down" institutional approach that may increase that tendency. What follows is a discussion of some important reforms undertaken to shift the constituency of police and courts from the state to the citizenry, with achievements and failures duly noted.

Demilitarization and Repoliticization of Law Enforcement

A pathbreaking study of policing in sub-Saharan Africa by Alice Hills proceeds from the core assumption that the behavior of a state's police is a reflection of a regime's character and "a general barometer for political development."[9] Hills examines the effects of political change in the early 1990s—cautious liberalization, rather than the more ambitious goal of democratization—on public police in a half-dozen African countries. She concludes that the limited change she found in state policing (though she identifies varying patterns of adaptation to postcolonial states) mirrors the lack of political development in these countries—Uganda, Eritrea, Ethiopia, Namibia, Somalia, Somaliland, and Democratic Republic of Congo—more generally. Hills distinguishes between state uses of police to maintain public order—repressing public dissent—and civil order—the management of ordinary crime within limits set by law and human rights.[10] Her standards for measuring liberalization include reducing the role of coercion in police activity, a sensitivity to the needs of the policed population, and detachment from state concern with threats to internal security. By these standards—and in contrast to the countries she studied—South African progress toward the development of a police force that honors its primary obligation to protect and serve citizens reflects well on the democratizing character of the post-apartheid regime.

There was a lot of room for progress. One commentator has called the former South African Police—now symbolically renamed the South African Police Service (SAPS)—"an icon of white-minority rule," and Nicholas Haysom, a legal advisor to Nelson Mandela, has characterized its blatantly political role prior to 1994 as "an internal military campaign."[11] Both critics and defenders of the police presumed that its role in ordinary crime prevention and control—which followed standard Western practices in white (and, to a lesser extent, Indian) areas—was a distant second to enforcing apartheid laws. Police were unresponsive to reports of crime in the townships, and residents were even arrested when they reported crimes. Police violence was common and could usually be justified under the law; if not, the police were often undeterred, operating with autonomy to exceed even the mandates of the state that unleashed them. If the police acted to prevent mass disorder, it was primarily in the form of suppressing popular demands for political change. (They provided public order at "white" events like rugby matches and New Year's Eve celebrations.) Beyond the well-publicized brutalities of the Sharpeville massacre (69 people dead and 180 wounded by police firing from their station house and from a Saracen armored car) and the Soweto uprising (176 people dead within the first week) the police were instigators or instrumentalities for the worst oppressions of the regime—torture, political detention, forced removal. To the extent, furthermore, that a so-called third force within the police assisted the Inkatha Freedom Party's attacks on ANC members and United Democratic Front supporters in townships and "homelands," the police actually fomented mass violence. As a result of these patterns the police were seen as part of the enemy, pillars of the hated regime to be toppled in the liberation struggle.

Neglect of ordinary police protection accompanied repression as part of the legacy of apartheid. Routine law enforcement was often simply missing in the black communities; during apartheid as much as three-quarters of the country's police stations were in white areas.[12] The current, widely accepted Western ideal of police work as furthering public safety through order maintenance first and crime-fighting second did not exist, and if it had, the South African Police could not have begun to realize it.[13] Constables—those in the lower police ranks, equivalent to enlisted men in the U.S. Army—were (and still are) poorly paid, equipped, and trained. When the *kitskonstabels* (instant constables) were incorporated into the regular SAPS after apartheid ended, it became apparent that thousands on the bottom rung of policing were illiterate and tens of thousands could not drive. Their credibility as crime fighters was undermined by rampant crime and corruption in the ranks.

The winds of police reform began blowing before apartheid's end when ex-president F. W. de Klerk took office. In an address to top-level officials at the national police college in January 1990 he announced that police would no longer be used for political ends. "You will no longer be required to prevent people from gathering to canvass support for their views," he said. "This is the political arena and we want to take police out of it. We don't want to use you any more as instruments of certain political goals."[14] This view was expeditiously reinforced by the amendment of security legislation, investigations into police violence, and the formal dissolution—many members were, however, reassigned—of the infamous Security Branch.

But limits on police transformation were endemic in early years of the democratic transition. The negotiated settlement included a commitment to retain civil service workers for five years; and even when vacancies occurred in leadership positions, the new government did not have qualified aspirants for them. The best candidates for top police jobs were middle-management officials from the old regime who were considered to be relatively untainted by its abuses. Affirmative action was unlikely to bring many blacks into management positions in the SAPS any time soon; those that were qualified tended to prefer the greater material rewards of the private sector, where they were now in demand. Recruits for entry-level positions would simply be incorporated into the old apartheid-era forms of policing, "shifting the goal posts without altering the rules of the game."[15] Lack of resources and the resignation or retirement of some experienced staff—most notably detectives with investigative experience—made prompt professionalization of the SAPS impossible; and consideration of a fundamental reorientation of policing—ceding the bulk of order maintenance to private and community groups, for instance—was too threatening to be seriously considered. The complexities of folding the ten police forces of the apartheid-era "homelands" into the SAPS made the task of rapidly instilling uniform standards of sensitivity and accountability nearly impossible.

Nonetheless, progress toward the liberal democratic ideal has been significant. "Clean" police officials were found to direct a service that would focus on routine crime control and social order rather than political enforcement. An academy for detectives opened in 1997 to build investigative expertise, and detective units were reorganized so that detectives would provide leadership and assistance to local police stations—though not without internal conflict.[16] Efforts were made to redefine public order policing—part of the "high policing" that remains as political protection in even the most democratic societies.¹⁷ Political violence emanating from official police action ended almost immediately. (Unofficially, however, police continued to foster violence through aiding the factions in interparty fratricide, particularly in KwaZulu-Natal.) Western European and North American democracies provided funds and personnel for human rights training for line officers and station commissioners—previously called "commanders" in line with the military orientation of the police. And the Commission of Inquiry into Public Violence and Intimidation (generally known as the "Goldstone Commission," for its chair, then Appellate Division judge Richard Goldstone), set up in 1991 to investigate the sources of public violence, gave notice that the police and the military would not be immune from sanction for dirty tricks. Notwithstanding the pressures to reject political enforcement, police culture is famously resistant to change. The South African accomplishment is particularly notable in light of the difficulties—in law enforcement and elsewhere—of putting new wine into old bottles. Many senior police officials from the old order have shifted political gears to serve the new government ably, and those that haven't have largely been eased out. Racial integration of the SAPS has occurred at management levels—the majority of the constabulary was black even before the end of apartheid—though not as fast as blacks in the force would like and not without tensions. By 2002 the national director of public prosecutions, Bulelani Ngcuka, could credibly note the irony that the old-guard police are now protecting those who used to be considered enemies of the state.¹⁸

South Africans generally see the detachment of public policing from the state ideology of apartheid as the depoliticization of policing, and to the extent that police are now expected to be racially impartial in their application of the law, this is understandable nomenclature. But a more accurate term for democratizing is *repoliticization,* the replacement of the old politics of racial separation and repression with a new politics of inclusion and respect for human rights. Democratic repoliticization also means accepting dissent as a feature of political life and rejecting the use of criminal justice operatives and mechanisms to suppress it.

The government's use of the police to quash real or imagined subversive activity has been tested on several occasions, with differing results. The bad news is that in 2001, when tensions within the ANC led to criticism of President Mbeki by three prominent party members, the minister of safety and security announced, with great fanfare and no evidence, a police investigation of the "plot." Although the outcry that followed led Mbeki to rebuke the minister, the incident was troubling evidence that the government was prepared to use the police to repress apparently legitimate dissent.¹⁹ And protests at the 2002 World Summit on Sustainable Development by the Landless People's

Movement and groups protesting cutoffs of electricity for nonpayment and mortgage foreclosures were met with armed resistance from police, leading some observers to suggest that class apartheid had replaced the racial kind.[20]

The good news is that a resurgence of white, right-wing extremism has been handled with relative restraint as well as competence. In September 2002 a large cache of weapons was found in a truck in the Northwest province and a Limpopo doctor was arrested for plotting to overthrow the government. In striking contrast to the habits of apartheid governments, ex-president Nelson Mandela met with the head of the right-wing Freedom Front to discuss measures to be taken in preventing and sanctioning the violence of political extremists.[21] A month later eight bombs went off in Soweto, killing one person, and subsequently the perpetrators allegedly tried to blow up a bridge and a hangar for SAPS helicopters. Members of a far-right white group called Boeremag (Afrikaans for "Boer force," as in an army) were suspected.[22] The police investigation was meticulous and generally measured, though some oppositional groups complained that police raided (with warrants) members of other right-wing organizations and defendants allege that privileged documents were seized. There were no charges of illegal arrest or torture of defendants during interrogation. (Allegations of police abuse have been made on other occasions since 1994, however, most notably during the investigations of Pagad, the vigilante group accused of Cape Town bombings in the late 1990s.) The raids of "Operation Zealot" yielded weapons and prevented what would surely have been a bombing with many fatalities. For the time being at least, and for threats from the white right-wing, consultation and due process had largely replaced repression and brutality as a strategy for dealing with dissent.[23]

Demilitarization, too, while not complete, is well under way, also initiated by de Klerk in 1989 when he abolished the National Management System, an overarching repository for coordination and direction of security activities in all agencies of the apartheid government.[24] Some of the changes are merely cosmetic. Gone is the primary emphasis on military drill that characterized police training from the time of the South African War; the military titles have also been dropped. The rectangular armored vehicles—military Casspirs with gun ports—that struck terror into the hearts of demonstrators in the past have largely been retired. The SAPS retains many paramilitary qualities of style and structure (as do the police of many democracies), but their purpose is to maintain discipline and command structure; the Anglo-American model of the officer who exercises a good deal of discretion on the beat is not popular. The paramilitary hierarchy is important to "promote efficiency," says a deputy commissioner, rather than to serve as a surrogate army defending the state.[25] In the view of some observers, however, the SAPS now has too many managers—there are now more inspectors than constables—and too little discipline.

Most important are the steps that the military has taken (now the South African National Defence Force, or SANDF) to sever the entanglements with the police. Although South Africa was never ruled by the military, military men have led it, and the relationship of the military to state leaders was increasingly cozy as apartheid-era insurrection dictated more repressive security policy. During the 1960s a civil defense force was created—first as part of the Department of Justice and then incorporated as a section of the South African Defence Force (SADF)—to aid both the military and its "sister organization," the South African Police, in meeting threats from internal insurgency.[26] The military and the police were empowered to work in conjunction to combat anything labeled as terrorism—which could cover a lot of ground—and the military's strategic plan of 1973 required the SADF to assist the police whenever needed in political enforcement.[27] The interpenetration of the two forces also extended to operations outside the country, with police supporting the Rhodesian security forces engaged in counterinsurgency and assisting rebels in Mozambique after it became independent.

The Boeremag investigation illustrates both the importance of separating the police and the military and the extent to which that separation can be effective. Police investigators were not prevented from arresting several current and former military officers, though their guilt is yet to be proven. In contrast to many countries that have undergone regime change, where the military remains a threat to stability, SANDF is generally loyal to the new government. Racial transformation in the military is occurring more expeditiously than in the police; only 28 percent of noncommissioned officers were white as of August 2003, and although two-thirds of senior officers are still white, the force is committed to further integration through attrition.[28] Putting military discipline and the practical need to accept the inevitable ahead of their past practices, white soldiers trained to battle the *swart gevaar* ("black peril") and black rebels from the armed wings of the ANC and the Pan Africanist Congress (PAC) have managed sufficient reconciliation to work together, despite occasional clumsy attempts at resistance.

Major organizational changes are limiting the relationship of the SANDF and the police.[29] The military now provides a total of about 2,350 men to supplement the less-well-trained, less-disciplined police force. It participates in "Operation Crackdown," the concentration of law enforcement resources in the police stations of 145 high-crime areas (about 10 percent of the total). It has also been called in to assist police in what is essentially a peacekeeping function in the "taxi wars," and where there has been ongoing violence against predominantly white farmers; about 1,500 members of the military patrol the country's borders. Commando units, part-time reservists sometimes accused of brutality, currently patrol in rural areas and participate in police roadblocks to control drugs, weapons, and drunkenness on the highways. In response to concerns that internal military deployment was becoming a permanent condition, the military has specifically adopted the goal of shifting its constituency. Its strategic plan for 2003–5 defines its transformation as the embrace of civil control and "a change in defence posture, from offence to defence."[30] It foresees complete withdrawal from the military support role for police by the end of the decade; the commando units will be shut down. Although the strategic plan still formally announces cooperation with police as a priority, the military's responsibility for internal order maintenance is already quite limited. The SANDF has a role in policing internal order only in extreme disturbances or in situations, like natural disasters, where personnel shortages for guarding a troubled area makes deployment of soldiers a necessity. Troops were also used in 2001 to keep people away from a flooded river, for example, and to deter squatting on private land that had been rumored to be available for settlement.

Few law enforcement functions are ever performed with perfect neutrality, nor should they be. Political and social judgments infuse many of the daily decisions of the typical police officer, and as carriers of the most overt policies of coercion that the state enacts, the police are bound to its must fundamental political commitments. Nonetheless, some police functions have more political significance than others, and performing them in a neutral manner—or, in the case of South Africa, in a manner that promotes the liberal transformation embodied in the new constitution—requires greater political understanding. Crowd control, for example, is generally a more politically complex task than intercepting burglars or patrolling neighborhoods. In a liberal democracy part of the police role is to protect the public's exercise of its rights of free expression, notwithstanding that the nature and extent of those rights will vary from country to country. Sensitivity to this aspect of maintaining public order is often difficult when crowd control includes restraining people—either those who are exercising those rights or those who oppose that exercise—from damaging property or other people. It requires that, in the interest of professional responsibility for the law and for public protection, the officer accept the right to protest (whether from personal conviction or obedience to the commands of superiors) and set aside private opinions that may be at variance with those of the protesters. Evaluation of public order policing provides, therefore, an important indicator of the extent to which police in a transitional society have been repoliticized and demilitarized.

Before 1990 the principal task of public order policing in South Africa—by what was then called the Riot Unit—was to defend the apartheid state (sometimes in concert with the military) against subversion from within. From the time of the Soweto uprising in 1976 each police division included a riot squad, and after the police strike of 1986 they were supplemented by the *kitskonstabels,* a hastily recruited force of blacks who patrolled the townships with extreme brutality. In 1991 the Internal Stability Division replaced the Riot Unit; while it was no longer charged with enforcing the racial repressions of apartheid, its behavior did not change substantially. It still used excessive force—live ammunition as well as tear gas—in dispersing crowds, and it was indifferent to (and usually ignorant of) the purposes of public gatherings. Looking back in 1998, a public order policing supervisor noted: "The aim of the police was always to disperse crowds, regardless of their purpose. The police were not interested in what the protest was trying to achieve or if there were legitimate goals."[31] Particularly in the African townships the containment of hostile crowds continued to engage police in pitched battles through the mid-1990s.

But policy reform and professional leadership have brought major change to public order policing. The tone was set by the preamble to the Regulation of Gatherings Act, which provides that "every person has the right to assemble with other persons and to express his views on any matter freely in public and to enjoy the protection of the State while doing so."[32] The police appear to have taken this directive to heart; David Bruce, the country's leading authority on police brutality in the post-apartheid period, says that police killings during demonstrations are now very rare. Monique Marks has studied police organization and change in South Africa and the rest of the southern African region; her recent ethnographic work with the public order policing unit in Durban examines organizational, behavioral, and attitudinal patterns in an urban division that has confronted a number of challenges in policing contentious crowd events. She reports that training in crowd management, managerial directives that dictate restraint, planning for the policing of particular events, and providing officers with information about those plans have had significant effects. While there have been a few public events at which the police used unnecessary force (in at least one case, with fatal results), the overall picture is of a force being retrained and reconditioned since the mid-1990s to behave with restraint and to learn to manage rather than repress crowds. Behavior may be less controlled, however, when police are not under close supervision in public spaces, and attitudinal change has not kept pace with behavioral change. Marks found that the Durban public order police often yearned for "action," by which they meant violence, and their disdain for the demonstrators they were assigned to manage (and protect) was evident in a survey of 142 of them; almost half agreed with the statement, "People who take part in public protests are generally troublemakers."[33] Marks's conversations with officers patrolling African townships (a secondary crime prevention assignment undertaken when they are not policing public events or demonstrations) indicate resentment at the "hands-off" stance they are now required to take and nostalgia for the bad old days when, as one inspector put it, "We would go into [township] areas that were on fire. . . . We would beat the living daylights out of those youngsters. They were just like barbarians ... We really worked in those days and we had excellent commanders."³⁴ Marks concludes that, within the Durban unit at least, "patterns of behavior have changed significantly, yet old and redundant ways of thinking have endured."³⁵

Judicial Accountability and Independence

Judicial accountability and independence take on particular importance in a society only recently emerging from rule by an autocratic and monolithic state. On the one hand, judges must be held to the obligation of furthering the core principles of the new political system—in the case of South Africa, the ideals of dignity, equality and freedom embraced in the preamble of the new constitution. On the other hand, the new leaders must not lean on their judges to do their political or personal bidding—either directly or indirectly, by creating an environment where a judge's tenure or livelihood is threatened for not meeting political expectations—raising the specter that transformation has merely meant the substitution of one group of lackeys for another. The ideas are closely related. Truly independent judges may defend themselves against interference when interpreting rules by invoking accountability to the principles of the new order.

Allister Sparks, one of the country's most distinguished journalists, and others of similar respectability have defended the historic autonomy of the South African judiciary, and it is true that support among many judges for British traditions of independence was strong throughout the twentieth century. In apartheid South Africa, however, the government's appointment of judges and magistrates assured that most occupants of the upper and lower bench—although there were notable exceptions, especially in Natal and the Western Cape—were white Afrikaner males socialized to support the regime.³⁶ The late Dullah Omar, minister of justice from 1994 to 1999, called the judiciary of that period "the handmaiden of government," and few would dispute the testimony of Arthur Chaskalson, South Africa's chief justice (and head of the Constitutional Court), before the Truth and Reconciliation Commission (TRC): "Any examination of the role of law in our society in the last thirty years must start from the recognition that law was the primary tool used to give effect to apartheid."³⁷ The government's interest in strict enforcement of apartheid laws by magistrates and judges yielded the desired results most of the time, with particularly brutal outcomes in periods of crisis.³⁸ Some members of the South African judiciary had always chafed at the repressive and inegalitarian legal order they were expected to impose; at least two judges of the upper courts resigned in what was interpreted by some to be a protest of conscience, and others tried to mitigate apartheid legislation by interpreting it as narrowly as possible.[39] But judgments that buttressed the apartheid regime were the norm. The courts' failure to recognize either the role of individual rights in the rule of law or the needs of South Africa's mostly black population was justified with the positivist notion that the judicial role was merely to apply neutral principles to existing law without regard to its political significance. Yet most judicial officers applied principles that were anything but politically neutral.[40]

The apartheid laws are gone and so are most of the old-line judges who carried them out. Despite a campaign of opposition by many sitting judges, the late judge Ismail Mahomed—chief justice of Namibia and at the time deputy president of the Constitutional Court and widely considered to be a jurist of distinction—became the first black chief justice of the Supreme Court of Appeal in 1998.[41] Blacks and women have been appointed to the higher courts in significant numbers, even more so to the magistrates' courts. But it has not been easy to steer a path between assuring the maximum commitment to the new order—which would dictate tight central control of judicial behavior but undermine the reality and the perception of the judiciary's first allegiance to the law—and allowing judicial independence that might threaten that commitment. Angry debates about both accountability and independence have taken place both on the bench and in the press. Periodically the government criticizes judges and magistrates for not working hard enough, and the judges respond by saying that the government doesn't understand their duties or their schedules and that, in any event, their workload is not the justice minister's business. Judges and magistrates have been accused by some of clinging to old values and loyalties and by others of toadying to the ANC as the political party that dominates the executive and legislative branches of government. Nonetheless, the new South African government has created institutions designed to balance accountability and independence for judicial officers in magistrates' courts as well as the higher courts. And judicial perspectives have shifted accordingly.

Some of the institutions and practices that have furthered these goals are authorized or mandated by the constitution. Unlike the United States Constitution, which merely suggests judicial independence through separating governmental powers in the text, the South African language is explicit; the constitution states, "The courts are independent and subject only to the Constitution and the law" and that "[n]o persons or organs of state may interfere with the functioning of the courts."[42] The power of judicial review ensures that a parliamentary system of government need not mean a parliament immune to constitutional challenges, and the South African parliament has not sought to weaken that power. Assisted by the Constitutional Court and a heavy dose of self-regulation, the judiciary and the magistracy are adapting to new directives and new faces, transforming themselves in ways that are consistent with the values of the new democracy. Political conflicts and ideological backsliding have occasionally tainted the courts, and cultural change has not always kept pace with institutional change, especially in the magistrates' courts, where control by the executive branch of government was tighter in the apartheid past.[43] But internal reforms and external controls and protections have made the composition of the courts, the regulation of judicial behavior, and the protection of judicial independence in South Africa among the more successful of its democratization projects.

Oversight of South Africa's judicial officers is complicated by a history that separated upper and lower courts in many respects. Until recently, the magistrates, who staff the lower courts, where over 95 percent of criminal cases are heard, were selected from a different pool (the ranks of prosecutors, rather than senior trial counsel) than were the judges, who hear the most serious cases and appeals from the magistrates' courts. They generally qualified as lawyers through a less rigorous university curriculum supplemented with training by the state's Justice College. They were dependent on the state in the most fundamental respects—as civil servants, employees of the Department of Justice whose jobs included administrative duties like administering estates, overseeing elections, and granting liquor licenses. (This practice was a holdover from the old *landdrost* system of powerful local administrators inherited from the Dutch.) Magistrates' prestige was (and is) low, and their working conditions were (and are) generally poor. Their lower professional status was determined not only by their lesser education, limited jurisdiction, and meager pay but by the likelihood that most of their work involved criminal (and, to a lesser extent, civil) matters that were most often the problems of the poor, black majority. Generally beginning their careers as prosecutors, they were not often considered eligible for appointment as judges. They were overwhelmingly white; the director-general of the Justice Department testified before the TRC that, in 1991 as apartheid was dying, there were only three African magistrates.[44]

Judges of the upper courts, however—the Supreme Court (now called the High Court) and its Appellate Division (now the Supreme Court of Appeal)—were chosen from the ranks of senior counsel, equivalent to the higher classification of barristers in England. Coming from more privileged backgrounds than most magistrates, they had received a university LL.B. and established a well-regarded private practice as advocates. Their elite status and their guaranteed tenure and salaries gave them theoretically greater independence from political executives in Pretoria. But while they may have been spared direct political interference—the "telephone justice" that some say controlled judicial decisions in the Soviet Union—apartheid architects found ways to ensure that this independence proved more apparent than real. Terrorism and internal security legislation locked judges into draconian decrees, with little room to exercise discretion. The priorities of the executive branch also provided remedies for judicial autonomy; during the late 1980s judges of the Appellate Division who were not sympathetic to the government were rarely assigned by the chief justice to sit on cases interpreting the emergency regulations of the internal security laws.[45]

Transformation in the judiciary has included efforts to bring the two kinds of judicial officers closer together. Magistrates now hear cases of rape and murder as well as of minor crimes; the regional (as opposed to district) courts can sentence an offender to incarceration for up to fifteen years or to a fine of up to three hundred thousand rand (about forty-three thousand dollars).[46] Institutional dependence on the executive branch of government is significantly reduced; magistrates are no longer employees of the Department of Justice, and the minister of justice no longer has complete discretion over their appointment or suspension. With respect to both the judiciary and the magistracy, independence has been enhanced by opening up the pool of potential judges and magistrates. In the interests of bringing blacks and women into the judiciary, the career ladder leading to the position of judge has widened to include experienced attorneys (the equivalent of solicitors in the British system), advocates without senior status (equivalent to British barristers), and magistrates, at least where they have received the LL.B. Inclusion has been gradual, to be sure; out of the forty-five black or female judges appointed between 1994 and the end of 1999, only seven had served as magistrates.[47] And the fundamental distinction of role and status has been maintained; a 1999 proposal to merge the magistracy and the judiciary that met with dismay from judges of the upper courts has been quietly shelved.

(It should, however, be noted that service at the two court levels is still a very different experience. In 2002 Judge Mbuyiseli Madlanga described it this way:

> A criminal court magistrate's lot is unenviable: a heavy case load, numerous postponements and consequent part-heard matters, long hours, difficult working conditions, relatively inexperienced legal practitioners, interpreters and investigating officers, rudimentary library facilities, and an often unsavoury physical working environment. A particularly stressful feature of such a magistrate's task is the high percentage of accused persons who do not have the benefit of legal representation and who often have language problems and cultural and educational difficulties in presenting a passable defence. The whole scene differs radically from the high courts where . . . undefended accused are usually such from choice. The high court case load is usually lighter, the human and material support resources considerably better, and the general atmosphere infinitely more conducive to fair judicial proceedings.)[48]

If access to justice is a measure of judicial accountability, then South Africa has a long way to go. And behavioral independence of magistrates is surely impeded by working conditions that make the leisured consideration of all elements of a case an unknown luxury. Judges of the upper courts have also made the connection between adequate resources and their ability to make efficient and independent decisions. A statement issued in 2003 by Chief Justice Arthur Chaskalson on behalf of all High Court judges noted, "Some judges have no offices, many have no computers, secretarial assistance or other basic facilities. In many instances, judicial officers are not provided with the basic facilities necessary for the performance of their functions."[49]

The new government has chosen to steer a path between the populism of elected judges and the centralization and elitism of executive control of the judiciary by setting up two regulatory institutions—one for the higher courts and one for the magistracy—to promote accountability and protect independence. The Judicial Service Commission (JSC) is a constitutional creation—a body of twenty-three representatives of the judiciary, the legal profession, and the executive chaired by the chief justice.[50] It is charged with nominating judges for the president's appointment and given the authority to advise the president "on any issue relating to the judiciary or the administration of justice."[51] It may recommend to parliament the removal of a judge "if it finds that the judge suffers from an incapacity, is grossly incompetent or is guilty of gross misconduct," and by inference, therefore, has the authority to discipline judges.[52] (No judge has been removed, however, since Union [1910] made South Africa one country.) A subcommittee considers complaints about judges, which have not, in its judgment, amounted to misconduct that warrants a recommendation of removal. A bill to establish a procedure for receiving and reviewing complaints against judges for behavior that is not impeachable was drafted by the Department of Justice and Constitutional Development and was pending in parliament in late 2004.

The Magistrates' Commission was established by legislation in the final days of apartheid and, although not named in the final constitution, was clearly contemplated by it in a provision that calls for the enactment of law that "must ensure that the appointment, promotion, transfer or dismissal of, or disciplinary steps against, these judicial officers take place without favour or prejudice."[53] It is headed by a judge and, in parallel to the JSC, includes representatives of the legal profession and the state, magistrates, and the head of the Judicial College that trains them. Its independence is somewhat constrained by the authority of the justice minister to appoint magistrates, but he or she must consult with the commission when making appointments. The Magistrates' Act sets forth the conditions for disciplining or removing a magistrate, and regulations that supplement the act describe examples of misconduct for which a preliminary investigation may be ordered by the Magistrates'

Commission, followed in most cases by a hearing to determine whether a magistrate's alleged offense warrants disciplinary action or a recommendation to parliament for removal.[54] The list of sins for which proceedings may be initiated in the Magistrates' Commission is sweeping enough to have been challenged in court, but the Constitutional Court has rejected the challenge, leaving it to the commission to determine what constitutes misconduct.[55] (In fact, most cases that come before the commission involve charges of drunkenness, traffic violations, or a magistrate's being "negligent or indolent in carrying out his duties.")

Between April 1994 and May 2002 the commission conducted misconduct investigations and hearings for forty-seven magistrates, the results of which were then referred for decision to the justice minister. During that period the minister issued sentences (short of removal, which only parliament can decree) that included reprimands, delayed promotions, and suspensions.[56] (Prosecutions in court for fraud, drunk driving, and other crimes were also brought, which generally led to a commission proceeding, since conviction of a criminal offense is grounds for a finding of magisterial misconduct.) The commission's powers were, however, enhanced in 2002 by a Constitutional Court finding that the assignment of sanctions by the minister interfered with judicial independence.[57] The commission was ordered to perform that function, and it has now sentenced magistrates in several cases. The strains of adapting to the new order have sometimes been evident in these proceedings; a disciplinary hearing and court case brought against the chief magistrate of Pretoria in 2002 for intimidation and *crimen injuria* (defamation) pitted newly appointed black and old-line white magistrates in his court against one another.[58] While the higher courts have greater security of tenure and remuneration than magistrates' courts—the government cannot fire them or reduce their salaries or benefits—magistrates are assured a measure of financial security in that only parliament can reduce their salaries or remove them.[59] If this occurs, it can be appealed to the higher courts, giving the judiciary a role in the protection of the independence of its junior institution.

The JSC was created, in part, to convey the message that judicial appointment would not be simply a way of ensuring compliance with government dictates. The constitution permits it to establish its own procedure and to recommend for appointment any "appropriately qualified woman or man who is a fit and proper person," a standard that also applies to the appointment of magistrates.[60] It also provides that at least three of the six members of the JSC designated by parliament from among its members must belong to opposition parties, and both lawyers' groups and law teachers are to designate members as well. As it currently operates, the JSC also displays its functions of both making judges accountable and protecting their independence by making its interviews with judicial candidates open to the public.[61] This transparency is important for assuring the public that the mandate given to the appointing powers to choose judges who "reflect broadly the racial and gender composition of South Africa" is being honored.[62]

The transparency of both appointment and disciplinary proceedings for judicial officers occasionally reveals continuing strains of adjustment to both the values and the policies of the new government. It may be particularly true in South Africa that "society's divisions run through its courts."[63] Abiding attitudes about race and apartheid associations often provide an undercurrent in meetings of the JSC and occasionally bubble up to cause a public flap. While the press and the politically attentive public—a large and vocal group for a country with a high degree of poverty and illiteracy—decry the challenges and insults that are played out in the courts, they attest to a free and open exchange that would be the envy of many democracies, whether embryonic or mature. With all their problems, the courts enjoy a high degree of legitimacy, partly attributable to the degree of publicity of their operations.

An example of the playing out of old tensions and new values occurred in April 1998 when two candidates—both sitting judges, one in KwaZulu-Natal and one in the Eastern Cape—came before the JSC for the post of deputy judge president of KwaZulu-Natal. One was a judge of long standing, an Afrikaner who had formerly been a member of the Broederbond, the secret society to which many apartheid leaders belonged and which stood for the kind of Afrikaner nationalism the country has now repudiated. The other was a recently appointed African judge whose reputation for a somewhat casual attitude toward his professional duties provided the ammunition for a group of his colleagues who opposed his advancement. Fourteen of the nineteen judges sitting in the province signed a letter to the JSC expressing their view that as a "junior judge" Judge Vuka Tshabalala would not be able to command their respect if he were to be given the job of leading them. (Important background facts are that at the time Tshabalala would have been the first black deputy judge president in the country and that the judge president was nearing retirement, at which time the deputy would be his likely successor.) The JSC meeting where the two candidates were interviewed began formally enough but soon became explosive, with angry exchanges about whether Judge Booysen's former membership in the Broederbond was a disqualifying factor in considering him for the post and whether the judges' letter was an inappropriate (and racist) communication to the JSC.[64] The commission could not come to a conclusion as between the candidates, and the matter was held over until the next meeting six months later, at which time Tshabalala prevailed. (He is now the judge president of the province.)

What matters most here is not that issues of affirmative action and past political associations remain to some extent unresolved in South Africa but that the exposure of sites of conflict through the operation of public and representative institutions is a normal and uncontroversial practice. While the opposing judges' letter about Tshabalala was widely disapproved, no one in authority called for their resignation, suggesting institutional respect for their independence. As for accountability, the public play given to the meeting conveyed to Judges Booysen and Tshabalala—and to other potential judicial candidates—the message that behavior and associations relevant to judicial performance would be considered in the appointment process. In another instance of a publicly visible solution to a vexing political problem involving the judiciary, President Nelson Mandela set up a commission to investigate racism, nepotism, and mismanagement in the South African Rugby Football Union, whereupon an apartheid-era judge rejected it as an abdication of executive responsibility and an "administrative action" in violation of the constitution. The decision was insulting to the president in that it included findings that his testimony was not credible. The Constitutional Court overruled the High Court judge, finding his opinion guilty of "material misdirection" and "fallacious" reasoning, but the tone of the decision was measured, and the government took no action against either the particular judge or the remaining old-line judges who still made up the bulk of the judiciary.[65] Similarly, an outburst by one of the "hanging judges" against the abolition of the death penalty was received as worthy only of journalistic note and seen as a contribution to an important national policy debate.

The newly appointed multiracial Constitutional Court set a standard of commitment to independence from the start. The first case it heard found the death penalty unconstitutional, despite widespread support for it among both blacks and whites—and probably among most government ministers.[66] In a 291-page opinion, the court initially refused to certify the proposed final constitution, forcing the Constitutional Assembly to reconsider the text.[67] Despite those decisions and the high reputation of the court both within South Africa and internationally, it has detractors who question its independence. When the South African Rugby Football Union case came to the Constitutional Court the union's president requested that the entire court recuse itself on the basis of his view that its members would be biased against him because they had been appointed by President Nelson Mandela (who had brought the appeal), because of their presumed sympathies with the ANC, and because of the friendship of Nelson Mandela and the family of Arthur Chaskalson, the chief justice.[68] This attack on the institutional integrity of the court was widely regarded as outrageous, but there were some commentators in the press who asserted that, as a general matter, the court was indeed unwilling to offend the party in power.[69] While many thought the charge misguided at the time, it would now be preposterous. Since the court's early cases rejecting the death penalty and sending the initial constitution back to the framers for revision, the court has made many rulings that were either wildly unpopular with the public or administratively problematic for the ruling party. In 1999 it supported the right of prison inmates to vote and rejected a local government's effort to block scholarships for schools with mostly white students.[70] Most important, it ruled the following year that the ANC government must take reasonable measures, given its resources, to effectuate the right to adequate housing—in this case "to devise, fund, implement and supervise measures to provide relief" to people living in desperate conditions in a field.[71]

While the court has continued to display its independence of parliamentary and executive action, it may still have difficulties having an effective last word. A July 2002 decision finding that the government had a constitutional obligation to prevent mother-to-child transmission of HIV and ordering the government to make nevirapine available to HIV-positive pregnant women was a test of both the court's fidelity to independence and the government's respect for that independence.[72] There have been no recriminations from the Ministry of Health, which lost the case (and, in fact, the minister of justice has praised the outcome), but neither local nor national public health agencies rushed to comply with the decision. (The *Mail and Guardian,* in its annual rating of government ministers for 2002, gave the health minister an F for her handling of the AIDS crisis and described her as continuing "to give the impression that she suffers from Aids denialism.")[73] A year later an investigative report found chaos and confusion—"a shambles," as one anonymous health official described it—in the distribution of nevirapine in most provinces, despite the decision.[74] Now that the South African cabinet has approved an operational plan for giving free antiviral drugs to anyone who needs them—more than five million people are estimated to be infected with the virus—the situation for HIV-infected mothers will probably improve, although there is controversy over whether nevirapine alone or a more expensive cocktail of drugs will be distributed.[75] In any case, effective treatment of the pandemic will come about only indirectly because of the Constitutional Court decision; the government's plan for a nationwide AIDS program was largely the result of public pressure, spurred in large part by the Treatment Action Campaign that brought the constitutional case and continues to monitor government policy.

There seems little reason for concern that other South African courts will be subject to the kind of harassment from parliament or from the executive branch of government that Zimbabwe has suffered.[76] Any attempt by the government to influence High Court or appellate decisions is likely to be noted and criticized by press and public. At one level the battle for institutional autonomy for the judiciary and magistracy has clearly been won. A more exacting test of the courts' independence, however, will be whether their moral and constitutional authority will be enough to force compliance with rulings that are controversial or expensive to implement. And, with respect to the behavioral independence and accountability of individual judges and magistrates, there will continue to be value conflicts that pit the old habits against new mandates. Assessments of these conflicts, furthermore, will not always yield clear answers.

Two widely publicized cases decided in 1999 illustrate some of the complexities of these issues for the High Courts and the Supreme Court of Appeal. In one the Reverend Allan Boesak was found guilty of fraud and theft of over two hundred thousand dollars in funds donated to Boesak's Foundation for Peace and Justice. Boesak had "wrongfully and unlawfully appropriated money intended for the children of South Africa," said the judge in sentencing him to six years' imprisonment; "[h]e treated the money as his own," using it to buy luxuries for himself and his wife.[77] Boesak had been an antiapartheid hero, a powerful orator—one scholar likens his style and substance to that of Martin Luther King—and a founder of the United Democratic Front.[78] During his trial powerful friends from the days of the liberation struggle came to his aid: Nelson Mandela publicly expressed doubt about the state's case and raised money for his defense; the minister of justice criticized the prosecutor for bringing the case; and Archbishop Desmond Tutu sent the judge a telegram urging a lenient sentence. These considerable lapses in institutional independence, however, did not affect the behavioral independence of either the trial judge or the Supreme Court of Appeal, which affirmed the judgment on three of the four counts charged.[79] While a few objections were raised to Boesak's imprisonment on the ground that he had performed great service to the liberation struggle, the general view was that, as an editorial put it when he later applied (unsuccessfully) for a pardon, "Forgiveness in the context of a political solution is not the same as forgiveness for criminal acts that stem, not out of political injustice, but out of personal greed."[80] The courts' handling of the case was widely regarded as a credit to the judicial system, a sign that even a liberation hero is not above the law.

The other case involved a rape sentence in apparent violation of a 1997 law providing for life imprisonment for the rape of a girl under sixteen unless "substantial and compelling" mitigating circumstances could be found.[81] The legislation was unpopular with magistrates and judges as a curb on judicial discretion, and the trial judge had departed from the mandatory life sentence and given a man only a seven-year prison term for the rape of his fourteen-year-old daughter. He justified the sentence in part by noting that the defendant had no record of sexual aggression outside his family, a comment that was interpreted as diminishing the seriousness of the rape. The public outrage over the judgment and what was viewed as a callous rationalization of it focused on the need to make judges accountable for their decisions especially in light of South Africa's history of neglecting the safety and dignity of women and children. A parliamentary committee threatened to summon the judge to answer for his decision, and some called for his removal. Judicial independence, however, prevailed over public fury. As one commentator put it, "Vigorous public protest, criticism from the profession, and the corrective mechanism of an appeal are far preferable to hasty, ill-conceived calls for impeachment."[82] The Supreme Court of Appeal did make a correction; it ruled that the judge "materially misdirected himself in imposing the sentence of seven years" and increased the sentence to twelve years.[83] But the judgment merely disagreed with the weighting given to mitigating and aggravating factors in the defendant's behavior and did not impugn the trial judge's commitment to justice.

More was at issue in this case than a sentence that seemed to many an inadequate punishment for a crime that has given South Africa the reputation of being the rape capital of the world. And the Boesak case was about more than the moral lapses of a leader in the liberation struggle. South African judges and magistrates have had to adjust to new imperatives—for example, enhanced protection of women and children and the prevention of corruption in the infant democracy—even as they adjust to a different balance between independence and accountability. It is significant that although the appellate court in the rape case held the trial judge accountable by overruling his sentencing decision, it followed his lead in rejecting the legislative mandate of life imprisonment, indirectly reminding the public and the parliament that making sentencing decisions without interference is an aspect of judicial independence. With the Boesak case, too, the judicial branch showed itself to be both accountable—intolerant of fraud and theft—and independent—resistant to pressures emanating from powerful figures consumed by liberation nostalgia. The new democratic environment requires judges to navigate a thicket full of political and jurisprudential brambles. In this context, sympathy for the trial judge is surely warranted; in these two cases it happens to have been the same person, Judge John Foxcroft of the Cape Town High Court.

Integrity of Criminal Justice Operatives

Few modern citizens believe in the perfect congruity of law and justice. Yet even the most ardent legal realist assumes that the criminal law sets some moral standards for individual behavior. And it follows that those who enforce the law must be imbued with those standards and with a sense of public duty. Whether police and judges see themselves in this position and endeavor to conduct their professional lives in a manner that honors the public trust and reflects a common moral consensus is one of the questions that must be answered in the affirmative in a constitutional democracy. Part of shifting the constituency of criminal justice institutions in the transition from an authoritarian regime is establishing the confidence of citizens that police and judges themselves live by the moral, legal, and professional standards that they are charged to uphold. So the reality and the perception that the personnel of criminal justice are criminal, corrupt, or indifferent can undermine democratization.

The South African experience of attempting to ensure the personal and professional integrity of criminal justice functionaries is similar to that of demilitarizing and repoliticizing police and establishing a balance between judicial accountability and independence. The post-apartheid government has undertaken significant institutional reform that seems likely, in the longer term, to ensure that police and judges honor the moral imperatives of a liberal democracy. (South Africa is rated 48th among 133 countries in a 2003 index of perceived corruption, with Finland number 1 as the cleanest and Bangladesh number 133 as the most corrupt.)[84] Even in the apartheid past personal moral turpitude was a rarity in the judiciary and the magistracy, and the expansion of opportunities for blacks and women in judicial roles has not changed that. Significant problems remain, however, with a law enforcement legacy that continues to perpetuate a culture of exploitation in the police, where routine encounters with citizens matter in establishing the regime's legitimacy.

If there is an integrity issue with respect to magistrates and judges, it is not one of widespread crime or corruption. Respondents in the Afrobarometer survey of 2002 were less likely to say that "most" of them were corrupt than to come to that conclusion with respect to elected leaders, government officials, and police.[85] A few charges of corruption and minor crimes have been brought against magistrates, but that is to be expected, with about fourteen hundred magistrates nationwide (as compared with fewer than two hundred judges). Alcohol problems, however, are common enough to cast a pall on the magistracy. Johannes Meijer, the magistrates' commission official who oversees misconduct hearings for magistrates, estimated in 2000 that 80 percent involve charges of drunkenness on the road or the bench or absenteeism attributable to a hangover.[86]

When the character of judges or magistrates comes into question, it is often a question of cynicism or indifference rather than of corruption. In 1998 the overburdened, underresourced court system suffered further injury when prosecutors and magistrates began resigning in the middle of trials, forcing the state to rehire them to complete the cases at the higher rates paid to private-sector lawyers.[87] And disparate sentences have revealed a few racially motivated decisions and occasional sympathy for apartheid-era thugs, particularly in the early post-apartheid years. In 1999 a judge suspended a ten-year sentence for four white men, members of the right-wing organization AWB (the Afrikaner resistance movement), who had been convicted of a particularly vicious murder in which they dragged a defenseless black hunchback out of his car and beat him to death; the lenience was justified on the grounds that the accused had been conditioned to be racist and that they were remorseful.[88]

When outrageous judgments occur, they generally get wide circulation in the press.

South African reforms intended to buttress the integrity of its criminal justice operatives have not, however, met the challenges of crime and corruption in South African police precincts. While the constitution is silent on matters of police integrity, the 1995 legislation that establishes the powers and functions of police outlines with great specificity the penalties for police who are convicted of crimes; basically, those who are sentenced to imprisonment without the possibility of a fine are summarily discharged.[89] In addition, the minister for safety and security is authorized to develop regulations for the conduct of police and bring disciplinary proceedings pursuant to them.[90] The legislation also creates the Independent Complaints Directorate (ICD) to "investigate any misconduct or offence allegedly committed by any member [of the SAPS]"; the ICD "may, where appropriate, refer such investigation to the Commissioner."[91] Finally, at the level of official rhetoric, the SAPS has explicitly embraced its constitutional duty; the preamble of a recent annual report asserts its commitment to "protect everyone's rights and to be impartial, respectful, open and accountable to the community; use the powers given to us in a responsible way; provide a responsible, effective and high quality service with honesty and integrity."[92]

Yet the law on the books is not the same as the law in action. To many South Africans the police are a criminal class. When the SAPS reported in 1998 that on average police were three times more likely to commit crimes than civilians, many of the crimes noted were extortions or thefts made possible by the power they have over civilians. Police often find criminal opportunity on the job; the head of a vehicle theft unit runs a chop shop, an investigator of gun crimes sells illegal weapons on the side, cops who take fingerprints falsify them for a fee. But police are also sometimes involved in larger criminal enterprises. They may be in league with local gangs or vigilante groups, and occasionally the station house becomes a center of organized crime, with police assisting in robberies, hijackings, and murders. In 2000 the residents of Kwa-Mashu, a township near Durban, asked the SAPS to shut down a police station that that the community saw as a den of criminals. "It is not only staffed by incompetents," said the deputy chair of the community police forum, "It is the major source of crime in our area."[93] Police have been accused of taking part in the taxi wars and participating in a series of still-unsolved bombings that took place over a two-year period in the Cape Town area. The entanglement of police and criminals is evident in stories of retribution taken against people who report police abuses. The pattern seems to be that police brutalize a criminal suspect, who then files a complaint of assault, and if the police are convicted, the complainant is beaten or tortured or murdered by someone else.

Corruption is also a substantial problem, one that long predates the current period.[94] The offenses include accepting bribes and protection money, stealing evidence and police dockets, aiding prisoners to escape, and sometimes grander schemes as well. During the years 2001 and 2002 the SAPS investigated 2,370 cases of alleged corruption, resulting in 1,331 criminal prosecutions and 641 internal disciplinary hearings.[95] In 2003 a police inspector in the Johannesburg area was accused of claiming a fifty-thousand-rand reward (about seven thousand dollars) for a fictitious person who had supposedly assisted in the arrest of the area's most-wanted murderer.[96] Recent research found that corruption in inner-city areas where illegal markets thrive and police benefit from them is so widespread that local residents assume they must pay to the police a "street tax" of money or drugs or sexual favors.[97] Some surveys suggest that at least half of the population either believes that police take bribes or have been exposed themselves to police corruption. These perceptions may be inaccurate; Afrobarometer surveys have found that South Africans are less likely to encounter corruption among public servants than is popularly thought, and less likely to think their government officials are corrupt than they were in the mid-1990s. The self-reported incidence of experiences with police corruption is higher, however, than in other kinds of encounters with public services—for instance, efforts to obtain an official document or get a child into a school.[98] South Africans are discouraged by the continuing corruption, which they attribute primarily to police. They were among the most pessimistic of citizens from forty-five countries surveyed by Transparency International in 2003; 51 percent expected corruption to worsen within the next three years.[99]

It is impossible to be precise about the actual amount of corruption that occurs. Most is not reported, since often the police officer is accommodating a criminal suspect who does not want the transaction known. And it is difficult to know what the official data mean; the SAPS reported that there were 1,041 prosecutions in 2000 for police corruption, with 195 convictions, while the ICD received only 106 complaints of corruption in 2002–3, obviously a tiny fraction of the actual total.[100] It is also difficult to know whether corruption is on the rise. Even though the number of complaints taken to the ICD was so small, it represented an increase of 253 percent in just one year, which may reflect a growing awareness of the complaints procedure and increasing trust in the ICD, rather than an actual jump in incidents.

These records, along with field reports and the observations of criminal justice researchers, suggest that the rise in complaints against police, whether to the ICD or to the police themselves, may be a positive sign.[101] The Institute for Security Studies found in 2003 that crime victims were more likely than in 1998 to report their victimizations for some crimes—notably theft and assault, but not robbery—to police, suggesting that the legitimacy of law enforcement could be established, however tentatively, even if the police continued to be largely ineffective against the scourge of violent crime.[102] Now South Africans appear to be more confident that they have a role in assuring the integrity of law enforcement, that filing a complaint against police no longer entails assuming intolerable risks.[103] Participation in the structures and mechanisms established by the government presumably furthers public safety and expresses faith in the new democracy.

It seems likely that widespread corruption will continue as long as police are so poorly paid, trained, and equipped. In addition, their occupational conditioning comes from a time when the population was regarded with suspicion rather than respect; it will probably take a generation to erase the expectation of many constables and officers that community residents present opportunities for exploitation. Incorporating the police forces of the ten "homelands" into the SAPS is an additional challenge, as the culture of corruption was particularly strong at all levels of those puppet governments. Finally, members of the SAPS have not been confronted with good role models. In the bad old days a constable might look the other way rather than enforce the pass laws, for a fee; the higher-ranking officer might be in league with a criminal syndicate. Apartheid law enforcement was corrupt at the core; the murderous security police commander Eugene de Kock dipped into a secret fund—estimated at nine million rand (then about $2.5 million)—to support the lifestyles—holidays as well as weapons—of the deadly Vlakplaas unit (see chapter 3).[104] These days, with the exception of the former national head of organized crime policing, who pled guilty in 2002 to charges of filing fraudulent expense claims, the senior police management seems to be clean. But continuing corruption investigations into the behavior of other national officials, particularly relating to the government's forty-three-billion-rand arms deal of 2000, have fed the general public impression that public functionaries are untrustworthy. Provincial officials, too, are frequently unmasked as stealing from the public and from the public fisc, and polls show low levels of public trust in them.[105]

Fundamental Fairness: Respecting Due Process and "Freedom and Security of the Person"

The yearning for human rights in South Africa was a mantra that echoed through the liberation movements of the early and middle twentieth century. As apartheid collapsed and the millennium approached, it became a mass chorus. It is, therefore, not surprising that the new government and the organizations of civil society that supported it have laid great emphasis on building a culture of rights. Although for many of the clans and ethnic groups that make up the South African population the Western notion of individual rights is somewhat alien, there is widespread recognition that it was, to a great extent, the vehicle of deliverance from the sufferings of apartheid and is therefore to be respected as a guarantee of dignity. The great South African satirist Pieter-Dirk Uys says it very simply: "Human rights is the right to be human."

The South African constitution provides very comprehensively for fairness in the operations of police and courts. Its bill of rights contains two separate but related clusters of protection. Section 35, dealing with "arrested, detained and accused persons," guarantees such rights as humane treatment by police, legal representation, adequate accommodation in detention, and family visitation for prisoners. The right to a fair trial includes not only the formal elements of due process that would be familiar to Americans—the right to be informed of all criminal charges, to be tried in public, to be presumed innocent, and so forth—but also "a concept of substantive fairness which is not to be equated with what might have passed muster in our criminal courts before the constitution came into force."[106] The other cluster of rights, to "freedom and security of the person," is even more encompassing. It covers encounters with state officials and private citizens as well and resonates strongly with a population that has lived through a brutal past and anticipates a democratic future.[107] It aligns liberty with basic dignity by including the rights "(a) not to be deprived of freedom arbitrarily or without just cause; (b) not to be detained without trial; (c) to be free from all forms of violence from either public or private sources; (d) not to be tortured in any way; and (e) not to be treated or punished in a cruel, inhuman or degrading way."

Much of the impetus for a priority on these rights came from the treatment of apartheid's victims by the criminal justice system. Justice Pius Langa, then-deputy chief justice, in the case that declared the death penalty to be unconstitutional, made clear the congruence of political oppression and brutal law enforcement during apartheid:

> The history of the past decades has been such that the value of life and human dignity have been demeaned. Political, social and other factors created a climate of violence, resulting in a culture of retaliation and vengeance. In the process, respect for life and for the inherent dignity of every person became the main casualties. The State has been part of this degeneration, not only because of its role in the conflicts of the past, but also by retaining punishments which did not testify to a high regard for the dignity of the person and the value of every human life.[108]

The new constitution, therefore, provides as comprehensive and progressive a recital of formal procedural rights for people who get into trouble with the legal system as can be found anywhere in the world. The corollary to that is the aim of educating citizens to the rewards of a system that guarantees "dignity of the person" and the active acknowledgment of the suffering of crime victims.

Once again the picture is one of considerable institutional achievement, with implementation far more difficult and tenuous than policymaking. To a great extent, the government has followed up on the constitutional promise not to abuse state power over the individual when the stakes—the personal liberty and safety that are challenged when a law violation is alleged—are highest. Legislation and court decisions that protect criminal suspects and defendants against the villainies of an authoritarian justice system are unequivocal. In the context of protecting a woman's rights to dignity and "freedom and security of the person" the Constitutional Court has put prosecutors and judges on notice that when the common law does not reflect the "spirit, purport and objects of the Bill of Rights," the courts have a duty to take affirmative steps to develop it so that it does.[109] Despite widespread support for the death penalty from the public and virtually all of the opposition parties, the government has refused to entertain the amendment of the constitution that would permit it. The right to legal representation is guaranteed by the constitution, and the state will assign a lawyer to an indigent defendant and pay for the defense "if substantial justice would otherwise result."[110]

But the impediments to realizing the ambitions of the constitution's protection of human rights are formidable and various. Sometimes they are primarily a lack of resources—either for staffing the structures and mechanisms of protection or for educating the public as to their significance and how they can be activated. Sometimes the implementation problem is a manifestation of the resistance to change found in organizations everywhere, the universal difficulty of acquiring new habits in settings where risk of physical danger or professional rejection is great. (Chapter 9 discusses the current "get-tough" policy direction.) And sometimes old habits hold sway, subverting the core objectives of ensuring equality, dignity, and freedom. The constitutional plea for healing past divisions, after all, is not a concrete plan of action.

Current standards for obtaining a confession from a criminal defendant—both their formulation and their implementation—suggest the pattern. The South African common-law tradition prohibited coerced confessions and protected the right to remain silent. But police practice during apartheid relied heavily on torture or duress during interrogation to obtain confessions, and the courts often turned a blind eye with the legal presumption that confessions were voluntary—and therefore admissible in trial—unless proved otherwise by the accused, clearly an impossibility in most cases.[111] The post-apartheid Constitutional Court's very first judgment rejected this presumption as inimical to the guarantee of a fair trial and the presumption of innocence.[112] Other official policy statements have underscored the shift in perspective. The 1995 Police Service Act provides that an SAPS member "may use only the minimum force which is reasonable in the circumstances."[113] Warnings of the defendant's right to remain silent are constitutionally guaranteed; a Constitutional Court judgment in 2003 underscored the necessity of the right, noting the country's "dim past of torture and intimidation during police custody."[114]

But some of these requirements make extraordinary demands on those who actually operate the criminal justice system, and the costs of honoring them—court delays and failed prosecutions—are high. A defense challenge to the voluntariness of a confession—and they are now common, according an Institute for Security Studies monograph—can slow down a trial with a separate hearing where the prosecutor attempts to meet the burden of proving that the confession was freely made.[115] Similarly, the prosecutor can no longer rely on the presumption that if drugs are found in the vicinity of a defendant, they were actually in his or her possession.[116] Even an experienced prosecutor—of whom there are now very few—will have difficulty persuading a defendant on the witness stand—if he is willing to testify at all—to acknowledge possession of the drugs. Martin Schönteich, an experienced prosecutor and researcher, has concluded that conviction for possession of unlicensed weapons has become almost impossible since the Constitutional Court's rejection of the presumption of the Arms and Ammunition Act of 1969 that an illegal gun found in someone's home or car is in his or her possession.[117]

Compliance with constitutional mandates is much easier to monitor in court proceedings than in police precincts or in township streets. Torture and other forms of brutality during arrest, interrogation, or detention continue to occur, though it is impossible to know how frequently. Some human rights lawyers in the late 1990s alleged that brutality had increased since the end of apartheid, and one critic has charged that the undeniable fact of rampant violent crime in South Africa has actually emboldened the police to violate the rights of suspects.[118] Immigrants are particularly vulnerable; footage of police dogs being set upon defenseless Mozambicans as a kind of spectator sport in 1998 horrified viewers around the world. The ICD was notified of 528 deaths during the fiscal year 2002–3 of people in police custody or killed as a result of police action.[119] (Most deaths are the result of the use of force by police, but some are suicides, assaults by private citizens, or injury or disease unrelated to the contacts with police; police killings are, furthermore, not necessarily illegal.)[120] It should be noted, however, that that number had decreased by 40 percent since data were first kept in 1997–98, when the ICD announced that such deaths were occurring at a rate of sixty per month.[121] (Another report of police shootings during that period estimated that, in addition, more than thirteen hundred people each year were injured.)[122] While the trend may suggest a drop in the worst kinds of abuse, it may instead reflect a reduction in other causes of death for those in custody. The ICD recorded an increase in reports of torture in 2001, and its 2002 report on the prevention of torture recommends that police be required to report all alleged criminal acts of police to the ICD. (Presently the SAPS is legally required to report only deaths in custody or attributable to police action.)

One troubling finding of the ICD report for 2002–3 is that 293 of the deaths were attributable to police shootings—generally of unarmed suspects trying to flee. In some cases the dead were juveniles or persons being sought for minor crimes; in one case a defendant tried to escape while being escorted from the court to a holding cell. In none of the cases investigated were the police endangered by the conduct of the accused. One may attribute this police behavior to the legacy of apartheid practice and the jitters that must accompany the job of law enforcement in such a crime-ridden country, but a lack of political will for implementing policy reforms is also evident. Many of the incidents reported by the ICD and by researchers at the Centre for the Study of Violence and Reconciliation also reflect a lack of training in the procedures appropriate to a human rights culture and a failure of police management to command the discipline that respects that culture.

They also suggest the difficulties of making legal change a lived reality and the ambivalence that may attend even the reform of a law that is obviously repugnant to the new order. During apartheid (with precedent dating back to the mid–nineteenth century) criminal procedure law allowed the use of lethal force—even by a civilian and even against a child—to stop a fleeing crime suspect.[123] Immunized from prosecution by the law, police frequently shot and killed unarmed suspects; legend has it that even children stealing apples were mowed down. Denounced by human rights groups as a tool of apartheid oppression even before the new democracy was born, the law was challenged in court in 1995 by the mother of a ten-year-old boy who was shot and killed by police who were chasing him for hunting doves. Though the lower courts acknowledged that the notorious Section 49 might be held to be invalid under the new (actually the interim) constitution, it refused the application for removal to the new Constitutional Court on the grounds that a revision of the law was pending.[124] That revision—sponsored by the Department of Justice among others—was indeed enacted by parliament in 1998, providing that lethal force was justified only to protect the life of a police officer or private citizen or to prevent future threats to life.[125]

But the law had powerful opponents. Although the national police commissioner had, in 1997, issued an internal order to the effect that force used by police should be proportional to the seriousness of the suspected crime, the directive was described as an interim measure and was not widely distributed. The SAPS complained of inadequate resources to train officers in how to handle fleeing suspects if the new law were to go into effect. They also argued that it would render them ineffective and could not be reconciled with the tremendous community pressure to catch criminals by all available means. A belligerent minister for safety and security opposed it on the basis of "massive violent assaults against the police."[126] (It is true that violence against police has been widespread, with 185 deaths in 2000, both on and off duty; but the new law would not prevent the use of force in self-defense.) President Mbeki deferred to law enforcement concerns and failed to sign off on the legislation.

In May 2002, after four years of administrative dithering and delay, the Constitutional Court found Section 49 to be a violation of the rights to life, dignity, and bodily integrity and imposed a standard embracing the proportionality principle—that the officer's response to a suspect's flight should reflect the seriousness of the harm or potential harm presented by the situation. An officer could use deadly force to make an arrest only when he or she reasonably believed that the suspect posed an "immediate threat of serious bodily harm" or had committed a crime that caused or threatened such harm.[127] Although the court remarked that the 1998 law could be put into effect immediately, it was only in July 2003 that the president signed it. While no challenge to its constitutionality seems likely and training of police now includes instruction in what they can and cannot do when using force with suspects, whether police will honor the new standard remains to be seen.

An assessment of judicial commitment to human rights encounters many obstacles. At every level it is difficult to obtain useful information. All but the most serious cases are tried in the magistrates' courts, which do not publish judgments and are rarely studied. Official data on the performance of the lower courts include only referrals to court (not arrests), withdrawals from prosecution (because of insufficient evidence, missing witnesses, and the like), and convictions. As a general matter magistrates' observance of constitutional limitations on criminal procedure is monitored only by the opportunity for appeals, which is rarely exercised. The anxiety about general lawlessness in South Africa appears to be so intense that research on due process and fairness as an aspect of the courts' performance is neglected in favor of the study of why cases are not prosecuted and what accounts for the relatively low rate of convictions.[128] Finally, with a few exceptions, neither magistrates nor judges were willing to testify before the TRC on the role of the judiciary in perpetuating apartheid, an exercise that might have produced a self-imposed standard against which to measure present performance. The five top judges sitting in 1997 who did submit a statement were aware of the importance of acknowledging human rights abuses in the legal profession, "not as an end in itself, but as a prerequisite to the discharge of our present and future responsibilities for the achievement of constitutional goals; democracy, human dignity, freedom and equality."[129]

The shortcomings of research and documentation have meant that examining how the courts have discharged those responsibilities in criminal matters is a speculative enterprise. It requires taking a top-down view, examining the perspective taken by the Constitutional Court on both procedural questions and substantive rights. Anecdotal evidence from lawyers and social workers with experience in trial court proceedings provides only a limited view of the extent to which the ethic of a rights culture has permeated the lower reaches of criminal justice.

In the early post-apartheid years the Constitutional Court set aside a number of legislative decisions made by the previous governments that could not meet human rights standards of the new. "[O]ld rules and practices can no longer be taken for granted," the court announced. "[T]hey must be subjected to constant re-assessment to bring them into line with the provisions of the Constitution."[130] The Criminal Procedure Act of 1977—neutral on its face but harboring the potential for many oppressive outcomes—took a particularly hard drubbing. The court threw out a section that had enabled the summary conviction of political defendants during apartheid, a presumption that a confession made before a magistrate was voluntary.[131] Noting that "[a] culture of authority which legitimates the use of violence is inconsistent with the values for which the Constitution stands," the justices also held that juvenile whipping was "a cruel, inhuman and degrading punishment" and that the section authorizing it violated the right to protection of one's dignity and the right to freedom and security of the person.[132] A provision that denied a prisoner who did not have legal representation the right to an automatic appeal from a magistrates' court was held to violate the right to a fair trial as well as the guarantee of equal protection of the law.[133]

The Constitutional Court also engaged in a kind of constitutional housecleaning by nullifying a number of provisions in old laws that negated the presumption of innocence. It threw out a section of the Drugs and Drug Trafficking Act that provided that a person found in possession of 115 grams of marijuana (*dagga* in South Africa) was deemed to be dealing in the drug; the burden of proving the contrary would fall on the accused.[134] Similarly, it disallowed the presumption in the apartheid-era Gambling Act that the presence of cards or dice in a place or on a person indicated that proscribed gambling was occurring.[135] Requiring a person to come to court and provide evidence to rebut these presumptions, the court said, would violate the general right to a fair trial and the rights included in it to silence and to be presumed innocent until a prosecutor had established guilt beyond a reasonable doubt. (It is puzzling that the prosecutors in these cases—representatives of the new democratic state—were defending the draconian policies of the bad old days.)

The constitution provides the right to legal representation paid for by the state to any arrested, detained, or accused person "if substantial injustice would otherwise result."[136] The court has not yet been called upon to interpret this vague standard, which is bound to present a major challenge.[137] Unless the definition of substantial injustice is very narrow, the right will be too costly to implement. A quick check of newspaper accounts in 2003 suggests that indigent defendants charged with the most serious violence are offered free legal aid in most cases, at least in urban courts. And an early sign of the High Courts' commitment to that goal was the release in 1998 of a man convicted of hijacking—a frightening crime that had been on the rise—because he had not been informed of his right to a lawyer. Yet with most defendants in the magistrates' courts unrepresented and the lack of state resources to subsidize legal services for the poor, the right to a lawyer is likely in the short term to remain more theoretical than real. The shortage of lawyers to represent defendants is also one of the causes of the appalling backlog in South African courts—almost fifty thousand detainees awaiting trial in September 2003, some of them for several years.[138]

There are, however, significant efforts to realize the promise of free legal aid for criminal defendants. The publicly supported Legal Aid Board has reorganized so that, with its own complement of full-time, salaried lawyers, it no longer needs to rely solely on more expensive private attorneys. With forty-four legal assistance centers (as of March 2003) around the country and plans for sixteen more, as well as a legal aid officer in every magistrates' court, it has vastly increased its services since 1994. The Legal Resources Centre, the country's preeminent public interest law firm, and law clinics in universities take some criminal cases on a pro bono basis. And the Law Society for the Western Cape—the professional association for attorneys—has begun to require that all its members do a minimum of three days of pro bono work annually; if implemented nationwide and directed to serving in criminal cases, this policy would contribute significantly to easing the shortage of lawyers for poor people accused of crime. Of considerable political interest are two situations in which the Legal Aid Board, amid great controversy, footed the bill in high-profile cases. By providing partial support for the private legal team defending liberation hero Allan Boesak in 1999 and, in 2003, paying the legal expenses of the right-wing Boeremag defendants, the board has sent a message that the principle of assistance for those who cannot pay (often honored in the breach, to be sure) will apply without regard to the political sympathies of the accused.

Criminal defendants have many grievances besides insufficient legal representation. Even when lawyers are assigned to them, they may wait for months or years for their cases to be heard; where defendants must sit out the delay in detention, they can justly assert that fundamental rights have been denied. Prosecutors and judges are accused of keeping bankers' hours; an audit conducted by the office of the national director of public prosecutions in 1999 found that serious cases—those that ended up in the High Courts—took an average of 520 days to proceed from the first court appearance to sentencing.[139] The lack of support services in the magistrates' courts worsens delays, prisoners awaiting trial must do so in very cramped conditions, and the risk of violence between inmates is high. While there are relatively few allegations by prisoners of assaults by wardens and guards in the overcrowded prisons—582 recorded in a total prison population of more than 185,000 in 2002—it may be that there is much brutality that is not reported for fear of retaliation.[140]

Where intense criticism of court decisions in criminal cases arises, it is generally in the form of outrage about acquittals or what are perceived as light sentences. Even without a victims' rights movement of the kind that has developed in the United States in recent years the South African press and public exhibit particularly keen concern for crime victims. The dominant punishment rationale is often retribution, with strong support for long sentences—or sentences seen as proportional to the seriousness of the crime—that are deemed to be the only proper tribute to the dignity of the victim. In the case of the right-wing defendants who had beaten the hunchback to death, the Court of Appeal rejected the lenient sentence of the trial court (it may do this only when the sentence is "disturbingly inappropriate" or grossly disproportionate to the seriousness of the offense) and resentenced the accused to twelve years' imprisonment (with two years suspended for time served). The opinion rebuked the trial court judge for giving too much weight to the defendants' situation "without balancing these considerations properly against the very serious nature of the crime committed, the many very aggravating circumstances that accompanied its commission, its actual and potentially serious consequences for others, and the interests and legitimate expectations of the South African community at a very crucial time in its transition from a manifestly and sadly racist past to a constitutional democracy premised on a commitment to a constitutionally protected and expressly articulated culture of human rights."[141] As with many cases in today's South Africa the human rights issue here is thus the affirmative grant of protection for the victim rather than the concern with holding the government accountable through the negative protections of due process.

Commitment to the rule of law is a hallmark of constitutional democracy, and South Africa has certainly made that commitment. But the rule of law can be simply the convenient strategy of powerful political actors rather than a means of restraining government power. Given South Africa's particular concern with victims and the country's history of brutal repression of blacks and the whites that championed their cause, it is not surprising that the public and some legal observers were angered by the outcome of several court cases that failed to convict apartheid criminals. In 1996 Magnus Malan, the former minister of defense and a protégé of apartheid prime minister P. W. Botha, was acquitted along with fifteen other defendants of the 1987 slaughter of thirteen people. The victims, mostly women and children, were attacked as they slept in what was described by the prosecution as political vengeance intended for an ANC supporter and principally carried out by members of the rival, more conservative Inkatha Freedom Party. The judge found that the prosecution was lackluster and the evidence insufficient for a conviction, and indeed the prosecutor had failed to prove his contention that the attack was authorized by the government by calling as witnesses police and military officials who might have sealed the defendants' fate. Even though Malan had carried out the apartheid government's "total onslaught" strategy against antiapartheid activists Nelson Mandela resisted pleas to intervene in the case and announced support for the verdict. However, given the magnitude of the massacre and its presumed source, adherence to the rule of law in acquitting the defendants seemed to many to be less a constraint on the government impelled by the prosecution's failure to rebut the presumption of innocence than a convenient choice for a judge (and a passive prosecutor) sympathetic to the accused. "South African law has been like this and it's always going to be like this. Murderers go free," said the brother of the man whose house was raided.[142]

Echoes of the case reverberated six years later when Wouter Basson—a chemical warfare expert dubbed "Doctor Death" because of his reputation for killing antiapartheid activists—was acquitted on forty-six charges of murder, assault, fraud, and drug dealing. With Magnus Malan attending the trial to provide Basson with moral support and the brother of the leader of the right-wing Conservative Party as the sitting judge, observers of the case could be forgiven for suggesting that some prosecutors and judges are still not beyond using the requirement of proof of guilt beyond a reasonable doubt to absolve former abusers of human rights. Arguing that the state had not made its case against Basson, the Supreme Court of Appeal refused to retry the defendant, but the Constitutional Court ruled that there were constitutional issues raised by the charges of judicial bias and that the Supreme Court of Appeal erred in refusing to allow the state to appeal the trial court's decision.[143] As of this writing it is not clear whether Basson will be retried.

Despite failures of implementation, the ordinary citizen clearly believes that a turnaround in the state's respect for human rights has occurred. A greater willingness to go to the police when a crime occurs and an increase in the demand for legal assistance both testify to the general view that the institutions of criminal justice are now committed to public protection. This shift of attitude does not, however, mean that people are forgiving of inept or lazy police or of lengthy court delays and sentences perceived as too lenient. The public is now much more concerned about the effectiveness of police and courts in controlling crime than about their political legitimacy. (It may be that this shift has occurred so rapidly in part because for many the courts enjoyed some legitimacy even during apartheid, unlike police.) Justice for victims—usually defined as a long sentence for a violent offender—is seen as an important right, and the appellate courts are prepared to enforce it, particularly when the victim is especially vulnerable, as in the cases of the defendant who had raped his fourteen-year-old daughter and the whites who had beaten the black hunchback to death.

In fact, if journalistic accounts and anecdotes on the ground are to be believed, the public thinks that the police and courts charged with carrying out the mandates of the constitution give suspects and defendants *too many* rights. The constitution is often denounced as "criminal-friendly." "It is unthinkable that state funds should be used to fight criminals and at the same time be used to defend the criminals in court," a letter to the editor of *Business Day* complained in 2003, giving expression to the views of many.[144] This perspective helps explain the high degree of vigilantism in many parts of the country and probably supports the police assertion that the public wishes them to have free rein with suspects. In this respect, the criminological environment looks strikingly like that of many Western countries: the popular view is that the niceties of due process are expendable if police are not catching enough criminals and judges are not incarcerating enough offenders for sufficiently long periods to control crime. Criminologists are likely to assail the presumed connection between unrestrained law enforcement and a reduction in crime; the prevailing academic view is that police cannot prevent most crime and that incarceration rarely rehabilitates or deters. But the direction of South African citizens' criticisms suggests that once the state's coercive forces are not directed against them, they will support their vigorous exercise—unmodified by human rights protections—against others that they view as wrongdoers.

A Note on Representation

South Africa is unique among recently democratizing countries in the extent to which the old regime was driven by an ideology of race. So the task of bringing the majority racial group into the government adds a special dimension to the challenges of democracy building. But South Africa is hardly the only country undergoing transition in which ethnic and political rivalries dominate political life. Representation of a country's various demographic groups in official decision-making does not constitute political transformation; only the quality of those decisions and the values behind them can accomplish that. But the presence in government of faces and names and backgrounds that ordinary citizens recognize as mirroring their own has both instrumental and moral benefits; it can help to resolve cultural and political conflict through reduced suspicion of the government, and it exemplifies an aspect of self-government. If the major demographic groups do not share in the actions and transactions of criminal justice institutions, they cannot be democratically legitimate. And greater sympathy for the problems of law enforcement and courts is likely if the citizen feels some identification of race, ethnicity, gender, class, or ideology with police, judges, and prosecutors.

It therefore seems worthwhile to note that South Africa has made significant progress in bringing blacks and women into positions of influence in the criminal justice system. Despite the retention for five years of many civil servants required by the negotiations that ended apartheid, police and courts are well on the way to realizing the constitutional mandate that "[p]ublic administration must be broadly representative of the South African people, with employment and personnel management practices based on . . . the need to redress the imbalances of the past to achieve broad representation."[145] Attrition and job creation have brought three (of five) black deputy commissioners into the SAPS, as of 2003, and seven (of twelve) black divisional commissioners. The constabulary has long been predominantly black, and the national police commissioner and the minister for safety and security are both African.[146] (It should perhaps be noted, however, that of the top eighteen positions in the SAPS only four are held by women.) The national director of the prosecuting authority is black, as are many of the members of the elite team of prosecutors and investigators, the Scorpions (officially known as the Directorate of Special Operations), that was formed in 1999 and enjoys great prestige in its pursuit of high-profile offenders, whether they are denizens of organized crime or corrupt public officials. As of early 2003, 44 percent of the legal personnel of the National Prosecuting Authority were women, slightly more than half of whom were black.[147]

Integrating (or "transforming," as South Africans would say) the bench has been slower because of the shortage of well-qualified black and female lawyers who are willing to forgo lucrative opportunities in the private sector. While blacks were never formally prohibited from entering the legal profession during apartheid, the barriers were formidable. Latin was required for admission to the study of law but was not taught in black schools. A university education was required for becoming an apprentice in a law firm, yet many universities, particularly those in urban centers, were not open to black students. Nelson Mandela, in his autobiography, writes of his law practice with Oliver Tambo in the 1950s, "[E]ven as we practiced and fought and won cases, we always knew that no matter how well we pursued our careers as attorneys, we could never become a prosecutor, a magistrate, a judge."[148] Later, under the Group Areas Act, black lawyers were not allowed to practice in "white" areas; stories of black lawyers who had to borrow the offices of sympathetic white colleagues when they needed to interview clients—including the future chief justice of the Supreme Court of Appeal—are legion.

This history, and the resulting lack of exposure to a wide range of professional opportunities, has dictated that true race and gender representation on the bench has taken what many regard as too long to achieve. The creation of new opportunities in the magistracy has occurred more rapidly than in the judiciary; blacks and women had already begun to integrate its ranks before the end of apartheid, and the appointment process could be managed more efficiently by the government. Nonetheless, there have been complaints that judicial assignment to civil cases is more likely to go to whites, while the criminal courts—regarded as hardship posts—are more likely to be staffed by blacks.[149] The slower pace of integrating the upper courts has been a source of frustration for many South Africans, but enlarging the pool of judicial candidates required structural change in the legal profession and a process by which black and female lawyers (and legal academics, who had previously been excluded from judgeships) could acquire the experience generally considered technically necessary to ascend to the bench. Very soon after the end of apartheid attorneys were empowered to appear for clients in the upper courts, and both experienced attorneys and magistrates became eligible to apply for judgeships. With some reluctance advocates endorsed these changes, which broke open the elite ranks of the legal profession. By early 2000 training courses for judicial aspirants were under way, and new judges were attending an orientation course that instructed them in such matters as the management of trials, writing judgments, and judicial ethics. It has become standard practice to give black and female judicial candidates who lacked the professional experience that apartheid had denied them but who otherwise showed professional promise a kind of apprenticeship as acting judges before making permanent appointments. As one prominent judge sees it, although the new judges are less experienced in the law and have less understanding of "court craft," the bench is enriched by the diversity they bring to it, and their training has improved since the early post-apartheid days.[150]

In July 2003 the chief justice announced that there were 214 judges—sixty-one black males, twelve black females, thirteen white females, and 128 white males.[151] This meant that 40 percent of the higher judiciary was black or female, still not fully representative in a country that is 75 percent black and more than 50 percent female. It represents, however, a major step toward race and gender transformation in a single decade; it is less likely every year that the bench will be described as "male and pale," as one Supreme Court of Appeal judge put it with a sigh in early 2000.[152] Until 1990 there was not a single black judge (and only two women); the late Ismail Mahomed, who later became the country's deputy chief justice and president of the Supreme Court of Appeal, was appointed later the following year. Furthermore, blacks have assumed leadership roles in the judiciary very quickly. All the judge presidents of the judicial districts (roughly corresponding to the provinces) are now African, and Pius Langa, the successor to Arthur Chaskalson, South Africa's first post-apartheid chief justice is African. The Supreme Court of Appeal has been slowest to integrate; the death of Judge Mahomed in 2000 left it once again a province of white males, though two Africans, one Indian, and two women have been appointed as of this writing. The Constitutional Court, created in 1994 to hear only constitutional matters, currently consists of eight men and two women (with one vacancy); three judges are white, six African, and one Indian. There is as yet no coloured judge on either the Supreme Court of Appeal or the Constitutional Court.

The magistracy has integrated more rapidly than the judiciary, perhaps because the requirements for education and experience were less stringent and the pool of eligible candidates was therefore larger. The new government, eager to advance blacks who had been held back by apartheid laws—blacks were prohibited from serving as magistrates or prosecutors in courts where whites appeared, for example—also had more control over the appointment process. Of 1,779 magistrates serving (in both district and regional courts) as of May 2004, 1,275 were men and 504 women; 49 percent were black.[153] The racial breakdown was as follows:

White	903
African	648
Indian	130
Coloured	98

Of the twenty-three chief magistrates, who are responsible for the leadership of lower courts in a large region, five were women; 61 percent (fourteen) were black.

Conclusion

South Africa has made great strides in repoliticizing the police, assuring judicial independence and accountability, purging corruption and bias from police and courts, and honoring human rights in the operations of criminal justice. In shifting the constituency of justice institutions from the state to the citizens it has conformed to basic ideals of its constitutional democracy. As a result, despite lingering police corruption, dreadful court delays, and widespread public ignorance about the new rights culture, the criminal justice system has acquired legitimacy that was lacking for most of South Africa's history. Nonetheless, it has disappointed both the ordinary citizen who hoped for a respite from the violent crime of a society with a history of repression and inequality and the reformer who saw it as a potential source of public empowerment. The ability of the justice system to fulfill the promise of democratic *performance*, as opposed to democratic *procedure*, is still unrealized. Whether the continuing scourge of violent crime and the failures of the justice system to respond to it effectively will be a source of destabilization for the country remains to be seen.

III Deepening Democracy through Social Ordering
Theory and Practice

7 Public-Empowering Justice
Resource for a New Democracy

> The stress on transformation is at the heart of the strong
> democratic conception of politics.
> —Benjamin Barber[1]

> Governance is now everybody's business.
> —Les Johnston and Clifford Shearing[2]

A PERSISTENT THEME in this book is that, to the greatest extent consistent with the inherently coercive role of the state and the rights-oriented constitution, democratic criminal justice in South Africa requires a direction that empowers citizens to make crucial decisions about responding to crime and disorder—a national program that gives them the freedom and the resources to participate in making their communities safer. The view that developments in criminal justice reflect the process of democratization, and that public empowerment in that area is an important part of the process, is based on the confluence of ideas in political science and criminology and on observations of the history of community life in both established and embryonic democracies. This chapter discusses the potential accomplishments and limitations of a commitment to public-empowering criminal justice policies and practices in light of recent thinking about community policing and restorative justice and, more generally, about participatory and deliberative democracy. Deliberative democracy brings people together to reason; community policing and restorative justice (and related programs) bring them together to act. Jointly, they express a yearning for a more participatory political life and the faith that ordinary people can chart a course for regulating their own behavior in many situations.

Experiments in public-empowering criminal justice are taking place in many parts of the world. In the United States and many other countries—Australia, New Zealand, and Japan, as well as western Europe—attention has turned to the local potential for preventing and dealing with some kinds of crime. The community as well as the individual victim suffer from social disorder, the reasoning goes, and community forces (as well as structural changes that improve the lives of potential victims and offenders) may be best able to deal with that disorder and the crimes it spawns. The argument does not exclude the professional roles of police, prosecutor, judge, and jailer, but it assumes that they can, in many instances, be diffused in a variety of local initiatives in which ordinary citizens participate or even take the lead. The approach appeals to democratic attributes quite different from the pluralistic competition that creates accountable, transparent, rights-oriented institutions of governance. It calls on citizens to cooperate, rather than to compete; it aims for group consensus rather than majority victory. Civil society shares power with the state in some spheres and acts independently in others. Although public-empowering justice does not turn away from vindication for victims and punishment for offenders, individual remedies for crime and disorder are secondary to the goal of community harmony.

What is meant by "community" in this discussion is both less and more than some uses of the term. As "the most fundamental and far-reaching of sociology's unit-ideas," the notion of community has been defined by philosophers and sociologists to encompass all deeply rooted human relationships, collective and individual, that transcend the roles and associations formed by choice and law.[3] At a more practical level, it also denotes the administrative and geographic boundaries of city neighborhoods and rural hamlets. In discussing community policing I will assume the conventional contemporary use of "community" to mean a legally bounded area over which public police exert authority; but for the purpose of presenting a frame within which public-empowering justice could develop, I will use a definition of community that closely conforms to the one embraced by prominent advocates of community justice, Todd Clear and David Karp. They conceive community as "a quality of social existence: an indication of solidarity, shared practices and traditions, and emotional connectedness."[4] Attachment to multiple kinds of community varies in intensity over time and according to shifting priorities. Relevant communities are not bound by the ascribed status of family and ethnicity and faith, nor do they encompass all realms of modern life. They are the environments in which modern citizens work and play and live—environments where we should feel safe and secure.

From both theoretical and practical standpoints public-empowering justice is particularly important to consolidate democracy in countries in transition from authoritarian regimes. It can help to mend the social fabric in damaged communities, whether because it helps to reduce crime or simply because it gives citizens a role in working—sometimes on their own, sometimes with the state—to improve the conditions of their lives. It can foster understanding of inclusive, participatory ideals that shape vibrant democracies (and begin to counter some traditional attitudes, like the subservience of women, that impede democratic progress). These conclusions apply with particular force to South Africa, where apartheid's scars are visible in the flesh of social life everywhere, particularly in the urban townships where violent crime is epidemic, and where democracy must bridge cultural chasms to flourish. In addition, participation in this kind of social ordering furthers both the mutuality and the autonomy that are at the heart of substantive ambitions for democracy. It signals what Benjamin Barber calls "strong democracy," self-government where "the possibilities of transforming private into public, dependency into interdependency, conflict into cooperation, license into self-legislation, need into love, and bondage into citizenship are placed in a context of participation."[5] Limitations exist on how much can be achieved and under what conditions, to be sure, but neither social control nor democracy is perfectly achievable under any formulation. And, whether from cultural background or political experience, South Africans—particularly the African populations—have traditions of participatory self-government to draw on as they take control of some justice functions.

Criminal Justice on the Defensive

In the Anglo-American democracies, and to a lesser extent in a number of western European countries, criminal justice policy is in what several criminologists have called a "watershed" period.[6] Old institutions are crumbling or being restructured and new ones—sometimes with seasoned roots—are emerging. Policing is no longer primarily a state function; in many countries—among them the United States and South Africa—private providers of policing outnumber those sponsored by governments. Under attack are the welfare state attitudes that, for a generation, tempered a classically punitive perspective on wrongdoers. In reaction to that period, the moralistic perspective prevails once more and dictates long, mandatory sentences—especially in the United States, but also in England and Canada—for even relatively minor offenses. Cynicism has displaced ambitions for the rehabilitation of offenders; criminal justice professionals view the management of the risks they present—through incarceration and surveillance—as the best that can be achieved.[7] The prevention of crime through redistributive and welfare policies—job-training programs and financial incentives for employers willing to take a chance on the unskilled, public assistance based on need rather than desert—is now largely thought to be futile. The minimalist view that is currently fashionable advances what is called situational or environmental prevention, efforts to defend communities with locks and "defensible space" architecture and neighborhood watch activities, quite independent of a focus on the sins or problems of those who made that defense necessary.[8] And doubt has assailed the ideals of professionalism in law enforcement. Now that the primacy of crime-fighting in policing and discretion in judicial decision-making is under fire, role definitions and purposes in these occupations are increasingly unclear.

Although its dimensions and implications differ in countries in transition from authoritarianism, the criminal justice crisis is not limited to Western democracies. Police and courts from Brazil to Poland are seen as ineffective at controlling crime and brutal or biased in relating to the public. Sometimes democratization is blamed for the breakdown of crime control; eastern Europeans complain that the openness of democracy and the new market society have brought them unprecedented crime problems like gangs, organized theft, and prostitution. On the other hand, police and courts often contribute to violence, as in Latin America, signaling limits to democratic consolidation; much of the urban violence that has plagued Brazil since the early 1990s is attributable to the military police, whose repressive traditions often prevail over attempted reforms.[9] Corruption in the police and the judiciary is routine in Africa and South America. Vigilantes both threaten and protect communities who cannot get help from state institutions. Human Rights Watch regularly decries the gap between policy and performance in countries like Nigeria, where, despite official declarations of reform and international aid for training in potentially violent encounters like crowd control, brutality and torture by the police are rarely punished.[10] In many countries the corruption of the police and courts is inseparable from general state corruption and is therefore unreachable without revolution.

The criminal justice crisis includes not only its perceived inability to control crime but also its frequent neglect or abuse of those it is theoretically designed to protect. As they have gained professional authority and political power, women all over the world have protested the justice system's indifference to widespread rape and domestic violence. American police brutality, born of excessive zeal in the pursuit of lawbreakers, especially blacks in inner-city neighborhoods, is well known. Even in the relatively peaceful Netherlands, where bicycle thefts and shoplifting are serious offenses and police are prohibited from using devious methods to obtain a confession, the practice of isolating and interrogating the accused in a small room with photos of the victim covering the walls was used for a decade until public attention brought a stop to it.[11] In democratizing countries distrust of police and judges is a predictable obstacle to be overcome as new regimes try to find a new balance between the role of criminal justice in representing the state and its responsibility to protect the public. Habits of brutality and bias die hard even when the directives change. The deadly police violence that has accompanied democratization in Brazil since the mid-1980s still includes beatings and shootings of the homeless and activists who represent them.[12]

Criminal justice is also open to the charge that it is manifestly incapable of responding to the criminogenic effects of political and economic changes occurring around the world. In the Anglo-American democracies, particularly the United States, the political mind-set that sees poor people and criminal offenders as sinners and losers in a sink-or-swim marketplace rejects the modest welfare state policies that may formerly have reduced incentives for some kinds of crime. Globalization has few remedies for the displacements and despair it fosters as agricultural subsidies in rich countries deprive people of their livelihoods in poor ones. Research on the effects of trade policies on crime is still scant, but revealing incidents abound. Peruvian coca farmers, whose crops were being eradicated so that Peru could get preferential trade status under the United States Andean Trade Promotion and Drug Eradication Act, protested violently—and some turned to the cultivation of opium poppies instead.[13] And the opening of borders not only provides new opportunities for transnational crime but destabilizes communities, as smuggled guns bring more violence and the importation of women and girls brings new sex businesses.

To a considerable extent, the worldwide criminal justice crisis is one of confidence. Public opinion tends to overestimate the severity of crime and underestimate the severity of the state's responses to it. And media reports greatly exaggerate the incidence of violent crime relative to property crime in both industrialized and developing countries. David Garland's magisterial and persuasive analysis of crime in our time argues that as a "normal social fact" crime has become a symbol of larger forces that characterize late modernity in Western societies and undermine, for both the public and officials, faith in the institutions of the welfare state.[14] Responses to these changes, Garland concludes, constitute a social and political realignment that embraces economic neoliberalism and social conservatism and has redirected social policy in general and penal policy in particular. While this conclusion surely has validity for the United States and the United Kingdom, the countries that formed the basis for Garland's study, a simpler observation is also valid.

Over the past generation officials, scholars and—to a lesser extent—citizens have become aware, in varying degrees, that crime is, to a considerable degree and in the countries where it can be studied, independent of what the criminal justice system does to contain it. In the United States, for example, it now seems quite clear that neither increasing police patrol nor improving response time will significantly reduce crime.[15] And, for many kinds of offenders poised to commit a property or violent crime, the prospect of punishment does not deter, even when it seems relatively likely.[16] If we had comparable research in other countries, it would probably suggest that the rules and rationales of crime control policy have less effect on crime than does the countries' culture, political economy, or degree of political stability. All over the developed world and in many developing countries some kinds of crime appear to have risen, yet crime policies vary tremendously. In countries like Japan and Switzerland victimization has remained relatively low despite lenient policies.[17] In Singapore it is low also, but there the penalties for even minor crimes—some readers will recall the flogging of an American youth for scrawling graffiti—are harsher than would generally be permitted in a constitutional democracy. The United States is admittedly the outlier of Western states, with its high homicide and robbery rates driven in part by easy access to guns and by economic and social deprivation.[18] Despite a substantial drop in the 1990s for reasons that are still in dispute, crime remains relatively high there, resistant to punitive policies and resulting record incarceration rates (which have increased much more than crime). The inescapable conclusion in looking at a typical Western democracy is that its criminal justice system—and probably that of less-studied countries as well—cannot make a very large dent in ordinary crime.[19]

This does not mean that police cannot catch offenders or that courts cannot convict and sentence them. But dispatching criminals to probation or prison is not the same as reducing crime. (For that to occur the traditional rationales for punishment—deterrence, incapacitation, and rehabilitation—would have to be more effective than we know them to be. The reality is that potential offenders may discount evidence that some must pay for their sins, successors to the miscreants in custody may quickly fill in for them, and convicted offenders may learn nothing more effective in prison than more sophisticated kinds of criminality.) The activities of capture and containment will always be largely symbolic because structural factors determine what kinds of crime will occur and because there is so much slippage in even the most efficient justice system. To begin with, the vast majority of wrongdoing goes undetected; surveys have shown that most people—Americans, at least—have committed some sort of offense, and all but a few get away with it.[20] Crime is often detected but not reported—either the victim doesn't think it important enough to report or doesn't have enough faith that police and courts will respond.[21] Furthermore, routine and inevitable flaws in the process—some human, some institutional—will result in attrition from it. Reluctant witnesses cannot be forced to testify, and ambiguous evidence will rarely persuade a judge or jury of culpability. Finally, constitutional democracy builds in contradictions to its general aim of protection for the law-abiding majority—the presumption of innocence (made operational in criminal trials by the standard of proving guilt beyond a reasonable doubt), constraints on state intrusions into personal privacy, limits on what the police can do to get a confession. A study of the criminal justice process in New South Wales, Australia, illustrates the case filtering that occurs; it found that out of every 156 crimes (limited to breaking and entering, motor vehicle theft, robbery and assault) only 1 resulted in a prison sentence.[22]

The public—and the politicians that represent them in a democracy—doesn't buy the symbolic nature of official efforts to bring the culprits to book. Especially in an era of economic and political insecurity—both national and global—people want present victimizations sanctioned and future victimizations prevented. And when it doesn't happen, they blame defects in state service delivery rather than acknowledging inherent limitations in what official institutions can do to bring about and maintain domestic peace. Garland describes the general public attitude in the United States and the United Kingdom as "an 'absolutist' conception . . . that demands justice, punishment and protection, whatever the cost."[23] South Africans share the demand; in a 2002 survey a huge majority (82 percent) reported dissatisfaction with the government's efforts to control crime, and when people are asked why there is so much vigilante activity the common answer is that vigilantes can do what government will not or cannot do.[24] In recent decades politicians have seized upon public impatience and anger (and the media attention given to crime) to demand that police be given greater license and that courts impose harsher penalties for even minor crimes. All over the world prison is the preferred sanction for serious crime, especially in developing and transitional countries and in Anglo-Saxon countries, according to the International Crime Victim Survey conducted by the United Nations.[25] The tendency toward greater punitiveness is developing in Europe as well, sometimes analyzed as the "Americanization" of crime control policy.[26] As with the American pattern, it is those at the margins of economic and social life who are targets—immigrants and foreigners in Europe instead of black and brown citizens in the United States.[27]

Our limited statistical picture does not give us a clear picture of whether or not the world has really become a less law-abiding place in recent years. Official crime data, which do indeed show higher crime rates over the past generation, are notoriously bad in most countries, partly because they are based on only the crimes that are reported to police. Furthermore, the frequency with which people report crime to the police depends on the degree of confidence they have in the justice system.[28] Only a small (but growing) number of countries and the United Nations conduct studies of victimization, which are based on interviews with a representative sample of residents and are probably more reliable than police data. Crime becomes easier to report with every technological advance in communications—first the availability of telephones, then the computerization of records; as a result, some of what appears to be a crime wave is surely at least partly a reporting wave. Increases in reported crime may also reflect a country's growing ability to pay for police to record offenses. And definitions of what is criminal are anything but fixed; they tend toward expansion, reflecting public or political views about what behavior deserves sanctioning. Definitional differences among countries also make international trend data problematic, though some general patterns are discernible, like increases in theft in eastern European countries in the early years after the breakup of the Soviet Union.

Despite the data problems that make many conclusions about international crime trends suspect, developments in social and economic life in some countries support official reports of rising violent and property crime around the world.[29] The experiences of democratic transition and the emergence of a country from civil wars or bloody regional conflicts seem equally criminogenic. (In the countries of Central America criminal violence now exceeds the political violence of the past, and the end of the cold war brought bloody new struggles over resources—diamonds in particular—to a number of African countries.)[30] Greater availability of firearms increases the likelihood that an assault will be fatal. Greater physical mobility of desperate people adds to the misery of the slum and exposes comfortable suburbanites to predatory acts they only read about in the past. Wider gaps between rich and poor—especially where television is easily accessible and displays the disparity—heighten the sense that there is little to lose from a burglary that might meet the material needs of young people who have no hope of satisfying them legitimately. Democratizing countries are also often embracing free trade, economic restructuring, and other features of unbridled global capitalism. The pressure to be globally competitive has forced businesses in many countries to shed workers, and in an environment of reduced employment combined with expanded personal freedom criminal incentives abound. (While high unemployment is often associated with increases in some kinds of crime, other kinds depend on employment—embezzlement, public corruption, and corporate fraud, for example. But that kind of crime—although it too takes its greatest toll on ordinary citizens—rarely generates the public and political outcry that follows uncontrolled street crime.) Finally, as national borders become ever more porous, transnational opportunities for smuggling, fraud, and the distribution of drugs and arms present new challenges to law enforcement, both national and international.

It seems incontrovertible that in many parts of the world criminal justice as conventionally conceived is neither providing basic physical security nor treating victims and offenders justly nor maintaining social order in a way that enriches the quality of life. If that situation continues, the consequences will be severe for the comfort of citizens of Western democracies. For other parts of the world they will be more dire. Where police and courts are not respected, the hard-won legitimacy of countries in transition to liberal democracy may be at risk. Representative democrats, after all, delegate the management of the polity to such officials; their performance is an important aspect of the credibility of such a political system.

The Policy Watershed

With such persuasive evidence of an authority crisis in criminal justice worldwide it is not surprising that major policy shifts have been occurring over the past decades. It is hard to trace a direct line of cause and effect from disillusionment to transformation, but some patterns of response emerge. While there is considerable variation from country to country in the degree and nature of the changes and the patterns are clearest in the democratic West, they can also be seen in some democratizing countries. What we might call "watershed responses" seem to have taken two directions. One is the embrace of harsher approaches—"zero tolerance" policing, punishments for all but the most trivial of offenses—by the state. Current get-tough programs reject the prospect of human improvement through offenders' contacts with police, courts, and prisons. Instead, they endorse police sweeps as management of the inner city, harsh punishment for its own sake or for its utility in keeping malefactors off the streets temporarily.[31] The other reaction is the fragmentation of policing and judging into practices that are sometimes public, sometimes private, and often an amalgam. In an implicit rejection of the Weberian assumption that states are defined in part by their monopoly of the use of force, many contemporary governments have ceded to private industry and civil society some part of the functions of crime prevention, order maintenance, dispute resolution, custodial supervision, and incarceration. "Policing now belongs to everybody," say David Bayley and Clifford Shearing; and when prison management is contracted out to private corporations and probation supervised by community groups, the same could be said of sanctioning.[32] It is a peculiar era with the two trends operating in tandem: the state tightens the noose on individual behavior even as neoliberal impulses encourage the proliferation of private sources—corporate security and citizen volunteers alike—to secure community spaces.

Data from the United States and the United Kingdom and from a few European countries suggest the development of the punitive policy trend, tempered—or, some would say, supplemented—by an orientation to corporate and community involvement in maintaining order. But dangers abound in extrapolating from the world's most studied—and, for the United States, most punitive—countries to others with very different cultural habits and political attitudes. The United Nations has tried to elicit trends in the behavior of criminal justice systems in dozens of countries through surveys conducted every five years. They give us a few clues, although the United Nations Office on Drugs and Crime, which conducts the surveys, warns that "to use the figures as a basis for comparison between different countries is highly problematic."[33] Industrialized nations appear to arrest, prosecute, and convict offenders at higher rates than developing countries with, however, fluctuation over time that defies generalization.[34] Some of the eastern European countries that came into being with the dissolution of the Soviet Union appear to have addressed rising crime and attendant public dismay in the early 1990s with punitive policies—especially the Russian Federation, where prison admissions in 1994 reached 1,542 per 100,000 population.[35] (By comparison, the comparable rate for Hungary was 178, similar to rates for western European countries, which are quite stable.) An assessment of the incarceration rate by world regions suggests an upward trend in the period 1990–94 for New World countries (Australia, Canada, New Zealand, and the United States) as well as for countries in transition.[36] Taken together, these snapshots could indicate an international trend to try to stem crime by being more punitive. But the United Nations surveys are based on very incomplete data for individual countries, and rates for all steps in the justice process are susceptible to a number of different explanations. It may be, for instance, that the industrial countries are more aggressive in pursuing lawbreakers because they have the resources to do so. Or it may be that high prison admission rates reflect multiple admissions in a single year for many individuals or conceal high rates of parole releases; both situations would indicate that prison sentences are used for short-term discipline rather than longer-term segregation.

Nonetheless, it is hard to avoid the impression of a world that is embracing increasingly harsh penal policy, particularly in English-speaking countries and in countries emerging from authoritarianism. The turn to "law and order" politics in the United States and Britain is well known. The contest is no longer between lenient and punitive perspectives on how to deal with criminals but rather who can be toughest; both Republicans and Democrats in the United States and Conservatives and Laborites in the United Kingdom have embraced longer sentences and the "zero tolerance" notion for minor crimes.[37] Concerns about the costs and efficacy of the welfare state are surfacing in western European states as well as in the English-speaking world, and the preference for the punitive state over the welfare state has become contagious.

Some export of the "get tough" perspective—much of it from the United States—is under way, either through active consultation or by emulation. The United States Drug Enforcement Administration has more than two dozen field offices around the world; New York City's colorful former mayor Rudy Giuliani has been much in demand in Mexico and elsewhere for his administration's apparent success in riding herd on so-called quality-of-life offenses. As for countries in the throes of democratic consolidation, their citizens are appalled by crime that appears to have increased—or has at least become more visible than in the closed societies of dictators.[38] They often demand crackdowns on crime, a response that at first seems an anomalous and masochistic throwback to the bad old days but may simply indicate the human tendency to have recourse to the familiar.

Punitive policy approaches in democratizing countries do not necessarily give criminal justice operatives free rein. Reform of police and courts is high on the agenda of democratizing countries all over the world. Newly elected leaders vow to end police corruption, legislative bodies pass legislation to modernize and professionalize law enforcement, and nongovernmental organizations press transitional governments to end detention without trial. From the favelas of Brazil to the townships of South Africa officials have tried—with varying levels of commitment, it must be noted—to replace the gangs and vigilantes that conduct extralegal forms of often-violent policing with state-sponsored policing that assures fair, responsive public protection.[39] Assistance in the reform of institutions appropriate to a democracy has become globalized, with governments of developed countries (and their private foundations) providing judicial and police training to less developed ones. Scotland Yard and several Scandinavian governments have paid for and provided police training in post-apartheid South Africa, for example, and over the past decade the United States Agency for International Development (USAID) has supported the initiation of oral trials—more transparent and accessible than those with only written records—in several Latin American countries. International assistance in training police can sometimes serve as an incentive to persist with democratic reform when it faces local setbacks.[40]

As confidence in the crime control effects of arrest and incarceration has dwindled, crime prevention strategies have become complementary to the punitive, retributive policy approach. But in a time of shrinking budgets and socially conservative politics Western governments do not define prevention as redistributive policy that addresses the poverty and inequality that provide incentives for some kinds of crimes. Altering the physical environments where people conduct their daily lives—improving locks and lighting in urban neighborhoods, mounting closed circuit TV cameras for better surveillance of commercial areas—is cheaper and more visible—and thereby more politically salable—than tackling structural conditions. What is called the situational prevention strategy is based on the theory that most personal and property crime is opportunistic—"normal social fact" rather than deviant behavior reflecting deprivation or pathology—and can be prevented by reducing the immediate opportunities that present themselves.[41] The focus of criminological attention is no longer on the offender and his or her circumstances but on the criminal event; the purpose is not to make the guilty pay but to make the law-abiding secure.[42] (The principal theorists of what is called the "routine activity approach" describe the preconditions for the kind of crime they think to prevent as "the convergence in space and time of *likely offenders, suitable targets,* and the *absence of capable guardians*"—a fancy way of saying that susceptible people commit the crimes to which they have access when no one is in charge.)[43] Private security has long operated on the situational crime prevention principle; governments are latecomer participants. But this kind of prevention is now popular public policy in the United Kingdom (particularly) and the United States, and it has taken root in Scandinavia, the Netherlands, and Australia. And in democratizing Brazil responses to violence have included defensive architecture that segregates, protects, and conveys social status.[44]

There is considerable criminological debate about whether the situational approach actually reduces crime or merely displaces it to other locations, and whether it is effective in the most crime-ridden locations, the areas that presumably need it most.[45] (An influential review of American crime prevention measures found that "in study after study evidence emerges that crime prevention programs are more likely to take root, and more likely to work, in communities that need them least.")[46] And where some see this kind of crime prevention as protection, others see it as intrusive surveillance or needless, fear-inducing reminder of the risk of victimization. But no one disagrees that, even where governments sponsor preventive measures, public cooperation—and in many situations active public involvement—is necessary to implement them, whether they involve screening people for admission to buildings, moving youth recreational programs out of high-crime areas, or improving security systems in convenience stores.

In this respect situational crime prevention is part of the other trend—besides greater punitiveness—that is taking hold around the world. As scholars, practitioners, and ordinary citizens in the West have become increasingly disillusioned with the capacity of state institutions to protect or correct, they have turned to private sources of social ordering. Increasingly, profit-making security services supplement (and sometimes replace) public police, and commercial litigation these days is often conducted through privately sponsored mediation or arbitration. But the pluralization of roles in criminal justice extends beyond the market to include citizen participation—usually on a voluntary basis, but not always—in maintaining order, providing security and adjudicating some kinds of social conflicts. While its proponents often see this development as valuable assistance to conventional state services of policing and judging—police who say they cannot do their jobs without community input or judges who welcome alternative dispute resolution for the relief it gives to clogged courts—they also have a larger vision. They would reverse the usual assumption about the ultimate responsibility for social ordering; the new theory is that criminal justice institutions can best realize their limited contribution to controlling crime and maintaining order by assisting the public.[47]

In focusing on the sins of individual suspects and offenders, the coercive license of the police and the adversarial court process are narrow approaches that do not go to the heart of the problems of crime and disorder, according to this perspective. Criminal justice officials—police, prosecutors, probation officers—and neighborhood workers and residents should exchange information relevant to the protection of the community and assume equal and shared responsibility for developing longer-term priorities and strategies to promote community safety. Emphasizing service to the community over control of individuals, these partnerships aim to keep low-level crimes and disputes out of the formal court system through identifying places and people that are in trouble and reducing opportunities for crime. It is presumed that local skills and knowledge of local conditions can be harnessed to address quality-of-life issues, not just crime. When an offense is committed, community residents are empowered to establish their own mechanisms for minimizing the disruptions it causes, bringing victims and offenders together to acknowledge the harm that was done, negotiate a fair penalty to be paid, and mobilize resources to restore the guilty party to a position of respect in the community.

The best known of these participatory reforms is community policing.[48] Initiated in Britain, it has spread to many countries of the world. In the United States, a federalist system where law enforcement is generally thought to be a local matter, enthusiasm for it is so strong that the federal government subsidizes it. Community policing means vastly different things to different implementers; for the purpose of this discussion I will presume, with Bayley, that it is a prevention-focused program that involves consulting with community residents, adapting to local needs, mobilizing the public in pursuit of order, and solving problems before they turn into incidents that require police reaction.[49] The approach does not engender universal acclaim. Even generally supportive observers worry that its service orientation weakens crime-fighting capacity and that the close relationship with citizens encourages corruption or diminishes the authority that police need when they assume their crime-fighting function. Doubters consider community policing incapable of altering embedded police culture to respond openly and cooperatively to citizens' needs. And what if those needs are expressed as demands for dealing with suspects (or neighbors who are not even suspect) in ways that deny their constitutional rights to association, privacy, or due process? One critic notes that community policing can be both democratic and disciplinary, with the assistance it provides to communities tempered by larger power struggles over questions about which communities are valued and what will be done to protect them.[50]

Restorative justice gives public involvement in social ordering an even more important role. Bucking the modern paradigm of social conflict as law violation that sets up a contest between state and offender, proponents focus on harm rather than rules and argue that social injury is a matter for collective healing without retributive state interference.[51] The alternative perspective gives rise to a great variety of practices—family group conferences in New Zealand, mediation programs in American cities, sentencing circles in Native American communities. Restorative projects bring offenders (sometimes referred by a court, sometimes by police, sometimes by a civic group) together with their families and neighbors and often with their victims to confront their acts and take responsibility for them through a commitment to make restitution in some way. Unlike the formal processes of prosecution and sentencing, the victim has an active role and the desired outcome is healing instead of punishment (though penalties are usually applied and enforced).[52] The restorative mechanisms occasionally operate in precincts and courts but more often in community centers, schools, and even homes and businesses. Concerned immediately with after-the-fact attention to disruptions of community life, restorative justice also seeks to enrich the contributions that criminal justice and other public agencies and private groups make to future community harmony; sanctions for offenders often involve working for a prescribed period on community projects. In Britain a form of restorative justice has been adopted for most first-time juvenile offenses, and the home secretary has called for expanding the concept to deal with adult criminals.[53]

Criminologists who support these participatory forms of policing and judging explain and justify the movement in somewhat different ways. For Clear and Karp the goal is recovering community, addressing social forces that produce crime through enlisting the involvement of people and institutions—victims, offenders, onlookers, justice officials—in preventive and restorative activities. Their strategies would foster partnerships between state and citizen that honor principles of equality, inclusion, mutuality, and stewardship—the public-spiritedness that puts collective good ahead of personal comfort.[54] While their vision—they call it "community justice"—does not reject the relevance of individual guilt (for the purpose of clarifying the normative standards of the community as much as for sanctioning offenders), it focuses primarily on improving the quality of community life—on the repair of places, rather than people. Community justice covers a multitude of initiatives, including but not limited to both community policing and restorative justice. (Clear and Karp present a "thought experiment" that envisions a community center in a low-income community where projects develop crime prevention plans, broker services to victims, mentor children of prison inmates, supervise offenders doing community service sentences, convene sentencing circles, provide after-school activities for kids, and so on.) Members of the community, crime victims, and offenders come together to work to reduce local crime risks, alleviate damage done to crime victims, and reintegrate offenders into the life of the community. "It redefines the justice objectives away from traditional, disinterested law enforcement toward an activist, involved system that treats crime as a community problem to be unraveled."[55]

Other conceptions rely more on political theory. Shearing comes to participatory justice through an analysis of shifts in late-modern governance, the exercise of control over individual behavior by state and nonstate sources alike. He and Les Johnston argue that a paradigm of risk management—largely operationalized by private-sector efforts to forestall threats to corporate security—can have progressive effects on poor communities. It can contribute a preventive, future-oriented focus to supplement the traditional emphasis on social control that employs symbolic strategies of deterrence and retribution.[56] Risk reduction strategies dictate a multiplicity of sites for governance; "the state is but one player—albeit an important one—in a complex network of governing agencies."[57] This trend presents an opportunity for ordinary citizens—particularly the poor, who rarely get the benefits of private security and are often short-changed in the allocation of police resources—to manage their own security and justice. In doing so they become a node in the network of governance, which also includes the corporate sector and nongovernmental organizations. Since a risk-based approach elides the distinction between policing and judging, Shearing promotes a model of justice that focuses on citizens resolving disputes without the usual designation of victims and offenders; he calls it "peacemaking." A practical application of these ideas is under way in South Africa and is discussed in the final chapter.

Criminologists who support these community-oriented strategies have much in common. They reject the adversarial and punitive model of state-centered criminal justice; centralized, professional reactions to individual incidents, with their focus on the culpability of the offender, do not respond adequately to the damage done to communities by crime and disorder and the insecurity that results. They are reluctant to rely principally on even the best expertise provided by criminal justice professionals and are confident that ordinary citizens can competently make essential decisions about maintaining order. At the programmatic level, they see the institutions they are building—the Community Justice Center (Clear and Karp) and the Peace Committee (Johnston and Shearing)—as forces in community development. They see the public as more than a passive recipient of services; community participation in crime control becomes a limited form of direct democracy.

The recent shift to participatory approaches for policing—for both fighting crime and preventing it—and for dispute resolution involving criminal matters is largely a Western development. But the preventive thrust behind community policing is not so new, and restorative justice is often associated with ancient and non-Western traditions. In 1829 Sir Robert Peel saw the success of his new Metropolitan Police in their ability to prevent crime, and they were instructed that a secure community would reflect better on them than the capture and containment of criminals.[58] Traditions among ancient Hindus, Navajos, and the Maori of Australia and New Zealand are said to support restorative, rather than retributive, approaches to dealing with deviants. John Braithwaite, whose work provides a trenchant theoretical justification for restorative justice, asserts that it was the "dominant model" of criminal justice in human history until the Norman Conquest.[59] In both strategy and program, the current approach departs in important respects from Western criminal justice of recent centuries. It concentrates on neighborhoods—one scholar calls it a "turn to the local"—while formal, contemporary criminal justice relies on centralized authority.[60] It reflects Peel's concern with improving the social health of a community. It backs away from the twentieth-century emphasis in the West on professionalism by decentralizing the work of security and justice in important respects; both policing and the adjudication of minor crimes become responsibilities shared by formal institutions and informal structures.

The criminal justice system is expected to be responsive to citizens in new ways; its responsibilities include the correction of criminogenic conditions as well as reaction to socially harmful incidents. So police are expected to note and report physical decay in neighborhoods, assist neighborhood residents in remedying dangerous physical and social conditions, and work with other local service providers to find activities that keep restless teens busy and content. Taking steps to seal the dilapidated building where drug sellers congregate is as important an aspect of policing as making arrests for dealing. Mediation replaces adjudication in many cases, on the theory that healing the rupture that a crime causes in a community is more likely if the offender apologizes to the victim and remains in the community to make restitution or atone in some other way. Finding services for both victim and offender becomes a community alternative to a penal sanction for some sources of disorder. At the core of participatory criminal justice is the realization that crime and disorder are, in part, responses to a social and economic environment and that citizens, as both objects and subjects of that environment, have a right and a responsibility to influence its effects.

This kind of social ordering includes a variety of relationships between state and citizen. It does not replace the standard liberal institutions but reaches beyond the individual protections they profess to provide and challenges them in some respects. It does not reject the role of the state but reduces the emphasis on specialized, professional managers of crime problems.[61] It does not abandon the retributive foundations of conventional criminal justice but applies them in a different way—through the emphasis on acknowledgment of guilt by an offender in a restorative justice program, for instance.[62] The state role, however, is in the technical support and sponsorship it provides; the initiatives get their legitimacy from civilian involvement, whether in the planning stage or in operations. Sometimes this means citizens deputized as auxiliary authority for the state, as in the creation of police precinct councils that offer neighborhood intelligence to help police solve crimes, the establishment of community reparative boards (as is done in Vermont), or the use of lay assessors to advise a judge. Sometimes it means nonstate initiatives where neighbors keep each other under surveillance or dispense forms of popular justice with mores and procedures that relate only indirectly to what would be found in an official tribunal.

Redefining the roles of state and citizen cannot be done without great tension. Criminal justice practitioners typically characterize participatory justice as assistance that brings them closer to the communities they serve. The state's usual presumption is that a community orientation makes police and courts more efficient in honoring their professional and constitutional mandates. (Budget imperatives play a part too; secure custody is generally more expensive than a community sanction.) There is also an underlying objective, shared by both the state and the citizens, of repairing relationships between justice institutions and damaged communities that have felt overlooked or victimized by institutional behavior like police brutality, or depleted by policy developments like harsh sentences for minor crimes that remove or marginalize potentially productive young people.

But the state and involved citizens may part company in conceiving the meaning of the new theory of justice as they think about who is assisting whom. Where criminal justice officials usually see the goal of community participation as increased efficiency and legitimacy for their professional assignments, at least some groups see their own empowerment. The state, they argue, is their resource as well as their regulator. The state cannot merely "responsibilize" the public, enlisting it in the performance of duties previously assigned to police and courts. Privatization in this view must grant to citizens an oversight role for police and courts; the state must follow civil society in efforts to integrate community policing, restorative justice, and other initiatives into larger community development plans; it must be prepared to regard citizen groups as political players if and when the service-providing aspects of participatory justice evolve into demands for policy change.

Some Directions for Public-Empowering Justice

In the preceding pages I have used the terms *participatory justice, community-oriented justice,* and *community justice* to designate the new ideas and their programmatic emanations. These terms suggest the stimulation of public participation in usual and unusual justice-related activities as well as a shifting of the roles of criminal justice operatives to a community orientation. But, taken together, the programs that have sprung up can do more than assume collective responsibility for much social ordering. They can shape local norms as well as reflect them; they can press for personnel changes in police units as well as joining in surveillance activities; they can demand resources for justice-related services—health care, environmental cleanup, education—as well as brokering them for victims and offenders. It is the potential for advocacy tied to service provision that justifies my label—public-empowering justice—for the new perspective and its institutional forms. Whether policy influence will be substantial or trivial will certainly vary from place to place, affected by the extent and vigor of popular involvement, the responsiveness of local elites, and the general political culture. A crucial variable is the degree to which law enforcement simply co-opts the community-based projects, turning them into eyes and ears for police and prosecutors, acquiring volunteer recruits to state functions instead of assisting civil society in managing its own problems. Community policing and restorative justice alone are unlikely to build significant grassroots political or economic power, although projects that see themselves as part of a development effort may become a force to be reckoned with as local governments grapple with issues of education, the environment, and public health. While the greatest successes may be won in relatively stable, affluent communities, the aim of building political power at the local level through public participation in justice activities is especially important where people's opportunities to make decisions about their collective lives have been few and, as a result, they have been voiceless.

It is far from clear that either the partnerships of state actors and residents—the community policing and community justice programs—or nonstate mechanisms that seek to regulate behavior more informally can make a significant contribution to crime control. There is no indication that the tinkering of the state with its institutional behavior in many jurisdictions has produced significantly different patterns of crime or disorder; New York City police officials would probably say that the dramatic drop in violent and property crime during the 1990s was achieved *despite* the city's short-lived community policing program rather than because of it. (Rudy Giuliani, the city's mayor at the time community policing was abandoned, and his police commissioner, William Bratton, derided it as social work inappropriate for police and embraced instead the hard-line, in-your-face approach of "zero tolerance" policing.)[63] The general view is that it works best in the neighborhoods that need it least, but in some poor American neighborhoods community policing has apparently contributed to maintaining order.[64] Research has not supported victim-offender mediation as effective at reducing recidivism, although young offenders may commit fewer crimes after encountering their victims or they may commit only lesser offenses.[65] Furthermore, it is possible that community-oriented programs merely transfer responsibility for preventing crime to its potential victims, detracting attention from the state's indifference to criminogenic conditions in communities.

But for advocates of public-empowering justice crime reduction is not the only benefit to consider; as Clear and Karp note, "We want more from our justice system than mere adversarial victories."[66] To the extent that major goals of policing are to foster an aura of security and legitimacy, community policing in many locations can been deemed a success; it appears to make people feel safer and improves their views of police.[67] Although the general public and some officials feel that restorative justice lets offenders off too easily, these are usually the views of people far removed from the actual negotiations that take place in Australia's family group conferences or at Vermont's community reparative boards. Satisfaction among both victims and perpetrators with the procedures and the outcomes of victim-offender reconciliation sessions in which they participate is generally high.[68] From an economic point of view, local initiatives may be popular as a way of containing criminal justice budgets. So in light of the failures of official social control and the interest in alternatives for at least some situations, experimentation with citizen participation in policing and judging is likely to continue. It is therefore worth considering how the trend might contribute to justice as well as legitimacy, to democracy as well as to professional efficiency.

The public-empowering features of criminal justice in a contemporary democracy are of two kinds, separate but sometimes overlapping. The first are state initiatives with heightened democratic objectives—greater transparency and accountability in activities of law enforcement, crime prevention, and dispute resolution. Most important, they supplement the official social control function with active public participation in decision making—something more than the cooperation of the compliant citizen—about how to maintain order and handle malfeasance. Although the law of the state continues to structure the relationships that characterize these measures—the arresting authority for police is not challenged, for example, nor the scope of matters permissible for judicial notice—citizens are empowered by acquiring enhanced voice and oversight in the institutions that carry out that law.

The second kind of empowering features of democratic justice function at a greater remove from the state. They are not independent in the sense that they defy the laws of the state or operate outside its authority, but they are not primarily organized or operated by state actors. They are regulated by civil society—usually local nongovernmental organizations—so that their missions and operations do not violate human or constitutional rights, and their activities may be conducted in cooperation with (and even funded by) the state; coordination with police and probation, for instance, is often crucial. They may, however, also apply traditions of social ordering that are at variance with institutional practices formalized by the state, particularly those that are most overtly retributive or adversarial. Their operations may operate in accordance with values shared by the state but with a different emphasis, as when an informal dispute resolution puts the restorative element ahead of the retribution, deterrence, and rehabilitation justifications for "old justice."[69] The difference in perspective plays itself out in the scope of matters under consideration by the different institutions, the ways they are considered, and the role of follow-up to the events that brought the matter into consideration in the first place. The lay assessors in a magistrate's court (a state project) will evaluate only criminal charges; the elders in a street committee (civil society) will handle criminal and noncriminal disputes and will usually be indifferent to the legal distinction. When the joint efforts of public and community police have led to formal arrest and prosecution, the citizens have effectively finished with the suspect; citizens who take part in a restorative justice program, on the other hand, will continue monitoring the behavior of the person who has victimized an individual and disrupted a community as well as keeping an eye on others who are thought to have contributed. Nonstate initiatives represent the recognition that in many societies a plurality of avenues to justice is the only way.

Arriving at this conclusion may result from a limitation of resources to deliver state justice to all, popular rejection of the legalist models of Western justice, or a diversity of cultures that cannot be represented with the values of a single sovereign power. But on a more theoretical level it may also constitute an endorsement of David Held's view that the best of modern democracies require what he calls "double democratization," where state sovereignty is maintained to preserve the principle of autonomy for individuals but the people must be sovereign too, with authority over a broad range of rights and the resources (health, skills, political access) to give them effect.[70]

The public-empowering model has significant limitations. It cannot address structural problems that threaten public safety: it cannot provide jobs or education or alter a state's priority for deficit reduction over social spending. A political economy that minimizes inequality and insecurity requires both political commitment and an investment of the state's resources that goes far beyond the funding that public-empowering justice initiatives may require. The devolution of responsibility for some social control functions usually located within liberal institutions may, in fact, merely add to citizen duty without conveying increased power. A less active form of participation, after all, is also a feature of liberal criminal justice, as when the public cooperates in the investigation of a crime or witnesses provide the crucial evidence in a criminal trial. And state policing can be community-oriented without conveying authority to the public in the sense that its professional aims include sensitivity to community needs in the provision of a protective service.

But the implications of assigning to the public as well as the professionals collective responsibility for policing and judging include the potential for becoming a part of community development through strengthening the public voice. When the state decentralizes criminal justice resources and recognizes that individual victims and members of a community wounded by crime can chart their own course for greater safety and security, it is engaging in a redistributive process, ceding rights and authority to an involved public in its decision-making role. Admittedly, such a shift has not occurred in many established democracies and will seem a costly, ephemeral, and politically threatening goal for many democratizing states. But its embrace, at a time when criminal justice has lost authority around the world, may be an essential part of assuring legitimacy and justice for both mature and embryonic democracies.

It is important to note that some of the initiatives that may be defined by their proponents as public-empowering justice are not particularly progressive. Victims may want rights—the opportunity to influence sanctioning authorities with dramatic and frightening statements of the impact crime has had on their lives, for example—that become concrete only in the formal justice process and make an already punitive system more so. Residents beleaguered by drugs and assaults in their neighborhoods may promote zero-tolerance policing and prosecution that have the contradictory result of intensifying the traditional programs of capture and containment without bringing greater peace or social cohesion to the communities that support them. Community policing has not usually involved citizens in core decision-making; they remain recipients of service, a passive role supplemented with opportunities—or obligations—to give police information about local criminals and criminogenic conditions, to provide symbolic support for police activities, and to trumpet their concern about crime through the neighborhood. Popular justice can take a retributive turn and inflict punishments—flogging, for example—that clash with the protection of rights provided by liberal justice systems. And those suspects, victims, and observers who choose community dispute resolution programs—they must always have the option *not* to participate—will have to sacrifice some of the due process protections provided (at least in theory) in Western courts.[71]

Unintended consequences may also pervert the objectives of public-empowering strategies that are otherwise reintegrative and fair. Community programs may "widen the net," particularly where they rely on referrals from the police, so that more minor offenders are swept up into the traditional criminal justice system. This could happen as police and prosecutors become more aware of problem areas and problematic people identified in local programs. Another risk is the possibility that restorative justice will be used as an add-on to traditional punishments, with the offender doing time as usual and subsequently being referred to the supervision of a community program.⁷² Indigenous values that get support from community decision-making may oppress women or immigrants. In many communities participatory justice activities turn out merely to supplement traditional roles of police and courts—ironically, in the communities where healing and public empowerment are the most needed. Community policing often has the most positive impacts—better relations between citizens and law enforcement, reduced disorder (no one really knows whether it reduces serious crime), lower levels of fear—in affluent areas where people have a strong, material stake in their neighborhood and the population is homogeneous; an evaluation of community policing in Houston, Texas, found that its benefits accrued primarily to whites and homeowners.⁷³

Yet the opportunity for these new activities to contribute to the deepening of democracy remains. Brian Forst notes that "the community policing movement amounts to a return to fundamental democratic principles of governance: that the police *serve* the public, that they are *accountable* to the public, and that the public has a *voice* in determining how the police will serve them."⁷⁴ A similar analysis applies to the development of restorative and community justice alternatives to traditional court processes. The joint efforts of families and victims and offenders to repair harm in their communities respond to immediate public needs more directly than the formal criminal justice system, and the individual decisions that emanate from those efforts contribute to a larger democratic expression of preference for standards of conduct in the local community. Regardless of whether public-empowering justice directly effects a reduction in crime, it extends a limited kind of sovereign authority to involved citizens.

Public-Empowering Justice and the Problems of Transition

The question must now be asked whether public-empowering justice is generally desirable and feasible for democratizing countries. Can public participation in crime prevention and dispute resolution further democratization in countries emerging from authoritarian rule? Does it have as much potential for enhancing community peace and safety as in more settled democracies? Consolidating a fledgling democracy is a process of deepening commitments made in the initial transition, including the development of a civil society active enough to make its interests felt by the new government. A responsible program of community justice empowers civil society, enabling citizens to become more than the passive recipients (or the targets) of a public good—official social control—which is only indirectly authorized by their representatives. The orientation theoretically contributes to building strong democratic habits and to a greater understanding of democratic possibilities. And participatory mechanisms that can help to mend broken and divided communities without violating human or constitutional rights should reinforce the accountable, transparent, rights-oriented institutions of justice that are requisites of the consolidated liberal democracy.

Western programs of community policing, restorative justice, and community crime prevention, to mention just a few, cannot be exported reflexively to countries with very different cultures, political traditions, and levels of economic development. States in transition have special circumstances with implications for citizen involvement in justice. Many developing countries, for example, have very recent histories of popular justice, some of them constructive and some brutal and repressive. Both the political past and the economic present are likely to affect the ease with which democratizing countries can accommodate public-empowering justice along with the liberal protections of police and judges who are accountable, uncorrupted, and respectful of human and constitutional rights. Cultural factors are relevant, too; in traditional societies where women are expected to defer to men and younger people to their seniors, participation will have a different quality and pose different challenges. But if democratic transformation means that citizens can now have more say in determining the conditions of their lives, and social order is an important aspect of community life, an obvious conclusion is that the public can (and should) share both responsibility and authority for maintaining it. Granted, a social ordering function that involves civil society so centrally—bypassing the state or challenging it at times—creates new political power centers. But perhaps new democracies can adjust to that more easily than established ones.

The arguments for and against the development of public-empowering policies and practices in democratizing countries are necessarily speculative, since the approach has not been tried consistently anywhere and since its particulars would invariably be shaped by political and cultural conditions that vary both among and within different countries. But some problems are obvious, effects of both past oppression and present chaos.

The functions of public-empowering justice may be politically alien for both newly democratic citizens and the officials who will have to accommodate them. Authoritarian regimes breed subjects, not active citizens; past compliance with the rule of obedience to sanctioning authorities will often be a habit that is difficult to shed. On the other hand, where insurgents against the old regime have taken over order maintenance functions, they may be reluctant to share their powers of governance in responsible citizen action. Police and judges are also unlikely to yield with ease the authority they have enjoyed in a highly coercive system. Becoming operationally accountable to community needs and demands may be galling; the British government, supported by the police, "gutted" the recommendations for a community-oriented policing in

Northern Ireland before a new system could even be tested.[75] Police culture worldwide is famously closed and resistant to change, while judicial independence often serves as a defense against challenges to judicial power. Residual mutual distrust between officials and citizens is likely to impede the cooperation that is necessary for partnerships in crime prevention and dispute resolution. Even in established democracies the state assumes that it can define and implement strategies of public ordering with little citizen interference; if it has been difficult for public-empowering initiatives to get a toehold in these societies, it may seem an even less likely outcome in new democracies. Finally, the lack of a legal culture that is understood and accepted by most people is likely to pose problems in fashioning public-empowering activities that honor the constitutional values of the new nation while seeking solutions to local problems. Otwin Marenin points out that in established democracies shared norms, both substantive and procedural, can guide change in policing practice and philosophy, but democratic states in embryo are evolving their politics even as they create the institutional forms that express those politics.[76]

Countries in transition are likely to have burgeoning crime problems. Disorder may be attributable to the opening of borders, the granting of new freedoms, and the increased availability of opportunities for risky or illegal entrepreneurship. In countries where there has been a long period of widespread rebellion against a colonial or authoritarian power, there may be a whole generation of insurgents who are shut out of the new society and who now substitute criminal violence for the political violence that was justified by a liberation movement. The social chaos of postauthoritarian societies can easily spawn retributive justice that neither shifts the constituency of police and courts from the state to the citizenry nor empowers people to take charge of most social ordering in their communities.

Economic problems of postauthoritarian societies also have consequences for public-empowering justice. New democracies are likely to be poor and will therefore have difficulty providing resources for new police priorities, financial support for community justice programs, and stipends for some kinds of citizen participation. Police training in new democracies will be difficult because of the reorientation that will be necessary in persuading police that their primary constituency has shifted and that their priority is to serve the public rather than to control it. The introduction of community policing will require adding to that task training in the particular features identified as appropriate for that country—to say nothing of the task of merely defining the phenomenon. (Bayley, whose academic expertise on policing is second to none, expressed the frustration of many critics when he said of community policing that it "often seems less a program than a set of aspirations wrapped in a slogan.")[77] Whether restorative justice programs are heavily regulated by the state or operate quite independent of it, their focus on deliberation and on group decision-making can be expensive; countries that are experimenting with lay involvement in justice functions are learning that it is not a cheap alternative to professionalism.[78]

But the problems mentioned above also suggest qualities in democratizing countries that may increase the receptivity of both state and citizen to new approaches and enhance the likelihood of effectiveness for public-empowering justice. There is very little indication that new democracies' struggle for professionalism and political neutrality in conventional criminal justice systems yields greater confidence in their effectiveness. From Russia to South Africa the general public feels that police and courts are not protecting them from crime. Russians continually complain about being less safe in their neighborhoods in recent years, and respondents polled in 2003 felt that organized crime in their country had more power than the president.[79] The leading public opinion survey in South Africa, conducted approximately every other year since the first democratic election, described the rise in public concern about crime as "meteoric" during the first four years, and the data bear out that characterization; when asked in late 1994, "What are the most important problems facing this country that government ought to address?" 6 percent of respondents mentioned crime, a share that ballooned to 65 percent by April 1999.[80] In its March 2002 survey of twelve African nations the Afrobarometer Network found high distrust of police (64 percent of respondents), somewhat less of courts (52 percent).[81] This lack of confidence is hardly surprising, given that most democratizing countries are economically strapped and therefore cannot provide protective policing or speedy trial to all, with the predictable result that affluent neighborhoods are better served than poor ones, where the need is usually greatest.

Some of the antagonism that citizens in new democracies feel toward criminal justice operatives is not dissimilar to that felt in established democracies. There is at least theoretically no reason why the perceived inability of the justice system to provide safety and order cannot provide the impetus for the kinds of policy developments that constitute the movement for public-empowering justice in Western countries. Improvement in the performance of the liberal, individualistic justice system as generally conceived in democratic countries—greater efficiency as measured by improved clearance rates, speedier trials, and higher conviction rates—is unlikely to assuage communities' anger at the justice system's distance from and indifference to criminogenic conditions that residents see close at hand. Funding and training for community policing and neighborhood dispute resolution projects may say more to newly enfranchised citizens about the state's commitment to self-government than a rights-oriented court system and well-trained patrol officers and investigators, especially if the new institutions operate at considerable distance from their daily reality.

A major concern of some democratizing countries is the presence of or potential for vigilantism. Groups of citizens may become cop, judge, and jury when they think a crime has been committed, or they may hire self-styled enforcers to find suspects and pass summary judgment with some form of violence. Informal justice in democratizing countries may have its origins in self-policing traditions of the distant past, and it may have reemerged during a period of political unrest as a way for the community to protect itself against a perceived oppressor—as in Northern Ireland—or as compensation for government neglect of community safety, as in South Africa.[82] It may have played a role in building solidarity for an insurgency or liberation movement. It may have been a feature of the authoritarian past, as in Brazil, with police and gangs indistinguishable influences on community life. It may have recourse to violence regularly or only occasionally, and when it imposes punishments, it may observe distinctions based on gender, age, and seriousness of offense.

A democratizing country's prior experience with informal justice, or vigilantism—the distinction is often one of perception—can be both an impediment and a benefit to a public-empowering program. To the extent that vigilante groups have become permanent features of a social landscape and are perceived as providing a valuable service (and profit financially from it, as some do) they are unlikely to submit gracefully to the regulation that will be necessary to develop a responsible system of participatory justice. On the other hand, ad hoc groups—outraged neighbors who come together on occasion to hunt down a suspected thief or child molester—may be already working in informal partnerships with police and magistrates and will welcome the prospect of additional resources and expertise that flow from a country's commitment to public-empowering justice. Furthermore, a community's prior experience with any kind of informal justice, whether violent or benign, suggests that residents are willing—perhaps eager—to be more than simply consumers of social control services defined and provided by the state. It is, of course, essential that criminal suspects be provided access to the formal justice system if they feel they would be better protected by it than by a street committee or sentencing circle.

The idea that public-empowering justice can build upon and regulate what may have been brutal or arbitrary forms of nonstate policing and judging is hardly new. The Patten Commission created for the reform of policing in the context of Northern Ireland's "Troubles" acknowledged that "networks of policing nodes" that included self-styled enforcers, rather than a single public police force, had become the norm in the province and recommended the creation of a Policing Board that would regulate both the state police and the nonstate "nodes" and the adoption of budgets that would allow for the support of policing not undertaken by the state.[83] The new Rwanda government, acknowledging that formal courts were inadequate to try the thousands of

Hutus charged with assaulting and killing eight hundred thousand Tutsis in 1994 and hoping for reconciliation as well as retribution, turned to a modern version of the traditional, restoration-oriented "gacaca" court system in 2002 "to help the country move along."[84]

Another aspect of the experience of countries in transition bodes well for the introduction of public-empowering justice. Democratization often succeeds civil war or other internal strife, and as a result the view presented to citizens of the new order is dichotomous: peace has replaced violence, accommodation will take the place of resistance, the people will be respected rather than repressed. While this state-building myth may turn out to have little substance, it can nonetheless provide an atmosphere receptive to innovation. The prospect of change on the ground is congruent with the new image of a country in recovery when the messages sent are that restorative justice makes for more peaceful communities, community policing brings reconciliation to residents' relations with the state, and public-empowering justice in general relies on the ideas and judgment and competence of local people.

Viewed individually, the arguments for public-empowering justice are all quite partial. But perhaps they can be creatively combined within a framework that applies with particular force to countries in transition to democracy.

As noted earlier in this chapter, the argument from effectiveness—that public-empowering justice will be significantly better at reducing crime than more formal approaches—has serious limitations. There is simply too much undetected crime in any modern society—and perhaps particularly in one that is in economic chaos, as are most countries in the process of democratization. The structural causes of crime, too, are beyond the reach of even the most dedicated community peacemakers. (As an empirical matter, there is nothing in the record of community justice efforts so far that indicates a direct and significant impact on crime levels.) Over time, however, if community policing consistently identifies and corrects some criminogenic neighborhood conditions and informal dispute resolution keeps some community tensions from turning into open conflict, public-empowering justice may be able to take credit for a modicum of crime prevention.

Similarly, the argument from efficiency isn't likely to be very powerful in the short term. It's very difficult to know what kind of bang for your buck you are getting when you are funding objectives as vague and broadly defined as crime prevention and community safety. Measuring budget savings from the substitution of participatory justice programs (generally administered by nonprofit groups under contract) for expenditures on police and courts is a narrow way of evaluating the economic rationality of investment in the social ordering of a community. It addresses only the effects on one pocket in state coffers of the general trend of pluralizing sources of crime control, and it doesn't do that very well. Those effects will cut across expenditure categories if the community is doing its job and the political system is responsive—increased mental health expenditures as the result of new referrals, for example, or increased sanitation costs because the public and the community police have determined that cleaning up empty lots in urban areas is good crime prevention. In addition, public-empowering programs can be as labor-intensive as formal processing; the costs of training participants, developing regulatory schemes that reflect concern with local conditions, and brokering services for justice-related problems that arise cannot be overlooked. Lay participants may not be—and perhaps should not be—willing to serve for long periods as volunteers. And the inefficiencies of democratic deliberation may increase the cost of programs that are so closely tied to local dynamics. Participants who are actively engaged are likely to be continually debating the standards, values, procedures, and outcomes that define their task. Finally, to the extent that these programs really empower participants and give them a voice in the governance of their communities, local officials may find themselves faced with costly new service demands that will be politically awkward to reject.

Then there's the argument from legitimacy—the position that only through the reorientation of criminal justice toward support of public participation can the state's efforts to control crime be understood and appreciated. Of course one of the benefits of community policing and restorative justice should be improved relations between citizens and the state that is directed to protect them. A public that has become better informed about criminal justice principles and practices by working on problems of social ordering is less likely to support symbolic, politically motivated policies and more likely to have confidence in the justice system.[85] This, too, however, is a narrow view, more concerned with getting acquiescence than justice; it assumes that the task of public-empowering justice is to reinforce the legitimacy acquired through the process of policy adoption by elected representatives.

But in this area representative democracy has very limited value for beleaguered, high-crime communities undergoing political transformation. Representatives are simply too distant and too inaccessible to be immediately responsive to the daily agonies of crime and disorder in communities lacking the social glue that, in traditional associations, enabled them to maintain order informally. Furthermore, many new democratic citizens are likely to be suspicious of the commitment and the competence of their representatives, either because they are unfamiliar with the workings of the new political system or because past experience with representation has been one of betrayal. So what is needed is a different kind of argument from democracy, one that supports public-empowering justice for these communities because it delivers on the promise of political transformation. It must be an argument that supports an alliance between state and citizen to engage cooperatively in the production of public safety and security, with the goals of justice, legitimacy, and effectiveness. It must acknowledge that in this area the definition of democratic self-government goes beyond the choice of political leaders to embrace an active and continuing role for citizens in making decisions about policy and practice.

Public-Empowering Justice and Deliberative Democracy

Over the past two decades political scientists have shown increasing interest in the idea that republican democracy is incomplete without citizen deliberation over its outcomes—government by the people through greater involvement in managing the society than the vote provides. The heterogeneity of the modern polis, combined with its reliance on technology to convey political messages, creates a political environment in which participation through voting or demonstrating is often an atomistic and isolating activity. Neither the promise of choosing representatives elected in fair, competitive contests nor the protections afforded by a rights-oriented constitution ensure the active engagement of democratic citizens in influencing important policy directions—or even in choosing among political candidates, as low turnout rates in some countries suggest.

Without such engagement, the argument goes, the collective judgments of a democracy lack moral authority; they coerce opponents into compliance without an opportunity either to explain their position or to discover common ground with proponents. According to this view deliberation among citizens—"the process of mutual reason-giving"—fills the gap.[86] It enriches the enterprise of political choice and also instructs and bonds the participants. The aim is not consensus that leads directly to policy—only the most limited form of direct democracy is exercised here—but a richer experience of citizenship that rationally and respectfully articulates interests to influence policy choices. Recommendations from deliberating groups should not amount to a "right to instruct" their representatives, but political outcomes should reflect participation that extends beyond the vote to public discussion in a variety of forums.

Deliberative democracy theorists are often trying to revive the spirit that they see as having informed the creation of the American democratic republic. They rely in part on a particular reading of American political history—principally the comments and correspondence of James Madison—to find that the ideals of the framers of the United States Constitution included the belief that citizens' representatives should rely on reasoned discussion at all levels to arrive at important policy decisions.[87] They see public deliberation in politics as both a brake on governmental power and an antidote to sound-bite politics. They argue that media polls, direct-mail campaigns, and political advertising have replaced deliberative activities, that party conventions and floor debates are meaningless as opportunities for reflection and exchange, and that democratic politics must be more than the expression of momentary majority preferences. While judicial and legislative debates are occasions for deliberation, the theorists find deliberative democracy in civil society also. Face-to-face interaction among ordinary citizens is necessary to foster political cooperation and to give participants an informed voice in democratic decision-making.

Exploration of the institutional uses to which this concept of democracy could be put has frequently focused on the procedural attributes of democracy. One example is the "deliberative opinion poll" proposed by James Fishkin. In this exercise a representative sample of citizens is brought together for several days before an election to interact with each other and with candidates before they are polled, "bring[ing] the face-to-face democracy of the Athenian Assembly or the New England town meeting to the large-scale nation-state."[88] The supposition is that such a mechanism can improve the quality of information and value choices that people bring with them into the voting booth and strengthen the connection between them and their representatives.

Some theorists also stress the importance of bringing substantive principles of democracy—equality and dignity, for instance—into deliberation over policies that will shape citizens' lives. Amy Gutmann and Dennis Thompson point out that the legitimation of public policies on such issues as abortion and the rationing of health care resources cannot occur without public debate that takes into consideration those values and the weights given to them by different groups affected by the policy.[89] The core principle of deliberative democracy, they argue, is reciprocity, the obligation of citizens to give each other reasons that justify the imposition of a policy on those who did not support it. Reciprocity will often be incomplete without the inclusion of both procedural and substantive principles; as an example, considerations of equity as well as a majority endorsement must accompany a decision to allocate scarce resources to primary health care rather than to an organ transplant program.

In the view of Gutmann and Thompson, "the moral authority of collective judgments about policy depends in part on the moral quality of the process by which citizens collectively reach those judgments."[90] Where the stakes are particularly high—where life and liberty are at stake, as in foreign policy and criminal justice—that process warrants close scrutiny. Deciding such policy issues on the basis of the aggregated preferences of political representatives or their bureaucratic delegates alone consigns citizenship to the expression of private, individual views. Liberal democracy and deliberative democracy approach collective choice in different ways: the former bundles together disparate viewpoints, resulting in a judgment that favors the dominant one; the latter channels opinions into a product of mutual accommodation. Liberal democracy reflects individual preferences; deliberative democracy balances them.[91]

The sensitive issues of criminal justice—setting standards for circumstances and methods for arresting and charging, determining suitable roles for victim and accused and penalties appropriate for particular behavior, balancing individual retribution and community restoration, and so on—cry out for mutual accommodation. The Aristotelian ideal of citizenship included judicial participation. Modern theorists sometimes use decisions about capital punishment—whether to have it at all, what means of execution to use—as hypothetical subjects for democratic discussion.[92] Yet reasoned argument among and between citizens and their representatives is notable for its absence in actual criminal justice policymaking. In any society citizens will have varying views on what police behavior is acceptable in making arrests and how harshly a young thief should be dealt with—and by whom. Airing a wide range of attitudes at the grass roots and conveying collective decisions on these matters to political representatives and public administrators is an indispensable supplement to judicial consideration and legislative debate with respect to them. Furthermore, what the range of permissible topics should be can itself be a matter of deliberation—whether police personnel decisions can be shared with a community police forum, whether the allocation of crime prevention funds is appropriate for community consideration, whether sentencing circles can determine sanctions for serious violent crimes, whether community forums have the authority to call for the mandatory use by magistrates of lay assessors in criminal trials. "Deliberation is the most appropriate way for citizens collectively to resolve their moral disagreements not only about policies but also about the process by which policies should be adopted. Deliberation is not only a means to an end, but also a means for deciding what means are morally required to pursue our common ends."[93]

The punitive program of criminal justice policy that has prevailed in many countries in recent years is often presented as an expression of the will of the people, and it is this view that continues to make crime politics salient as elections approach. But "punitive populism" is a product of hasty judgment based on poor information. It is fueled by an unrealistic sense of what the criminal justice system can really do to protect people, sensational reports of hideous crimes, and the urgings of political candidates who are prepared to manipulate public fear.[94] It proposes abstract solutions for concrete problems. It has symbolic power not only because of individual fears of victimization but also as a stand-in for larger, underlying social and economic insecurities.

Without the fuel for punitive populism people tend to be quite sensible about approaches to crime. (Admittedly, the research that presents a more complex picture of public viewpoints is largely studies of Americans, but there are not compelling reasons to think that Americans would be so different from others in this respect.) The general public and political portrayal of what people want from their law enforcement agencies—speedy arrival at the scene of a crime and speedy apprehension of its perpetrators—leaves out what they tell police about immediate and routine needs in their neighborhoods—for attention to the daily threats to order and security. When it comes to punishment we know that people become less hard-line about crime as they learn more about offenders and the contexts in which their crimes are committed. Interviewees in Ohio who were asked generally whether they favored a "three strikes and you're out" law in their state were far more likely to express support for life sentences than when given vignettes and asked to choose among a range of punishments for three-time offenders.[95] Juries are famously reluctant to pronounce a capital sentence—even though disbelievers are weeded out in the voir dire—when they learn the full particulars of a case. Familiarity, in this context, breeds understanding rather than contempt.

These tendencies suggest benefits that could flow from the more nuanced views of crime that attend a deliberative approach to criminal justice. Reasoned discussion between police and public of how to protect communities is more likely, in most situations, to produce preventive environmental strategies than support for unrestrained police sweeps. Studies conducted in Canada, the United Kingdom, and the United States have found that victim-offender mediation in community settings satisfies victims more than the formal procedures of state courts, even though the offender's penalty will almost surely be less severe.[96]

Deliberative democracy is difficult to effectuate when the issue at hand is a global one—international environmental controls, for instance—where many policymakers are outside the sphere of influence of discussants. Even when the debate is about candidates for state or national office the connection between deliberation and outcome is somewhat attenuated; the interests of participants in deliberation may be too varied and their backgrounds too diverse to easily find common ground, and the results of deliberations may lose something as they are conveyed to other, distant deliberators or policymakers. But, with some exceptions like constitutional mandates and national sentencing policies, justice policy and practice are largely matters of local concern. They have immediate relevance for citizens' daily lives, and the constituency for resolving many problems is small enough to permit the face-to-face interaction that makes deliberation meaningful to its participants. The voluntary associations of civil society can provide space within which a form of local governance can flourish—citizens guiding one another to achieve shared goals, with state intervention only to preserve individual autonomy or prevent harm to others.[97]

In departing from the liberal perspective that endorses democracy because of its celebration of individual autonomy, proponents of deliberative decision-making are sometimes accused of giving short shrift to rights. But aggregating preferences in a different way need not prevent the imposition of constraints on the political choice that results. "Rights will be often be pre-conditions for the deliberative process," notes Cass Sunstein; constitutional prohibitions against discrimination and the fundamental requirements of due process, for example, have to be presumed as deliberation on criminal justice policy and practice occurs.[98] This position is still consistent with deference to collective decision-making; an earlier democratic process, after all—the adoption of a constitution or rights-creating legislation—has presumably established the rights to be respected.[99]

Of course deliberation also has potential negatives. Its outcomes will not necessarily be just. One theorist worries that the compromises that are necessary for participants to make a collective choice will render the enterprise susceptible to co-optation by the powerful.[100] And the mere fact that decisions are reached through public deliberation rather than bureaucratic or legal decree may not reduce the degree to which they are simply symbolic—for example, punitive sanctions that don't reduce either crime or the fear of it in the future. The discussion may drive people apart rather than bring them together; Sunstein has suggested that deliberation may result in what he calls "group polarization," the phenomenon that, rather than arriving at mutually accommodating positions, participants—clinging to their concepts of themselves or unable to break out of a narrow range of arguments—adopt more extreme views in the direction of those they had coming into the discussion.[101] Particularly relevant for tense, crime-ridden communities, deliberative democracy does not promise that respectful mutual exchange over political questions will displace the conflicts that characterize modern nations. In fact, it is those conflicts that make deliberation particularly important. A greater danger is that inherently conflictual power relations in the society will negate the benefits of deliberation. If participatory talk and action modifies those power relations in even a small way, the promise of democratic deliberation and community-oriented criminal justice will be realized. But if it does not contribute to social justice, the frustrations that result may prove counterproductive and contribute to further apathy and atomism, dividing communities and increasing crime.

This discussion of a theoretical justification for public-empowering criminal justice is most immediately relevant for citizens' role in influencing policy formation and decisions regarding policy implementation. But deliberation is of the essence in the justice system's daily operations, too. Many of the processes of justice, after all, whether guided by liberal or deliberative democracy, involve citizens—as victims, witnesses, jurors or assessors or lay magistrates, volunteers of various kinds, and defendants. Their responsibilities for deliberative participation—in jury room debates, trials, interrogations—are, however, fundamentally passive and increasingly marginalized, as plea bargains determine most judicial outcomes and technological advances in forensic science increase reliance on technical evidence. What Adam Crawford calls the "socially transformative logic" of participation in criminal justice is a more active, inclusive form of responsibility in which citizens not only recommend what the state should do but also make decisions about social ordering that supplement—and sometimes replace—those of the formal system.[102] So the public acquires a voice not only in determining what community problems police should address but also in deciding how those problems should be weighed in considering the extent of harm done by offenders. "Active responsibility . . . calls upon active participation. As such active participation is a desirable element of deliberative democracy."[103]

Deliberative activity provides an education in democracy that is particularly relevant for countries in the throes of political transformation. For people who have merely submitted to mandates imposed by a distant and often hostile state, sharing information, weighing policy options, and expressing preferences are vital contributions to the consent that defines self-rule. Participants can become better informed as to political considerations that are newly relevant to their status as democratic citizens. Both theoretical and empirical work suggests that deliberation over public choices fosters in participants a commitment to impartiality with respect to others—and an acceptance of policy solutions that are impartial and inclusive—as well as an inclination to supplement self-interest with consideration of the public interest.[104] And deliberation, as it explores the relationships of state and citizen—an inevitable aspect of participation in social ordering—may spur trust in the democratic process by rendering it more familiar.

Culture is relevant, too. The public in many countries in transition may be more comfortable with a deliberative process that engages them in addressing problems of crime and disorder than citizens in more established Western democracies. The presumption of liberal democracy that decisions are reached through the aggregation of individual preferences may not sit well with people whose experience of group decision-making in traditional communities has been a process whereby individual preferences were modified and channeled into consensus through collective judgment. The deliberative process enables people in transitional countries to decide whether the procedural protections provided by liberal democracy are adequate to deal with the problems of crime and disorder that they face and what supplements or alternatives to institute. Some of the concerns that have been raised about the unworkability of deliberative democracy in large, diverse societies are unlikely to apply in local settings where populations may not be culturally or politically homogeneous but are likely to be united on the need for safety and security.

Conclusion

The ultimate challenge of public-empowering justice as an aspect of democratization is to work out the problems of coexistence with the rights-oriented institutions that embody the shift from authoritarian rule. There are, to be sure, contradictions inherent in the development of separate but interlocking spheres. The greater power of the state—its formal authority, its resources—militates against both the citizen influence that makes community policing an effective partnership and the independence on which the restorative justice process depends. The liberal ideology that protects the individual runs counter to the restorative approach, which subsumes the individual's interest into those of the community at large. As a practical matter, risks abound: that the state will dictate the contributions of civil society, resulting in an expansion of formal social control and increased frustration of community participants; that citizens will tire of cooperation with a system that does not address structural inequality and deprivation.

But living with these tensions is not impossible. Looking at a group of southern African states Wilfried Schärf concludes that "the more legitimate (and sensitive to the needs of the poor) the regime, the more the 'non-state-type' structures will be integrated into the formal system, or at very least tolerated by it."[105] New modes of reciprocal accountability must evolve and be accepted by both the operatives of the formal criminal justice system and the citizens whose activities supplement and sometimes supplant that system. As citizens assume more responsibility for social order and acquire more power to demand greater protection, new definitions of professionalism in policing and judging will evolve, and the challenge to the state will be to accommodate without losing the respect for individual dignity at the core of constitutional democracy. Adapting to plural institutions and theories is not for the political purist or the politically timid.

8 Participation Thwarted
South African Failures

> Development in Africa is not likely to be very fruitful if the justice systems of the respective countries are not in tune with the needs of the population. Development can achieve some results if the state system adapts to the needs of the citizens and if it allows itself to be enhanced by the non-state forms of responsible ordering.
> —Wilfried Schärf[1]

IT IS HARDLY SURPRISING that the dawning of post-apartheid democracy brought with it interest in citizen participation in social ordering, whether in partnership with government or independent of it. In the past, South African communities had often taken the law into their own hands, bypassing the state—or being ignored or egged on by it—in their pursuit of safety and peace. Two hundred years ago Africans largely maintained their own social order with broad participation of tribesmen (not women) as well as chiefs. Sachs comments that "in traditional African society every man was his own lawyer, and his neighbour's too, in the sense that litigation involved whole communities, and all the local men could and did take part in forensic debate."[2] And as the white Dutch settlers left Cape Town and became farmers in isolated rural areas, they imposed and enforced their own laws on each other and on their underlings. Under colonialism blacks in Natal and elsewhere were permitted limited self-regulation through customary law applied by the chiefs' courts, subject to "repugnancy" clauses that revoked authority when the law offended Western legal sensibilities—condoning witchcraft and polygamy, for instance. The "native policy" of the Black Administration Act of 1927 recognized the existence of indigenous courts (primarily in the rural areas, where customary law still held sway) but incorporated them as the bottom rung of the state system.[3] This policy, part of a containment strategy to discourage urbanization and unrest, gave the chiefs the authority of officials but diminished them as indigenous leaders. During apartheid the government actually encouraged the conservative tribal courts (called *makgotla*) that imposed harsh punishments on dissidents and rebellious youth. Some of the chiefs' courts still exist, though their influence is much reduced and the law they impose reflects Western standards as well as tribal customs and values.

To a considerable extent, the use of nonstate mechanisms to keep order and resolve disputes in South Africa (and in many other countries) has responded to brutality or neglect by the state. That was certainly the case when resistance to apartheid spawned many forms of popular justice. People's courts in the townships often inflicted violent penalties on people perceived as traitors to the antiapartheid cause, while organized and representative tribunals affiliated with political organizations (offshoots of the street committees that provided much local governance) held proceedings similar to Western trials or supervised mediation sessions.[4] Sanctions varied. Whipping and other physical punishments—the worst was "necklacing," putting a rubber tire soaked with gasoline around the neck and then lighting it—became common in the mid-1980s, particularly when young men were in charge. But a restorative philosophy usually reigned, with wrongdoers assigned to community tasks of various kinds and assured that they would be welcomed back into the fold. While these structures often acted primarily as disciplinary weapons to ensure solidarity in the liberation struggle, they also functioned to address ordinary crime—thefts, assaults, burglary—as well as noncriminal issues like quarrels over inheritance or the use of scarce communal resources.[5] (The most serious violent crimes were generally referred to police.) Without a formal justice system that was considered legitimate, popular justice flourished as a form of governance for many communities.

As apartheid collapsed, community justice shifted focus; challenging the power of the old state gave way to shaping power in the new one. "Popular justice in the 1990s was no longer an attempt to prefigure a new state, but to normalize and to impose principles of its own sovereignty at a community level."[6] In addition, late-stage apartheid reforms had begun to introduce an element of responsiveness to ordinary people's needs for access to the formal justice system—notably small claims courts and mediation. So the stage was set for going beyond the crucial step of shifting the constituency for the criminal justice system—the liberal, rights-oriented approach—to embracing public participation in crime prevention and sanctioning. In loosening its monopolistic grip on the maintenance of law and order the new democratic state would both informalize its own practices and acknowledge new powers for citizens.

But this formulation of the objectives of South African post-apartheid planners is much too simple. For one thing, the ideological range of those making the plans was very great, and the positions from which they saw public-empowering justice were very different. Officials—some of them holdovers from the apartheid regime—tended to view the development of ways to involve the public as a means of acquiring greater legitimacy for a discredited system and a supplementary resource for police and judges who would remain the primary and authoritative providers of official social control. Citizens, on the other hand—including scholars and activists with strongly communitarian ideals—were eager to do more than merely participate in the social ordering of the new society. They wanted power as well as responsibility—to oversee the performance of a government still staffed in large part by representatives of the former oppressors, to mitigate the harshness and arbitrariness of apartheid law enforcement, to direct justice resources to the majority poor, to ensure delivery of the constitutional promise of dignity and equality for backs and women. And not very far in the background was the anger and suspicion that the victims of apartheid felt in dealing with the institutions—and sometimes the individuals—that had oppressed them.

Beyond the divergent institutional goals of the planners were fundamental differences in perspectives on what constituted the social order to be achieved. The representatives of the official institutions of Western criminal justice tended to assume that arrest and punishment of individuals were the desired outcomes of intervention into a criminal incident. Citizen groups and their representatives, on the other hand, derived their aspirations from African traditions and from their recent experience of self-regulation. While they did not reject formal authority for handling the most violent crimes, they put a high priority on preventing disorder through informal measures of surveillance and mediation. They were not so ready to attach the label of "crime" to troublesome behavior in the community, and they were satisfied with restitutive solutions to much social harm—return of stolen goods to their owner, for instance, and payment of medical expenses for an injury.[7]

This range of visions and definitions in planning post-apartheid criminal justice—to say nothing of limited resources to institute new programs and practices—necessitated compromises. The pool of shared idealism that conceived of justice as coproduced by state and citizen was shallow, and officials of the formal system were, not surprisingly, reluctant to concede control over resources or authority to nonprofessionals who had recently been their antagonists. So the common objective of greater public participation in maintaining order yielded efforts to bring lay influence to bear on the formal system, rather than "popular justice" that would have been relatively autonomous. The incorporation of participatory elements in the formal justice system was nonetheless potentially public-empowering. And the steps taken during the early post-apartheid period did not preclude the development of parallel institutions of self-regulation that would maintain social order in many situations.

But the post-apartheid South African government has not, after all, made a sustained and substantial commitment to public-empowering justice. Its plan for community police forums—mandatory for all precincts in the 1993 interim constitution—was initially conceived as a partnership between the state and the citizenry. The South African Police Service (SAPS) would provide assistance to communities in identifying and correcting problems of crime and disorder, and the communities would provide police with information and monitor their local policies and practices. Now, with the exception of affluent white suburbs that can afford to provide material and moral support to their police precincts, community policing has generally become the haphazard use by police of citizens to supply intelligence in fighting crime. The use of lay assessors in criminal trials—heralded as an important aspect of judicial transformation, a way to give blacks and women immediate influence on justice—has dwindled, even though both citizen representatives and justice officials (even the last apartheid minister of justice) initially supported it. Legislation considered by the cabinet in early 1998 to make lay assessors mandatory in trials for crimes against persons died on the vine. Plans to regulate the community courts that functioned to keep order during the liberation struggle have never materialized, though a proposal languished at the South African Law Commission for several years. An ambitious government plan for crime prevention has stimulated some community activity, and there has been a limited effort in some areas—notably the Western Cape—to coordinate local public services to that end. Public participation is, however, marginal to the effort; the constitution describes crime prevention as the job of the police, and police seem to define crime prevention as simply crime-fighting efficiency; they measure their performance in this area with data on crimes reported and arrests made.[8] Private projects of restorative justice and dispute resolution are under way, but they reach only a tiny fraction of the population, and their financial support comes primarily from foreign governments, small discretionary grants within the social welfare bureaucracy, and modest local funding. The national government prefers to commit its resources to increasing professionalism—with an emphasis on managerial efficiency—in the police, the National Prosecuting Authority, and the courts.[9] As a result of poor service delivery from the formal criminal justice system and a lack of investment in participatory programs, a great variety of nonstate structures has sprung up, many of them dispensing summary justice in brutal forms and relating to police, if at all, in an atmosphere that one observer describes as "fraught with suspicion and rivalry."[10] These bodies often constitute yet another crime problem that the police and courts cannot effectively address.

The remainder of this chapter looks at efforts to install several forms of public-empowering justice—their genesis and decline—and posits some explanations for why this aspect of democratization failed to evolve. Problems of both theory and implementation plagued the efforts of the new South African government to empower citizens in protecting their communities. Confusion about the significance of the proposed initiatives enabled preexisting divisions between criminal justice operatives and citizens to simmer just below the surface of apparent agreement on aims and strategies. A lack of resources for training and upkeep plagued the programs of both community policing and lay assessors, and their novelty created suspicions about their effectiveness. Police and judges (including the magistrates of the lower courts) felt threatened by perceived incursions on their professional turf, even though they also proclaimed support for the supplementation of their functions that the new institutions could potentially provide.

But in the end the failures of public-empowering measures came not principally from within criminal justice but from the larger political culture: symbolic politics that dictated a muscular state response to crime, single-minded adherence to Western—particularly Anglo-American—constitutionalism, and pressures to deliver conventional services expected of powerful Western democracies in a neoliberal era.

Community Police Forums

Even the late-apartheid South African government of the early 1990s was embracing globally trendy developments in policing. "Some two or three years before the elections we started moving towards implementing principles of community policing," reported Louis Eloff, deputy national commissioner of SAPS, one of the "clean" officials retained in the new government.[11] But the label can apply to a wide variety of ideals and practices, and community policing often appears to be what Bayley characterized as "a set of aspirations wrapped in a slogan."[12] Police officials in that period saw it primarily as a matter of public relations and an opportunity to elicit information from community people that would help in fighting crime. Antiapartheid activists were scornful of this approach, which they saw as co-optation pure and simple; "they [police] would go out and have a braai [barbecue] in a township with the leaders."[13] A 1991 strategic plan for the South African Police proposed a new division of police-community relations and community liaison bodies, but at meetings held with community people pursuant to this development the police did not respond to their concerns seriously or allow them to chair meetings.[14]

Ironically, the ubiquity and vagueness of the community policing concept, rather than rendering it unimaginable for the embryonic democracy, may have permitted people with very different visions to come together to plan a program for the new government. It also carried the seeds of defeat for those who had a more ambitious view of the role of the public in determining how the state would protect the new society. A prominent American observer has commented that "[t]he astonishing success of constitutional design in South Africa was possible largely because people of one view were constantly in discussion with people of opposing views."[15] But a gorgeous design is no guarantee of a workable building, and the planners of post-apartheid policing were contractors working with different materials. The police saw a top-down consultative role for community residents, while the academics and representatives of prominent nonprofit organizations like the Centre for the Study of Violence and Reconciliation (CSVR) and the Institute for Democracy in South Africa (IDASA, originally the Institute for a Democratic Alternative in South Africa) envisioned community police forums (CPFs) as a public-empowering opportunity that would help consolidate the South African democracy. The creation of CPFs was a handy way for the SAPS to cordon off a program that was somewhat peripheral to their central tasks; for the more progressive post-apartheid planners it was to be, rather, a visible symbol of the changed perspective that would permeate the entire SAPS mandate.

In anticipation of regime change and the opportunity to govern, the ANC had begun to shape its strategy for building the social infrastructure of the democratic state. Its document "Ready to Govern" set forth "A New Approach to Policing," which stressed the service orientation of the new police and included the directive that "[p]olice priorities shall be determined in consultation with the communities they serve."[16] One of the post-apartheid planning committees was composed of criminologists, activists, and legal scholars interested in adapting the theory and practice of community policing as practiced around the world to the democratization of South Africa. They favored an approach where local groups would dictate priorities and strategies to cooperating police. The members of the committee brought to their task the experience of a larger group of transition planners whose goals included the creation of civilian oversight bodies in many realms.[17] These people held differing ideological positions and operated from a variety of institutional bases. Some were legal reformers previously involved through NGOs in such issues as prisoners' rights and legal representation for the poor, and some came from a group of critical criminologists that had been working for many years to develop a criminology for the democratic South Africa they envisioned. They shared "a commitment to community-based research and to solutions that favoured local autonomy."[18]

The same commitment did not exist among the police officials who would be responsible for implementing a participatory program. To them community policing was a matter of the style they adopted in relating to the public, rather than a vehicle for control of order maintenance in which citizens would set the terms of a partnership with the state. They endorsed the idea of consultation on services to be delivered, but when push came to shove they saw themselves as still firmly in charge, rejecting nonstate control of efforts to enhance community safety. As Deputy Commissioner Eloff put it, "It's simply a process of collaboration, not who is in charge of whom. . . . You want to take the needs of the community into consideration as far as you can, but whatever people say about democracy, we are a law enforcement agency. We have to find a balance between the needs of the people and higher level needs of the government in terms of . . . stability and security of the state."[19] For him the notion of community bodies as civilian oversight for police was "nonsense."

Several factors influenced the choice of CPFs as the dominant model within SAPS for community policing. The availability of funding from foreign governments steered the planners toward a Western-style state-centered program, though in some parts of the country planners tried to avoid that influence, aware that South African conditions and needs were very different from those of countries like the United States and the United Kingdom.[20] On the other hand, a vision of democratic policing as a more communitarian process shaped the preference of the activists and academics for bottom-up citizen mobilization around community protection in even the poorest areas. They drew on the long tradition of organized self-help in many black communities—civic associations, street committees, the self-defense units created by young people to fill a vacuum in law enforcement during the apartheid years—and on their conviction that the police who had been instruments of oppression for so long could only be contained by the vigilance of citizens.

The final choice was dictated in part by pragmatic concerns about what SAPS would accept. Many police were genuinely relieved not to have to enforce apartheid any longer and endorsed community policing in theory, at least as to its value in improving community relations. Minutes of early planning meetings and interviews with some of those that participated suggest, however, that they were also doubtful of its efficacy and uncomfortable about the increased visibility it might bring to police operations. The outcome was a hybrid model of community policing—a state-centered and centralized program that was, however, to be guided by the values and voices of civil society. Police could incorporate it into a traditional Western vision of crime control as an opportunity for community help in gathering intelligence and improving public relations; and the activists and scholars who participated in policy planning could somewhat naively see it as an arena of local democracy. Some of the latter group simply overlooked the contradictions in the plan. "In 1994 the transition was very fresh," said Mduduzi Mashiyane, an organizer who worked in Durban, Johannesburg, and Pretoria on a range of urban safety projects. "A culture of organization and mobilization made CPFs exciting."[21]

There is no typical CPF, but some organizational characteristics are common. Each CPF must have a written constitution, a code of conduct, and an annual general meeting; and both police and residents must be involved. Community members are usually representatives of organizations (sometimes political, more often not) within the precinct, though membership is open to all. A community relations officer from the police is a member—usually very influential, although not permitted to be the chairman—and often the station commissioner participates. Area and provincial boards coordinate the individual CPFs.

An active CPF meets monthly; working committees and subcommittees may meet more or less often. Meetings are formal in structure, with minutes taken and rules of order observed in theory if not in practice. Between 1994 and 1999 I attended meetings (sometimes several in one place) of a dozen CPFs in three South African provinces; in my experience, attendance varied from four people to fifty.[22] Meetings were sometimes orderly, more often chaotic and tense. Where there is significant racial, ethnic, or political diversity in a CPF, meetings are likely to be arenas of conflict, which may be resolved or not. Issues raised in meetings include inadequate police protection (response time, patrol routes, allocation of police time, etc.), police crime and corruption, alcohol-related crime in local shebeens, vagrancy, street children, drug trafficking, thefts from businesses, family violence (rape and incest as well as wife-beating and child abuse), police personnel practices (including the choice of a new station commissioner), and how to spend money allocated to the CPF (including many complaints about the lack of transportation funds for community members coming to meetings). Although all community members are volunteers, some spend many hours each week on CPF matters. Participants in CPFs in the major urban areas have received at least some training and technical assistance, which is rare in the more remote areas.

Taken together, official documents and experience on the ground reflect very clearly the South African government's waning commitment to community police forums as the new political order evolved. The 1993 interim constitution provided as follows:

> The functions of community-police forums referred to in subsection (1) may include—
> a. the promotion of accountability of the Service to local communities and co-operation of communities with the Service;
> b. the monitoring of the effectiveness and efficiency of the Service;
> c. advising the Service regarding local policing priorities;
> d. the evaluation of the provision of visible police services, including—
>   i. the provision, siting and staffing of police stations;
>   ii. the reception and processing of complaints and charges;
>   iii. the provision of protective services at gatherings;
>   iv. the patrolling of residential and business areas; and
>   v. the prosecution of offenders; and
> e. requesting enquiries into policing matters in the locality concerned.[23]

The potential role of the CPFs, as set forth by this language, made community accountability paramount in many respects. The provisions for monitoring police, influencing policing priorities, and evaluating police services suggested lay control of law enforcement and went beyond most Western conceptualizations of community policing. Rhetorically, at least, this concept was embraced by the ANC government that came to power the following year. The new minister of safety and security, Sidney Mufamadi, in his initial policy statement announced that "community policing . . . must be made to permeate every aspect and level of policing."[24]

Initially, many early CPFs tried to influence local SAPS personnel policy, resource allocation, and enforcement priorities. Two CPF meetings observed in black townships outside Cape Town in July 1994 included citizen complaints about the disciplining of a black officer by his white supervisor, a request for more regular police surveillance of business establishments, and a demand for police to respect the street committees' ability to deal with minor offenders outside official state mechanisms. Community CPF members were vocal and unapologetic in their demands, and their complaints of racism in the way the black officer was handled were accompanied by the assertion—vigorously resisted by the police—that the community should be included in hiring, discipline, and firing decisions.

A year later the Police Service Act, enacted pursuant to the interim constitution (Section 214), used less confrontational language to describe the desired relationship of the CPFs and the police. Of crucial importance now were "establishing and maintaining a partnership," promoting "communication" and "cooperation" between the SAPS and the communities it serves, and encouraging "joint problem identification and problem-solving."[25] While accountability to the community was still the principal objective, it was to be accomplished indirectly, apparently a retreat to the usual Western autonomy of police decision-making. Improved police-community relations and local oversight are side by side as CPF responsibilities; this would seem to be a contradictory set of goals even in a country without South Africa's history of tension and conflict between citizens and police.[26] The same orientation is evident in the "Community Policing Policy Framework and Guidelines" issued in 1997 by the Department of Safety and Security. It assumed that community policing was a "collaborative effort" and envisioned "an active partnership between the Police and the community through which crime, service delivery and police-community relations can jointly be analysed and appropriate solutions designed and implemented." It embraced "the key strategy of community consultation" through CPFs, which "are intended to assist the police."

The 1998 "White Paper on Safety and Security" (in effect until 2004) reinforced this shift in CPF functions from oversight to assistance.[27] Community policing has became principally an instrument of crime prevention, vaguely envisioned as "[a]ssisting with the development of targeted social crime prevention programmes" or more concretely endorsed as providing intelligence for police and other officials ("[i]dentifying flashpoints, crime patterns and community anti-crime priorities"). Although the foreword insists that national police policy is still "underpinned by the philosophy of community policing" and some CPFs are still functioning, community members and activists involved with CPFs often insist that the rest of the white paper belies this statement. It stresses the involvement of elected representatives of municipal government in setting priorities for police, signaling a fundamental shift in responsibility for police decision-making at the local level. And as a practical matter the policy influence of CPFs in most communities had waned by then, the range of their activities had narrowed, and participation had dwindled. (Some affluent white suburbs were the exception, as well as parts of the Western Cape where training and technical assistance were still supported locally and by foreign governments.) A meeting attended in Mitchells Plain in April 1998 was dominated by police officers who provided information to community residents about recent crime patterns in the township and heard complaints about police unresponsiveness to crime reports. Nothing about either the atmosphere or the agenda suggested that community members of the CPF were involved in police decision-making. An interview with police afterwards confirmed the impression that CPFs were seen as useful "eyes and ears" to help police ferret out the wrongdoers of the community and identify "hot spots" for the new orientation to problem-oriented policing.[28]

Criminologists and NGO workers in South Africa who have been deeply involved with the development of community policing acknowledge that the functions of CPFs as their advisory group originally conceived them had narrowed by the late 1990s. Police consult on some matters with the CPFs that still exist, but CPFs have not survived as mechanisms of police accountability. Proponents of the original institutional plan cite many obstacles to its effective operation: confusion about mandates, mutual distrust between police and citizens, and the power imbalance between community people and the SAPS. They note that many of the problems stemmed from insufficient resources—not only for meetings, training, and special projects, but also to get broad community participation. The CPFs rarely reached the marginalized people who needed them most; citizen members of CPFs in black townships were often the more affluent people in the community—teachers and social workers, retired people with state pensions who could afford to volunteer their time. It might be said that what remains of the CPF program has exacerbated the gulf between rich and poor in South Africa; some white, middle-class communities have continuing participatory relationships with police—contributing much-needed equipment to local precincts, planning joint projects, directing security to troubled areas—of a kind that is impossible in poor communities. Even in the communities where resources are adequate the problem of mutual distrust became crippling. A 1999 research report concluded that "trust remains the primary challenge faced by the majority of South Africa's police stations and the people represented at CPFs. . . . at these localities, the continuous grappling with developing trust results in little or few improvements to actual service delivery, increasingly negative public perceptions of safety and security . . . and little actual reduction in crime."[29] (It should be noted that distrust included both the legacy of political suspicion and reactions to contemporary police brutality and corruption. Distrust between different political and racial groups within communities also contributed.)

Somewhat surprisingly, the academics and activists who worked so hard to make their vision of community policing effective did not generally see the failure of CPFs as the result of a power struggle between police professionals and civil society groups in which the police were the victors. They have expressed sympathy with the shortage of police resources that made the maintenance of CPFs merely an additional burden, rather than a resource, and they do not condemn the foreign donors for terminating their support after a few years. Some have said that, even if the government had been more supportive, the fragmentation and division of poor South African communities would have been a significant obstacle to assuming the roles they expected of citizens.[30] They noted that the political climate had changed very soon after the first democratic elections in ways that worked against the CPFs and that they were naive to assume that their vision could prevail over resistance to it from SAPS and merely passive interest from the Ministry of Safety and Security. But hindsight has also provided understanding of the political dynamics that operated from the start. As Elrena van der Spuy, a criminologist at the University of Cape Town, put it several years later, "It was a struggle over who steers and who rows the boat. The cops thought that all the community actors could be co-opted, and we progressives were suspicious of all state actors. . . . We embraced a romantic communitarianism not yet shaped by the realities of bureaucratic and state structures."[31]

The program produced some consequences that were positive, or at least compensatory. Grassroots efforts to work with police revealed and fostered community leadership that had not previously been acknowledged. A number of younger people found in community policing a way to move up and out of the township—an advance for them but a mixed blessing for the communities deprived of their talents and vigor. Working with CPFs gave to some an important rung on the career ladder; Zelda Holtzman started as a community organizer committed to both popular justice structures and to community policing, then went first into the national government to promote affirmative action and then into provincial government in the Western Cape, where she was deputy police commissioner for several years.

Looking back in 1999 Janine Rauch, a policing expert who has worked in the new government as well as with several NGOs, felt that the major achievement of the planning period was not agreement on a particular model of community policing but "bringing police face-to-face with their clients" and fostering the principles for which the early CPF program stood—"the preservation of respect for the community, a consultation process."[32] At that point she favored the development of other mechanisms to make the police accountable to the community. The Independent Complaints Directorate would investigate and publicize incidents of police brutality and corruption as well as deaths in custody or "as a result of police action" (during arrest, investigation, etc.), of which there were 681 that year.[33] Rauch and others now saw the debate over the public's participation in policing as part of a larger commitment to crime prevention expressed in the 1996 National Crime Prevention Strategy. The CPFs had operated in isolation, they concluded; interdepartmental projects that involved the delivery of health and education and correctional services should engage police and make them more responsive at a local level. In the Western Cape (and later the Eastern Cape and KwaZulu-Natal) the CPF movement evolved into a network of such projects, called community safety forums (CSF) and largely supported by the United Kingdom and by local government. Described by Schärf as an effort "to enable poor people to participate in planning and implementing large-scale development projects which will increase the quality of life in their area, and in the process hopefully also reduce crime," they attempt to coordinate the activities of national, provincial, and local social service and law enforcement agencies.[34] Although this integrated service delivery scheme has enabled the creation of safety plans tailored to the conditions of the particular communities it serves, it has not attracted more than a sprinkling of citizen representation.

What has been lost by the demise of the CPF movement? The government's decision to back away from the original roles of CPFs, given their theoretical and operational problems, does not, of course, mean that other approaches to enhance police performance were not valid. In fact, better training, the creation of municipal police forces, and redeployment of specialists to local stations has probably improved the crime-fighting capability of the SAPS. But public participation in policing has largely been sacrificed. No alternative form of community policing has taken its place, and the concept has not had a significant effect on SAPS service delivery overall.[35] (It should perhaps be noted that a persistent problem with community policing in other countries as well is the difficulty of integrating other police functions into it, creating a "split force" where those assigned to solve community problems get little help from patrol officers or specialized units.)[36] Neither officials nor activists have made an issue of the fact that the legislative mandate of the Police Service Act for active forums is largely ignored. One of the arguments made by both officials and activists to justify the shift away from community policing was that it had not improved the level of trust between police and citizens; the public doubted the integrity of police and blamed them when arrests did not result in convictions, and the police had no confidence in the competence or political neutrality of residents.[37] But the alternative emphasis on professionalizing the police, which removes them from much close contact with the public, has not yielded trusting communication either. The SAPS has acquired a legitimacy that it lacked in the apartheid and colonial past in the sense that no open resistance to police activity now exists, but the cooperative consideration of threats to community safety is rare.[38] Furthermore, the lack of an active civil society engaged in public deliberation over policy directions for police has made it easier for the elites of the post-1999 government to redefine police priorities to embrace a "back to basics" approach and has enabled the police sweeps of Operation Crackdown, which, since 1999, have resulted in mass arrests but few convictions. The tough talk that has accompanied this focus has been popular in the townships beleaguered by violent crime, but it does not foster close scrutiny of police activity. Political transformation no longer includes institutional reform that places the values of democratic accountability, openness, and participation at the center of policing. To quote the preamble to the proceedings of a 2003 conference on police accountability, "[P]olitical and public attention to oversight issues appears to have faded."[39]

Lay Assessors

The prospect of a newly inclusive society affected late-apartheid politics in many ways. Leaders of the regime rushed to reform a legal system that was thought, even by its operatives, to lack legitimacy. They proposed several initiatives to increase access to courts and give ordinary citizens—that is, the oppressed black multitude who would now become the majority of the polity—a voice in the processes of justice. Mediation for labor and community disputes was introduced in the 1980s, and a small claims court enabled litigants to plead their cases without the expense of a lawyer or the cumbersome procedures of the higher courts. As the transition to democracy approached, the minister of justice recommended using lay assessors and lay judges in civil and minor criminal cases; in a 1991 parliamentary debate over mediation legislation he announced that "it is envisaged that members of local communities will become more intimately involved with the administration of justice."[40]

The intimate involvement anticipated by the minister was not for the purpose of encouraging popular, nonstate mechanisms for resolving disputes or handling criminal matters. The sentence that followed the one quoted above reveals his attitude toward that approach: "This will assist those communities' leaders who wish to rid their communities of the scourge of the people's courts." Public participation in judging would be an auxiliary function to formal processing by courts of the state, adopted for the purpose of validating that system rather than democratizing it or making it more just. Only the state could define or supply justice, and community participation would reinforce that authority.

So the passage of the 1991 Magistrates' Courts Amendment Act was not a triumph of popular sovereignty.[41] Nor did it usher in a new era of pluralism in which the state and private citizens would share responsibility for judging. In fact, the real motive for the enactment seems to have been expedience. A training document for magistrates instructing them in the implementation of the act casts it solely in terms of assistance to the court in decision making. Jeremy Seekings, whose research conducted in 1997 with Christina Murray is the sole study of lay assessors in South Africa, notes that in this early phase, "[t]he use of lay assessors is presented as a technocratic reform, not a transformation of the court system."[42] Whether because blacks resisted participation in the system that had subjugated them or because magistrates could choose not to use assessors, lay assessors were rarely appointed.[43] In one area east of Johannesburg the senior magistrate pressured those who served under him to use assessors and enlisted the help of prominent Africans to recruit willing assessors with the message that serving in this role would enhance access to justice; but this was the exception.

After the 1994 elections, however, the legislation, along with a constitutional endorsement of "the participation of people other than judicial officers in court decisions," provided an avenue for establishing the legitimacy of the courts under more favorable circumstances.[44] The new minister of justice, Dullah Omar, was committed to making the courts representative in terms of both race and gender, and in particular he thought lay assessors would "enable more and more people to identify themselves with the judicial system."[45] He appointed a committee of the chief magistrate of Cape Town and two prominent attorneys to set up the system, and a pilot project began to operate in the Western Cape. By August 1995, even before the completion of a pilot project in the Cape, the committee reported that lay assessors were being widely used in four provinces and in parts of a fifth, and less than a year later the minister announced plans for new legislation to make the system mandatory throughout the country.

The decision to adopt this particular form of lay participation seems to have been determined by the fact that it seemed both familiar and relatively harmless to the government officials and their advisors who considered the matter. It was familiar because assessors had been used in criminal trials at least since Union in 1910, though they were "experts" who sat with the judge or magistrate—lawyers and former judicial officers, by and large. It seemed harmless because there was still a lot of leeway for magistrates to choose *not* to use assessors (except in murder cases in the regional courts, where they were required) and because it was both less expensive and less threatening than the alternative of a jury, an option that was never seriously considered.

For American and British readers accustomed to a jury system, the rejection by South Africa of this form of lay participation bears examination. Although the jury has been in decline in the United Kingdom for fifty years, hearing only a tiny percentage of cases, it is fundamentally a British institution, "the glory of the English law" according to Blackstone. Theoretically it provides more than a popular evaluation of decisions made along the line from an arrest to a prosecutor's summation. It is also intended to confer legitimacy to criminal justice as implementer of the law and a brake on judicial power. And for some it represents the epitome of self-government, "in which everyman and everywoman must take upon themselves the serious role of judgement of their peers."[46] In these roles it is, as Tocqueville noted, a "pre-eminently political institution."[47]

Juries have not caught on in many countries for a number of reasons. There is no necessary correspondence between democracy and the existence of a jury. Poland had juries before Communism collapsed and still does; Japan suspended its jury system in 1943 and, when writing a new constitution after World War II, it "was not thought necessary to a well-ordered democracy."[48] Russia, which used juries in the late nineteenth century but abolished them at the time of the 1917 revolution, has revived the jury in the post-Soviet era.

Juries are often considered unreliable, expensive, and incompetent. Lawyers and judges, eager to protect professional standards and ever mindful of incursions on their territory, are often opposed to juries. An American judge of the school of legal realism wrote of the jury trial, "A better instrument could scarcely be imagined for achieving uncertainty, capriciousness, lack of uniformity, disregard of previous decisions—utter unpredictability."[49] And, at the time when the question of instituting lay participation in the magistrates' courts of South Africa was at issue, Ellison Kahn, a prominent legal scholar, entitled a much-discussed five-part article, "Restore the Jury? Or 'Reform? Reform? Aren't Things Bad Enough Already?'"[50] In it he argued that the legitimacy that a jury might convey to a justice system was outweighed by the general incompetence of juries—attributable to lack of education or professional training or to language barriers—and by the costs that a jury system would incur. He also expressed concern with the risk of nullification—the situation in which juries vote their conscience or their prejudices instead of following the law—and assumed that jurors would be more subject to irrationality in their judgments than judges or assessors drawn from the legal profession. His trump card was a list of lawyers and judges—heads of legal societies, distinguished academics—who opposed the reintroduction of juries into the South African legal system.[51]

The jury has an uncomfortable history in South Africa. While black jurors with education and property were allowed in the colonial Cape, they were rare in pre-Union Natal, and in the Boer republics (Transvaal and the Orange Free State) jurors were required by law to be white and male. The national Criminal Procedures and Evidence Act passed in 1917 reinforced this diversity by requiring that jurors be voters (excluding all women and black men except in the Cape) but otherwise created uniform provisions for jury service in the provinces. In effect jurors had to be white males between the ages of twenty-five and sixty who were literate in one of the two official languages (English and Afrikaans), owned property or had a substantial income, and had not been convicted of a serious crime. Most professionals were exempted from jury service, so the juries generally consisted of white farmers, tradesmen, artisans, and clerks. Despite a lack of research on jury behavior, anecdotal evidence is strong that juries often pitted white Afrikaner farmers against black urban defendants, making a mockery of any notion that a suspect's case was evaluated by peers. Kahn cites the 1926 memoir of a judge who says he was "astonished by the verdict" in a case where a white jury acquitted a black man of a rape charge, suggesting the unlikelihood of a jury outcome that could counter entrenched racial bias.[52] An accused person could choose to be tried by a judge instead of a jury, and in this event the judge could (but was not required to) use "expert" assessors to assist him in fact-finding. Gradually, this option replaced the jury in most cases. Furthermore, parliament began to restrict the use of jury trials legislatively—in 1948 by allowing the minister of justice to mandate a nonjury trial in cases that required an understanding of bookkeeping or accounting; in 1954 by shifting the presumption so that the accused had to request a jury in a higher court trial; in 1962 by prohibiting jury trials in sabotage and terrorism cases—a measure perhaps convenient for averting the possibility of hung juries that might result from white liberals sympathetic to defendants engaged in the liberation struggle. In 1969 the jury was abolished outright.[53]

Did the jury fall into disrepute in South Africa because it was thought to be unjust or irrational or because it was inconvenient for judges and magistrates? Seekings sees professional self-interest at the root of the abandonment of the jury in 1969; lawyers and judges could easily do without the wild card that juries represented in the legal process.[54] Perhaps the same could be said for the new government's failure to restore them in the 1990s; in the post-apartheid era juries would have to be multiracial and multicultural, and women could not be excluded. Managing the process would be even more complex and conflictual than in the bad old days; the South African legal community was almost universally opposed. The "juries" of the informal courts in the townships gave notice of how erratic and arbitrary a sizable group of ordinary citizens could be. And the costs of setting up and maintaining a jury system—for compensating jurors, recruiting the jury pools, conducting juror qualification assessments, evaluating exemption claims, and so on—would be prohibitive. The adoption of a system that called for fewer than the twelve jurors required in an American criminal case would have reduced expenses somewhat, but in a country with such great ethnic and cultural diversity the larger jury might be necessary to balance perspectives, take into account all relevant influences, and convey a sense of fairness.[55]

The model of public participation in the lower courts that emerged from post-apartheid planning was a compromise that responded to diverse interests. It was less costly than a jury and easier to control, a stopgap measure of reform for the magistrates' courts until more judicial officers of color could be appointed. It had the potential to transform the lower judiciary in both senses—conferring instant "representivity" and affecting attitudes in the courtroom. Where the power of judging had been entirely in the white hands of magistrates appointed during apartheid, black assessors—very few were white—now acquired it virtually overnight, at least with respect to the determination of guilt.[56]

The 1991 legislation that authorized the appointment of lay assessors demonstrated great deference to the discretion of magistrates by allowing for considerable variation in the way the system operated.[57] A magistrate could choose to use either one assessor or two or none, except that the use of two assessors—either lay or expert—was mandatory in murder cases unless the accused objected, in which case the magistrate had the discretion to proceed without assessors or to appoint either one or two assessors. Senior magistrates could choose assessors themselves or—the method preferred by the Department of Justice—turn to a locally representative district assessors committee made up of leaders of community organizations. Assessors could participate in all stages of a proceeding, or only during trial; they could sit with the magistrate all the time or only be called when needed; or magistrates could choose not to use them at all. Assessors could ask questions of witnesses during a trial, usually through the magistrate but sometimes on their own—or not. They could be consulted on the bench in full view of the public (furthering transparency) or could adjourn to magistrates' chambers or even the tearoom (perhaps furthering candor and deliberation) for discussion of a case. They sometimes served almost full-time, more often only a few days a month. Sometimes they received training in basic legal principles that are relevant for criminal cases, more often not.

Supplemented with directives from the Department of Justice and guidelines prepared by the Justice College, the legislation did, however, dictate some commonalities. A magistrate was permitted to appoint assessors, in the words of the statute, "if he [*sic*] deems it expedient for the administration of justice."[58] To determine that, he (or she, though there were few women until the late 1990s) was to take into account the cultural and educational background of the defendant, the seriousness of the offense charged, and the likely punishment if the defendant were convicted, and "any other matter or circumstance which he [*sic*] may deem to be indicative of the desirability of summoning an assessor or assessors."[59] The magistrate could choose lay assessors (described by the Justice Department as persons "without experience in the administration of justice") to evaluate matters of fact—not legal questions—and to vote on guilt and advise on sentencing. Majority rule determined the vote on the determination of guilt, so in the event that two assessors participated in the trial they could outvote the magistrate. (If one assessor participated and voted differently from the magistrate, the magistrate's vote prevailed.) Although it is not mentioned in the legislation, appointment of politically active assessors and illiterates was discouraged. The government was responsible for compensation to the assessors for expenses and a stipend, the amount to be determined by the minister of justice. (In fact, that amount was very low—up to about one hundred rand [approximately twenty dollars] a day at the time when the use of lay assessors was at its zenith—but it was still more than many laborers in South Africa make in full-time jobs.)

Because there has been so little research on the South African lay assessor system—and because lay assessors were widely in use for such a brief period—it is difficult to generalize about its effects. Whether it improved either the quality of justice dispensed by the magistrates' courts or public perceptions of that justice is a question that awaits more rigorous attention than can be provided here. But Seekings's work and interviews I conducted in the Western Cape in 1997 and 2000 suggest both strengths and limitations in the use of lay assessors as a public-empowering development in the criminal justice system of the new democracy.

It is possible to describe in general terms the characteristics and attitudes of assessors appointed between 1994 and 1997, the period when their use was most aggressively promoted. They were disproportionately middle class and well educated in the communities they represented, and many were professionals—teachers, social workers, accountants. They tended to be older—many were retired—and they were more likely to be male than female (six out of every ten were male in the Seekings study). They were thoughtful about their assignments, divided on whether or not specialized training was necessary to perform them with maximum competence. Some wanted a decision-making role in sentencing; others were glad not to have that responsibility. Seekings found that 75 percent of assessors believed that their use should be compulsory in all but the most minor cases, but also found them divided on whether there should always be two assessors to provide the constant possibility that they could overrule the magistrate.

As with the government officials and civil society representatives, assessors had varying justifications for the new system. Many believed that their presence was legitimizing the court system. "People can see that the decisions are not all made by rich white people," an assessor said to me in 1997.[60] Another commented, "I feel the public realizes that the lay assessor is one of them, from amongst them and sitting with the magistrates makes the accused and his kinfolk more relaxed and accepting." Many assessors also believed that they could affect the procedures and outcomes of justice, often by increasing the court's sensitivity to context. "I live in the township," said one, "and I'm used to violence and know most of the living condition of most of the accused persons and thus I think I would be able to judge an accused from an informed position." They sometimes felt they had an educative role with respect to the magistrate, "to make the magistrate see things more humanly than basically legally." And, finally, they felt they were making a contribution to democracy. "There is an opportunity now for communities to get involved in the judicial process," one assessor told me; and another offered, "This insures that there is transparency in the judicial process." Although I certainly did not interview a representative sample of assessors—self-selection of interviewees ensures that the interviewer will speak with the most eager and articulate—I came away with a strong sense that commitment to a democratic enterprise on a variety of bases transcended any interest in the modest material rewards and the status of being an assessor.

It should not be assumed that the assessors' view of their greater identification with the accused necessarily meant that they would be more lenient. Although generally there was agreement between magistrates and assessors, the former said that assessors tended to be more punitive than they themselves were—more ready to convict and favoring more severe penalties, especially where crimes of violence were involved. A chief magistrate maintained that assessors were reluctant to grant bail. Assessors often agreed that they were tougher on defendants who were terrorizing a community; in response to Seekings's questionnaires they were more likely than magistrates to say that the courts were too concerned with defendants' rights and less likely to give priority to them than to the protection of society.[61] (It is not clear whether this finding reflects the selection criteria for assessors or their lack of commitment to or understanding of their new constitution, or something else.) On the other hand, many assessors said that they were less punitive than magistrates where the charge was acquisitive crime and suggested that their perspective was preferable when crime was something like stealing food because they were better able to understand the need. Seekings surmised that as assessors gained experience, their attitudes became less punitive, perhaps reflecting a more nuanced view of the causes of crime and the effects of punishment. A college composition written in 1996 by a particularly thoughtful woman assessor illustrates the deepened understanding that comes from experience:

> Assessors can only be an advantage to the accused and complainant because they come with insights of everyday life in the community which might seem improbable to magistrates, prosecutors and attorneys. The assessors, though expected to be objective and to deal with the facts of the matter, are also able to raise perspectives relevant to the community from which the accused and complainant originate. This widening of access to justice democratizes our courts.[62]

From the beginning a majority of magistrates resisted the lay assessor program. Sometimes they raised theoretical objections, arguing that lay assessors limited judicial independence and that there were other ways to ensure accountability, transparency and representivity in the courts.[63] Most magistrate respondents in the Seekings study felt they understood the problems of ordinary people and "the community" (i.e., black areas in their magisterial districts), perhaps explaining in part their view that public participation in judging was unnecessary. Some saw a fundamental contradiction in the contributions of professionals (magistrates and expert assessors) and community representatives. The professionals are tied to a logic of legal rationality that values an impartial judgment with respect to whether the defendant is guilty of the illegal behavior charged, which they believed could be determined only with the training and perspective of the lawyer. Lay assessors are to be used for the purpose of providing context that may contribute to the understanding of the behavior of the accused, not whether or not the act was committed. The value of community representatives in judging is thus most relevant at the time of sentencing, they argued, when the severity of the sanction may well depend on the circumstances of the commission of the act or the environment in which it occurred.[64] But the assessors had no power at the time of sentencing, only an advisory role that is often ignored.

Magistrates had less abstract quarrels with the system too, frequently resenting the way it was being implemented or denigrating the quality of the assessors. They objected to the fact that two assessors could outvote them on the question of guilt—although that almost never happened—and as a result they rarely chose two assessors. (One magistrate I interviewed, however, justified his unwillingness to use two assessors with the rationale that assessors only reinforced the original views of the magistrate, so why bother with more than the single assessor that would lend authority to his judgments for black observers.) Many felt that assessors were ignorant or too emotional or that they could not be "objective," at least not without legal training. They asserted that accused often rejected the use of assessors, though it is unclear how widespread that was or why it occurred. Assessors often tried to go beyond their evaluation of the facts to make judgment on the law, magistrates alleged; "most of them know what they must do, but they always like to go a bit farther," said a senior magistrate.[65] Complaints included a lack of reliability—assessors sometimes didn't show up to complete a trial or fell asleep during the proceedings—and concern that assessors knew the litigants and did not then disqualify themselves. Sometimes the magistrates saw assessors as not representative enough because they were among the more privileged of their peers, other times as *too* representative of their communities and therefore incapable of independent judgment. Most of the time their objections boiled down to extreme discomfort over lay participation as an incursion on professional responsibility and authority. They thought assessors should be assisting them, and assistance did not include independent judgments of any kind.

Resistance was certainly not universal. Seekings found that magistrates who used assessors routinely often felt very positive about them, not so much because of the cultural benefits of their closeness to the communities of the victim or accused but because it was useful to have another viewpoint. Whether positive attitudes predated the experience with assessors was not clear, but Seekings quotes one magistrate as saying, "I was hostile at the beginning. It was forced on us—and it was this that caused the hostility, but now I think that, if you have the right person, it's good. It's working well, with some of them. Some are excellent."[66] When I asked both magistrates and assessors why there tended to be agreement on issues of fact, most said that in cases where decisions were not immediately obvious they had good deliberations that produced consensus. Assessors did not tell me that magistrates pressured them or that they felt intimidated.

Even among the more positive magistrates, however, enthusiasm was waning by the time of my second round of interviews in 2000. They cited serious problems of implementation, mostly related to problems of resources, competence, and coordination that beset the general functioning of the magistrates' courts.[67] Preoccupied with delays in court processing, unpaid pay increases, and basic problems of courtroom infrastructure like nonfunctioning toilets and phones, they complained that lay assessors slowed the proceedings still more. Demand on the courts had increased, too. Legislation passed in 1998 added jurisdiction over more serious crimes; magistrates could now try crimes for which the penalties were up to three years in the district courts and fifteen years in the regional court.[68] The confusion of litigants and officials about how to proceed under the new dispensation had so clogged the courts that the addition of lay assessors merely seemed irrelevant and costly, another drain on resources that were already insufficient.

Unlike community policing, the lay assessor system was abandoned through omission, rather than by policy statements that backed away from the reform. Chief magistrates did not press the use of assessors, and magistrates simply stopped appointing them. Nowhere on the website of the Department of Justice and Constitutional Development can any mention of lay assessors be found, although the ministry is responsible for the creation and maintenance of the lay assessor system. A prominent judge says, "Lay assessors never had a powerful champion."[69] The legislation to make their use for violent crimes mandatory simply died. One explanation that has been proffered was that the community committees that were to be set up to nominate assessors could not be organized, but the failure to accomplish that seems merely evidence of a lack of political will to make it happen rather than an insurmountable administrative obstacle. Perhaps if the proposal had been supported by the higher court judiciary, it would have passed, but judges too were resistant to the idea of lay assessors even as an option, much less as a requirement.

South Africa's failure to institute lay assessors in the magistrates' courts is sometimes attributed to a lack of clarity—about the reasons for introducing public participation in judging and how it should be done.[70] There was indeed considerable variation in the ways the proponents of lay assessors thought of the institution. The politicians who wished to legislate mandatory use of assessors in some cases considered it a matter of legitimizing the lower courts, while the Department of Justice bureaucrats who issued guidelines and other materials for the assessors saw them as an enrichment of the court's capacity to do justice. Those documents, however, display contradictory conceptions of the role of the assessors; the application form for lay assessors states at the top, "It is a service, not job creation!" but the code of conduct calls them "judicial officers" and warns the reader not to comment on "matters pertaining to his/her profession." The academics and activists wanted lay assessors to reflect democratization—its respect for the communities and cultures from which defendants and victims came, its sensitivity and respect for rights. In their view, justice would be done (the professional view) and would be seen to be done (the political view) as concomitants of the less instrumental belief in lay participation as valuable for its own sake.

But the collapse of the lay assessor initiative resulted from united resistance by the actors in the drama of setting up a public role in the courts rather than chaos caused by a squabble among them. Within their particular arenas of power, legislators, bureaucrats, and magistrates set aside their divergent views about the purposes of lay participation and came together to give the idea a quiet burial. The lay assessors program was a casualty of the legal profession's certainty that preserving "expertise" in their bailiwick was more valuable than introducing popular participation. Once the country experienced the triumph of the first democratic elections in 1994, legitimacy that had seemed elusive before the end of apartheid proved to be within reach without the bother of managing lay assessors. In the parts of the country where it was implemented, the lay assessor system immediately brought a new look to the lower courts: "Since its inception approximately two years ago, there has already been a marked improvement in eradicating the perception of the 'white face of justice,'" a Department of Justice official commented in 1998.[71] But lay assessors were promptly supplemented by the appointment of black magistrates and prosecutors, and what legitimacy crisis there had been with respect to the lower courts faded. One of the members appointed by the minister of justice to the original committee that designed the pilot project—now a chief magistrate—told me in 2000 that the system was never intended to be permanent, that in future "the need for lay assessors will fall away because people will have trust and confidence in the presiding officers."[72] It is hard to escape the conclusion that the professional arrogance of lawyers (including many on the left) trumped the ideal of greater democracy in court processing when it was put to the test. As for the aim of contributing not only to the appearance of justice but to justice itself, the overwhelming administrative problems in the lower courts had taken such priority by the end of the decade that—at least for the magistrates that I interviewed—the question seemed too hypothetical to be taken seriously.

Again it seems appropriate to ask what is lost by the government's abdication of responsibility for this form of public participation in criminal justice. Magistrates and others in the legal profession may be correct in thinking that the fairness of the lower courts can be increased with other measures that make their proceedings more representative and more sensitive—the appointment of "expert" assessors who are black or female and come from the communities of most victims and accused, or greater use of witnesses to reflect community views. If the courts are no longer perceived as instruments of oppression, the legitimacy argument collapses as a justification for lay participation. But in several different forms, the argument from democracy remains. Lay participation of the sort that non-"expert" assessors can provide increases the accountability and transparency of court processes. It embodies the consent to be governed in as direct a way as voting. Magistrates often make the argument that lay assessors simply don't understand the complexities of weighing evidence, applying presumptions, and evaluating the credibility of witnesses. But assessors are the public, and if the public cannot understand the basics of criminal proceedings, it cannot effectively rule itself. If lay assessors cannot master the intricacies of a criminal trial for the purpose of evaluating a factual situation, revision of the legal system should be in order. If they are competent, however, their participation in determining guilt in a court of law is a particularly meaningful attribute of citizenship because it engages people in a process of deliberation over how the order of the society is to be preserved.

Lay participation has another important function in a newly democratizing country—to provide citizen oversight of trials of crimes committed to support the prior authoritarian regime. Surely court decisions that reflect the perspectives of ordinary citizens on political crimes are an important part of the cleansing of the past, corollary to the release of political prisoners that usually accompanies regime change. Although it will be said that lay assessors would tend to be vindictive and rule unfairly on the behavior of their former oppressors, there is no evidence that ordinary citizens are any less objective with regard to the matters of fact on which they would rule than lawyers or judges. And it might be argued that in determining the guilt of apartheid defendants lay assessors would be more likely to judge fairly than those judges and magistrates who are holdovers from the old regime. As mentioned in chapter 6, in 2002 a conservative Afrikaner judge acquitted Wouter Basson—universally known as "Doctor Death" because of the number of assassinations he had allegedly carried out or ordered as head of the apartheid military's top-secret chemical and biological warfare program—on forty-six charges of murder, attempted murder, theft, fraud, and drug dealing. Brother of the leader of the Conservative Party, the judge appeared throughout the thirty-month trial to have prejudged the case, continually emphasizing his belief, despite mountains of damning evidence, that the state's arguments were trivial or unfounded. Accused of bias, he refused to recuse himself; he also refused to use assessors (either lay or expert).[73] Although the state made a number of blunders in prosecuting the case, the South African public and press responded with widespread indignation to the acquittal. The judgment was upheld in the Supreme Court of Appeal, however, because the state could find no legal basis on which to fault the judge.[74] What Wim Trengove—one of the country's most distinguished lawyers, who presented the appeal before the Constitutional Court—described as "flawed judicial process" might have been less so with the appointment of assessors.[75]

Nonstate Justice

The participatory justice initiatives that South Africa embraced and abandoned depended on relationships between state and citizen that turned out to be very lopsided. Community policing that was supposed to include joint problem definition and priority-setting did not lessen the dominance of the state after all. Most CPFs that remained after the late 1990s were mere intelligence-gathering appendages to the police; a few, generally in affluent neighborhoods and in parts of the Western Cape, were able to run community safety projects, largely because residents could supplement police budgets to provide sophisticated equipment and communications devices. Lay assessors, always auxiliaries to official judging, had almost no impact on the procedures or judgments of the courts. While the laws changed and the directives for enforcement reflected the new democratic order, the institutions of criminal justice remained essentially unaffected by public participation. The state was still firmly in charge of criminal justice, with citizen oversight limited to the liberal protections—essential but remote—of separated powers and judicial review.

But formal, state-run institutions are not the only source of justice practices in the post-apartheid society.[76] Many nonstate bodies deliver social control and sanctioning—undifferentiated functions, unlike the Western justice system—sometimes with the blessings of the state, sometimes in defiance of it, most often ignored by it. In some rural areas traditional courts (also called chief's courts or customary courts) still hold sway, dispensing justice that is arbitrary by modern standards. The private sector provides security services for profit; it has been estimated that there are four times as many private security employees as public police.[77] Vigilantism is widespread in South African townships, inflicting quick and decisive physical punishment on guilty—or innocent—parties (see chapter 4). Sometimes it is hard to distinguish from ordinary private security because it emanates from very well organized groups that operate over long periods and charge fees to victims for finding and beating suspects; but ad hoc groups of citizens impatient with the inefficiency and delay of the official justice system also take the law into their own hands.[78] Neighborhood watches, which in some communities far outnumber the police, are sometimes benign, sometimes violent.[79] Street committees and informal community courts—often comprised of older, respected citizens acting as village elders once did—resolve a variety of social conflicts in some communities, though their influence has waned since they are no longer a linchpin of the liberation movement.[80]

Nonstate justice bodies are not necessarily antagonistic to the state's efforts to control crime and disorder. They often act cooperatively: private security companies whose mission is the prevention of crime will usually report the offenses they observe to police; and street committees, which rarely make the distinction between civil and criminal matters, refer matters involving serious interpersonal violence for formal prosecution. The state enables many informal practices, even to the extent of permitting the use of indigenous law by certified chiefs, who receive stipends; the constitution recognizes the possibility of extrajudicial institutions and protects the right of people "to participate in the cultural life of their choice."[81] Police participate in nonstate justice—directly by giving evidence in community courts and indirectly by using neighborhood watch groups to expand a precinct's surveillance capacity. Sometimes they simply set aside the constraints of their formal role to track down and inflict violent punishments on a suspect at the request of the presumed victim. The fluidity of relationships between state and nonstate justice often permits great selectivity as to what is reported to the formal system and what is handled *ex-judice*.

From its birth the democratic South African state has been ambivalent about most of these forms of nonstate justice. The ANC has been leery of challenging tribal chiefs that still have some authority in the rural areas, despite their refusal to support equality for women. With high crime rates and little capacity to do much about them, the government has recognized the inevitability of self-help from many sources. Several police officials—station commanders and higher—whom I spoke with in 1997 predicted (off the record) that vigilante activity and unregulated community dispute resolution would grow if crime did not diminish, even if the efficiency and effectiveness of law enforcement improved. While they tended to repeat the public view that criminals operate with impunity because of the restraints placed on police and courts by the new constitution, they also pointed to divisions within the society that generate conflict beyond the reach of the formal justice system and would do so even if police and courts could be tougher on suspects and defendants. The ubiquity of alcohol and the paucity of jobs would still trigger domestic violence, they felt, and the lack of legitimate avenues for advancement for unskilled blacks would still foster drug gangs and the syndicates that stole luxury cars at gunpoint. Violence in the few legal areas of entrepreneurship that did not require education or capital, like group transportation—taxi wars have brought death to innocent riders as well as to competing drivers—was to be expected. Given both the structural causes of crime and the limitations of formal criminal justice institutions, the informal mechanisms—like the informal economy—were a useful supplement. Magistrates, on the other hand, generally thought informal justice was second-class justice that lacked the safeguards of formal processes and was tolerated only because it was cheap and served the poor.

The criminal justice operatives saw nonstate structures as exceptional—necessary deviations from the norm of formal justice. Participants, on the other hand, and a number of scholars and social activists supported nonstate bodies with more affirmative arguments, stressing values that were presumed to flow from the informal justice sector. They noted that resolving conflicts through consensual rather than adversarial proceedings, as the street committees and similar bodies generally have done, is an approach better suited to communities where people must live together in close proximity once action has been taken. The informal structures handled a wide variety of disputes—assaults, thefts, breaches of trust, issues of succession—without making distinctions between what Western legal systems consider criminal and civil. They treated most matters that came before them simply as problems to be solved within the community, avoiding the retributive discourse of crime and punishment that would label the perpetrator as an outsider. Their supporters saw them as drawing on participatory and restorative traditions that were part of indigenous South African cultures.

Since 1994 there has been consideration of state sponsorship and regulation of some of the nonstate justice structures to create responsible, accountable mechanisms that would operate alongside the formal legal system. Planners of the new order have recognized that in a country with such diverse cultures, deeply embedded, a single set of practices—indubitably stemming from Western traditions—does not take into account the many visions of justice that prevail in South Africa's black communities. They know that informal justice provides social support as well as control and that township institutions "set and reproduce the values and norms by which the majority of residents live."[82] And they understand that, to a certain extent, the use of nonstate formations to deal with crime is filling in for the state's incapacities. So proposals for community courts have floated around the legal community for most of the past decade. Workshops were held around the country in 1998 to assess popular support for them—it was strong—and to obtain suggestions for how the state should support them. The premier of Gauteng at the time, Mathole Motshekga, was a vigorous proponent, arguing that a mechanism for sifting serious crimes from minor matters that should be dealt with outside the formal system was needed: "When a hungry child walks past a house and steals a piece of bread do we really need to bring it to the police and send the youngster through the criminal justice system? For some things, communities need to impose their own moral authority."[83]

Debates about the relationship between state and nonstate structures have centered on whether community courts should be incorporated into the formal system and regulated by it or whether the state should supply support and guidance that ensures compliance with basic constitutional principles but allows a good deal of procedural discretion in line with the cultures of the citizens using the informal system.[84] Problems inhere in both approaches. Incorporation would have such advantages as providing state assistance with serving summonses and permitting appeals to the formal court system, and judgments would be enforceable. Training and inspections would lessen the possibility of conduct that would violate the constitution. But the organic quality of the existing structures would be lost, and resistance to the formal system might simply lead to the re-formation of nonstate bodies. The political and cultural diversity of South Africa's black population militates against the straitjacket of a single, state-centered system; the South African Law Commission has proposed a separate tier of dispute resolution forums that would accommodate a variety of cultural and political allegiances. Finally, the Justice Department noted that the creation of one hundred to three hundred new state courts with paid personnel would be prohibitively expensive.[85]

The alternative option would leave control of the informal justice bodies in the hands of community participants, but it would increase accountability by providing for minimal surveillance by local government (and some involvement of established NGOs) and requiring that serious crimes be referred to state courts. It would guarantee access to justice that many people in townships and villages feel they do not have and would keep the user-friendly qualities that residents see as advantages over the formal justice system. It would be much cheaper, providing some organizational resources to community groups but retaining the volunteer basis on which most participants serve. From the government's perspective, however, the courts would still be outside the system that carries out the new constitutional order; they would, in fact, not be considered to be courts, but rather dispute resolution centers with the capacity to deal with a wide range of community problems. Given that community courts of the past were subject to local political pressures and were often biased against young people, women (especially in the traditional courts), and immigrants, the planners worried that the looser connection of this option to the formal system might result in denial of the constitutional right to an "independent and impartial tribunal or forum."[86] The guarantees of due process would also be largely suspended, though a person would have the option to be brought before a formal court rather than the community tribunal. Schärf expressed the dilemma this way:

> The choice thus boils down to one between effective social control and social support on the one hand, and due process, coupled with a splitting of civil and criminal matters, on the other. The first would have to remain outside of the state's family of courts because it cannot squeeze into existing legal categories, the other becomes a state-sponsored lower tier of courts.[87]

But this debate has proved to be academic. Despite the South African Law Commission's proposal for "community forums" in 1999, legislation was never introduced into parliament, and the commission's project committee on alternative dispute resolution has not moved on its proposal for the support of responsible dispute resolution projects. The interest in restorative approaches that was behind the proposal for community courts has been channeled to the safer arena of juvenile justice. (One observer notes the irony that the idea of restorative justice has been "marginalized" when the Truth and Reconciliation Commission was sold to the public as a restorative institution.)[88] In September 2002 the minister for justice and constitutional development introduced into the National Assembly a Child Justice Bill, legislation that provided for diverting many youthful offenders from the justice system and calling for a widened range of sentencing options and restorative procedures. Youth organizations were confident of its passage and began to design programs based on its provisions. A year after the bill was introduced the Portfolio Committee on

Justice and Constitutional Development was holding informal hearings on the bill, and the 2004–5 budget for the Department of Justice and Constitutional Development included a modest allocation for child justice programs. As of September 2005, however, the bill was still in committee.

Whither Participation?

It is easy to conclude at this point that there is now simply no state support for public-empowering justice initiatives. This would not be quite accurate. The national budget for 2004–5 includes an allocation for the establishment of parole boards comprised of citizens making decisions about the release and reintegration of prison inmates; the new system went into effect in October 2004. Provincial departments of community safety still provide a modicum of support for CPFs, which have clearly been dropped, however, as a national priority. Nongovernmental organizations that are sponsoring restorative justice or community dispute resolution programs have managed to find funding from local governments or national departments other than those principally responsible for justice initiatives (the Department of Justice and Constitutional Development and the Department of Safety and Security). And sponsors of these projects point to the government white papers that have expressed support for alternative justice mechanisms in the fight against crime.

But support for broadly participatory activities and organizations appears to be primarily rhetorical and worth very little in practice; financing is meager, and the necessity of cobbling together marginal funding sources keeps the progressive programs small and local. The Community Safety Forums that succeeded CPFs were funded by the British in the hope that they could be mounted around the country; despite expressions of support at all levels of government, it hasn't happened. The fact that to a small but significant degree civil society has stepped in where government defaulted does not seem likely in the near future to spur national commitment to forms of public-empowering justice.

At one level the reluctance of the ANC government to invest in public-empowering policies—whether as part of the state-centered system (community policing and lay participation in criminal trials) or as innovations outside the formal institutions (community courts or restorative justice projects)—is understandable. The resistance of police and judges who have adapted in large measure to enormous changes in the past decade surely weighs heavily in considering proposals that depart significantly from the Western models of professionalism and legal formalism adopted by the laws and constitution of democratic South Africa. And new demands on the personnel of the criminal justice system have made their tasks much more complicated. To provide the police training that is needed to function in a democratic society is expensive; to add to that the orientation of community groups—to the workings of formal justice, to the potential and limitations of alternative programs—increases the burden. Building a criminal case has become far more complex since police and prosecutors can no longer rely on (often coerced) confessions; it is only in the last few years that sophisticated investigations for complex crimes have become possible, in large part because the Scorpions—the elite unit of the National Prosecuting Authority—swing into operation when high-profile offenses are alleged (see chapter 6). Increased access to justice is benefiting victims and complainants, to be sure, but it also has administrative drawbacks. Now that people feel freer to bring their grievances and injuries to the courts and the requirements of due process apply when they are there, the criminal process moves more slowly and often threatens to break down completely. (Public rebuke of judges and magistrates for sitting on the bench too few hours in a day recurs with tedious regularity, though there seems to be little difference in this measure of judicial performance between South Africa and the advanced industrial countries it seeks to emulate.) Along with joblessness, poverty, and AIDS, the social chaos that has accompanied the democratic transition—not so different from that of many other countries—has exhausted reformers and put the new political powers on notice of the fragility of the new dispensation.

To abandon the commitment to public involvement in shaping democratic justice in South Africa is also, however, to turn away from a fragmented but suggestive history of popular participation in social ordering even in the worst of times. The consensual traditions of African communities are still powerful enough that Nelson Mandela expressed admiration for them when he was president. People still remember the widespread experience of self-regulation that characterized the liberation struggle; an activist from Imbali told Daniel Nina in 1999, "[W]e . . . see the people's courts playing a nation-building role. . . . They are not a temporary phenomena [*sic*] related to the struggle against apartheid. They will continue to play a role because people feel more comfortable in the people's court than in the formal courts."[89] ANC documents that endorse participatory democracy with respect to criminal justice include the Freedom Charter of 1955, written in an intense period of collective self-examination, and the document issued in 1992 as the ANC was on the brink of political dominance, which puts great emphasis on the role of the public in policing.[90] Most recently the Truth and Reconciliation Commission expressed the confidence of South Africa's democratic leaders that by illuminating the past, the voices of ordinary people would share in defining a peaceful future.

Nonetheless, a *laager* mentality—gathering around the wagons rather than reaching out to discover and develop talents for self-regulation—has prevailed. Two tendencies—both of which reflect habits of the oppressive past—must be added to the institutional problems cited above as explanations.

The democratic South African state has chosen to retain a great deal of central control. Government ministers in charge of criminal justice policy saw the public as assisting the practitioners even when the participatory measures were introduced; but pressures to transform necessitated a brief flirtation with concepts of public empowerment through partnerships, oversight mechanisms, and affirmative action. The justice system rode to legitimacy on the coattails of the new, popularly elected government; when that was established the professionals could ensure a return to relatively traditional institutions. The state's resistance to the reformers was in part a defense of turf: the terrain of decision making was not to be invaded unless it was necessary to give ground for the purpose of institutional survival. Local government was not well established, and trust in provincial officials, even from the same party, was low. Two or three years after the end of apartheid institutional survival seemed to require reducing the risks from decentralized programs, a "back to basics" movement that would redefine the public's interests as consumers rather than producers of public order.

The other tendency is a culture of distrust that has outlasted apartheid. Police who were being asked to work as equals with citizens often found that an absurd expectation; they regarded CPF members as politically motivated at best, criminal at worst. Although residents of crime-ridden communities were willing to make the effort to work with police, the reservoir of suspicion was deep and dark, reinforced in the late 1990s by personal experiences of corruption, media reports of brutality, and statistics that exposed police as among the criminal classes.[91] Magistrates, too, doubted the capacity and integrity of the lay assessors with whom they were asked to share one of their core responsibilities, the determination of criminal guilt. And even the perspective of the post-apartheid minister who initially proposed lay assessors suggests that he had little confidence in the contributions to justice that they could make; he viewed their utility as "help[ing] to establish the legitimacy and credibility of our courts" and even then only until affirmative action could place blacks and women in judicial positions.[92] Little wonder that nonstate justice programs, which would empower the lowest rung of civil society, were not candidates for national investment.

Many of the reformers who initially supported—and worked very hard for—the public-empowering features of criminal justice in their new democracy now consider their demise inevitable. "We were naive," says policing expert Janine Rauch of her efforts to establish the CPFs.[93] "Over-zealous" is the word chief magistrate Gadijah Kahn uses for the efforts that she and her colleagues made to launch the lay assessor program, first as a pilot project in the Western Cape and then as a national program.[94] In 2003 University of Cape Town law professor Christina Murray, whose work with Jeremy Seekings is still the only study of lay assessors, concluded, "To ask them [the lower courts] to do another administrative thing—arrange lay assessors—was never a good idea. They hardly manage to get prosecutors in courts! Rosy-eyed idealism gave way to the realities of practice."[95]

None of these dedicated people, however, denies the relevance of the failed innovations to democratization. And a prominent scholar of policing notes that a variety of approaches to that function can be accommodated in a democratic state. "In a society with very divergent population groups, a multiculturalism shaped by apartheid, should not the accommodation of social differences also recognize the relativity of the policing or social ordering process—that what is unacceptable in one community may be acceptable within the social ordering process of another community?"[96] Organizer Mduduzi Mashiyane noted wistfully in 2001 that CPFs, at their most effective, gave residents a responsible role in protecting themselves and blunted vigilantism as "the community's defense mechanism."[97] He and his colleagues in the NGOs that pushed for public-empowering policies all assumed that the symbolic politics of crime control and the practicalities of implementation in a time of social turmoil had superseded the claims of participatory democracy.

It is tempting to conclude that if South Africa—the economic engine of the African continent, the beacon of democratic transformation at the end of the twentieth century—cannot move in the public-empowering direction as it deepens its commitments to democracy, then no other country can. From this perspective, the lesson from the South African experience is a caution about being overambitious with regard to institutional reform that engages the public. On the other hand, a democratizing country concerned with establishing mechanisms of social order that both elites and ordinary citizens can believe in—particularly states where police and courts in the past were primary instruments of repression—might take away from the South African experience a different conviction: that greater political will from the start and an educative process that engages the population in setting new standards of justice and building new institutions will make it easier to develop "double democracy" and stay the course when political and administrative problems arise.

IV Post-Post-Apartheid Challenges

9 Wielding the Big Stick

> If we are serious about economic growth, the eradication of
> crime must be implemented with utter ruthlessness.
> —Thami Mazwai[1]

> A government that routinely sustains social order by means
> of mass exclusion begins to look like an apartheid state.
> —David Garland[2]

IT WOULD BE HARD to exaggerate the democratic euphoria of the vast majority of South Africans in the early 1990s. Ordinary people in townships and villages celebrated the chance to vote and the new society their votes would usher in; scholars and dissident observers of apartheid convened endlessly to fashion a bold new constitution; and antiapartheid activists basked in their hard-won success. The watchword of "transformation" embraced change that went beyond the establishment of formal requirements of democracy— majority rule in free and fair elections, broad suffrage and access to political candidacy, free and open political communication. Sweeping liberal rhetoric extolling dignity and equality as well as the long-standing socialist commitments of the ANC called for the overhaul of old institutions that had enforced apartheid and the creation of new ones that could empower those victimized by it.

Police and courts were targets for institutional reform even before the 1994 election put an official end to apartheid. In January 1990 F. W. de Klerk, the last apartheid president (just elected by the white minority that knew its days in power were numbered), told South African police that they would no longer be used for political ends.[3] Academics and activists vowed that policing would become democratically accountable and publicly visible—"a source of protection, empowerment and liberty."[4] The dreaded Internal Security Unit would be dismantled and detention for political ends would be ended. The new constitutional court would include blacks and women and legal scholars and would put flesh on the skeleton of the brave new society outlined in the constitution. The newly integrated lower courts would deliver fair and merciful judgments, assisted (and, in limited circumstances, overruled) by ordinary citizens in criminal cases. The reformed criminal justice system would merge indigenous traditions and Western standards for the rule of law. Law enforcement teams from Western democracies would provide sophisticated training in criminal investigation and other functions that had been neglected in apartheid policing, and international donors would help South Africans develop and regulate innovative forms of social control and divert lesser offenders from prison. The development of a culture of rights was appealing not only as protection against the authoritarian brutality of the apartheid regime but also as foundation for building racial, political, and social equality. The ideals of accountability, transparency, representation, and participation that spurred reform were intended to underscore the redistribution of rights and benefits that would accompany the creation of an electoral democracy.

The national mood shifted quickly, however, and so did the reformers' vision of criminal justice performance. Perhaps the disillusionment was an inevitable result of the failure of both law enforcement and the new ANC leaders to understand that the violence that characterized the last days of apartheid could not be vanquished merely by regime change.[5] Although formal reforms of the justice system have endured and provide the base for a rights-oriented system, their reach is very limited and they do not provide a level of protection from crime and disorder that satisfies either the public or the politicians. Within a year of the triumphant national election that formally ended apartheid, political discourse at the highest levels of government pointed the way to a new, punitive criminal justice program.

Crime had become a political issue by the time of the first democratic local elections in 1995. The ANC slogan for those contests was "Tough on crime; tough on the causes of crime," and the Democratic Party promised, "More cops, less crime." A few years later a prominent black judge announced that "if it is the fault of the Constitution that criminals escape arrest and conviction then it must be revisited."[6] By the end of the decade the trend was more pronounced. Although faith in South Africa's democratic future had not erased memories of abuses by police and courts, their image as apartheid's enforcers had receded. The legitimacy crisis they had earlier faced—and which had spurred many creative proposals for a peaceful society—had been replaced by a crisis of confidence, a widespread belief that the criminal justice system was ineffective at addressing the new democracy's violent crimes—murder, robbery, rape, and domestic violence. Charges of inept law enforcement had replaced concerns over the trustworthiness of the police, even though corruption was widespread and it was common knowledge that crime rates for the police were higher than for the population in general. Although there were a few widely publicized incidents of race-based sentencing and callous remarks from the bench, lenient sentences and a bill of rights thought to be too protective of criminals had become far more salient issues than judicial fairness. (Even judges committed to constitutional democracy were complaining that the constitution provided too many "technicalities" that enabled criminals to go unpunished, and the minister of safety and security had vowed to track down criminals "by all means, constitutional or unconstitutional.")[7]

Responses to the crisis of violent crime varied. Ordinary citizens weighed in with strong support for harsh measures, including overwhelming support for reinstituting the death penalty, which was held unconstitutional in 1995.[8] Many supported national and local vigilante groups as more effective in controlling crime than police and courts. Although a common response to reports of a vicious crime is opposition to bail, the ubiquity of vigilantism has also led to perverse positions. Occasionally community people have paid a suspect's bail so that when he is released they can apply their own forms of summary justice—in at least one case killing him by dousing him with petrol and setting him on fire.[9]

Elites have found less violent but equally unambiguous ways to send the same message. Affluent whites, who had been protected from most violent and property crime by apartheid laws that controlled the movements of the majority, have used the white-dominated media to call for harsher criminal penalties; many cite the fear of crime as a reason for emigrating. Media crime reports have become more lurid since the end of apartheid, in part because reporters are now more likely to cover the townships, where criminal syndicates flourish and domestic violence is epidemic. Journalists are not so quick to assume that the solution to the crime problem is a more punitive approach—many are mindful of constitutional imperatives and the worldwide human rights standards that support them—but they continually remind readers and viewers that the South African economy depends on domestic and foreign investors who may be deterred by reports of theft and violence and encouraged by reports of "efficiency" in crime control.

As for the professionals, police have fallen back on their professional culture, focusing on technocratic reforms intended to make them more efficient crime-fighters and rejecting crime prevention approaches in favor of better investigation and intelligence capacity. Improved management to counter the new threats of international organized crime and "urban terrorism" has been the priority.[10] The courts have retreated in some important respects from the high moral ground of the constitution's procedural protections of defendants, as we see later in this chapter. And the politicians busied themselves with passing laws that would send a message to the world as well as to South Africans that the new democracy would not be crippled by violent crime.

South Africa's "tough on crime" legislative program looks strikingly like the approach embraced by the United States over the past generation. It relies on aggressive law enforcement, limited defendants' rights, and harsh penalties. While it may bring occasional victories against a criminal syndicate or temporarily rout immigrant drug dealers from urban neighborhoods, it provides little protection for most communities. Without a corresponding redistributive economic program to bring jobs and homes to South Africa's poor black majority the limited resources that South Africa can commit to crime control are unlikely to significantly affect the country's climate of violence. Furthermore, harsher sentences and aggressive policing may be racially selective, as they have been in the United States, harking back to apartheid-era repression and threatening the liberal democracy they were intended to enhance. Finally, to the extent that "get-tough" measures respond—directly or indirectly—to pressures for reduced social spending, lower taxes, and balanced budgets, they represent a decision to prioritize South Africa's participation in the global market over strengthening the capacity for social control in civil society.

The Current Crackdown

It is important not to portray the punitive program that has taken shape since 1994 as monolithic. At the operational level programs like pretrial release for minor offenders have taken root, and the ANC government has held firm in resisting demands for reinstituting the death penalty. Resource constraints have kept prison building and aggressive police patrol in check. But the law-and-order legislative direction—intensified after 1999 when Mbeki the technocrat replaced Mandela the peacemaker as president—is evident at every turn. And public opinion supporting those policies has affected Constitutional Court decisions on defendants' rights, even though the judges agree that a bill of rights, by its nature, counters majority sentiment in favor of the protection of unpopular interests.[11]

Bail Reform

Enforcing apartheid required that courts acquire firm control over accused persons, which the law enabled. Detention without trial was common, the defendant bore the onus of showing why he or she should be released on bail, and bail was unavailable for a number of both ordinary and political crimes. Transition planners, mindful of unbridled abuse of defendants in the past, were determined to ensure their rights in the new dispensation. The new constitution—the 1993 interim document that was later revised and its successor formally approved by the Constitutional Court—reversed the burden of proof to grant a defendant the right to release on bail "unless the interests of justice require otherwise."[12] This limitation clause was apparently too vague for magistrates making bail decisions, and parliament sought to clarify standards for the decision with a 1995 law that retained the burden of proof on the prosecutor and the court to show why someone should be detained but set out factors to be weighed and allowed the magistrate to hold the accused for a limited time while collecting evidence with which to assess the suitability for release.[13] Honoring the constitution's presumption of innocence, the law allowed defendants charged with all crimes to apply for bail release.

Within two years the government reversed course. Faced with public objections to the perceived laxity of bail release, the drafters of the final constitution (1996) reverted to the apartheid standard, putting the onus for showing why bail was appropriate on the accused, providing a right "to be released from detention *if* the interests of justice permit, subject to reasonable conditions."[14] In 1997 legislation imposed on the accused in serious cases the burden of showing "exceptional circumstances" justifying bail; prosecutor and police would not have to make the case for detention. As a result, release from pretrial detention is now virtually impossible for defendants charged with serious crimes like rape, murder, major fraud, or theft and drug dealing.[15] Objections from most human rights groups in South Africa (the South African Institute of Race Relations, the Human Rights Commission, the Legal Resources Centre, the National Association of Democratic Lawyers, Lawyers for Human Rights) were unavailing when the law was tested in the Constitutional Court. Although several judges worried during oral argument that the "exceptional circumstances" clause imposed too heavy a burden on the defendant and the magistrate, the court, in an uncharacteristically timorous judgment, voted unanimously to support the law.[16] Influenced by vigilante attacks arising out of public anger over crime, the court was willing to uphold a provision that allowed a magistrate or judge to withhold bail if the release of the accused would "disturb the public order or undermine the public peace or security."[17] As one commentator wrote,

> In essence, Kriegler [the judge writing the decision] is telling us that the accused should remain in jail because people have little respect for the criminal justice system and take justice into their own hands. It is doubtful whether a constitutional court the world over has ever before denied an accused person his freedom with a glib reference to the force of mass lawlessness.[18]

Minimum Sentences

Until 1997 South Africa had not had a mandatory penalty since the abolition of the death penalty, which was required for murder between 1917 and 1935, after which parliament effectively abandoned manditoriness by legislating increasingly long lists of "extenuating circumstances" that could mitigate the sentence.[19] But in 1997 the outcry over violent crime led the post-apartheid parliament to enact a law that mandated lengthy minimum sentences for serious offenses—from fifteen years for first offenses of rape or robbery to life imprisonment for crimes like killing a police officer or gang rape.[20] A departure from the minimum was possible only if warranted by "substantial and compelling circumstances."[21] At the outset the law was strictly applied. Between January and October 2001 sixty-nine mandatory life sentences were imposed for the rape of children.[22] That year, however, the Supreme Court of Appeal took on the task of determining a precise definition for the standard by which a court could decide to deviate from the legislative prescription. It opined that judges were not precluded from the usual considerations that might suggest leniency—a previously law-abiding life, for example—in concluding that the mandatory sentence would be "unjust or, as some might prefer to put it, disproportionate to the crime, the criminal and the legitimate needs of society."[23] While this gave judges some leeway, the law is wildly unpopular among them as limiting the discretion that is at the heart of the judicial function. Both magistrates and judges felt (and continue to feel) that the prescription of minimum sentences robs them of the chance to consider varying degrees of culpability determined by the characteristics of the offender and the context in which the punishable conduct occurred.[24] "What do parliamentarians know about sentencing a rapist?" a judge asked a journalist at the time of the constitutional test of the law. "Sitting in Parliament you cannot see the tragedy of individual lives, or the expression in the accused's eyes. All you can think of is how much the electorate will love you for throwing away the prison keys."[25] The authoritarian connotation of harsh, mandatory punishments imposed by a central government law also made many in the ANC uncomfortable; "prescribed minimums" is the preferred euphemism among some in the government.

The Constitutional Court once again sustained the punitive approach with a unanimous decision endorsing the mandatory sentencing scheme. It ruled that the curb on judges' decision-making did not compromise judicial independence, pointing out that even in the United States, a country more committed to the separation of powers than South Africa, the legislative body was permitted to set mandatory sentences and limit the reasons for evading them.[26] Although the lower court had not made an issue of whether the mandatory life sentence constituted a violation of the constitutional prohibition of cruel or degrading punishments, the Constitutional Court raised it and indicated acceptance of the standard adopted in other countries that would reject a sentence only if it were "grossly disproportionate" to the offense. In reaching this conclusion the opinion also forestalled the argument that mandatory sentencing violated the right to dignity guaranteed by Section 10 of the constitution. The Court did not consider whether there was a rational relationship between the mandatory sentencing policy and the objective of reducing violent crime.

Asset Forfeiture

The Prevention of Organized Crime Act went into effect in January 1999, enabling police to address organized crime before it occurs—criminalizing association with a gang or other criminal group and requiring citizens to report suspicions of racketeering activity.[27] It includes the Proceeds of Crime Act, which allows the police to seize property if there is reasonable suspicion that it is the fruit or instrumentality of a crime, whether or not its owner has been criminally charged.[28] (Since the application for a confiscation order is a civil proceeding, it does not trigger a presumption of innocence. To defend against the forfeiture of assets the defendant must show that they were acquired legitimately.) The sweep of the law is very broad, covering anything that could be directly or indirectly used to commit a crime; as one commentator noted, "A thief traveling in his car with suspected stolen car radios stands to lose not only the radios but his car and the garage he parks it in."[29] After two court decisions ordered the return of seized property to apparently guilty defendants, parliament made the law applicable retroactively.

To implement the legislation an asset forfeiture unit was created in 1999 within the National Prosecuting Authority. Its aggressive operations—shutting down brothels, seizing game farms and luxury cars from prominent businessmen, attaching the assets of apartheid's notorious "Dr. Death"—have given both tabloids and sober newspapers like *Business Day* exciting tales of legal derring-do, only slightly deflated when the courts have found them excessive. When seized assets are forfeited, the proceeds are either returned to crime victims—one hundred million rand (about $15 million) between 1999 and the end of 2002—or deposited into the Criminal Assets Recovery Account—sixteen million rand (about $2.5 million)—for use by police.[30] The media attention and the possibility of extra resources for criminal justice provide a strong incentive to apply the law as broadly as possible—which, given the law's definition of a "criminal organization," is very broad indeed. As one critic commented, "Under the existing wording, it is possible that certain political parties could be classed as 'criminal gangs,' and their members persecuted. Whether you should cheer or mourn the passage of the Act depends on how highly you rate the capabilities and fairness of the government."[31] The practical discovery that crime can be useful to fund crime-fighting may, in fact, supersede those concerns.[32]

Although lower courts have struggled with the interpretation of the law and have occasionally thrown out seizures of assets for various reasons, the Constitutional Court has not ruled directly on the constitutionality of the asset forfeiture law. In a decision that dealt narrowly with a procedural detail, however, it described the scheme and its purposes without any indication of disapproval and, noted that "it is now widely accepted in the international community that criminals should be stripped of the proceeds of their crimes."[33] Recently the Supreme Court of Appeal consolidated three cases in order to explicate the phrases "instrumentality of an offence" and "proceeds of unlawful activities," which describe the property that is subject to seizure. Relying heavily on the Constitutional Court's description of the law *as though* it had been endorsed, the Court of Appeal sought to narrow the range of situations in which a seizure would be permissible by reading the phrase "instrumentality of an offence" to mean that "the property must play a reasonably direct role in the commission of the offence," providing a rational connection between the seizure and the purpose of the law.[34] (None of the seizures that were the subject of the three cases met the test, and the lower-court decisions invalidating them were upheld.)

Both parliament and the Constitutional Court have effectively approved policy in this area that seems to contradict the liberal constitution's emphasis on due process. Neil Boister points out that legal confiscation as practiced in South Africa risks the flaws of asset forfeiture in the United States: law enforcement motivated by revenue potential rather than the control of crime; use of civil procedure for penal effect; and confiscation of property whose owner may not have been involved in crime, among others.[35] Even the head of the asset forfeiture unit has acknowledged constitutional difficulties with his program. "We have expected to lose the constitutional aspect for some time," he told *Business Day* after a High Court decision had found that a seizure had violated a defendant's right to reply to his accusers and the constitutional right to privacy, "which includes the right not to have possessions seized."[36]

Police Crackdowns

Lacking demonstrable results from either traditional crime control methods or the innovative, communitarian projects conceived in the early days of post-apartheid euphoria, successive law enforcement officials have trumpeted saturation campaigns against the bad guys. In June 1996 National Police Commissioner George Fivaz announced his "sword and shield" initiative to hunt down high-priority offenders and provide more visible and comprehensive protection of communities. He vowed to arrest ten thousand of the country's most wanted criminals within thirty days; to no one's surprise the goal was not met. Three years later the new minister of safety and security, Steve Tshwete, asserting that "the time for games is over," launched a "ruthless and aggressive" campaign against organized crime, gun laws, and car hijacking, which consisted of sweeps in targeted neighborhoods that netted many arrests but could not be sustained.[37] In early 2000 the new police commissioner, Jackie

Selebi, announced a three-year strategy—Operation Crackdown—to target 124 crime "hot spots" and reorganize the South African Police Service into units that would address their particular crime problems, somewhat like the much-heralded SATCOM program in Brooklyn, New York.[38] Supplementing this would be a high-intensity focus on particular crimes like taxi violence and attacks on farmers. (The approach was the most visible aspect of the National Crime Combating Strategy, a plan that is often referred to but rarely honored.)[39] The police sweeps that followed in Johannesburg and Cape Town netted several thousand arrests of illegal immigrants and low-level drug offenders as well as the confiscation of illegal guns and stolen cell phones. In 2002 the Pretoria police announced that they had arrested fifty thousand people in one month, setting up twenty thousand roadblocks and searching fifty thousand homes and vehicles.[40] While human rights groups and individuals have complained of brutality during raids, which are sometimes conducted jointly with the military, the public often welcomes them as signs that law enforcement is ridding their communities of undesirables.

Raids have been conducted not only to find serious offenders and confiscate guns and drugs, however, but also to roust squatters and intimidate political protesters. In 2001 the Pan Africanist Congress exploited the sluggishness of the government's land reform effort and the desperation of homeless people by promising plots of privately owned and municipal land for a nominal fee to the first comers. To resolve the ensuing crisis the government chose a law enforcement solution—bringing in police and private security to evict people by demolishing their hastily constructed shacks—despite the Constitutional Court's directive to the government nine months earlier to make "reasonable" efforts to provide temporary solutions to homelessness.[41] A year later the government took extraordinary measures to contain dissent at the United Nations World Summit on Sustainable Development—arresting activists in advance from the Landless People's Movement and the groups protesting the country's AIDS policy and the cutoffs of electricity and water; banning demonstrations; and, when a march was finally permitted, bringing out guns and dogs to police its route. Before the summit began police had fired stun grenades into a protesting crowd, injuring three people.

Supplementing these law enforcement crusades, President Thabo Mbeki has taken investigation of some priority crimes out of the hands of the police. Created in 1999, the directorate of special operations—nicknamed the "Scorpions"—is an elite force of about five hundred prosecutors, investigators, and accountants often likened by commentators and government officials to the FBI, which has vast investigatory powers and is overseen by the national director of public prosecution. The new government wished to counter the fragmentation and chaos that accompanied the post-apartheid task of incorporating the homelands police into the SAPS and to focus resources on crimes that had a high impact on the country's economy. It was thought necessary to build an institution that was not tainted, as the police and prosecutors were, with the implementation of apartheid, and which could come into being with the values of the new constitution paramount. "We value efficiency *and* democracy," says the Scorpions' spokesman. "We deliver the same services to all."[42] Its focus on economic crime and political corruption has sent the message that the National Prosecuting Authority will be as tough on the comfortable as on the poor.[43]

Impacts

Support for the big-stick approach of the past few years is by no means universal. Criminologists, constitutional lawyers, and people with a continuing sense of apartheid history have worried that a collision may yet occur between basic constitutional protections and the government's need to prove the impossible: that its justice system can control crime. But concern about the specter of South Africa as a police state—or at least a country only rhetorically committed to human rights where suspects and offenders are concerned—does not, by and large, come from the people most affected by violent crime. For most South Africans the values of due process in criminal justice are too abstract to carry much weight. They are looking to the effects of the get-tough program on the ground.

Although official data report a recent drop in the crimes of murder, vehicle theft, and commercial burglary and some experts agree that violent crime has stabilized, these are incomplete and tentative findings.[44] Even if they do indicate that crime is coming down, the trend cannot be attributed to the get-tough approach. The universe of offenders is very large; even with tougher policies only a small number are caught. More than half of the suspects are not prosecuted, not necessarily because of system incompetence but because the state decides that the cases are too weak to be brought to trial. Finally, defendants are acquitted in a small percentage of cases—75,445 in 2002 as opposed to 327,142 convictions.[45] (This "sieve effect" operates in the United States and the United Kingdom much as it does in South Africa. With the exception of convictions for murder, the percentage of reported crimes that result in conviction is not dramatically lower in South Africa than in those countries.)[46] The reality of few convictions for serious crimes even in a relatively punitive policy environment suggests limits on punishment theories of incapacitation and deterrence. South African gangs have enough appeal among young men without other employment prospects to be assured of replacing those sent to prison with eager recruits who are likely to be unfazed by the remote possibility that they too might go that route. As for police strategies, a generation of research in other countries has demonstrated that, while police may avert a criminal incident in individual situations, there is little that police can do to have an effect on crime overall—not intensifying patrol, not responding more quickly to citizen calls, not improving investigative capabilities.[47] While the police raids of Operation Crackdown have resulted in many arrests, few are for the crimes that most bedevil South Africans in their daily lives; furthermore, the saturation campaigns are too expensive to be comprehensive or to be sustained for long. Most ordinary police functions—patrolling, guarding, rushing to accidents—do not involve fighting crime; although the number of crimes recorded annually per officer rose by 65 percent between 1994 and 2003, at the end of that period the average number was still only 25.6 crimes recorded, or a little more than two per month.[48]

The primary impacts of the get-tough program appear in its effects on the prison population. Between 1996 and 2003 the incarceration rate rose from 280 per 100,000 population to 402.[49] The numbers of people with lengthy sentences—ten years or more—increased by almost 35 percent between 2001 and 2003.[50] Explaining these increases as an outcome of increasing violent crime seems only partially plausible; violence grew very substantially in the late 1980s and early 1990s but did not occasion a corresponding increase in imprisonment. Prison crowding has reached alarming proportions as the daily average prison population rose 65 percent between 1996 and 2003. The Department of Correctional Services acknowledges that, as of March 31, 2003, the prisons exceeded their capacity by 78,507 people, while in 1994 the spokesman for the department put the overpopulation number at 16,794; this increase occurred despite additional beds provided by the construction of new prisons.[51] Denial of bail and the failure of defendants to be able to raise even low bail clogs the courts and prisons with persons awaiting trial and causes violations of the right of defendants to a speedy trial. Delays in moving cases through the courts are apparent; 58,144 prisoners were awaiting trial at the end of March 2003, up from 41,435 at the end of 1997.[52] While the percentage awaiting trial overall in 2003 was 30.6 percent, in some facilities—the most crowded ones—the percentage was as high as 45 percent. The courts have released a number of prisoners held for long periods awaiting trial, and some—for example, a woman who was detained for more than six years—have been bailed out by prisoners' rights organizations.[53]

The impact of the big-stick approach that affects ordinary South Africans most is the symbolic reassurance it provides. Crime—particularly the violent kind that threatens such a large part of the South African population—is a powerful condensation symbol; that is, as a public issue it evokes the emotions that accompany a specific situation, a criminal event.[54] Punishment has symbolic power of the same kind, suggesting that enemies are vanquished and, at least in most modern cultures, the innocent are protected. Messages from the state that are perceived as protective have great political power. "Political forms . . . come to symbolize what large masses of men need to believe about the state to reassure themselves."[55] And it appears that the hard-line messages and the police sweeps have been popular with the general public.

Approval of the police rose as Tshwete's tough talk reverberated across the country, and residents of townships beleaguered by violence were only too willing to allow police sweeps in their communities that netted arrest and detention of the predators among them. (Many were not truly predators; the demonization of young township males and immigrants has justified indiscriminate targeting of many who were arrested and released.)[56] The legislation and court decisions that limited defendants' rights were popular with those who thought the constitution was partly to blame for high rates of violent crime. "Tshwete and Selebi were cowboys with aggressive rhetoric that the public liked," says Ted Leggett, a senior researcher formerly with the Institute for Security Studies. "The public view of police improved though nothing had changed."[57] A Human Sciences Research Council public opinion poll conducted in November 1999 indicated that an increasing proportion of the public believed the government was getting control of crime—a perception that was erroneous, if crime report data for that period is to be believed. That view was attributed to "the tough high profile stance adopted by Minister Steve Tshwete since his appointment as Minister of Safety and Security after the June [1999] elections."[58] The populist rhetoric of national criminal justice officials may also have been popular because people who were so inclined could read its subtext as approval of the vigilantism that seemed to many to be a more efficient way of controlling crime than through the cumbersome procedural niceties of the state system.

Symbolism is important not only in the response of citizens to government crime control programs but also in officials' design of them. A sequence of interviews with Willie Hofmeyr, first head of the asset forfeiture unit and now deputy national director of public prosecution, suggests some patterns.[59] In 1996 Hofmeyr described a criminal justice system so underresourced and incompetent and a public so concerned about crime that he worried that the issue threatened to destabilize the state. He viewed blacks as having little concern with individual rights and the majority of whites as generally opposing the black government. To address this crisis—he noted that blacks were more concerned with crime than with housing, generally considered a dire need—the government would have to start having "immediate and direct impact" on crime and could not afford the time or expense of education in the rights orientation behind the constitution or of innovations like lay assessors. Raising conviction rates was the priority, and the cultural and institutional changes that would honor rights and involve the public in bringing justice would have to wait for the longer term.

When I talked to Hofmeyr in 1999 and 2000 he continued to justify the get-tough program as necessary for political stability and legitimacy but from a somewhat different perspective. Coming down hard on violence against women and children was necessary "to preserve democracy"—part of commitment to gender equality—and sending the message that the ANC was not soft on crime was a way of quelling the rumor (presumably among whites) that the party wanted to redistribute wealth to the poor and that crime was one way to do that. Crime was no longer a surrogate for general political threat or instability (whites were "starting to relax about Mbeki," he noted in 1999) but rather an impediment to joining the international mainstream where professionalism required aggressive action against economic and transnational crime as well as a "zero tolerance" posture on quality-of-life offenses. Hofmeyr's focus on affecting public perception had become more specific: he endorsed the Scorpions enthusiastically in 2000, noting that even a few high-visibility operations would reassure people as to the government's commitment of protectiveness. Addressing another general concern, he pointed out that there was little risk of abuse and corruption among the Scorpions because they were tightly controlled from the central National Prosecuting Authority. While he acknowledged that the unit's accomplishments were primarily symbolic, he held out hope that with improvement in detective work as well as better-trained police and more prosecutors the justice system could reduce significantly the incidents of gang crimes, carjackings and domestic violence. He continued to assert that a rights culture was alien to South Africans of all classes and colors but seemed optimistic that its importance could be established "after people feel confidence that the government can protect them."

The Iron Fist in the Grip of the Invisible Hand

Violent crime is without doubt a looming threat for all South Africans and a terrifying disruption in the lives of many, particularly township residents and women. But it is also a public relations problem for the new democracy, for good reason. Fear of crime can be as serious a threat to peace and stability as crime itself. And since 1994 the government's problem has reached beyond the fears of residents to affect perceptions of South Africa outside the country. The outcry at home that propels harsh policies is echoed by worries in the boardrooms and travel agencies around the world that crime in South Africa adds intolerable risks to investments and vacations there. While there are several explanations for the iron-fisted criminal justice policies of post-apartheid South Africa, all of those that are plausible revolve around the reality of the perceptual damage done by the image and the fact of South Africa as a violent society.

Some will argue that the elites of the post-apartheid government—legislators, judges, the ministers of safety and security and of justice and constitutional development—have committed themselves to draconian policies in the belief that they will significantly reduce crime and make South Africans more secure. Perhaps for a few who cling to traditional theories of punishment this is the case. But well-publicized research over the past generation has cast doubt on the strength of the relationship between the severity of punishment and crime rates, at least in countries that profess to be rights-oriented democracies.[60] Most criminal justice policymakers in South Africa know that, and most are aware that only a combination of various strategies will alter the social conditions that give rise to the country's high crime rates. The violence that has riddled South Africa's poverty-stricken communities is so pervasive that even the most drastic measures that a democratic society could take to repress it could not be effective in the short term, and officials in post-apartheid South Africa are not ignorant of that fact.

A glance at the backgrounds of today's political leaders suggests that their life experiences had not prepared them adequately for assessing the crime control effectiveness of punitive policy directions. Those who remained in South Africa during apartheid—among them the first minister of safety and security, the low-key Stanley Mufamadi, and the relatively pacific first minister of justice, the late Dullah Omar—certainly lacked local evidence to support a connection between toughness and social peace; law enforcement during their formative years was aimed almost exclusively at the suppression of political resistance, not ordinary crime. The members of the ANC establishment who returned from exile had had a variety of experiences with crime and punishment. Their host countries had either been lower-crime societies (e.g., Zambia) or states with a long history of generally competent and restrained law enforcement (e.g., the United Kingdom). They had also, however, experienced the party's internal security practices, which, in particular periods and locations, meted out brutal punishments to those suspected of betraying the liberation movement. Neither group had dealt with the problems of "normal" crime and punishment, and the new dispensation did not dictate obvious policy directions for dealing with them.

The result was confusion about what course to pursue. Few of the officials I interviewed between 1996 and 2003—judges, police, or bureaucrats in the ministries of Justice and Safety and Security—believed that police sweeps or harsher penalties would result in a drop in crime, though they often thought that more efficient police work would. (There is, however, a paradox in this conclusion: that as police become more adept, the crime that now goes unreported will be revealed. As Leggett remarks, "Good police work in South Africa means finding this hidden crime, and, as police succeed in fulfilling this function, crime rates will necessarily go up.")[61] But they had badly underestimated the amount of crime and violence they would have to contend with in the post-apartheid era, and they did not know what to do beyond managerial improvements and get-tough policies, both of which could be only marginally effective.

Although political elites charged with finding solutions would be reluctant to attach the label of public relations to the problem, many acknowledge that the principal desirable outcome of get-tough policies is increasing public confidence. Victims of crime and the general population alike need to be reassured, they argue, and the common perception is that aggressive measures will be protective. In the view of Johnny de Lange, the former head of the parliamentary committee that deals with justice matters, it is an insult to victims to criticize the minimum sentencing scheme. "[P]eople want to see that law enforcement works," added Constitutional Court judge Albie Sachs in defending the *Dlamini* decision to withhold bail on the basis of the public disruption that releasing the defendant might cause.[62] Few would disagree with him, especially in light of evidence that in many cases vigilante activity arises from a widespread belief that police and courts will not deal promptly and decisively with wrongdoing. In this view upholding the rule of law is not demonstrating that rules have supplanted force but that the rules will be backed up with force.

Both the public rage over crime and the government's defensiveness are understandable. As apartheid collapsed so did its mechanisms of control, and what remained was not up to the job in a democracy. Demonstrable ineptitude in many police functions—a surprise after the effectiveness of the old SAP at putting down resistance to apartheid—is taking a long time to correct. Prosecutorial discretion in throwing out unwinnable cases—a normal aspect of professional practice in Western countries—appears in the new context to be weakness or indifference to crime. The chaos that characterized magistrates' courts during apartheid as well as afterward has come under the spotlight because service delivery to the poor people who come before those courts has now become a priority. And the demands on an already weak system threaten to overwhelm it. Consider the implications of the constitution's requirement that a defendant must be released unless the "interests of justice" would not be served. Initially there was no capacity for investigating the crime or criminal in time for the magistrate to make such a judgment, so many defendants were released (with or without bail) and the public outcry grew. Creating the Scorpions—an entirely new institution—seemed more efficient than trying to reform the old ones to handle high-visibility, high-impact crimes.[63]

The official view is unapologetic about the compromises on civil liberties that have been made in the adoption of the get-tough program. "We've had to revisit the idea of having the best human rights provisions in the world," said Hofmeyr as he took office as head of the asset forfeiture unit.[64] The government still defends the Constitutional Court's unpopular decision finding capital punishment unconstitutional, but in other contexts the general view is that necessity trumps defendants' rights. Dullah Omar, in an uncharacteristically bellicose moment, threatened to try to amend the constitution if bail was widely available.[65] Hofmeyr thinks the early ambitions of the Mandela government were misplaced and that the planners got their priorities reversed. He sees the get-tough program as a response to community fears to be undertaken while the state develops an efficient, modern criminal justice system—although others would say that deploying resources in the service of high-intensity crime fighting detracts from that task, which has the potential of some longer-term crime prevention effects.

The symbolic function of the criminal law (and the measures taken to implement it) is what matters here—its capacity to suggest to the public that it will be protected and to both potential victims and criminals that the state will be authoritative. These messages may have particular resonance with South Africans, most of whom have been, until recently, neglected by the criminal justice system and who are still doubtful about the state's capacity (and commitment) to improve their lives. Reinforcing this perception is evidence that the state is still relatively weak in two senses: in its capacity to deliver services—exercising power *with* society—and in its ability to get compliance with such routine regulation as user fees for electricity and television—exercising power *over* society. A symbolically effective declaration of leadership in criminal justice—whatever the merit (or lack of it) of the policies that leader embraces—addresses citizens' insecurity and speaks to both concerns about the weakness of the state; it promises to deliver a protective service and to do so with force. When Tshwete railed against criminals and threatened to ignore the constitution in bringing them to book, he not only spoke to a public yearning; he also reconstructed the threat people felt and reminded them to want more of his tough talk.[66]

How the public feels about its own safety is not the sole concern. For at least the first few years after the transition to democracy the government worried that violent crime and responses to it domestically would destabilize the country. White suspicion of the black government was still acute, and the ANC had to tread a fine line between meeting the concerns of whites and losing the support of the black majority. The likelihood that opposition parties would mobilize to oust the ANC at the polling place was small—the huge electoral majority of the first election guaranteed reelection—but a charge that the party was "soft on crime" could severely undermine public confidence. The larger worry was that the ambient noise of discontent over crime would encourage internal rebellion or external interference.

Fears of that kind of disruption have eased since the midpoint of Mbeki's first term, but others remain. The South African government desperately needs its professionals—doctors and other health care workers to respond to the AIDS pandemic, engineers to repair and construct its infrastructure, computer technicians to advance the information technology sector, teachers and trainers to develop the skills of people who have been left behind by the depredations and disruptions of apartheid and the resistance to it. Many who can contribute technical and managerial skills to the building of the new society have, however, left the country; official data report that 10,540 "economically active" people emigrated in 2003, more than in any year since 1994.[67] (This number is probably an undercount, since it reports only responses of those willing to say they were leaving the country permanently.) Some people leave because of concerns about employment and doubts that there will be adequate job opportunities for their children in a country run by blacks, and some because of crime. It will take another generation to replace fleeing whites with black professionals, managers, and technicians; the government would like to stem white flight, an objective it can promote with messages of protectiveness.

The other messages that constitute damage control for South Africa's criminal violence are those that trumpet the strength of the state. If the government cannot redistribute resources, it can at least show its authority through capture and containment of those who defy or evade its edicts. Increasing visible police activity in the form of raids to rout a community's bad actors, demonstrating a commitment to the control of organized crime through aggressive legislation (the 1999 Prevention of Organized Crime Act), and ratcheting up criminal penalties can be sold as improved service delivery, a sign that the state has taken command. The approach is also cheaper and politically safer in the short run than the "soft" approaches of crime prevention through community development, environmental target-hardening, and public participation in order maintenance.

The iron-fisted approach to crime control also gives notice of the state's responses to foreign needs and pressures. Organized crime is a plague to middle-class Mercedes-owners whose vehicles are stolen out of their driveways, but its implication as transnational crime that threatens security at the global level is equally significant. Here the targets of the messages of state authoritativeness are not only local citizens, prospective investors—guided by the credit ratings of agencies like Standard & Poor's—and tourists. Foreign governments and international organizations—the United States, the United Kingdom, and the United Nations, most prominently—also bring diplomatic pressure and technical assistance to bear on countries that seem to be weak links in the chain of international law enforcement.[68] With foreign aid in short supply and dependent on cooperation with Western nations trying to protect themselves from illegal drugs and weapons, South Africa has been eager to show that it can join the "advanced" nations in the war on organized crime. And doing so reinforces the punitive direction of local criminal justice policies, too.[69]

Sending the message that the state is doling out strong medicine to cure its crime problem also reaches beyond international bodies concerned with security to those with a stake in South Africa's economic future. The era of globalization has made explicit the link between the investor's expectation of a business environment conducive to profit and a country's dedication to the rule of law. (As Harvard economist Jeffrey Sachs puts it, "Market liberalization is the primary key to strengthening the rule of law.")[70] What this generally means is that contract and property rights must be secure, but noneconomic elements count too. The World Economic Forum's Global Competitiveness Report, for example, evaluates a country's productivity in terms of a broad range of influences on its firms' business environment, and the World Bank is now concerned with furthering good governance as an aim of its international aid projects.[71]

Investment in South Africa, whether by local firms or foreigners, is influenced by the perception that crime is a serious problem. Surveys by both the World Bank and the Development Bank of Southern Africa have found that South African businesses are constrained by the threat of crime. And USAID warns that patterns of crime and punishment in South Africa "have conspired to undermine investment and public confidence in a democratic government."[72] The Global Competitiveness Report for 2000 warned that South Africa, while described as the southern African region's "critical anchor," lacked "proper sequencing of socio-economic reform, for instance, around crime and unemployment."[73]

Investor concern with reducing crime, however, does not in and of itself compel a punitive program. And there is no evidence that international donor groups or investment rating agencies explicitly condition their aid or endorsement on particular policy directions; one cannot say, for example, that the International Monetary Fund (IMF) is a conduit for directives as to appropriate criminal justice measures. Crime reduction would be equally likely to generate foreign confidence whether achieved through a "get tough" strategy or through policies that emphasized development as crime prevention and looked to nonstate, community justice approaches to social control like civil policing structures, reparative probation, or the family-conferencing program that is popular in New Zealand. Such a conclusion does not, however, negate the importance of foreign influence on the route to be taken to achieve the desired end. Policy transfer is very much in vogue, and the elephant in the room is the American get-tough program.

In the policy environment embraced by South Africa shortly after the first democratic elections, however, taking the developmental, preventive road was neither quick enough nor muscular enough. The get-tough program fit better with neoliberal expectations the government was trying to meet through partial privatization of state assets, deficit reduction, and reliance on market dynamics for economic growth. Corollary to that macroeconomic direction were assumptions that crimes were the outcomes of individual choices to be addressed with penalties that would make clear the costs of those choices. Economic and social conservatism came together as part of the broader declaration that the state was capable of joining the globalization bandwagon. As a political scientist put to me in 1996, "We want to get a toehold on the First World."[74]

Margaret Hanson and James Hentz have looked at the policy dialogues in Zambia and South Africa as each country moved toward commitment to neoliberal macroeconomic strategies. They found that neoliberal ideas were not imposed on the countries, but that policy-related activities like technical assistance and negotiation of lending conditions created a policymaking atmosphere that led to neoliberal commitment.[75] The policy dialogue was of two kinds—negotiations between potential funders and recipients, and internal political debates. Financial coercion by the World Bank or the IMF, they concluded, was not necessary to get South Africa to embrace a neoliberal strategy. The developing partnership with business—strongly promoted by Mbeki but not rejected by Mandela either—was more than capitulation to international funding institutions or investors.[76] It represented in part an internal shift of loyalties in domestic politics, an ANC break with labor and other groups that supported a priority for development over growth.

The adoption of criminal justice policy direction may be viewed as an extension of the process summarized above. As South Africa donned the neoliberal cloak in economic policy, so it may have adopted the "get tough" strategy. The infusion of punitive ideas that were dominant in some of the countries whose investments were sought—particularly the United States, itself firmly in the grip of neoliberalism—and the acceptance of technical assistance from the FBI and other foreign law enforcement agencies may have combined with an implicit understanding of South African negotiators that American (and other) elites generally favor get-tough policies at home and would be likely to do so abroad. Surely that is what national police commissioner Jackie Selebi assumed when he said, at his investiture, that the South African Police Service had a duty to provide an environment conducive to economic growth.[77]

It would be a mistake to suggest that macroeconomic policy *determines* crime policy. Imperatives from other sources—the outraged demands of the public, media and political hype, professional self-interest of police and judges—combine to set the pattern. In the case of South Africa this dovetailing has defeated a broader view of the task of bringing security to a country in transition to democracy. The country's scramble to conform its political transition to worldwide expectations has included the adoption of a social control program that reflects the sink-or-swim premise of a state relying on market-led growth.[78] And likelihood that aid and investment are conditioned on this direction, while not stated, may be imputed. The fact that USAID links the high murder rate and the low conviction rate in its assessment of the impact on investment of the country's crime problem gives notice of the international mind-set that associates tough criminal justice policies with a successful market orientation.

A Turnaround in the Offing?

I have suggested that local anger over violent crime, pressure from the international security community, and the South African macroeconomic strategy constitute a penumbra of influences shaping the current program of harsh, state-centered crime control. As some of those influences abate, does the policy atmosphere change and with it the policies? Can the policies change even when the pressures remain, if it appears that the program is not yielding lower crime rates, greater public confidence, or international investment in the national economy? There is some evidence that government policymakers are no longer so committed to the big-stick approach in criminal justice, or at least that their views of what will strengthen security in crime-ridden communities are becoming more nuanced.

The turnaround—if that is what it is—is evident in both sentencing policy and policing strategy. As of late 2005 parliament had all but agreed on a version of the long-promised Child Justice Bill that would legislate diversion of many youthful offenders from the formal processes of the criminal court, ban pretrial detention for most young defendants, and prohibit life imprisonment for those under eighteen at the time of an offense or who turn eighteen before the completion of criminal proceedings.[79] It would enable restorative justice practices—mediation between victims and offenders and family group conferencing—far beyond their current use. Most arrests of children are for property crimes, which would no longer be punished with prison terms. The legislation expresses a clear intent to get away from a retributive perspective with respect to most offenses by youth under eighteen; its stated "Objects of Act" are to "protect the rights of children," "promote *ubuntu* (collective human dignity) in the child justice system," and "promote cooperation between government departments and other organizations and agencies" to make juvenile justice effective.[80]

A gentler approach to mandatory sentencing is also evident. Although the legislation has not been modified, judicial interpretation of the standard that justifies greater lenience than the prescribed penalty—where "substantial and compelling circumstances" exist—has changed. In April 2004 the Supreme Court of Appeal ruled that a lower-court judge should have deemed the history of abuse suffered by the defendant to be a "substantial and compelling reason" for departing from the mandatory life sentence for the contract killing of her domestic partner. The court accepted the conclusion of the international social science literature and the personal testimonies of a local social worker and researcher that "a well-known pattern" exists whereby "the mind of [an] accused is eventually so overborne by maltreatment that no realistic avenue of escape suggests itself other than homicide."[81] Even the dissenter in the case, while objecting vigorously to the suspended sentence imposed as an alternative to life, supported the idea that the dead man's "gross physical and psychological abuse" of the defendant should warrant departing from the mandatory life sentence.[82]

The recent willingness to consider contexts in which crime is committed extends to sensitivity about approaching different forms of crime differently. While harsh penalties are being retained for organized crimes and rape, for example, the state is seeking to develop preventive approaches to "social crime," defined as interpersonal violence not related to economic enterprise—domestic violence, assaults, murders by intimates. The government has vowed to support multiagency coordination of the kind that the community safety forums have been doing, suggesting that social services can temper as well as supplement the efforts of the security forces; in his State of the Nation speech to parliament in May 2004 Mbeki called for "enhanced integration between the security and social clusters to deal with the social roots of many of the crimes communities experience."[83] On another front, where police formerly took aggressive action against beggars and unlicensed peddlers in the cities (an approach that resembled the campaigns of New York City against "quality of life" offenses) a collaboration with crime prevention potential has evolved. The young men who wave drivers into a parking space and then collect a small fee are given brightly colored vests to show that they have been authorized to do so, and "informal traders" have been allowed to operate in designated market areas. These projects have recast one kind of petty crime as urban renewal.[84] They may reflect a gradual return to the perspective of the 1996 National Crime Prevention Strategy, initially conceived as a major priority for the new government that would, in the words of the first minister of safety and security, "go beyond a mere police response to crime . . . [and] pay proper attention to political, social and economic causes and manifestations of crime."[85]

Sometimes, however, a contradictory mix of perspectives predominates. Minister of Safety and Security Charles Nqakula is concerned with both crime prevention and aggressive law enforcement, a duality expressed in the recent commitment of the SAPS to sector policing, the strategy that assigns police permanently to small, demarcated distracts and emphasizes attention to community problems. The most recent formulation of policing policy (2003 National Instruction on Sector Policing) emphasizes community policing and crime prevention as a *follow-up* to Operation Crackdown—a policing strategy characterized by experts as "an uncomfortable coexistence of a 'social' approach to crime prevention alongside a tougher 'war on crime.'"[86] And Mbeki's State of the Nation speech to parliament in May 2004, while stressing commitment to ending the poverty that is associated with much crime, highlighted the fight against crime with a silly promise (reminding many of the grandiose vow in 1996 of the national police commissioner) to use "all legal instruments" to arrest the "top 200 criminals" within the next three months.[87]

Ambivalence over the balance between the rights orientation symbolized by the country's new constitution and more authoritarian directions exemplified by criminal justice policies continues. The Regulation of Gatherings Act, despite some revision in 1993, still gives the police broad powers to ban and suppress dissent; what social activists have called "an apartheid relic" permits police to declare illegal a gathering of more than fifteen people that has not been granted a permit.[88] The law has been used to authorize the arrest of marchers protesting inadequate housing and foreclosures for failure to pay mortgages and to repress demonstrations at the 2002 World Summit on Sustainable Development. Ironically, the government invoked the law to deny the Anti-Privatization Campaign a permit—and then to arrest those who defied the decision—to demonstrate at the opening of the new building housing the Constitutional Court.

Many of the influences that have set the course of post-apartheid criminal justice are evident in the history of the terrorism law that was initially discussed in 1995, drafted in 2000, redrafted in 2002 and again in 2003, passed by parliament, but not signed by the president until December 2004.[89] The impetus reflected in the early work of the South African Law Commission was the sense that, although acts of terrorism could be prosecuted with common and statutory law, it would behoove South Africa to follow the "worldwide trend ... to create specific legislation based on international instruments relating to terrorism."[90] The enterprise took on particular intensity with the still-unsolved bombings of 1998 and 1999 in Cape Town and the overheated rhetoric those crimes generated. "Urban terrorism" became the bugaboo, and then came September 11, which spawned new terrorism laws all around the world. Critics of the South African bill worried that the vagueness of the terrorist label would reach innocent people, suppress legitimate protest, and legitimize state tactics unworthy of the new South African constitution.[91] Well-publicized disputes over the legislation and the opposition of labor—the coalition of unions worried that the bill's definition of terrorist activity could include strikes—held up its implementation.

Conclusion

South Africa's get-tough program has policy particulars in common with the punitive program in the United States—minimum sentencing, asset forfeiture, and so on—but important differences of perspective drive the two countries. In the United States the punitive program mirrors a larger development, a reconstruction of social policy.[92] In reaction to an earlier reconstruction shaped by the New Deal and post–World War II national rebuilding efforts, ascendant conservatives from the 1960s onward chipped away at the assumption that the state had a beneficent role to play in the lives of the poor. Social control replaced social welfare as a dominant aim of the state; regulation of personal behavior superseded even the mildly redistributive policies that had served as partial compensation for the inequalities generated by capitalism. The civil rights protests and the urban riots of the 1960s mobilized adherents to the conservative movement, generating an interest in curbing demands of those for whom the promises of the liberal state had turned sour. Crime became evidence that liberal social policies had not worked; the poor were lumped together with offenders as dangerous classes—to use a term popular in the nineteenth century—and have been be further marginalized by measures of state control. (Using a typically bellicose American metaphor, we have gone from the war on poverty to wars on welfare, crime, and drugs.)

This dynamic does not apply to South Africa. While the current government's race to harness the dynamism of global capitalism has had at least short-term negative consequences for millions of poor citizens, it is not part of a strategy to divide and exclude, to consign the disadvantaged majority of South Africans to the status of surplus people. The misguided expectation of large amounts of foreign investment to spur economic growth is not tantamount to arrogant disregard for the welfare of citizens. Although the neoliberal policies described earlier have not brought the rising tide that lifts all boats, the government has not abandoned its poor. However inadequate the benefits provided in the past decade—water, electricity, housing, expanded child support grants—they signal a continuing intention to cushion the blows of a cruelly competitive market economy.

But a punitive criminal justice program suggests that, as the old order used aggressive police and punitive judges to work its political will, so will the new order use them as a primary resource in dealing with the problems of transformation. If the liberation struggle taught those who participated in acts of defiance against the apartheid state that problems were appropriately solved with violence, so the aggressive tactics of police and draconian penalties of a get-tough program may teach the population that the only way the state can be authoritative is through another kind of violence. In addition, get-tough policies further marginalize young black males, already victims of structural unemployment and the legacies of Bantu education. Benefits to victims are often tenuous; harsh treatments of present predators may provide a false sense of security if little is being done to change the life situations of those who may become future offenders. A community suffers from crime, to be sure, but also from indiscriminate police sweeps and harsh penalties that remove those who might otherwise have been among its productive members. If the "social crime prevention thrust" announced by Nqakula is to be meaningful in the second decade of South Africa's democracy, it will have to confront the adverse consequences of policies adopted in the first.

10 Democratic Justice and the Competent Citizen

> We have a first-world constitution in a third-world country.
> —Vuyo Baluma[1]
>
> [C]onflicts represent a *potential for activity, for participation.*
> —Nils Christie[2]
>
> In newly democratic or democratizing countries, where peoples are just beginning to learn the arts of self-government, the question of citizen competence possesses an obvious urgency.
> —Robert Dahl[3]

An infant democracy faces challenges from both violent crime and public and private responses to it. Citizens who see the new government as too weak to assure basic order may think repressive approaches make for greater domestic tranquility or disdain the state's role by relying solely on private security.[4] They may lapse into apathy or embrace anarchy or vigilantism in the face of uncontrolled violence. Steven Friedman has worried that a loss of confidence in the new order is particularly likely where crime is committed by organized groups of armed men who appear to be stronger than the state.[5] While a majority of South Africans are willing to accept the moral authority of the new democracy, trust in the country's political institutions is not solid. A 2002 Afrobarometer survey found that 22 percent of respondents said they did not trust police at all and 15 percent felt similarly about courts; only 18 percent of people surveyed in 2000 approved of the government's handling of crime, cited as one of the country's priority issues.[6] More recently, a national victimization survey found that increasing numbers of people do not feel safe in their neighborhoods, and more than half of respondents perceive an increase in crime in their areas, even as these surveys find that rates for some crimes people fear most, like assault and murder, have stabilized or are beginning to decline.[7] And confidence in the state is undoubtedly undermined by the experience with petty corruption reported by 5.6 percent of respondents in that survey—corruption defined as a request by a public official for money or a favor in return for a service.[8]

Crime threatens other aspects of democracy as well. If people are afraid to be out and about at night, they are unlikely to join political groups; victims of domestic violence are unlikely to participate in civic life, and if women are afraid to report crimes against them, they will not be effective advocates for policy attention to abuse. The prospect of victimization has implications for the promise of prosperity that is part of the appeal of modern democracy. Domestic and foreign investors hesitate to bet on a violent country, and visitors have second thoughts about vacationing there. Crime creates reminders of apartheid. The barriers erected around suburban neighborhoods and the private security the affluent hire to protect them from crime symbolize the class and race divisions that remain, despite the embrace of dignity and equality in the new constitution and the declared commitments of the country's elites to economic and political inclusion.[9]

As worrisome as crime for the maturation of democracy is state behavior that contradicts democratic principles. Police who have perpetrated political violence in the past may easily resort to criminal violence when confronted with the escalating crime that often accompanies democratic transition. Legislative enactments of harsh penalties and court decisions that narrow civil liberties send the message that punishment supersedes justice. Corruption and abuse within the criminal justice system make a mockery of public accountability and delay the process of converting the doubters into supporters of the new regime. A narrow professionalism—overreliance on technology in police operations, for example, and the application of criminal law and procedure that overlook contextual issues—distances the criminal justice system from those they are presumed to serve. A justice system that is not comprehensible to the polity in general cannot claim to be transparent, and, with its reliance on technical rules and specialized practices, inevitably discourages participation.

I support public-empowering measures as essential for a deeper substantive democracy. But shifting the constituency for police and courts, prioritizing security for all, and adopting (at least to some degree) the Western rights orientation, taken together, also address some of the problems cited above. It would be simplistic to assume that occasional clashes between the principles of liberal and more participatory approaches render them oppositional as a general matter. In the past few years the commitment to public protection has become more visible around the world as modern law enforcement strategies—the identification of "hot spots" for intensified patrol, "problem-centered policing," and intelligence-led concentration on organized crime—have been adopted. Some kinds of crime in South Africa appear to have leveled off recently—albeit at high levels—and others have declined, sometimes significantly.

While hard evidence is lacking that reductions in crime can be explained by managerial improvements in state criminal justice operations, the reforms of the past decade are not irrelevant to a stabilizing social environment. Restructuring in policing and prosecution is starting to bear fruit, particularly in the areas of complex and high-profile commercial and organized crimes—transnational drug trafficking, human trafficking, and high-level corruption—and in cases involving violence against women and children. What was a chaotic and brutal system where police were primarily assigned to regime maintenance has been reoriented and professionalized, although resource constraints limit both the training and equipment available to SAPS officers. A limited number of specialized crime-fighting units and officers trained in such areas as drug investigations have been deployed to local stations. Ancillary services, such as guarding government buildings and servicing police vehicles, have been outsourced, freeing up law enforcement personnel for order maintenance.[10] Conviction rates in both magistrates' courts and high courts have risen considerably since the late 1990s.[11] Delay in the criminal courts is still appalling—in 2002 the average case took more than two years to move from referral to sentencing—but a former Constitutional Court judge has been assigned to develop a case management model that will speed up the process.[12] (Given this general pattern it is particularly impressive that special attention to domestic violence and sexual abuse has resulted in a six-month turnaround time for some of those cases.)[13] Most cases prosecuted by the elite Scorpions result in conviction.[14] Saturday courts are supplementing the regular courts to make inroads on the shocking backlog of cases pending; the number of cases finalized doubled between 2001 and 2002.

The priorities chosen for criminal justice attention reflect, at least in part, awareness of the need to correct inequities of the past. New sexual offenses courts and the aggressive pursuit of child support cases signals concern about crimes against women and children. The Firearms Control Bill, which requires registration and background checks for new and current gun owners, finally went into effect in July 2004 after five years of debate and delay. Civilian oversight—from the Independent Complaints Directorate and the (much diminished) Safety and Security Secretariat—ensures that at least some police abuse is recorded and investigated. Procedural fairness accompanies both harsh and lenient sentences.

If these developments are necessary for democratic criminal justice, they are not sufficient—at least not in a country with vast inequalities and a colonial past, a country where citizenship is a novelty that must be constantly reinforced to be believed, a country where much of the populace has little contact with the institutions of criminal justice that are theoretically committed to protecting them. In failing to develop public-empowering policies South Africa has lost—perhaps only temporarily—an opportunity to enhance the meaning of citizenship beyond the choice of leaders and regimes. For all but the small minority of middle- and upper-class South Africans citizenship has yet to become a truly participatory status, a role in which ordinary people contribute to the regulation of collective daily life.

Lost Opportunities

The failure to implement public-empowering policies has had a number of costs. It is impossible to say whether a national commitment to community policing or lay participation in criminal trials or community justice centers would have reduced violence or brought about the order that South Africans yearn for. And perhaps a reckoning of the deficits to deepened democracy that are attributable to the government's indifference to these policies is too abstract to be persuasive to a polity besieged by security concerns. But over the longer term a public-empowering program has the potential to contribute significantly to the building of communities that do not breed disdain for the property and bodily integrity of other people. And in the interim it offers the experience of active citizenship. In contemporary South Africa official capacity for maintaining order, fighting crime, and resolving conflict is low. Policing (however defined) is still rarely visible or effective in many places, and court backlogs defeat even the most comprehensive and progressive legislation, like the Family Justice Act—hailed around the world for its potential benefits to women but almost meaningless in application as a tool for protecting and emancipating women. Empowering citizens to share with the state the performance of social control functions gives them a role that underscores their importance to the new order.

The paragraphs that follow describe the nature of several missed opportunities in South Africa's approach to democratizing criminal justice. They fall into the general categories of community building, rights education, and vigilantism prevention.

Community Building

Anyone who spends time in the company of black South Africans is soon aware of the profound divisions between people on the basis not solely of race—the focus of attention, both locally and internationally, during the antiapartheid struggle—but of class, ethnicity, clan, and political loyalty. Although the political conflicts of Inkatha and ANC supporters have died down (with occasional eruptions in KwaZulu-Natal), distrust between them is often keen; even within the ANC local factions struggle for dominance.

Intraracial divides are increasingly common as whites join the ANC and the income gap widens between privileged blacks and shack-dwellers. Sometimes people are divided along cultural lines—followers of ancestral traditions versus followers of modern trends, for instance. And there are, of course, the social stresses that flow from apartheid's dislocations—the forced removals that dispersed people who were once part of tightly knit neighborhoods, the separation of families resulting from labor demands that sent men into the mines and women into suburban kitchens. The legacies of violence from that era—generated within oppressed communities as well as visited upon them—linger a decade after its end.

Furthermore, relations within a given community between officials and citizens—often infused with suspicion based on past (and perhaps present) injustices and biases—may be conflictual. The distrust that attended early efforts at community policing, the reluctance of magistrates to implement lay participation in criminal proceedings, and the government's long delay in acting on the Child Justice Bill (all discussed in chapter 8) illustrate the difficulties of moving beyond old presumptions and grievances. Nonetheless, the post-apartheid task of binding communities that are poor and often lacking any organic identity is as fundamental as instilling a sense of nationhood in the populace—something that was accomplished with great success by the ANC (led by the beacon of Nelson Mandela's charisma). While structural changes that brought about prosperity might accomplish that goal, organization around a cause as important as social order can also contribute.

Of course a national commitment to public-empowering policies is an enormous job, requiring articulation of values that may be contested, negotiation among parties who may be antagonists, deliberation over ends and means that may be threatening. And, equally important in a country with so much poverty, it is beyond the capacity of conventional service provision by a government that is itself fiscally strapped. But without a more committed and persistent effort than has been undertaken to date by the post-apartheid government, criminal justice in the new constitutional democracy will remain a remote and hollow resource for most communities. Without participatory activities undertaken in an atmosphere of mutual respect and concern most new democratic citizens are unlikely to acquire a sense of collective purpose and popular authority. In South Africa, where everyone is familiar with the sight of affluent neighborhoods that control their own security, acquiring that sense is likely to be particularly important.

The opportunity to participate in building community in this way fits neatly with larger strategies that characterize much of recent Western life. As the anxieties of late modernism have dictated a policy focus on reducing and avoiding risks, and macroeconomic policy has turned toward market solutions for what were formerly conceived as state problems, the prevention of crime is increasingly considered a private responsibility. The unfairness of this emphasis is evident where some have the resources to protect themselves and others don't. But if government commits itself to crime prevention and dispute resolution that rely on community decision-making and community action, the privatization of some practices of justice and security can be a strongly democratic development.[15] Friedman has suggested that, while civil society is not an alternative to the state as an instrument of social and economic progress, it can contribute to the reconfiguring of a democracy by giving citizens a vehicle for participating in public life.[16] Strengthening civil society in the arena of security and justice can be part of ensuring that it takes its place with state and market to shape a more equal and democratic society.

Substantial resources, of course, must accompany this delegation of responsibility, but it is not clear that community crime prevention and community justice would be more expensive than the budget creep of law enforcement and corrections allocations that seems likely if present policies are pursued. And local residents must get help from the state in discharging their new duties. With the proper incentives, they will surely respond. Despite all the brutal disruptions of colonialism and apartheid, communal values remain alive in South Africa's poor townships and rural areas, long traditions of nurturance and self-protection that people have adapted as new challenges threatened them.[17]

Rights Education

An irony of the direction the South African criminal justice has taken is that in failing to develop a public-empowering program the government also lost an opportunity to encourage the rights culture that is at the heart of its claim to legitimacy. Early in its tenure the state sponsored forums of many kinds on a wide range of problems. Opposition parties sometimes derided the ANC's propensity to create a kind of standing committee on issues ranging from gender equality to preserving the forests and then take it on the road to be addressed by unemployed street sweepers and suburban madams alike. Primary in the effort to bring policy concerns to the general population were forums on the meaning of democracy—not only its procedural aspects but also the theme of human rights that propelled much of the liberation movement. Law students taught workshops on newly acquired rights; pamphlets that described how to exercise those rights were distributed and explained even in remote rural areas.

The quotidian demands of running a government and the ANC's preferences for centralized power have submerged many—though certainly not all—of these initiatives. Efficiency seems often to preclude the extensive deliberation that characterized the early days of democratic service delivery. But efficiency is not the only primary value where justice is concerned. Abandoning the early intentions for public-empowering policies retarded the process of educating the public to the relevance of the new constitution for the way criminal justice institutions behave. Most people have learned that—at least in theory and often in practice—they do not have to suffer police abuse in silence, but most have probably *not* learned that they can hold police and prosecutors to performance standards that provide protection. (It is worth noting that Alix Carmichele, who successfully sued the state for releasing on bail a man previously convicted of one violent crime and on trial for another who later attacked her, was white and middle-class, with resources and knowledge that gave her power to claim that the state had a duty to protect her constitutional rights to dignity and security.)[18] Due process is not a term or a concept that has much meaning in most South African communities, and the right to counsel is a hollow promise for most poor people. Misunderstandings about how the criminal justice system works often have dire consequences. Angry victims or their family and friends interpret release on bail as outright discharge, encouraging self-help in the form of a thrashing. A lack of appreciation for the role of crime investigation in ensuring fair treatment of suspects can lead community residents to identify the wrong person as a thief or assailant. Most corrosive is the prevailing view that constitutional rights threaten personal safety and are therefore to be rejected. Without a continual, collective examination of particular events and their contexts—an examination that can take place in community centers as well as in police precincts or courtrooms—the meaning of constitutional protections for both victims and offenders is likely to remain obscure among those most vulnerable to crime and disorder where they live.

Vigilantism Prevention

When affluent South Africans feel unsafe, they hire security guards. When poor citizens are fearful about crime or are victimized, they look to state police; but when they do not get satisfaction, as often happens, they turn to vigilante groups, organized or ad hoc. (Sometimes the line between security companies and vigilante groups is extremely thin or nonexistent, as with Mapogo, discussed in chapter 4.) One of the best arguments for a justice program that empowers the citizenry relies on an analysis of crime and democratization in South Africa derived from Lars Buur's anthropological investigation of community-based groups meting out punishment—often quite violently—to young males suspected of stealing.[19] Buur takes issue with the idea that those who engage in vigilante activity are defying the state or expressing antagonism toward those who are making it in the post-apartheid era. His study of informal justice in the townships (particularly New Brighton, near the city of Port Elizabeth) found that people in these groups thought of themselves as *assisting* law enforcement—enforcing a moral code where the police and courts couldn't cope and providing protection for residents perceived as innocents or as leaders. The treatment of young, male suspects (usually the most likely culprits, at least if the suspected offense was theft) was also part of a process of moral definition for the community—showing youth how they should act. These conclusions crop up in other literature regarding vigilantism, and NGO workers in the townships regularly report that vigilante justice that they witness usually arises either after police have failed to respond to a criminal incident or when there is no hope of getting a response because state resources are spread so thin.[20] (In other words, having recourse to community justice is not a rejection of the formal justice system but an attempt to fill a vacuum in its performance.) The popular television series *Yizo, Yizo* reflects similar attitudes. It deals with township issues from drugs and robbery to school budget cuts and how they affect the ambitions of high school students; and, although it stresses the importance of referring crimes to the police, it treats spontaneous vigilante justice as a righting of wrongs against respectable people—in one case a popular high school teacher.

Buur's interpretation of his data suggests that vigilantism may be a resource for public-empowering justice as well as a problem. He sees the Amadlozi, the New Brighton group, as imbued with a radically democratic service ethic; they see themselves as directly representing the community but only as long as it is satisfied with the way they discharge that service.[21] He points to the fact that the group's members are generally men who fought in the liberation struggle—in different factions, which makes their unity around fighting crime somewhat surprising—and, like the suspects they rough up, they are marginalized in the democratic and neoliberal present. Yet they and other groups who carry out the same function are "making the present anew and protecting a whole range of social and moral orders," assuming a role that is respected by the attentive public and creating an alternative sovereign much as they did when making the townships ungovernable for the apartheid state.[22] If the basis for this re-creation of a moral community is not hostility to the present government but rather the vacuum of social order it has left, surely the state still has an opportunity to engage with the agents of popular justice—if only it can do so with patience, flexibility, and imagination.

That engagement is likely to carry with it uncomfortable accommodations—acquiescence to investigation techniques and evidentiary standards that would not pass muster in the courts of the liberal-democratic state, negotiation with people who have committed acts designated by the law as crimes, and discussion of alternative law enforcement priorities with those who have impeded the state's pursuit of criminals. In 1996 the SAPS and the minister of justice considered an alliance with Pagad to pursue drug dealers in the Western Cape, but the effort fell apart, victim of professional vision that saw Pagad members only as a gang capable of lynchings and, later, of going on a bombing spree in Cape Town, South Africa's prime urban tourist attraction.[23] (It may be that government's rejection of a relationship with the group contributed to its transformation from a populist movement of anticrime activists—clumsy and misinformed, but well-meaning and lacking a political agenda—into a group that the U.S. State Department labels as antigovernment and anti-Western in its "Terrorist Group Profiles.")[24] The abrupt reversal from cooperation to confrontation precluded any modification of Pagad's aims or tactics that would have turned the group in a more responsible direction and serves as a reminder of the costs of failing to engage vigilantes.

Prospects for Change

Can South Africa recapture the public-empowering possibility? The record to date is not encouraging, and there are a number of continuing pressures working against it for the future. One is simply the shortage of resources and pressures to spend those that exist on new police hires, salary increases for police, expanding the Scorpions, and higher salaries for judges and magistrates. The national budget for 2004–5 reveals the priority; about twelve billion rand (approximately two billion dollars) is to be spent on "visible policing," of which "prevention" is a part.[25] The get-tough rhetoric has been toned down since Tshwete died, but public support for his aggressive approach is still strong. Mbeki's rhetoric reflects it too. He refers to the need for "moral regeneration" of South Africans and calls criminals in the shantytowns "brutish thugs"; in a recent debate in the National Assembly he referred to the "permissive atmosphere that encourages members of the community to do crime."[26] The failings of individuals still have more traction in criminal justice policymaking than the conditions in which they live and have been socialized. The state's reluctance to support a restorative justice approach to juvenile offending is evident in the many delays in parliamentary approval of the Child Justice Bill.

On the other hand, an attitudinal shift in the government's willingness to intervene in the operations of the market economy may signal an understanding that poverty and inequality breed criminal behavior and that development is part of a progressive criminal justice program. Mbeki seems to be newly receptive to strong relationships between law enforcement and related service providers—health, welfare, and education agencies—and between law enforcement and citizens. His speech to parliament in May 2004 included a reference to "enhanced integration between the security and social clusters to deal with the social roots of many of the crimes communities experience" along with hiring new police, setting up more specialized courts, and creating a national victim services program.[27] In that same month he announced an expanded public works program, addressing the backlog of infrastructure construction projects with the prospect of training and jobs for a million unemployed people in depressed parts of the country.[28] To the extent that these initiatives represent "social crime prevention" (defined rather vaguely in the 1996 national crime prevention strategy as activities that "reduce the social, economic and environmental factors conducive to particular types of crime"), they represent a supplement, if not an alternative, to the government's more narrowly administrative perspective on addressing crime.[29]

From this trend may come a greater receptivity to citizen involvement in criminal justice. Community safety forums that mix community crime prevention and public service delivery receive modest funding from some provinces. Deliberation over the forms and values of social ordering goes on in the victim-offender mediation that is done in some townships, and the parole system has been reformed to include community members and crime victims on the parole boards. These practices do not cohere in a national commitment to public-empowering justice, however, and activities in which the public participates do not necessarily engage them in democratic deliberation; the use of poor citizens as paid auxiliaries to police in Cape Town furthers visible patrol and creates jobs but does not involve them in planning or decision making.

An interesting example of public-empowering justice operates beyond the formal aegis of the state but in its shadow and on occasion in partnership with it. The Community Peace Programme (CPP), operating from the University of the Western Cape since 1997, uses local resources in poor communities to resolve individual disputes—quarrels over money, insults and threats, property offenses—and mount projects that address collective needs—for children's day care and recreation, community cleanup, health education. The program starts from the premise that people have skills and knowledge that they can use to manage their lives even in conditions of extreme poverty and inequality. It seeks to recast the conception of the poor as passive consumers of social services—which are woefully inadequate in South Africa's townships and villages—by setting up structures within which they can actively affect the governance of their communities.[30]

What is often called the Zwelethemba model (for the poor settlement near Cape Town where it was first developed in 1998–2000) has two core elements that the group calls PeaceMaking and PeaceBuilding.[31] Both rely on democratic deliberation. The first recognizes security as a priority area where citizens can make major contributions to governing themselves through the peaceful resolution of conflicts. CPP staff members go into (or, increasingly, are invited into) poor communities—most are in the Boland district, north of Cape Town—and offer residents the chance to set up a Peace Committee that receives reports of local disputes and facilitates agreements between the parties (PeaceMaking). Guided by a Code of Good Practice—a simple document that sets out the values and priorities of the program and expresses commitment to the constitution and the law—members of the Peace Committee hold a "gathering" in an informal setting at which they help the disputants and other community members explore the causes of the problem, seek resolution, and adopt a plan of action intended to prevent further conflicts.[32] The process is nonjudgmental, applies no force or other sanctions, focuses on the future, and involves no officials. The second element of the program "broadens the model from being a conflict management model to a governance model."[33] When longer-range community problems are raised (PeaceBuilding) the committee meets to determine whether community action could effect a solution and who might provide it. Peace committee members are paid for each dispute handled under the Code of Good Practice, and each dispute generates money for a PeaceBuilding Fund that goes toward the community development projects that the committee sponsors. Foreign governments and foundation grants fund the program with some support from local district councils; the CPP manages the finances, with the University of the Western Cape providing audits.

As of August 2004 twenty-one peace committees had organized more than nine thousand "peace gatherings," bringing about forty thousand people into the dispute resolution process and generating about 2.5 million rand (about four hundred thousand dollars) for the peace committees and the communities in which they operate. The CPP now gets requests to establish peace committees in other localities, and in three places in the Western Cape community peace centers have opened, with more planned over the next five years. Here police handle serious crimes but refer lesser conflicts for PeaceMaking gatherings; the community-building projects (PeaceBuilding) continue to rely on local resources. CPP staff and peace committees are mindful of simply becoming an adjunct to the police in the peace centers; the program's gatherings operate independently—disputants may still go directly to the Peace Committee—and the committees continue to see themselves as neighborhood organizations.

The practical aim of the Zwelethemba model is to address the "governance deficit" that afflicts poor South African communities. By controlling their own security and providing social services they are to bring resources into the community. While community crime prevention and dispute resolution are central to the model, it is intended to realize the goals of democratic theorists who see governance as a broader realm than that of government and who envision a democracy that steers itself at the local level through the energy and power of civil society.[34] This does not mean it is hostile to the state. Police and social service officials generally approve, according to John Cartwright, training and communications manager of the CPP; he notes that it is "good value for money—it supports the aims of local government without involving them in extra management or bureaucracy (which they don't have the capacity to supply in any case), and in particular it reduces demand on the police and releases them to do the kind of policing work they are trained for."[35] Local governments also like it, he maintains, because they can invest in projects that will have responsible citizen oversight.

But another purpose is the enhancement of competent citizenship. The program appears to advance at least two of the lost opportunities mentioned earlier in assessing the general trend of post-apartheid criminal justice: mobilizing people around community building and averting vigilantism by acting within the law to resolve conflicts. It reaffirms the constituency shift of the transition from an authoritarian state to a democratic one when it makes citizens the problem-solvers of first resort in the event of a conflict, with police and social service workers providing backup and technical expertise. Cartwright reports that peace committee members who participate regularly in the gatherings become more confident about the their ability to address local problems and to relate to officials. Assuming the social responsibility of promoting security involves the peace committees and the community members they mobilize to help in dispute resolution in a very direct form of self-government. In the words of CPP leaders, "The model seeks to explore novel ways of realizing democratic agendas central to local governance. In doing so, it promotes community self-directedness and empowerment—it deepens democracy."[36]

It is interesting to speculate whether this kind of program can make a contribution to democracy in the second decade of post-apartheid South Africa. On the one hand, Cartwright points out that the CPP is popular with officials formerly involved in the liberation struggle as a way of respecting and expressing local knowledge. At the national level the South African Law Reform Commission's committee on alternative dispute resolution regards it approvingly (Cartwright is on the committee), as does a top official in the Ministry of Justice and Constitutional Development. Yet there seems to be little interest in giving this sort of initiative priority for national funding, and it is easy to imagine that too much national regulation could defeat the informality and adaptability to local conditions that are among its strengths. And as a nonstate node in the network of governance that Johnston and Shearing identify (see chapter 7) the peace committees would lose their vitality if they could only row while the formal political institutions steered.

To date the relations between community participants and local officials have generally been cordial and productive. But community building that raises the political consciousness of citizens who feel aggrieved by policy directions taken by the state may raise the hackles of a national administration that has, to this point, governed from the center and emphasized growth through investment, market dominance, and fiscal restraint. In addition to the expense and the conceptual adjustments that public-empowering activities require, local and national officials must be prepared for the prospect that participants are likely to connect local problems of disorder with needs that are as pressing as security—for economic development and redistribution and for improved service delivery in health, housing, and welfare, areas related to problems of crime and disorder. What are now being called the "social movements" in South Africa—the Soweto Electricity Crisis Committee, the Landless People's Movement, and the Anti-Privatization Campaign, to name the major ones—are in reality demands for economic justice. The government largely rejects their claims and finds them embarrassing reminders of abandoned ideals of the liberation struggle. Initially, the ANC raised expectations of access to water and power and land, and disillusioned citizens who have inherited a tradition of protest are now rebelling when those benefits do not turn out to be universally available. A similar sequence is possible if public-empowering policies give rise to expectations of broader popular authority. Truly participatory policies may disrupt the quiescence on which democratic governance often relies.

Yet to neglect the public-empowering approach is to limit security and justice to those with the means to invoke the protections of due process, equal protection, and socioeconomic rights—suspects who can hire lawyers; suburbanites who can avert much victimization in gated, guarded housing developments; families that can have most disputes mediated by therapists, school counselors, and doctors. South African elites are justly proud of having created institutions that respect the rule of law. But the rule of law can be a force for general emancipation or a constraint on popular sovereignty. By enacting a constitution that goes beyond the standard liberal prescriptions to confer rights to substantive benefits that can ensure effective participation in setting policy agendas, South Africans have declared their intention to enable all citizens to enjoy such rights. Without the involvement of citizens at all economic levels in decisions about the control of crime and disorder—whether as part of the traditional apparatus of police and courts or operating at a distance from them but in collaboration—justice in the new South Africa will remain the province of the powerful. Full citizenship in this democracy demands more.

Notes

Preface

1. Foucault, *Power/Knowledge*, 29.
2. Constitution of the Republic of South Africa, Sec. 35 (2)(e); *August v. Electoral Commission; Van Biljon v. Minister of Correctional Services.*
3. Van Zyl Smit and van der Spuy, "Importing Criminological Ideas," 196.
4. Van Zyl Smit, "Criminological Ideas," 198.

Chapter 1

1. Chaskalson, "Bram Fischer Memorial Lecture," 199.
2. Waldmeir, *Anatomy of a Miracle*; Sparks, *Beyond the Miracle*; Friedman and Atkinson, *The Small Miracle.*
3. "April 27: The First Time," in *SA 27 April 1994*, 52.
4. Mattes et al., "Democratic Governance," 24–25.
5. This estimate is a projection based on the 2001 census. Statistics South Africa, www.statssa.gov.za. "Black" in South Africa includes several categories: Africans, who currently make up 79.4 percent of the population; mixed-race people referred to as "coloured" (8.8 percent); and East Indians (2.5 percent).
6. For essays that examine apartheid as both economic strategy and segregationist ideology, see Beinart and Dubow, *Segregation and Apartheid.*
7. Johns, *Protest and Hope*, 4–5.
8. Johns, *Protest and Hope*, document 23, "Constitution of the South African Native National Congress, September 1919," Chap. 3, Secs. 6 and 9.
9. Karis and Gerhart, *Challenge and Violence*, document 11, "Freedom Charter," 205.
10. Sparks, *Mind of South Africa*, 241.
11. Ramaphosa, "Negotiating a New Nation," 84.
12. See Bayley, *Social Control.*
13. Schärf, "Community Justice," 7.
14. Cawthra, *Policing South Africa*, 1.
15. Ellmann, "Law and Legitimacy," 426. Sixty-two percent of urban Africans surveyed expressed "a great deal" or "quite a lot" of confidence in the legal system, as compared with 79 percent of rural Africans and 75 percent of whites.

16. Internal Security Act of 1982, Sec. 29; Public Safety Act 3 of 1953 as amended, Sec. 3(1); Security Emergency Regulations, Proc. R. 97, Sec. 3 (1), June 1988.

17. Ackermann, "Human Rights," 95.

18. Ellmann, *Time of Trouble,* 4. For detail on judicial protection of emergency power, see chap. 3.

19. See Bittner, *Aspects of Police Work.*

20. For a particularly trenchant analysis of the limited effects of democratization on policing in sub-Saharan Africa, see Hills, *Policing Africa.* She points out that it is undoubtedly easier for police to adapt to increased repression than to democratization.

21. Bayley, *Patterns of Policing,* 60–62.

22. Constitution of the Republic of South Africa, Sec. 1(a).

23. *State v. Makwanyane and Another,* 1995 (3) SA 391 (CC).

24. "Address of the President of the Republic of South Africa, Thabo Mbeki, at the Opening of Parliament: National Assembly, Cape Town, 25 June 1999." See http://www.info.gov.za/speeches/1999/9906281018a1006.htm.

25. See Young, *Exclusive Society,* chap. 5; and Dixon, "Exclusive Societies."

26. Linz and Stepan, *Problems of Democratic Transition;* Diamond, *Developing Democracy.*

27. For the application of this position to the situation of South Africa at the end of apartheid, see Brogden and Shearing, *Policing.*

28. Sen, *Development as Freedom,* xii, 152–59.

29. Held, *Models of Democracy,* 302.

30. Hirst, *Associative Democracy,* 26.

31. See, for example, Garland, *The Culture of Control,* 87–89.

32. See Gutmann and Thompson, *Democracy and Disagreement.*

33. Schärf and Nina, *The Other Law.*

34. "Constitution of the Republic of South Africa," Secs. 26 and 27.

35. Bayley and Shearing, "The Future of Policing," 597.

36. Policy Coordinating and Advisory Services, "Ten Year Review," 25. This report contains other statistics regarding social and economic development since 1994.

37. Opinion is divided on whether the average income of blacks has risen since the end of apartheid. For the positive view, see Van der Berg and Louw, "Changing Patterns," 11–12; Patrick Bond interprets official data to conclude that both relative and absolute poverty has increased for Africans, at least. Bond, "From Racial to Class Apartheid."

38. Nattrass, "Unemployment and AIDS," 93–94.

39. Laurence, "Critical Moment."

40. Data for unemployment and economic growth rates can be found at http://www.statssa.gov.za/.

41. Nattrass, "State of the Economy," 3–4.

42. Dahl, "Why Free Markets Are Not Enough," 84.

43. Taylor and Mattes, "Public Demands on Government," 6; Human Sciences Research Council, *Public Opinion,* 24; "South Africans Now Want More Jobs and Less Crime," Human Sciences Research Council, November 30, 2000 (media release).

44. Schatz, "Pirate Capitalism," 45.

45. For an influential sociological exegesis of this idea, see Garland, *The Culture of Control.*

Chapter 2

1. Moodie, *The Record,* 5. Van Riebeeck's opinion was formed during his visits ashore when the ship on which he was a surgeon was stranded in Table Bay for a year. His views evolved somewhat during the decade in which he ruled the Cape; he once recommended that control over agriculture be given to free blacks, a suggestion apparently rejected by the company (Vereenigde Oostindische Compagnie) that sent him to establish the settlement in 1652. Davenport and Saunders, *South Africa,* 35.

2. Rotberg, *The Founder,* 127.

3. As Albie Sachs remarks, "Slave society created relationships and attitudes which were to endure long after the abolition of the legal forms in which they had first appeared." *Justice in South Africa,* 12.

4. Magubane, *Making of a Racist State,* 267–68.

5. De Kiewiet, *History of South Africa,* 20.

6. Stock theft has been common throughout the country's history—and continues to be. During a police crackdown between November 2001 and March 2002, 968 people were arrested for stock theft and more than 5.5 million rand worth of cattle and other stock were recovered. Media statement, South African Police Service, May 21, 2002.

7. For a lively and detailed account of these two emblematic conflicts between the English and the Afrikaners, see Le May, *The Afrikaners.*

8. Eybers, *Select Constitutional Documents,* 155.

9. For accounts of this period in South African history, see Katzen, "White Settlers"; and Thompson, *History of South Africa,* chap. 2.

10. Wilson, "The Hunters and Herders," 65.

11. Ibid., 60.

12. Ibid., 67.

13. Kolb, *Present State,* 38.

14. Ibid., 87.

15. Ibid., 90.

16. Ibid., 296.

17. Kolb's account is chilling: "All is, in a Manner, silent for a Minute or Two. More Time rarely elapses, after the Sentence, before the Captain, who is Chief Executioner, flies at the Prisoner, as in a Rage, and with one downright Blow on the head with his *Kirri,* lays him sprawling on the Ground. The Captain has no sooner deliver'd his Blow, by which he generally shatters the Prisoner's Skull, than the Rest of the Court falls on; each giving the Criminal several Blows, which they fetch with all their Might with their *Kirries,* on his Head, Belly and Sides. Tho' they quickly dispatch him, they follow their Blows till his Skull is broken all to Pieces and his Belly extremely swelled." Ibid., 296–97.

18. Dapper, "Kaffraria," 65.

19. Walker, *History of Southern Africa,* 32.

20. Sachs, *Justice in South Africa,* 18–19.

21. Walker, *History of Southern Africa,* 33.

22. Le May, *The Afrikaners*, 14.
23. Thompson, *History of South Africa*, 36.
24. Sachs, *Justice in South Africa*, 23.
25. Walker, *History of Southern Africa*, 85.
26. Quoted in Thompson, *History of South Africa*, 43.
27. Kolb, *Present State*, 40.
28. See the conviction records kept by the early Dutch commanders in Moodie, *The Record*, 251–54, 311–15, 380–84 in part 1, and 106–9 in part 3.
29. Brewer, *Black and Blue*, 15–16.
30. *State v. Williams* 1995 (3) SA 632 (CC).
31. Thompson, *History of South Africa*, 60. Much of the material in subsequent paragraphs is taken from this concise and excellent treatment of South Africa from precolonial times to the release of Nelson Mandela from jail in February 1990; and from Wilson and Thompson, *Oxford History*.
32. Walker, *History of Southern Africa*, 126; Keppel-Jones, *South Africa*, 46.
33. Eric Walker describes 1828 as the *"annus mirabilis"* of Cape constitutional history, when freedom of the press was embraced and a new judicial system was created. Walker, *History of Southern Africa*, 162.
34. Davenport, "Consolidation," 301. Legal reforms initiated by the British were intended as much to be reminders of imperial authority as to establish legal equality.
35. "Extension of Hottentot Liberties," Ordinance No. 50, July 17, 1828, in Eybers, *Select Constitutional Documents*, 26–28.
36. For a description of the complexities of ending slavery, see Davenport, "Consolidation," 305–10; and Walker, *History of Southern Africa*, 169–74.
37. See Nasson, "Bobbies to Boers," 236–54.
38. For a description of Cape legal practice and the role of judges, see Sachs, *Justice in South Africa*, chap. 2.
39. This institutional development was not accomplished without conflict. J. B. Pieres describes a scandal of the 1820s that included trials with no jury, no due process rights, and the prosecutor serving as judge. "British and the Cape," 478.
40. See Elphick and Giliomee, "European Dominance."
41. Theal, *History of the Boers*, 62.
42. The relationship between labor needs and the discourse of crime is apparent here. Pieres notes: "Knowing that they [Afrikaner farmers] could not express their complaints in terms of their demand for labour and their regret for the passing of slavery, they phrased their grievances around the problem of 'vagrancy,' which conveniently represented their demands for labour as if they were legitimate necessities of self-defence." "British and the Cape," 501. Similar arguments justified coerced labor enforced by vagrancy laws in the nearby Portuguese colonies of Mozambique and Angola. Agostinho, *Security and the State*, 39.
43. Elphick and Giliomee, *Shaping of South African Society*, 556. In fact Elphick and Giliomee cite a 1986 South African M.A. thesis to state that "as many as half of the convicted criminals in Cape Town were in fact European," a statistic that, if correct, may indicate either how relatively law-abiding the blacks were—they made up much more than half of the population—or how indifferent the officials were to crime where the victim was black.

44. Keppel-Jones, *South Africa*, 48.
45. Retief's comments were essentially a letter to the editor published in the *Grahamstown Journal* of February 2, 1837, and reproduced as "Manifesto of the Emigrant Farmers," no. 92 in Eybers, *Select Constitutional Documents*, 144.
46. Theal, *History of the Boers*, 63.
47. Ibid., 11.
48. See Schapera, "Law and Justice."
49. Hoernlé, "Social Organization," 70. See also Wilson, "The Sotho, Venda, and Tsonga," 158.
50. Schapera, "Political Institutions," 178.
51. Wilson, "Nguni People," 121–22.
52. Thompson, *History of South Africa*, 72.
53. Allister Sparks quotes an 1847 editorial piece from the *Grahamstown Journal* to show colonial zeal for conquest of Africans and their lands:

Let war be made against Kafir huts and gardens. Let all these be burned down and destroyed. Let there be no ploughing, sowing or reaping. Or, if you cannot conveniently, or without bloodshed prevent the cultivation of the ground, take care to destroy the enemy's crops before they are ripe, and shoot all who resist. Shoot their cattle too wherever you see any. Tell them that the time has come for the white man to show his mastery over them. (*Mind of South Africa*, 65).

54. Thompson points out that the limited franchise for Cape Colony blacks did not give them political power; "people who were not white never amounted to more than 15 percent of the electorate and never produced a member of the colonial parliament." *History of South Africa*, 65.
55. Art. 9, "The Grondwet of the South African Republic," February 1858, reprinted in Eybers, *Select Constitutional Documents*, 364.
56. Thompson, *History of South Africa*, 85.
57. Walker, *History of Southern Africa*, 192.
58. Thompson, *History of South Africa*, 96.
59. Sachs, *Justice in South Africa*, 90–91.
60. For an elegant exposition of the development of indirect rule and its origins in Natal, see Mamdani, *Citizen and Subject*, chap. 3.
61. Welsh, *The Roots of Segregation*, chap. 2. Much of what follows comes from this study.
62. For a succinct description and history of locations, see Davenport and Saunders, *South Africa*, 645–46.
63. Ordinance 3 of 1949, Clause 7. The "repugnancy clause" continued as a common way for colonial and apartheid regimes to limit the discretion of informal judgments.
64. Welsh, *The Roots of Segregation*, 157.
65. Simons, *African Women*, 28.
66. Welsh, *The Roots of Segregation*, 147.
67. Ibid., 139.
68. Ibid., 140.

69. Sachs, *Justice in South Africa*, 63–64. Sachs points out that it should not be assumed that most prosecutions in the late nineteenth century were for violations of the "special laws" aimed at controlling blacks. He cites records from the Cape Colony in 1894 that showed 7,700 prosecutions out of 47,000 were for those crimes.

70. Walker, *History of Southern Africa*, 647.

71. Sachs, *Justice in South Africa*, 51.

72. Ibid., 88. Sachs notes that in the Transvaal before Union the law specifically exempted whites from flogging and that only blacks were executed. Ibid., 81.

73. Walker, *History of Southern Africa*, 621. Keppel-Jones quotes a Transvaal chief as follows: "My grandfather woke one morning at his own kraal and found a white man who said, 'You are living on my farm and you must work for me.'" *South Africa*, 167.

74. Keppel-Jones notes that "the pass system was designed to retain labour on the farms and the mines where it was wanted, to permit migration to the towns while excluding those who failed to find employment, to keep in the reserves those who were not wanted elsewhere, and to safeguard the white townspeople against criminals at night." *South Africa*, 173.

75. Allister Sparks describes their living conditions: "The Khoikhoi labourers were accommodated in the slavenhuys, where they lived with the slaves and ate with the slaves, and by day they worked with the slaves. In all but name they became a subdivision of the slave force, and in that capacity were a part of the transition of South Africa's labour system from slavery to the contractual serfdom [of *apartheid*]." *Mind of South Africa*, 84.

76. Keppel-Jones, *South Africa*, 45.

77. Davenport, "Consolidation," 311.

78. Ibid., 172–73.

79. Thompson, *History of South Africa*, 118.

80. Brewer, *Black and Blue*, 16.

81. Agostinho, *Security and the State*, 37.

82. Thompson, *History of South Africa*, 166.

83. Ibid., 167.

84. Inaugural Address by J. Tengo Jabavu, president, The South African Races Congress, April 2, 1912, document 22 in Johns, *Protest and Hope*, 75.

85. Quoted in Meredith, *Name of Apartheid*, 36.

86. For a history of the use of passes before the apartheid era, see Welch, "Growth of Towns," in Wilson and Thompson, *Oxford History*, 196–202.

87. Meredith, *Name of Apartheid*, 33–35.

88. Thompson, *History of South Africa*, 150–51.

89. Extending the requirement of passes (by then called "reference books") to women was not enforced until the mid-1950s, at which time it brought about massive protests, including a march of twenty thousand women of all races on the Union buildings in Pretoria.

90. Quoted in Thompson, *History of South Africa*, 39.

91. Meredith, *Name of Apartheid*, 37.

92. For the idea of law enforcement as the maintenance of race relations in the nineteenth century, see Sachs, *Justice in South Africa*, chap. 2; and Brewer, *Black and Blue*, 14–36.

93. One historian notes that between 1911 and 1921 the value of industry increased by a factor of six and the number of employees in industry tripled. Keppel-Jones, *South Africa,* 172.

94. For the material that follows, I am much indebted to Brewer, *Black and Blue,* chaps. 1 and 2. It should be noted that until 1926 the South African Police was not the only national police force. The South African Mounted Riflemen, a paramilitary force of five regiments, was created at the same time as the SAP to operate in rural areas, exclusively to police conflicts between blacks and black resistance to white domination. Its gradual absorption into the SAP contributed to the military orientation of that force.

95. Grundlingh, "Protectors and Friends," 171–73.

96. Brewer, *Black and Blue,* 29.

97. Ibid., 31.

98. Nasson, "Bobbies to Boers," 240.

99. Ibid., 73.

100. For discussion of the colonial and civil policing models and the failures of the SAP to move from one to the other, see ibid., 5–10 and 101–4.

101. Nasson portrays the situation in Cape Town in the early twentieth century as "a rather remarkable picture of restrained, consensual policing in the empire." "Bobbies to Boers," 241–46.

102. Sachs, *Justice in South Africa,* 45.

103. South Africa Act, 1909, Secs. 95, 96, and 98. Decisions of the Appellate Division could be appealed to the British Privy Council until 1950.

104. Corder quotes the comment made by an apartheid-era judge on the reputation of South African courts over time: "I am told on good authority that the English judges, who are undoubtedly the most eminent judges in the world, consider only the South African judges as their equals." Corder, *Judges at Work,* 6.

105. Dugard, *Human Rights,* 36.

106. Corder, *Judges at Work,* 9–13.

107. Ibid., 167.

108. Ibid., 62.

109. See Marks, *Reluctant Rebellion,* chap. 9, for an account of reprisals taken against Africans for violent resistance to a poll tax imposed in 1906. She notes, at 226–27, that there were, however, objections by prominent whites to the Natal troops that killed indiscriminately, burned huts and crops, and stole livestock.

110. Sachs, contemplating the Appellate Division's capitulation in the 1960s to support for segregation, notes "the long-term trend which has been away from the English common law doctrine of assumed equality towards an acceptance of race discrimination, not merely as something harmless and neutral, but as something positively beneficial." *Justice in South Africa,* 147.

Chapter 3

1. Meredith, *Name of Apartheid,* 120.
2. Hahlo and Maisels, "Rule of Law," 12.
3. Chikane, "Children in Turmoil," 337.
4. Moodie states, "The divine agent of the Afrikaner civil faith is Christian and

Calvinist—an active sovereign God, who calls the elect, who promises and punishes, who brings forth life from death in the course of history. The object of his saving activity—the Afrikaner People—is not a church, a community of the saved, however; it is a whole nation with its distinct language and culture, its own history, and special destiny." *The Rise of Afrikanerdom,* xvii.

5. Dugard, *Human Rights,* 42.

6. Posel, *Making of Apartheid,* 7–8.

7. Quoted in Cole, *Crossroads,* 71. The state bureaucracy that oversaw the implementation of most apartheid policies had many different names over the decades. The Department of Native Affairs, a small department that predated apartheid, became a "great super-ministry whose tentacles extended into every aspect of government policy"; it then became the Department of Bantu Affairs under Prime Minister Verwoerd, then the Department of Bantu Administration and Development in the 1970s and, briefly, the Department of Plural Relations; in the 1980s it was euphemistically called the Department of Cooperation and Development. The quoted description of Native Affairs comes from O'Meara, *Forty Lost Years,* 68.

8. Ellmann, *Time of Trouble,* 5.

9. Although the National Party can be credited with winning the election, it was a shaky win. The party took sixty-five seats in parliament, as opposed to the seventy won by the United Party, and won less of the popular vote because of a districting scheme that gave representation of the rural areas, where the Nationalists were strong, greater representation. The party quickly made common cause with the Afrikaner Party, which had won nine seats, and later absorbed it. For election results from the 1930s until the mid-1960s, see Wilson and Thompson, *Oxford History,* 2:422–23.

10. Ibid., 45. See also O'Meara, "1946 Mineworkers' Strike"; and Davenport and Saunders, *South Africa,* 356–58.

11. Davenport and Saunders, *South Africa,* 370.

12. Quoted in van Zyl Smit, "Contextualizing Criminology," 3.

13. From a speech to the House of Assembly proposing that South Africa become a republic, January 25, 1944, quoted in Bunting, "The Origins of Apartheid," 24.

14. de Villiers, "Afrikaner Nationalism," 406.

15. For a description of the evolution of the ideology of apartheid before 1948, see Moodie, *The Rise of Afrikanerdom.*

16. de Villiers, "Afrikaner Nationalism," 406.

17. Brogden and Shearing, *Policing,* 49.

18. O'Meara, *Forty Lost Years,* 61–62.

19. Corder, *Judges at Work,* 47.

20. Omar, "Overview of State Lawlessness," 22.

21. For a scholarly discussion of apartheid laws, see Dugard, *Human Rights.*

22. Ibid., 59.

23. Ibid., 63. Sachs notes that South Africa moved to "separate and unequal" just as the United States was rejecting "separate but equal." *Justice in South Africa,* 142.

24. *Minister of the Interior v. Lockhat,* 1961 (2) SA, 587 (AD).

25. Davenport and Saunders, *South Africa,* 674.

26. Horrell, *Bantu Education to 1968,* 146. Expenditures for coloured and Asian children were 4.7 times greater than for Africans.

27. Dugard pointed out in 1978 that segregation in higher education was damaging to the society as a whole, not just to black students. "As a result of the closing of the 'open universities' to blacks, all white universities have become white 'tribal' institutions in which the cross-fertilization of ideas and cultures, generally associated with university education, is no longer possible." *Human Rights,* 85.

28. Criminal Law Amendment Act 8 of 1953, Secs. 1 and 2.

29. For a history of pass controls (from slavery days to the second state of emergency in 1986) as a means of enforcing relations of production that subordinated Africans during different historical periods and in different economic sectors, see Hindson, *Pass Controls.*

30. For a vivid, first-person account of how apartheid laws directly controlled the movements, residence, and employment of even a well-educated African with professional skills, see Modisane, *Blame Me on History,* 299–310.

31. Quoted in O'Meara, *Forty Lost Years,* 35.

32. For a history of the use of passes before the apartheid era, see Welsh, "Growth of Towns," 196–202.

33. Meredith, *Name of Apartheid,* 127.

34. Hindson, *Pass Controls,* 64.

35. Sachs, *Justice in South Africa,* 167.

36. For a description of the apartheid legal process in action in the commissioners' courts, see Jackson, *Justice in South Africa.*

37. Commissioner of Prisons Report, 1978, cited in Davis, "Criminal Justice," 12.

38. See Frankel, *An Ordinary Atrocity.*

39. This legislation was officially known as Section 21 of the General Law Amendment Act of 1962.

40. Sachs, *Justice in South Africa,* 224.

41. Dugard, *Human Rights,* 119, 255.

42. For the ordeals Winnie Mandela suffered from the security laws, see Sampson, *Mandela,* 244–49.

43. Sachs notes, "Security laws were justified as a temporary measure to deal with an emergency, but the situation which arose was that of a permanent emergency with signs not of respite but of vanishing liberty and permanent insecurity." *Justice in South Africa,* 253.

44. Internal Security Act 74 of 1982, Secs. 28 and 29.

45. Thomas, "Violence and Child Detainees," 451.

46. Public Safety Act 3 of 1953, Sec. 3.

47. Ellmann, *Time of Trouble,* 21. A useful summary of South African internal security laws and regulations is at pp. 15–25.

48. Brewer, *Black and Blue,* 299.

49. Brodeur, "High Policing," 513.

50. South African Police, 1988 Annual Report, 20.

51. Sachs, *Justice in South Africa,* 173.

52. O'Meara, *Forty Lost Years,* 193.

53. Brewer, *Black and Blue,* 191.

54. Annual Report of the Commissioner of the SAP, 1952, 3, quoted in Brewer, *Black and Blue,* 193.

55. Brewer, *Black and Blue*, 196.
56. Ibid., 200.
57. Newham, "Tackling Police Corruption."
58. Dugard, *Human Rights*, 165.
59. South African Police, Annual Report, 1988, 20. For greater depth on this perspective, see van der Spuy, "Political Discourse," 85–105.
60. Brewer, *Black and Blue*, 205, 207.
61. Criminal Procedure Act 51 of 1977, Sec. 49.
62. Rauch, Shaw, and Louw, *Municipal Policing*, chap. 1.
63. Van der Spuy, "Political Discourse," 93. This historian (M. Dippenaar), according to Brewer, acknowledged that in 1968 only one in ten SAP personnel was involved in criminal investigation. *Black and Blue*, 259.
64. One historian described the effect of Prime Minister Hendrik Verwoerd's Promotion of Bantu Self-government Act as follows: "This meant that the millions of Africans living and working in the urban and industrial areas of the country were being given a patently fictitious right to choose their government. Instead of being allowed to participate in the election of the parliament which actually ruled them they were to vote for the election of a government (with limited functions) in a distant Bantustan which they had very likely never seen and probably never would." Hepple, *Verwoerd*, 188.
65. Brewer, *Black and Blue*, 215–16.
66. Sparks, *Mind of South Africa*, 260.
67. Brewer, *Black and Blue*, 261.
68. Cawthra, *Policing South Africa*, 17.
69. Brewer, *Black and Blue*, 255.
70. Ibid., 257.
71. Ibid., 235.
72. Police use of vigilantes is discussed in Brewer, *Black and Blue*, 307–11; and Haysom, *Mabangalala*. In South Africa at this time the term referred to gangs of conservative blacks who attacked antiapartheid activists.
73. Seekings, *The UDF*, 31–32.
74. Hansson, "Changes," 30.
75. Sparks, *Mind of South Africa*, 343.
76. Davenport and Saunders, *South Africa*, 467.
77. South African Institute of Race Relations, *Race Relations Survey*, 1985, 208.
78. Brewer, *Black and Blue*, 290.
79. For a detailed history of the UDF, see Seekings, *The UDF*.
80. Cawthra, *Policing South Africa*, 28.
81. Brewer, *Black and Blue*, 274.
82. Cole, *Crossroads*, 51.
83. Ibid., 142.
84. Cawthra, *Policing South Africa*, 28.
85. Haysom, *Mabangalala*, 1. The South African Institute of Race Relations reported for 1985 that political violence claimed 879 lives and that "of this number 50.2 percent were residents killed by security forces and 31.1 percent people killed by

fellow residents." South African Institute of Race Relations, *Race Relations Survey,* 1985, 534.

86. Haysom, "Licence to Kill."

87. Brewer, *Black and Blue,* 299–300.

88. South African Institute of Race Relations, *Race Relations Survey,* 1985, 435. Banned individuals were confined to their homes or to designated areas, and selected people were denied permission to leave or enter the country. The national treasurer of the UDF was denied a passport, and Jesse Jackson was denied a visa.

89. Steytler, "Policing Political Opponents," 106–34.

90. Pauw, *Heart of Darkness,* 21.

91. National Party submission to the TRC, August 1996, http://www.doj.gov.za/trc/submit/np_truth.htm. The final report of the Truth and Reconciliation Commission, issued in March 2003, found this statement "indefensible." See the full report at http://www.news24.com/News24v2/ContentDisplay/genericFrame/0,,trc,00.html.

92. For details on the brutalities of other repressive regimes, see Corradi, Fagen, and Garreton, *Fear at the Edge.*

93. Pauw, *Heart of Darkness,* 153.

94. Pauw recounts the attempts of one of the commanders at Vlakplaas to kill another (ibid., 148–49).

95. Steytler, "Policing Political Opponents," 108.

96. Amnesty International, *South Africa,* 12.

97. In a speech at Pretoria Police College on January 17, 1990, de Klerk said, "You will no longer be required to prevent people from gathering to canvass support for their views. This is the political arena and we want to take the police out of it. We don't want to use you any more as instruments to reach certain political goals. . . . This is the direction we are taking and I want you to make peace with this new line."

98. Amnesty International, *South Africa,* 20.

99. Ibid., 32.

100. Welsh, "Outline," 12.

101. For a contemporary account of the charges that the security forces were involved in the violence and the government's responses, see Zulu, "Political Violence."

102. Charney, "From Resistance to Reconstruction," 762. See also Brewer, "Police in South African Politics," 258.

103. McBarnet, *Conviction.*

104. Posel, *Making of Apartheid.*

105. Roux, *Time Longer Than Rope,* 236.

106. Corder, *Judges at Work,* 2.

107. *Moller v. Keimoes School Committee,* 1911 A.D. 635, quoted in Dugard, *Human Rights,* 307.

108. *R. v. Radsha,* 1923 A.D. 281.

109. *Harris v. Minister of the Interior,* 1952 (2) SA 428 (AD).

110. *Minister of the Interior v. Harris,* 1952 (4) SA 769 (AD).

111. The term "pigmentocracy" to describe a state in which all political power is

concentrated in a minority race comes from Dugard, *Human Rights,* 7. Dugard also presents in detail the legal battle over the entrenched clauses, at 28–31; discussion of its politics can be found in Le May, *The Afrikaners,* 205–6 and 212.

112. *Minister of the Interior v. Lockhat,* 1961 (2) SA, 587 (AD), at 602.

113. Act 9 of 1956. The Constitution of 1961 reinforced the provision with the same language.

114. Suppression of Communism Act 44 of 1950, Sec. 1; *R. v. Sisulu and others,* 1953 (3) SA 276 (A.D.).

115. *Rossouw v. Sachs,* 1964 (2) SA 551 (AD).

116. *Schermbrucker v. Klindt N.O.,* 1965 (4) SA 606 (AD). For a discussion of these two cases, see Mathews and Albino, "Permanence of the Temporary," 16.

117. Legal scholars (Dugard, Mathews, and Albino) have suggested that if the Appellate Division had expressed strong disapproval of detention practices, parliament might have been deterred from passing still more repressive laws. A more political analysis, however, would suggest that the power of the National Party state was so great at this time that parliament could act with impunity, regardless of judicial pronouncements and the criticism of the government that might follow.

118. Sachs, *Justice in South Africa,* 255.

119. *Minister of Justice v. Alexander,* 1975 (4) SA 530 (AD). The lower court had ruled that the minister did not have to state his reasons but should give the court access to the documents on which he based his judgment; the Appellate Division was unwilling even to compel discovery so that it could judge whether the minister was acting in the public interest.

120. *State. v. Wood,* 1976 (1) SA 703 (AD).

121. *Minister of Law and Order and Another v. Dempsey,* 1988 (3) SA 19 (A); *Omar and Others v. Minister of Law and Order and Others,* 1987 (3) SA 859 (A).

122. Ellmann, *Time of Trouble,* 89.

123. Foster and Sandler, "Study of Detention," 452–53.

124. *Sunday Times,* October 12, 1997.

125. See, e.g., *Sigaba v. Minister of Defence and Police,* 1980 (3) SA 535 (TkSC).

126. See, e.g., *Momonial and Naidoo v. Minister of Law and Order,* 1986 (2) SA 264 (WLD).

127. *Minister of Law and Order and Others v. Hurley and Another,* 1986 (3) SA 568 (AD), 578.

128. *Omar v. Minister of Law and Order,* 894.

129. Ibid.

130. Act 51 of 1977, Sec. 112.

131. Ibid., Sec. 217. Section 218 further provided that if the confession was found to be inadmissible because not voluntary, police testimony as to facts revealed as the result of the confession—the location of a weapon, the means of illegal entry into a house or business—would be admissible.

132. Sachs, *Justice in South Africa,* presents figures from police reports on racial disparities in convictions and sentencing, at 153–56.

133. Ibid., 156.

134. Dugard, *Human Rights,* 125–26.

135. Schönteich, "Does Capital Punishment Deter?" 91; Dugard, *Human Rights*, 126.

136. Although the defendant, Professor Barend van Niekerk, was acquitted on the first charge on the basis of a lack of intent to demean the judiciary or the justice system, he was later convicted of contempt when he criticized lawyers and judges for not opposing detention provisions of the Terrorism Act. See Dugard, *Human Rights*, 292–99.

137. The quote is from Mahomed, "Address by Chief Justice I. Mahomed," 48.

138. South African Institute of Race Relations, *Race Relations Survey*, 1987–88, 509. The quote is from Adriaan Volk, minister of law and order.

139. In 1981 there were 74,267 arrests for pass law offenses. South African Institute of Race Relations, *Race Relations Survey*, 1982, 277. While the number of convictions is not available, it is safe to assume that the number is not significantly smaller, as a finding of guilt was virtually automatic in most cases.

140. Jackson, *Justice in South Africa*, 21–22.

141. Simpson, "Snake Gives Birth," 7.

Chapter 4

1. Quoted in Sparks, *Mind of South Africa*, 243.
2. Cock, "Political Violence," 66.
3. Jeffrey Arendse, elementary school principal in the Cape Flats, Western Cape, quoted in *New York Times*, March 21, 2003.
4. *Mail and Guardian*, November 23, 1998.
5. Ibid.
6. Hamber, "Have No Doubt," 5.
7. See South African Migration Project for materials on South African emigration since the end of apartheid. http://www.queensu.ca/samp/. A 1998 Human Sciences Research Council national survey of people who wanted to leave found that crime was the main factor for 54 percent of whites, a higher incidence than for other racial groups. A related finding, however, is that whites were overwhelmingly (83 percent) negative about the way the new government was handling the economy. *Saturday Argus*, October 10, 1998.
8. Public opinion data on crime are available from the Human Sciences Research Council, http://www.hsrc.ac.za/, and from Afrobarometer surveys, http://www.afrobarometer.org/.
9. Nattrass, "State of the Economy," 2. The unemployment rate is from Statistics South Africa, http://www.statssa.gov.za/.
10. Human Sciences Research Council media release, March 8, 2000.
11. Burton et al., *National Victims of Crime Survey*, fig. 17, 53.
12. *Business Day*, January 14, 2000.
13. *ZA Now*, November 4, 1999.
14. Schönteich, "Back to the Future?" 6.
15. Rule, *Public Opinion*, table 16, p. 26.
16. Ibid., table 17.
17. Mattes et al., "Democratic Governance," 10.

18. *The Times* (London), March 10, 2003. Ironically, by this date surveillance cameras, omnipresent security, and development projects had made the downtown area much safer, but good news travels more slowly than bad.

19. Agence France Presse, August 20, 1999.

20. February 7, 1999.

21. *ZA Now,* April 4, 1999.

22. Mbeki, "State of the Nation Address," February 8, 2002.

23. Paton, *Cry the Beloved Country,* 74.

24. Shaw, *Crime and Policing,* 2. See the subsequent pages for discussion of the relationship between apartheid policies and crime during that period.

25. Simpson, "Snake Gives Birth," 6.

26. Simpson, "Shock Troops and Bandits," 122.

27. Chaskalson's title was subsequently changed to chief justice of South Africa.

28. *The Independent* (London), February 7, 1999.

29. See, for example, Shaw, "Crime, Police and Public," 3.

30. These figures are extrapolated from the Criminal Justice Monitor of the Institute for Security Studies (South Africa) (www.iss.co.za) and from population data in the CIA World Factbook. (http://www.cia.gov/cia/publications/factbook/index.html). The population estimate available is for 2002. Published data from the South African Police Service have not been used because they are reported only for the period January–June in each year.

31. FBI Uniform Crime Reports, "Crime in the United States, 2001," 32. The discrepancy would be greater still if South African figures were available for the full year.

32. The rate for aggravated robbery has fluctuated from 218.5 per 100,000 population in fiscal year 1994–95 to 163 in 1996–97, 260.3 in 2000–2001, and 288.1 in 2003–4. SAPS data reproduced by the Institute for Security Studies at http://www.iss.co.za/CJM/statgraphs/agrob.htm. I have used this source because it is easier to access and read than the official data, which are available at http://www.saps.gov.za/statistics/reports/crimestats/2004/categories.htm.

33. "City Crime Trends," Nedbank ISS *Crime Index* 5 (2001) (1), fig. 4.

34. SAPS data reproduced by the Institute for Security Studies at http://www.iss.co.za/CJM/statgraphs/rape.htm. The U.S. figure is taken from FBI Uniform Crime Reports, "Crime in the United States, 2003."

35. *New York Times,* July 12, 1998.

36. Leggett et al., *Criminal Justice in Review,* chap. 1.

37. Burton et al., *National Victims of Crime Survey,* 107.

38. Leggett, "Improved Crime Reporting."

39. SAPS data reproduced by the Institute for Security Studies at http://www.iss.co.za/CJM/statgraphs/murder1.htm.

40. Burton et al., *National Victims of Crime Survey,* 105.

41. Leggett, "Improved Crime Reporting."

42. South African Police Service, Crime Information Analysis Centre, reproduced in Leggett et al., *Criminal Justice in Review,* chap. 3.

43. Leggett, "Performance Measures," 62.

44. *Southern Africa Business Intelligence,* August 25, 1995.

45. Leggett, "Improved Crime Reporting," table 1.

46. U.S. Department of Justice, *Criminal Victimization,* table 91. Reporting rates for burglary and car theft were 59 percent and 95 percent, respectively for South Africa and 51.8 percent and 79.8 percent for the United States. Forty-seven percent of South African victims of sexual assaults reported the crime, while only 30.5 percent of Americans did.

47. Neild, "From National Security."

48. Neild, "New Face of Impunity."

49. Tanner, "Will the State Bring *You* Back In?" 110.

50. See Dinan, McCall, and Gibson, "Community Violence and PTSD," 737.

51. South African Police Service, Crime Information Analysis Centre; FBI Uniform Crime Reports, "Crime in the United States, 2003." The figures for the United States are for the calendar year.

52. Louw et al., *Crime in Johannesburg.*

53. For the association of criminal violence in the 1990s with the political violence of the late apartheid years, see Hamber, "Have No Doubt."

54. United Nations Development Programme, "Human Development Report 1999," 42.

55. For work on organized crime in South Africa, see the publications of the Institute for Security Studies, especially Gastrow, *Organized Crime;* and Kinnes, *Urban Street Gangs.*

56. See Redpath, "Gang Landscape," 34–40. A good overview of the organized crime problem is available in Shaw, *Crime and Policing,* chap. 4.

57. United Nations Office on Drugs and Crime, "South Africa." See also the African section of the International Narcotics Control Board, "Annual Report."

58. Shaw, *Crime and Policing,* 71.

59. *Mail and Guardian,* August 2, 2002.

60. Recent information on drug use patterns for all of the southern African region can be found on the website of the International Narcotics Control Board, http://www.incb.org.

61. Masuku, "Prevention Is Better," 9. The data on which this article rely come from the National Injury Mortality Surveillance System, which does not record every death, so they should be interpreted with caution.

62. Louw and Shaw, *Stolen Opportunities,* 37.

63. See Mistry, Snyman, and van Zyl, "Social Fabric Crime"; and Louw and Shaw, *Stolen Opportunities.*

64. Interpol data may be found at http://www.interpol.int/Public/Statistics/ICS/downloadList.asp. They should be interpreted with caution, as countries vary in their reporting standards and crime definitions.

65. *New York Times,* January 29, 2002.

66. For a discussion of the relationship between sexual violence and HIV transmission, see Human Rights Watch, *Deadly Delay.*

67. For the official picture of crime rates by province between 1994 and 2004, see South African Police Service, Crime Information Analysis Centre, http://www.saps.gov.za/statistics/reports/crimestats/2004/province.htm.

68. Marks and Andersson, "Epidemiology and Culture of Violence." This dispro-

portion may be less in recent years, as some of the murders were the result of political violence in the liberation struggle of the 1980s.

69. Human Sciences Research Council, *Omnibus Survey,* 1995, as reported in Louw and Shaw, *Stolen Opportunities,* 14.
70. *Mail and Guardian,* September 14, 2001.
71. *Daily News* (KwaZulu-Natal), September 10, 2001.
72. "Protecting Children against Violence in Schools," 4.
73. Human Rights Watch, *Scared at School.*
74. Lucas, "Adolescence and Youth," 8.
75. See Lee and Seekings, "Vigilantism and Popular Justice."
76. See Haysom, *Mabangalala.*
77. See Dixon and Johns, "Gangs, Pagad and the State."
78. Schärf, "Non-state Justice Systems," 37.
79. Schärf, "Community Justice," 6.
80. Sekhonyane and Louw, *Violent Justice,* chap. 3.
81. See Pelser, Louw, and Ntuli, *Poor Safety.*
82. See Louw and Shaw, *Stolen Opportunities.*
83. For a powerful and nuanced journalistic picture of the interplay of violence perpetrated against and by South African farmers, see Steinberg, *Midlands.*
84. See Manby, *Unequal Protection.*
85. Schönteich and Steinberg, *Attacks on Farms and Smallholdings,* fig. 1.
86. *Mail and Guardian,* May 22, 1998, and November 2, 1998.
87. Masuku, "Policing the Police."
88. *Mail and Guardian,* February 4, 2000.
89. Chevigny, *Edge of the Knife,* 7.
90. Bruce and O'Malley, "In the Line of Duty?"
91. Neild, "Culture of Impunity," 228.
92. South African Institute of Race Relations, *South Africa Survey,* 2000–2001, 88. Between 1984 and June 2000 there were 24,547 deaths attributed to political violence, with the highest number in 1993 (3,794), the year preceding the first democratic election. By 1999 the number of deaths had shrunk to 325. For detail on deaths and injuries from political violence between 1990 and 1995, see Minaar, Pretorius, and Wentzel, "Political Conflict."
93. SAPS data reproduced by the Institute for Security Studies at http://www.iss.co.za/CJM/statgraphs/murder1.htm.
94. Masuku, "For Better and for Worse," 17. This article includes graphs showing rates of increase and decline since 1994 for many crimes.
95. Independent Complaints Directorate, Annual Report, 2001–2, 4.
96. Burton et al., *National Victims of Crime Survey,* 102.
97. Ibid., 105. Among victims surveyed, 4.2 percent were victims of assaults in 1998, 2.2 percent in 2003.
98. Nattrass, "State of the Economy."
99. *Business Day,* October 30, 2002.
100. "Document 75. Statement during the Rivonia trial, by Nelson R. Mandela, April 20, 1964." Karis and Gerhart, *Challenge and Violence,* 777–78.

101. Ibid.
102. Gerhart, *Black Power*, 285–86.
103. Ibid., 288.
104. Hamber, "Dr. Jekyll and Mr. Hyde," 350.
105. Gerhart, *Black Power*, 14.
106. Hamber, "Dr. Jekyll and Mr. Hyde," 352.
107. Pauw, *Heart of Darkness*, 11.
108. Ibid., 117.
109. Jackson, *Justice in South Africa*, 98.
110. Glaser, *Bo-Tsotsi*, 40.
111. Ibid., 40.
112. Vold and Bernard, *Theoretical Criminology*, 190.
113. Glaser, *Bo-Tsotsi*, 189.
114. Segal, Pelo, and Rampa, "Into the Heart of Darkness," 100. Interviews from this study of gang members provide a chilling glimpse into the normalcy of violence in the lives of these young men and those they come in contact with.
115. Simpson, "Reconstruction and Reconciliation."
116. Ibid.
117. *Business Day*, January 25, 2000.
118. *Mail and Guardian*, January 28, 2000.
119. For a variety of perspectives, see Glanz and Spiegel, *Violence and Family Life*.
120. Medical Research Council, "Every Six Hours," 2. The percentage is higher (50.3 percent) if only those situations where the relationship is known are taken into account. There is no reason to believe that 1999 was in any way unusual; if this is the case, these figures suggest that in South Africa 8.8 women per 100,000 over age fourteen are killed by their intimate partners annually, the highest rate ever reported in the world.
121. Campbell, "Social Identity and Violence," 211; see also Campbell, "Learning to Kill?"
122. See, for example, Plywaczewski, "Challenges of Policing Democracy," 146–48.
123. Beinart, "Political and Collective Violence," 456.
124. Hootnick, "Improvised Justice," 66.

Chapter 5
1. Held, *Models of Democracy*, 1.
2. Bayley, *Social Control*, 16.
3. U.S. Department of State, "Sierra Leone Country Report."
4. *African Law Today*, October 16, 1998. Rule changes included abandoning the requirement of a unanimous jury, allowing secondary sources as evidence in trial, and permitting trials to be held in the absence of the accused.
5. *New York Times*, February 2, 2002.
6. Saad Eddin Ibrahim, a sociologist at the American University in Cairo, whose institute had been training Egyptians in voter registration and election monitoring, was arrested in 2000, tried in a state security court, and convicted of illegally accept-

ing foreign donations and disseminating information to damage Egypt's interests. An appeal court voided the conviction in late 2002, and a new trial—his third, this time in a regular court—acquitted him in 2003.

7. See Human Rights Watch, *Behind Bars in Brazil,* 1998. Investigators reported in 1998 that in São Paolo and Minas Gerais police lockups—where conditions were terrible and torture and intimidation the rule—were used for the detention of convicted offenders as well as most criminal defendants.

8. Chevigny, "The Populism of Fear."
9. See Klug, *Constituting Democracy.*
10. Schumpeter, *Capitalism, Socialism and Democracy,* 269.
11. See Dahl, *Polyarchy* and *Democracy and Its Critics.*
12. Rawls, *Political Liberalism,* 228. Robert Dahl also came to the support of economic democracy through his advocacy of what he called "self-governing enterprises," collectively owned firms governed by those who work in them. See Dahl, *Preface to Economic Democracy,* 91–92.
13. See Gutmann and Thompson, *Democracy and Disagreement.*
14. Macpherson, *Democratic Theory,* 10.
15. Held, *Models of Democracy,* 314.
16. Huntington, *The Third Wave.*
17. Ibid., 258.
18. For literature on democratic consolidation, see Diamond, *Developing Democracy;* Linz and Stepan, *Problems of Democratic Transition;* and O'Donnell, "Illusions about Consolidation."
19. Neild, "From National Security," 2.
20. Ellmann, *Time of Trouble,* 64–70.
21. Two relevant surveys are "Afrobarometer, Round 1"; and Garretón, "Redemocratization in Chile," 146–58.
22. *New York Times,* June 2, 2002.
23. Diamond, *Developing Democracy,* 74.
24. See Pye, *Asian Power and Politics;* and Friedman, "Agreeing to Differ."
25. Huntington, *The Third Wave,* 311.
26. Schmitter and Karl, "What Democracy Is."
27. Dahl, *Polyarchy,* 26–27.
28. Diamond, *Developing Democracy,* 77.
29. "Key Findings about Public Opinion in Africa."
30. Gordon, "Democratic Consolidation."
31. Bayley, "Democratizing the Police Abroad."
32. This rather obvious statement concerning the relationship between criminal justice and the state is sometimes expressed as a tension between serving the state or serving the law. But the law is by definition a core project of the state, not autonomous and neutral, and part of democratization is law reform.
33. Klug notes that adoption of an American-style bill of rights has become a requirement for participation in global economic negotiations (*Constituting Democracy,* 80), but it should also be noted that the new constitutions may go farther than the typical, procedurally oriented Western bill of rights to attempt the guarantee of some sub-

stantive rights like access to medical care and housing, as the South African constitution does.

34. Joseph, "Democratization in Africa," 239.
35. Bayley, "Contemporary Practices of Policing."
36. Reiner, *Politics of the Police,* 4.
37. For a trenchant analysis of the continuing role of police in maintaining repressive state power in sub-Saharan Africa, see Hills, *Policing Africa.*
38. Reiner, *Politics of the Police,* 60.
39. *BBC Monitoring Europe,* August 14, 2002.
40. European Code of Police Ethics, IV (A) (13). http://www.coe.int/T/E/Legal_affairs/Legal_co-operation/Police_and_internal_security/Documents/Rec(2001)10%20European%20Code%20of%20Police%20Ethics.asp; emphasis added.
41. UN Code of Conduct for Law Enforcement Officials, Article 1(b). http://www.coe.int/T/E/human_rights/Police/5._Reference_Documents/p._Code_of_Conduct_for_Law_Enforcement_Officials.asp#TopOfPage.
42. For purposes of this discussion I am assuming that public accountability for judges does not generally include popular election. Although the bulk of lower-court judges in the United States are elected, the practice is not common elsewhere and is generally regarded as an oddity of direct democracy. One distinguished Canadian political scientist writes, "A system that requires judges to win popularity contests to retain office takes democratic accountability to the point of destroying judicial independence." Russell, "Toward a General Theory," 16. I do not know of any newly democratizing country that elects judges.
43. See Chodosh, "Emergence from the Dilemmas," 599–600.
44. The right to a fair and impartial hearing in a competent and independent court has been included in the Universal Declaration of Human Rights; the International Covenant on Economic, Social and Cultural Rights; and the International Covenant on Civil and Political Rights.
45. Russell, "Toward a General Theory," 8.
46. The degree of separation of the branches of government is by no means uniform in democratic countries. See *Certification of the Constitution,* pars. 108–13, for a discussion of variation in some Western states and the approach South Africa has taken on this matter.
47. Russell, "Toward a General Theory," 10.
48. Burbank, "Architecture of Judicial Independence," 317.
49. Bator, "Constitution as Architecture," 269, quoted in Burbank, "Architecture of Judicial Independence."
50. See Burbank and Friedman, "Reconsidering Judicial Independence."
51. Cardozo, *Nature of the Judicial Process,* 167.
52. Scheppele, "Declarations of Independence," 244.
53. Njoku, "Nigeria at 40."
54. Sayed and Bruce, "Boundaries of Police Corruption."
55. Oko, "Subverting the Scourge," 407.
56. "Police, Then Judiciary Most Corrupt Public Institutions in South Asia, Reveals TI Survey," press release, Transparency International, December 17, 2002,

http://www.transparency.org/pressreleases_archive/2002/2002.12.17.south_asia_survey.html.

57. See Cilliers, "Peace, Security and Democracy."

58. Pound, "Discretion, Dispensation and Mitigation," 926.

59. For a list of press complaints in Brazil about censorship and efforts to use libel and defamation law to suppress information, see the 2003 Inter American Press Association country report, http://www.sipiapa.com/pulications/report_brazil2003m.cfm.

60. For more information on investigative journalism in democratizing countries, see the website of the IAPA, http://www.sipiapa.com/default.cfm.

61. Universal Declaration of Human Rights, Article 11, http://www.un.org/Overview/rights.html.

62. UN International Covenant on Civil and Political Rights, Article 9, http://www.hrweb.org/legal/cpr.html; see Amann, "Harmonic Convergence?" 825, for the view that the covenant is likely to become "a central component of a new, global constitutional criminal procedure."

63. Mamdani, "Social Movements and Constitutionalism," 172.

64. Held, *Models of Democracy,* 305.

65. Schmitter and Karl, "What Democracy Is," 50.

66. *Trop v. Dulles,* 356 U.S. 86 (1958).

67. Held, *Models of Democracy,* 316.

Chapter 6

1. *Mail and Guardian,* June 1, 2001.

2. Mandela, *Long Walk to Freedom,* 544.

3. Sunstein, *Designing Democracy,* 68.

4. Constitution of the Republic of South Africa, Secs. 34 and 35.

5. Internal Security Act of 1982, Sec. 29; Security Emergency Regulations, Proc. R. 97, Sec. 3 (1), June 1988.

6. The enabling legislation of the South African Law Commission (now renamed the South African Law Reform Commission) is the South African Law Commission Act 19 of 1973.

7. Limits on the efficacy of the Independent Complaints Directorate are detailed in Bruce, Savage, and de Waal, "Duty to Answer Questions," 71–96. See also Pigou, "Monitoring Police Violence." It should be noted especially that the ICD can only investigate incidents that are reported to them, and Pigou reports that the police and the Ministry of Safety and Security have resisted what they consider "fishing expeditions" to uncover brutality in police station holding cells.

8. Two-thirds of South Africans feel that police and courts "have the right to make people abide by their decisions," according to a 2002 Afrobarometer survey. Mattes et al., "Democratic Governance," 3.

9. Hills, *Policing Africa,* ix.

10. Ibid., 70.

11. Cawthra, *Policing South Africa,* vii.

12. Shaw, *Crime and Policing,* 11.

13. Skolnick and Bayley, *New Blue Line.*

14. Cawthra, *Policing South Africa,* 39.

15. Brogden, "Indigenisation of Policing," 234.
16. Altbeker, *Solving Crime,* "Restructuring of the SAPS."
17. Brodeur, "High Policing."
18. This was the theme of his lecture at the International Conference on Crime, Justice and Public Order in London on June 18, 2002.
19. As one commentator put it, "[T]hose in the highest positions of power are capable of conflating internal lobbying and caucusing with a treasonous 'plot.'" Mattes, "South Africa," 28.
20. Bond, "From Racial to Class Apartheid."
21. *Business Day,* September 18, 2002.
22. For a history of the Boeremag, see Schönteich and Boshoff, *"Volk," Faith and Fatherland,* chap. 4.
23. The "softer" approach did not preclude the usual operations of prosecution and adjudication. As of this writing, twenty-two Boeremag suspects are being tried on charges of treason, terrorism, sabotage, and attempting to overthrow the state.
24. For an understanding of the National Management System's role and function in the apartheid state (and its demise as apartheid was crumbling), see Hansson, "Changes."
25. Louis Eloff, interview by the author, February 10, 2000.
26. Frankel, *Pretoria's Praetorians,* 101.
27. Brewer, *Black and Blue,* 251.
28. Henri Boshoff, telephone interview by the author, November 3, 2003.
29. Separation of the military from the police was part of a much larger shrinkage of the SANDF, which has lost many of its personnel through resignations and retirements. Defense expenditures declined by 57 percent during the 1990s, though they have risen again as South Africa justifies the purchase of planes, tanks, submarines, and a ground-to-air missile system as necessary preparedness for (unlikely) attacks on the southern African region. The defense budget exceeded sixteen billion rand (about $2.25 billion at the time) in 2002. Harris, "Irrationality of South Africa's Military Expenditure."
30. South African Department of Defence, Strategic Plan, v.
31. Quoted in Marks, "Shifting Gears," 241.
32. Regulation of Gatherings Act No. 205 of 1993.
33. Marks, "Shifting Gears," 252.
34. Ibid., 254.
35. Ibid., 256.
36. No statutory impediment to black judges or magistrates was ever enacted in South Africa, but an appointment of a black or a woman to the higher courts would have been unthinkable, and it was rare for the magistrates' courts until the end of apartheid.
37. Omar's comment was quoted in *Citizen,* August 15, 1998. Chaskalson's statement is reproduced in Chaskalson et al., "Legal System in South Africa," 22. At the time of his testimony Chaskalson's title was president of the Constitutional Court. It was later changed to chief justice of South Africa, in recognition of the court's role as the ultimate authority on constitutional matters.
38. See Ellmann, *Time of Trouble,* for a study of the decisions of the "emergency team" on the highest court during the mid-1980s.

39. For the debate over whether judges opposed to apartheid should have resigned, see Dugard, "Should Judges Resign?"

40. For a thoughtful discussion of the problem of introducing judicial accountability into South African courts at apartheid's end, see Cameron, "Judicial Accountability."

41. Justice Mahomed's official biography is at http://www.concourt.gov.za/judges/jdmahom.html.

42. Constitution of the Republic of South Africa, Sec. 165 (2) and (3).

43. For a study of magistrates' perspectives on their roles and functions during apartheid, see Gready and Kgalena, "Magistrates under Apartheid."

44. Ibid., 156.

45. Ellmann, *Time of Trouble*, 63.

46. Magistrates Amendment Act 66 of 1998.

47. This observation is based on my perusal of files held in the administrative office of the Judicial Service Commission, discussed below.

48. *Steyn v. State,* 2000 CCT 19/00, par. 18.

49. *Sunday Independent,* July 20, 2003.

50. Constitution of the Republic of South Africa, Sec. 178. Until 2001 the chief justice headed the Supreme Court of Appeal. But in that year the president of the Constitutional Court was designated chief justice of South Africa. The president of the Supreme Court of Appeal also sits on the Judicial Service Commission.

51. Constitution of the Republic of South Africa, Sec. 178 (5). Section 178 (1)(k) provides that when the commission is considering an appointment to the High Court (as opposed to the Supreme Court of Appeal or the Constitutional Court), it includes, in addition, the judge president of the judicial division in which the appointee would serve and the premier of the relevant province.

52. Constitution of the Republic of South Africa, Sec. 177 (1)(a).

53. Ibid., Sec. 174 (7).

54. Magistrates Amendment Act 66 of 1998, Secs. 13 (2), (3), and (4); Regulation 26 (1), (2), and (3).

55. *Van Rooyen v. State,* 2000 CCT 19/00.

56. This observation is based on my perusal of the list of proceedings held during that period, provided by the Magistrates' Commission.

57. *Van Rooyen v. State.*

58. The chief magistrate was suspended and convicted.

59. The Constitutional Court has described the relative importance of judicial tenure as an indicator of independence for the upper and lower courts: "Protection against removal from office lies at the heart of judicial independence. The fact that members of the higher judiciary have greater protection than members of the lower judiciary, does not mean that the protection given to the lower judiciary is inconsistent with judicial independence. That question depends upon the nature of the protection given to members of the lower judiciary viewed in the context of the functions that they are required to perform." *Van Rooyen v. State,* par. 161.

60. Constitution of the Republic of South Africa, Sec. 174 (1).

61. This openness is, in one respect, more theoretical than real. The meetings are

held in a posh hotel in Cape Town. Most ordinary South Africans would not feel comfortable in such a setting, and few attend unless a particularly prominent or notorious candidate is being interviewed. While records are made of the proceedings, they are not generally available. The press, however, is welcome and supplies the public with accounts of particularly noteworthy interviews.

62. Constitution of the Republic of South Africa, Sec. 174 (2).

63. Friedman, "Diversity the Antidote."

64. I attended this meeting.

65. *President of the Republic of South Africa and Others v. South Africa Rugby Football Union and Others,* 2000 (1) SA 1 (CC), pars. 33(c) and 105.

66. *State v. Makwanyane,* 1995 (3) SA 391 (CC).

67. *Certification of the Constitution of the Republic of South Africa,* 1996 (4) SA 744 (CC).

68. *President of the Republic of South Africa and Others v. South Africa Rugby Football Union and Others,* 1999 (4) SA 147 (CC).

69. See Friedman, "South African Citizens."

70. *August v. Electoral Commission,* 1999 (3) SA 1 (CC); *Premier, Mpumalanga v. Association of State-Aided Schools,* 1999 (2) SA 91 (CC).

71. *Republic of South Africa v. Grootboom,* 2001(1) SA 46 (CC), par. 96.

72. *Minister of Health v. Treatment Action Campaign,* 2002 (5) SA 721 (CC).

73. *Mail and Guardian,* December 20, 2002.

74. *Mail and Guardian,* June 27, 2003.

75. The Joint United Nations Programme on HIV/AIDS (UNAIDS) estimates that, as of the end of 2003, 5,300,000 adults and children (age 0–49) were living with HIV. http://www.unaids.org/en/geographical+area/by+country/south+africa.asp. Human Rights Watch estimates that by the end of 2005 six million South Africans will be infected.http://hrw.org/reports/2004/southafrica0304/4.htm#_ftn21.

76. In 2003 the chief justice, Arthur Chaskalson, took a very visible stand for judicial independence by joining with the other chief justices of the southern African region to decry the arrest and detention of a Zimbabwean judge who was charged with interfering with justice and corruption but was told when arrested that he had "embarrassed the government" by releasing a detained opposition leader who had been arrested for holding an illegal political meeting.

77. *Guardian,* March 18, 1999.

78. Seekings, *The UDF,* 58.

79. *Boesak v. State,* 2005 SA 105/99 (SCA). Because the court found the judgment on one count unwarranted and calculated a lower amount of stolen money, it reduced the trial court's sentence to three years' imprisonment.

80. *Business Day,* August 23, 2003.

81. Criminal Law Amendment Act 105 of 1997, Secs. 51 and 53.

82. "Sergeant at the Bar," *Mail and Guardian,* October 15, 1999.

83. *State v. Abrahams,* 2001 SA 88/00 (SCA), par. 15.

84. Transparency International, Corruption Perceptions Index 2003, http://www.transparency.org/cpi/2003/cpi2003.en.html. It should be noted that the index

reflects responses to polls and surveys regarding corruption among public officials and politicians generally, not views specifically relating to the conduct of criminal justice operatives.

85. Mattes et al., "Democratic Governance," 10.
86. *Mail and Guardian,* December 18, 2000.
87. *Mail and Guardian,* January 23, 1998.
88. *Business Day,* March 10, 2000.
89. South African Police Service Act, Sec. 36.
90. The South African government had hoped to break through the code of silence and mutual protection that characterizes police departments around the world by creating a civilian secretariat that would monitor police operations and, in the words of its enabling legislation, "promote democratic accountability and transparency in the Service." But the secretariat is accountable to the minister for safety and security, who honors the traditionally closed culture of police by preferring to go it alone without a civilian representative looking over his shoulder, and the office has been sidelined.
91. South African Police Service Act, Sec. 53.
92. Annual Report of the National Commissioner for 2002–3, part 1.
93. *Mail and Guardian,* February 4, 2000.
94. See Sayed and Bruce, "Boundaries of Police Corruption."
95. South African Police Service, Annual Report, 2003.
96. *The Star* (Johannesburg), October 30, 2003.
97. Newham, "Tackling Police Corruption."
98. See Mattes et al., "Democratic Governance," 13–14.
99. Transparency International, "Global Corruption Barometer Survey," 3.
100. *Business Day,* July 4, 2001; Independent Complaints Directorate, Annual Report, 2002–3, 50.
101. The same opinion is expressed in Leggett et al., *Criminal Justice in Review,* chap. 3.
102. Burton, *National Victims of Crime Survey,* chap. 6.
103. An interesting detail that testifies to public confidence that the police will not retaliate against complaints is the finding by David Bruce that, in the first five years of the existence of the ICD, the number of complaints that alleged poor performance by the police ("neglects duty or performs duty in improper manner" and "failure to perform duties and responsibilities," as opposed to assault, torture, corruption, or the like) increased fourfold and that by 2002 constituted 75 percent of complaints. See Bruce, "Gripes or Grievances," table 3.
104. See Pauw, *Heart of Darkness,* 110; *Mail and Guardian,* September 1, 1996.
105. Mattes et al., "Democratic Governance," 5–6.
106. *State v. Zuma,* 1995 (2) SA 642 (CC), par. 16. The right to a fair trial is protected by Sec. 35 (3).
107. Constitution of the Republic of South Africa, Sec. 12.
108. *State v. Makwanyane,* par. 218.
109. *Carmichele v. Minister of Safety and Security,* 2001 (4) SA 938 (CC).
110. Constitution of the Republic of South Africa, Sec. 35 (3)(g).
111. Criminal Procedure Act 51, Sec. 217(1)(b)(ii).

112. *State v. Zuma.* The confession at issue was made before a magistrate, rather than to the police, but that fact does not alter the significance of the holding.
113. South African Police Service Act, Sec. 13 (3)(b).
114. *Thebus v. State,* 2003 CCT 36/02, par. 55.
115. Schönteich, *Lawyers for the People,* 136.
116. *Mello v. State* 1998 (3) SA 712 (CC).
117. Schönteich, *Lawyers for the People,* 137.
118. Hamber, "Have No Doubt," 7.
119. Independent Complaints Directorate, Annual Report, 2002–3, 31. Since the evidence of murder is generally available, this number is likely to represent most of the actual total.
120. See Bruce, "Police Brutality."
121. *Cape Times,* October 31, 1998.
122. Bruce and O'Malley, "In the Line of Duty?" table 12.
123. Criminal Procedure Act 51 of 1977, Sec. 49 (1) and (2).
124. *Raloso v. Wilson,* 1998 (4) SA 369 (NCD).
125. Judicial Matters Second Amendment Act 122 of 1998.
126. *Mail and Guardian,* February 12, 2002.
127. *State v. Walters,* 2002 (4) SA 613 (CC), par. 52.
128. Data from 2000 and 2001 suggest that rates of cases referred to court are not significantly lower than in Great Britain, except for murder, and that the attrition of criminal cases from arrest to conviction and sentence is only slightly greater than for Britain and the United States (again with the exception of murder). Concern about the high level of crime drives a view that greater efficiency (defined as both a greater percentage of arrests and a higher ratio of convictions to arrests) can and must be achieved. See Leggett, "The Sieve Effect."
129. *Sunday Times,* October 19, 1997.
130. *State v. Williams,* 1995 (3) SA 632 (CC), par. 8.
131. *State v. Zuma.*
132. *State v. Williams,* par. 52.
133. *State v. Ntuli,* 1995 CCT/17/95.
134. *State v. Bhulwana,* 1996 (1) SA 388 (CC).
135. *Scagell v. Attorney General,* 1996 CCT 42/95.
136. Constitution of the Republic of South Africa, Sec. 35 (2)(c) and (3)(g).
137. The court has, however, suggested that its commitment to the right will extend to noncitizens by assuming that an illegal Tanzanian immigrant charged with plotting to blow up the United States embassy in Dar es Salaam had a right to legal representation when faced with deportation. *Mohamed v. President of the Republic,* 2001 (3) SA 893 (CC).
138. *Cape Argus,* September 25, 2003.
139. *Business Day,* September 7, 1999.
140. See Leggett et al., *Criminal Justice in Review,* chap. 6.
141. *State v. Salzwedel,* 1999 SCA 273/98.
142. *Toronto Star,* October 12, 1996.
143. *State v. Basson,* 2003 SCA 404/02; *State v. Basson,* 2004 (1) SA 246 (CC).

144. *Business Day,* July 2, 2003.
145. Constitution of the Republic of South Africa, Sec. 195(i).
146. South African Police Service, Annual Report, 2002–3.
147. National Prosecuting Authority, Annual Report, 49.
148. Mandela, *Long Walk to Freedom,* 131.
149. South Africa Human Rights Commission, *Enquiry into Racism,* 15. This report also concluded that racial hostility was common in the working environment of magistrates' courts, that some segregated facilities—tearooms and toilets—still existed, and that opportunities like merit awards and advanced professional education were more available to whites than to blacks.
150. Judge Edwin Cameron, interview by the author, June 18, 2003.
151. *Sunday Independent,* July 20, 2003. These statistics do not include acting judges, many of whom are black and female.
152. Judge Ian Farlam, interview by the author, February 16, 2000.
153. Data supplied by the Magistrates Commission of South Africa.

Chapter 7

1. Barber, *Strong Democracy,* 119.
2. Johnston and Shearing, *Governing Security,* 70.
3. Nisbet, *The Sociological Tradition,* 47.
4. Clear and Karp, *The Community Justice Ideal,* 60.
5. Barber, *Strong Democracy,* 119–20.
6. Garland, *The Culture of Control,* 102, uses the word to designate the abandonment of the rehabilitative ideal and social sympathy for the lawbreaker in favor of punitive polices. Bayley and Shearing, "The Future of Policing," 585, use it to describe changes taking place in policing—its pluralization and the consequent search by state police for where they fit in a world where social control that used to be defined as law enforcement is shared by many actors, private as well as public.
7. Feeley and Simon, "New Penology."
8. Clarke, "Situational Crime Prevention," 235–37.
9. Caldeira, "Building Up Walls," 60.
10. See Human Rights Watch, *The Warri Crisis,* which documents ethnic violence over the control of stolen oil in Nigeria's Delta State and the involvement of the security forces in aiding the ethnic militia that have killed dozens of people in what many local people call a war.
11. Van de Meeberg and Aronowitz, "Challenges of Policing Democracies," 293.
12. Cavallaro, *Police Brutality.* Protest against police killings continued into 2004.
13. Inter Press Service, September 12, 2002.
14. Garland, *The Culture of Control,* 106.
15. See Kelling et al., *Kansas City Prevention Patrol;* and Spelman, *Calling the Police.* These are the classic studies, but more recent work has replicated their basic findings.
16. Wilson and Abrahamse, "Does Crime Pay?"
17. For the findings of the 2000 International Crime Victims Survey, see http://www.unicri.it/icvs/. While comparative crime data are notoriously inadequate, these surveys are probably the most reliable. It should be noted that victimizations rose fairly sharply in the early 1990s in Netherlands but then fell by 1999.

18. For a thoughtful discussion of the causes of high rates of violent crime in the United States, see Currie, *Crime and Punishment,* 120–47.

19. By "ordinary" I mean to exclude white-collar crime and corruption, not because they are unimportant but because they are somewhat less immediate problems for democratizing countries than theft and violence that threaten people's daily security.

20. Self-report studies that show a high incidence of offending began in the United States in the 1940s; in 1947 Wallerstein and Wyle, "Our Law-abiding Lawbreakers," found that 99 percent of the people they surveyed admitted committing an offense punishable by sentences of at least a year; more recent and more sophisticated studies in the United States and the United Kingdom have confirmed the wide prevalence of some kind of offending. See Tittle, *Sanctions and Social Deviance.*

21. See U.S. Department of Justice, *Criminal Victimization in the United States,* 2002. As the seriousness of the crime increases, the likelihood that it will be reported does too, suggesting that lack of confidence in the justice system is not a serious barrier to reporting when the stakes are high. But the reporting rate for all violent crimes was still less than 50 percent in 2002.

22. Newman, *Global Report,* 75 (reporting on an original paper by Satyansu Mukherjee, 1996).

23. Garland, *The Culture of Control,* 112. He elaborates, as follows: "In this way of thinking, criminals should be prosecuted to the fullest extent of the law, the guilty should always be punished, dangerous individuals should never be released, prisoners should serve their full terms, and an offender's sentence should precisely reflect his offense. And somehow, at the same time, the innocent should always be acquitted, the rule of law upheld, and expenditure held within reasonable levels."

24. Mattes et al., "Democratic Governance."

25. Newman, *Global Report,* 114, fig. 4.11.

26. Downes, "The Macho Penal Economy." See Newburn, "Atlantic Crossings," for an analysis of the "policy transfer" of U.S. criminal justice measures to the United Kingdom.

27. Wacquant, "Suitable Enemies," 217–18.

28. For a discussion of the complexities of interpreting crime statistics around the world and some tentative conclusions about crime patterns in the countries that have participated in the United Nations Surveys of Crime Trends and Operation of Criminal Justice Systems (UNCJS), see Newman, *Global Report,* chap. 2.

29. The UNCJS reports a general increase for crimes reported to the police in both the 1980s and 1990s but also cites lowered rates in some countries. For example, 43 percent of countries surveyed reported a drop in robbery between 1990 and 1994, 41 percent reported a drop in theft, and 30 percent reported a drop in rape. During that same period forty-eight countries showed an increase in crime overall, with seventeen showing a decrease. Newman, *Global Report,* notes to tables F2.3 and F2.4, 287.

30. See, for example, Pearce, "From Civil War"; and Orogun, "'Blood Diamonds.'"

31. Garland puts it this way: "In vivid contrast to the conventional wisdom of the previous period, the ruling assumption now is that 'prison works'—not as a mechanism of reform or rehabilitation, but as a means of incapacitation and punishment that

satisfies popular political demands for public safety and harsh retribution." *The Culture of Control,* 14.

32. Bayley and Shearing, "The Future of Policing," 591.

33. United Nations Office on Drugs and Crime, "Eighth United Nations Survey."

34. See responses to the fifth, sixth, and seventh surveys of the United Nations Survey on Crime Trends and the Operations of Criminal Justice Systems for up to eighty-two countries (Seventh United Nations Office on Drugs and Crime, "Seventh United Nations Survey"). The trend is also reflected in reports of UNCJS in Newman, *Global Report,* chap. 3.

35. Newman, *Global Report,* table 4.4, 95; see also the discussion in box 4.3, 101. These figures are for admission of both detainees and convicted offenders.

36. Ibid., fig. 4.5, 102.

37. A retreat from the harshest penalties may be developing in the United States, as states realize that criminal justice expenditures contribute to the fiscal pinch that many are feeling. See Butterfield, "With Longer Sentences."

38. See Shaw, "Crime, Police and Public," 2.

39. Sometimes the state police cooperate with or co-opt vigilantes rather than replacing them, as when they have information that is hard to obtain otherwise or when resources are scarce for what would otherwise be policing supplied by the state. Whether this amounts to corruption or a modified kind of reform—bringing discipline to outlaws—largely depends on the particular situation.

40. See Bayley, "Democratizing the Police Abroad," chap. 4, for sensible lessons for governments providing assistance in police reform to democratizing countries.

41. See Clarke, "Situational Crime Prevention."

42. For a description of the general shift in criminological perspective, see Garland, *The Culture of Control,* 6–20.

43. Cohen and Felson, "Social Change," 588.

44. Caldeira, *City of Walls,* 274–82.

45. See Clarke, "Situational Crime Prevention," 28–33, for a sophisticated treatment of the displacement argument.

46. Sherman et al., *Preventing Crime,* chap. 2.

47. See Clear and Karp, *The Community Justice Ideal,* 24–32.

48. A vast literature has sprung up around community policing. For a recent synthesis, see Goldstein, "Toward Community-Oriented Policing"; among the critiques of the approach, see Manning, "Community Policing."

49. Bayley, *Police for the Future,* 105.

50. Lyons, *Politics of Community Policing,* 4.

51. An important catalyst for the development of this way of thinking about the criminal process was Nils Christie's 1977 article, "Conflicts as Property," in which he argued that the modern state, through its crime control methods, had appropriated conflict from those most involved, rendering them powerless over events that shaped their lives.

52. For a review of restorative and community justice theory and practice, see Kurki, "Restorative and Community Justice." On the use of restorative justice for youth, see Bazemore, and Umbreit, "Rethinking the Sanctioning Function." For a crit-

ical but friendly view of the assumptions behind restorative justice practice, see Daly, "Restorative Justice."

53. *Guardian* (London), July 23, 2003. For information on the Youth Offender Panels, see http://www.youth-justice-board.gov.uk/YouthOffenderPanels/.

54. Clear and Karp, *The Community Justice Ideal,* chap. 5.

55. Ibid., 16.

56. Johnston and Shearing, *Governing Security.*

57. Ibid., 144.

58. Ibid., 15.

59. Braithwaite, "Restorative Justice," 2. But for another view see Daly, "Restorative Justice," 61–64.

60. Stenson, "Rethinking Crime Control," 71.

61. Crawford, *Public Matters,* 30.

62. Daly, "Restorative Justice," 60.

63. Karmen, *New York Murder Mystery.*

64. See Skogan, *Disorder and Decline,* 117.

65. Schiff, "Impact of Restorative Interventions," 333.

66. Clear and Karp, *The Community Justice Ideal,* 151.

67. Cordner, "Community Policing." For a discussion of citizen response to community policing, see Skogan and Hartnett, *Community Policing, Chicago Style.*

68. See Braithwaite, "Restorative Justice," 20–35.

69. Daly, "Restorative Justice," 61.

70. Held, *Models of Democracy,* 316–20.

71. See Braithwaite, "Restorative Justice," 79–104, for a discussion of critiques and defenses of restorative justice.

72. Kurki, "Restorative and Community Justice," 241, 288. See also Australia experience described on 276.

73. Skogan, *Disorder and Decline,* 107–10.

74. Forst, "Privatization and Civilianization," 33.

75. *Irish Times,* November 25, 2002.

76. Marenin, "Democracy, Democratization, Democratic Policing," 311.

77. Bayley, "Community Policing," 225.

78. Crawford, *Public Matters,* 21.

79. "Who Are the Bosses in Russia?" CDI *Russia Weekly,* August 28, 2003.

80. "Opinion '99, The Public Agenda."

81. "Afrobarometer Round 1," 31. It is not clear whether this finding reflects perceptions of corruption or incompetence or both.

82. It is important to distinguish between the term *vigilante* as used during the liberation struggle in South Africa and as used now. Formerly, the term referred to right-wing black groups who supported the government and beat or killed political dissidents; currently it has the more conventional meaning of individuals or groups who take the law into their own hands to mete out brutal punishments to those suspected of crimes.

83. Shearing, "New Beginning for Policing," 388–89. The Patten Commission report announces, at 29 (Sec. 6.10), "We see the role of the new body going beyond

supervision of the police service itself, extending to the wider issues of policing and the contributions that people and organizations other than the police can make towards public safety."

84. *New York Times,* June 20, 2002. For a description of *gacaca* jurisdiction and the justifications for its adoption, see the report prepared by Prison Reform International at http://www.penalreform.org/english/frset_pre_en.htm. Case studies of current practice are also available on the PRI website.

85. Crawford, *Public Matters,* 10–12.

86. Gutmann and Thompson, "Deliberative Democracy Beyond Process," 35. Theoretical work on deliberative democracy can be found in Sunstein, *The Partial Constitution,* particularly chaps. 5 and 6; Gutmann and Thompson, *Democracy and Disagreement;* Mansbridge, *Beyond Adversary Democracy;* and Nino, *Constitution of Deliberative Democracy.*

87. See Fishkin, *Democracy and Deliberation,* chaps. 2 and 4.

88. Ibid., 4.

89. Gutmann and Thompson, "Deliberative Democracy Beyond Process," 41.

90. Gutmann and Thompson, *Democracy and Disagreement,* 4. Nino, in *Constitution of Deliberative Democracy,* at 121, puts it another way; he sees democratic process as "a surrogate of the informal practice of moral discussion."

91. See Miller, "Deliberative Democracy," 182–83.

92. Nino, *Constitution of Deliberative Democracy,* 136.

93. Gutmann and Thompson, *Democracy and Disagreement,* 4.

94. Crawford, *Public Matters,* 10–11.

95. Applegate et al., "Assessing Public Support."

96. Immarigeon, "Restorative Justice," 309–11.

97. Hirst, *Associative Democracy,* 44.

98. Sunstein, *The Partial Constitution,* 135.

99. For a detailed discussion of this issue, see Nino, *Constitution of Deliberative Democracy,* 136–43. Gutmann and Thompson would constrain citizen deliberation with procedural requirements that exclude arguments from a contested worldview (religious fundamentalism, for instance), reasons that cannot be made public, and policy recommendations that will be offensive to their representative's constituency; these constraints may be too limiting for many deliberative proponents.

100. Young, "Activist Challenges."

101. Sunstein, "Law of Group Polarization."

102. Crawford, *Public Matters,* 22.

103. Ibid., 28.

104. Nino, *Constitution of Deliberative Democracy,* 121–28; Ackerman and Fishkin, "Deliberation Day," 22.

105. Schärf, "Non-state Justice Systems," 14.

Chapter 8

1. Schärf, "Community Justice," 25.
2. Sachs, *Justice in South Africa,* 95.
3. van Niekerk, "Plurality of Legal Domains," 24–27.

4. There is a substantial literature on these developments. See Burman and Schärf, "Creating People's Justice"; Pavlich, "People's Courts"; Nina, *Re-thinking Popular Justice;* and Schärf and Nina, *The Other Law.*

5. It is impossible to deal here with the range of practices used, the varieties of sponsorship, or the political complications that arose. See Nina, *Re-thinking Popular Justice;* and Burman and Schärf, "Creating People's Justice" for case studies.

6. Nina, *Re-thinking Popular Justice,* 13.

7. Nina reports on the anticrime committees of the Eastern Cape during the early 1990s in *Re-thinking Popular Justice,* chap. 6.

8. Leggett, "What Do the Police Do?" See also the crime prevention section of the South African Police Service Annual Report, 2002–3.

9. For a sense of the priorities of the South African Police Service and the Department of Justice and Constitutional Development, which is responsible for the prosecutorial service and the courts, see the South African Police Service Annual Report, 2002–3, part 5; and Leggett et al., *Criminal Justice in Review,* chap. 4.

10. Schärf, "Non-state Justice Systems," 29.

11. Louis Eloff, interview by the author, February 19, 2000.

12. Bayley, "Community Policing," 224.

13. Jenny Schreiner, interview by the author, August 23, 1996.

14. Marais and Rauch, "Policing South Africa."

15. Sunstein, *Designing Democracy,* 50.

16. ANC, "Ready to Govern."

17. Among the oversight bodies are the National Secretariat for Safety and Security, the Independent Complaints Directorate (both directed at police), the Human Rights Commission, and the Commission on Gender Equality.

18. Van Zyl Smit, "Criminological Ideas," 203. After the elections a similar group, the Independent Advisory Team, advised the new minister for safety and security until the civilian Secretariat for Safety and Security was established.

19. Louis Eloff, interview by the author, February 10, 2000.

20. Goldman et al., "Evaluation."

21. Mduduzi Mashiyane, interview by the author, January 28, 1999.

22. The CPFs visited included Vereeniging and Sandton in Gauteng; Bonteheuvel, Gugulethu, Khayelitsha, and Mitchells Plain in the Western Cape; and Galashewe, Roodepan, and Victoria West in the Northern Cape. I also attempted to visit a CPF in Colesberg in the Northern Cape, but factional fighting was threatening its existence and no one showed up for the meeting.

23. Interim Constitution, Chap. 14, Sec. 221.

24. Pelser, Schneffler, and Louw, *Not Everybody's Business.*

25. South African Police Service Act, Sec. 18 (1).

26. Pelser, Schneffler, and Louw, *Not Everybody's Business.*

27. South Africa Department of Safety and Security, "In Service of Safety."

28. See Goldstein, *Problem-Oriented Policing.*

29. Pelser, "Challenges of Community Policing," 45.

30. Janine Rauch, interview by the author, April 16, 1998.

31. Elrena van der Spuy, interview by the author, February 14, 2000.

32. Janine Rauch, interview by the author, January 25, 1999.
33. "Annual Report of the ICD," table 2, http://www.icd.gov.za/reports/2000/conclusion.pdf.
34. Schärf, "Non-state Justice Systems," 30.
35. Other attempts to install community policing were attempted, generally funded by international donors. Foreign funds supported the Basic Training Pilot Program, the Western Cape Community Policing Project, and the Community Policing Pilot Project. See van der Spuy, "Foreign Donor Assistance," 352.
36. Pate and Shtull, "Community Policing Grows in Brooklyn," 410.
37. See Pelser, "Challenges of Community Policing."
38. It is not, however, unheard of. Soweto, for example, has a number of active CPFs, but their function is primarily limited to patrol and intelligence-gathering in which they act as a sort of auxiliary to the state police.
39. "Proceedings of the Civilian Oversight of the Police Mini-conference."
40. Quoted in Nina, *Rethinking Popular Justice,* 15.
41. Magistrates' Courts Amendment Act 118 of 1991.
42. Seekings and Murray, *Lay Assessors,* 37.
43. The act gave magistrates discretion as to whether to use assessors or not, except in murder cases in the regional courts, where the use of either lay or expert assessors was mandatory unless the defendant objected.
44. Constitution of the Republic of South Africa, Sec. 180.
45. Quoted in Seekings and Murray, *Lay Assessors,* 43.
46. Thompson, *Writing by Candlelight,* 169.
47. Tocqueville, *Democracy in America,* 282.
48. Lempert, "A Jury for Japan?" 38.
49. Frank, *Law and the Modern Mind,* 172–73.
50. Kahn, "Restore the Jury?"
51. Ibid., part 5, 337 n. 338.
52. Ibid., part 1, 686.
53. Abolition of Juries Act 34 of 1969.
54. Seekings and Murray, *Lay Assessors,* 18–19.
55. See Lempert, "A Jury for Japan?" 41–42.
56. Seekings and Murray, *Lay Assessors,* 2.
57. The following paragraphs rely heavily on Seekings and Murray, *Lay Assessors,* and on interviews conducted with magistrates and assessors in the Western Cape (Cape Town, Wynberg, and Mitchells Plain) in the fall of 1997 and February 2000. I also observed the use of assessors in trials over a two-day period in Wynberg in February 2000.
58. Magistrates' Courts Amendment Act, Sec. 93*ter*(1).
59. Ibid., Sec. 93*ter*(2)(a).
60. Assessors are not identified individually, unless noted, either because they were either interviewed in a group or made their comments in passing as I was observing trials.
61. Seekings and Murray, *Lay Assessors,* 148–49.
62. This quote comes from Lavona George, a Cape Town assessor interviewed in 1997.

63. See, for example, the arguments in Schönteich, "Compulsory Lay Assessors."
64. See an argument of this kind in *State v. Gambushe,* 1997 (1) SACR 638 (N), where the judge was skeptical about the ability of lay assessors to understand and apply the standard of proof of guilt beyond a reasonable doubt.
65. Jakob van Heenen, interview by the author, February 21, 2000.
66. Seekings and Murray, *Lay Assessors,* 94.
67. One issue that both magistrates and assessors were concerned with was the amount of preparation assessors should have to perform their tasks. One view was that they should be trained in basic aspects of criminal law and procedure, but countering that was the view that to professionalize them would negate the community focus that was intended to be their strength. This issue was resolved, as were many others, by the reality of lack of funds to provide training throughout the country.
68. Magistrates Amendment Act, Sec. 6.
69. Judge Dennis Davis, interview by the author, April 30, 2004.
70. Seekings and Murray, *Lay Assessors,* 164.
71. *Johannesburg Star,* April 16, 1998.
72. Gadijah Kahn, interview by the author, February 11, 2000.
73. Much has been written about this case. For a journalistic summary of the state's problems and the behavior of Judge Willie Hartzenberg, see "In the Dock with Doctor Death," *Mail and Guardian,* April 5, 2002.
74. *State v. Basson* (2003).
75. *Business Day,* November 5, 2003.
76. It is difficult to find a descriptive adjective that encompasses all the mechanisms that exist. *Informal* justice excludes the private security industry, and *nonstate* suggests that state justice is superior and everything else is exceptional; *popular justice* suggests that state functionaries are never involved. So I have ducked the issue of nomenclature by trying to use whatever seems functionally precise in the context of the discussion. See Schärf, "Non-state Justice Systems," 2–3.
77. Schärf, "Specialist Courts," 4.
78. Schärf sums up the state of vigilantism in South Africa as follows: "South Africa currently [January 2003] has a spate of vigilantism whereby suspects are summarily judged in a street hearing and then punished, even executed by various means [stoning, burning, beating, shooting, all of which sometimes preceded by torture to extract the confession]." "Non-state Justice Systems," 9.
79. According to Schärf, "In some high-crime residential areas the neighbourhood watches outnumber the police by 10 to one." "Non-state Justice Systems," 29.
80. Finding suitable nomenclature for these groups is difficult. Nonstate bodies that meet on an ongoing basis to resolve local problems, ranging from disputes over the use of a communal water tap to murder attributed to witchcraft, are variously called community courts, traditional courts, mediation centers, street committees, and yard committees.
81. Constitution of the Republic of South Africa, Secs. 30, 31, and 34.
82. "Popular Participation in the Administration of Justice," 19.
83. Steinberg, "Community Courts."
84. See South African Law Commission, "Community Dispute Resolution Structures," 22–25.

85. "Popular Participation in the Administration of Justice," 22.
86. Constitution of the Republic of South Africa, Sec. 34.
87. Schärf, "Specialist Courts," 25.
88. Graeme Simpson, interview by the author, June 16, 2003.
89. Sehla Mgubane, quoted in Nina, *Re-thinking Popular Justice,* 45.
90. African National Congress, "Ready to Govern." The document says, "Policing shall be based on community support and participation," and "Policing priorities shall be determined in consultation with the communities they serve," and "Policing shall be subject to public scrutiny and open debate."
91. See Pelser, "Challenges of Community Policing."
92. Seekings and Murray, *Lay Assessors,* 43.
93. Janine Rauch, interview by the author, April 6, 2000.
94. Gadijah Kahn, interview by the author, February 11, 2000.
95. Christina Murray, e-mail to the author, July 3, 2003.
96. Brogden, "Indigenisation of Policing," 223.
97. Mduduzi Mashiyane, interview by the author, July 19, 2001.

Chapter 9

1. *Evening Standard* (London), October 9, 1995.
2. Garland, *The Culture of Control,* 204.
3. Cawthra, *Policing South Africa,* 39.
4. Brogden and Shearing, *Policing,* 3.
5. Shaw, *Crime and Policing,* 24–25.
6. *Sunday Times,* August 22, 1999.
7. *Business Day,* January 14, 2000.
8. *State v. Makwanyane.*
9. *Sunday Times,* July 4, 1999.
10. See van Zyl Smit and van der Spuy, "Importing Criminological Ideas," 189–91.
11. In the context of declaring capital punishment to be unconstitutional, the chief justice, writing for a unanimous court, commented, "If public opinion were to be decisive there would be no need for constitutional adjudication. The protection of rights could then be left to Parliament, which has a mandate from the public . . . but this would be a return to parliamentary sovereignty, and a retreat from the new legal order." *State v. Makwanyane,* par. 88.
12. Interim Constitution, Sec. 25(2)(d).
13. Criminal Procedure Second Amendment Act 75 of 1995.
14. Constitution of the Republic of South Africa, Sec. 35 (1)(f); emphasis added.
15. Criminal Procedure Second Amendment Act 85 of 1997.
16. *State v Dlamini,* 1999 (4) 623 (CC).
17. Criminal Procedure Second Amendment Act 85, Sec. 4(d).
18. Steinberg, "Clumsy Foray."
19. Bouckaert, "Shutting Down the Death Factory." It should be noted that large numbers of death sentences imposed during the period when they were mandatory were commuted.

20. Criminal Law Amendment Act, Sec. 51 and Part I, Schedule 2.
21. Criminal Law Amendment Act, Sec. 51 (3)(a). See *Malgas v. State*, 2001 SCA 117/00 for an elaboration of the standard.
22. *Mail and Guardian,* November 11, 2001.
23. *Malgas v. State,* par. 22.
24. In a study of attitudes toward sentencing conducted in 2000 researchers found that 63 percent of magistrates and 100 percent of judges interviewed preferred the pre-act sentencing scheme to the minimum sentencing law, largely because of its restrictions on judicial discretion. Schönteich, Mistry, and Struwig, "Qualitative Research Report."
25. *Business Day,* March 28, 2001.
26. *Dodo v. State,* 2001 (3) SA 382 (CC).
27. Prevention of Organized Crime Act No. 121 of 1998.
28. Proceeds of Crime Act No. 76 of 1996.
29. Henderson, "The Heart Rejoices."
30. Leggett et al., *Criminal Justice in Review,* chap. 4.
31. Leggett, "New Crime Bill."
32. Boister, "Transnational Penal Norm Transfer," 279.
33. *National Director of Public Prosecutions v. Mohamed NO and Others,* 2002 (4) SA 843 (CC), par. 15.
34. *National Director of Public Prosecutions v R O Cook Properties,* 2004 (SCA) 260/03 par. 31.
35. Boister, "Transnational Penal Norm Transfer," 282.
36. *Business Day,* May 22, 2002.
37. *Mail and Guardian,* June 28, 1999.
38. Silverman, *NYPD Battles Crime,* 47–60. For a skeptical view of the crackdown approach to policing, see Steinberg, "Selebi Talks."
39. For a description of the National Crime Combating Strategy, see Leggett et al., *Criminal Justice in Review,* chap. 3; and Rauch, "Changing Step."
40. *News 24,* May 2, 2002.
41. *Republic of South Africa v. Grootboom,* 2001(1) SA 46 (CC).
42. Sipho Ngwema, interview by the author, July 23, 2001.
43. According to its mission statement, the Directorate of Special Operations has "committed itself to the investigation of matters, which are national in scope and concentrates on those crimes that threaten national security and economic stability." http://www.info.gov.za/structure/justice.htm.
44. A 2003 national victimization study supports the official data. See Burton et al., *National Victims of Crime Survey,* 17.
45. Leggett, "The Sieve Effect," fig. 1.
46. Ibid., table 1.
47. A summary of this research can be found in Bayley, *Police for the Future,* chap. 1.
48. These figures were extrapolated by Martin Schönteich and the author in June 2004 from police personnel data obtained from SAPS Communications Services, SAPS Management Services, and SAPS Efficiency Services; the data for recorded crime are

from the SAPS Crime Information Management Centre. Police numbers are calculated from the beginning of each calendar year, while crime data are calculated for the fiscal year, which begins April 1.

49. "Prison Brief for South Africa." The prisoner figure comes from the South African Department of Correctional Services; the general population figure is based on the UN estimate of 45 million people. By comparison, the incarceration rate for the Netherlands (country of ancestral origin for the majority of white South Africans) was 100 and for neighboring Botswana 327. As of 2002, the rates for the two countries with which South Africa used to share the top position during apartheid are 584 (Russian Federation) and 701 (United States).

50. South African Department of Correctional Services, Annual Report 2002, table 14.

51. See tables and text at http://www.dcs.gov.za/annual_report/Annual_Report2002/Programme2.htm and http://www.dcs.gov.za/annual_report/Annual_Report97/1_Safe_custody.htm. The 1994 overpopulation number comes from South African Institute of Race Relations, *Race Relations Survey,* 1994–95, 150.

52. Ibid., Annual Reports, 2002 and 1997.

53. Julia Mashele was charged in 1993 with hijacking, robbery, and possession of drugs along with sixteen other defendants. Four of the coaccused escaped, six were acquitted, and five were released without being charged. *Business Day,* December 23, 1999.

54. For discussion of the nature and uses of condensation symbols, see Edelman, *Symbolic Uses of Politics.*

55. Ibid., 2.

56. See Dixon, "Exclusive Societies," 219–20.

57. Ted Leggett, interview by the author, June 17, 2003.

58. Media release, Human Sciences Research Council, March 8, 2000.

59. Interviews were August 22, 1996; January 21, 1999; and February 9, 2000.

60. See, for example, Tonry, *Malign Neglect,* 19.

61. Leggett, "Performance Measures," 63.

62. Albie Sachs, interview by the author, January 24, 2001.

63. Sipho Ngwema, interview by the author, June 23, 2001.

64. Willie Hofmeyr, interview by the author, January 21, 1999.

65. *Business Day,* January 19, 1997.

66. A cogent analysis of the phenomenon of constructing political leadership of this kind can be found in Edelman, *Constructing the Political Spectacle,* chap. 2.

67. "Documented Migration, 2003."

68. Van der Spuy, "Foreign Donor Assistance."

69. See van Zyl Smit and van der Spuy, "Importing Criminological Ideas," 191.

70. "It Can Be Done: Growth in Africa," *Economist,* June 29, 1996.

71. See Thomas et al., *The Quality of Growth,* chap. 6.

72. United States Agency for International Development, "2005 Congressional Budget Justification," http://www.usaid.gov/policy/budget/cbj2005/afr/za.html.

73. World Economic Forum, *Global Competitiveness Report,* 2000, "Complex Terrain," 25.

74. Keith Gottschalk, interview by the author, August 23, 1996.

75. Hanson and Hentz, "Neocolonialism and Neoliberalism," 480.

76. "State of the Nation Address by the President of South Africa, Nelson Mandela," Cape Town, May 24, 1994.

77. *Business Day,* January 14, 2000.

78. Gordon, "Side by Side."

79. Child Justice Bill, B49-2002. A certain ambivalence about this approach, however, is suggested by the fact that this bill was introduced into parliament in 2002 and had still not been fully enacted in mid-2005.

80. Child Justice Bill, Sec. 2(a), (b), and (c).

81. *Ferreira v. State,* 2004 (SCA) 245/03, par. 10.

82. *Ferreira v. State,* par. 74.

83. Mbeki, "Address to the First Joint Sitting of the Third Democratic Parliament."

84. Palmary, "Shifting Safety Agendas," 38–39.

85. Remarks of Stanley Mufamadi at the first meeting of an interdepartmental committee assigned to design the National Crime Prevention Strategy, February 17, 1995, quoted in Rauch, "Changing Step," 10.

86. Dixon and Rauch, *Sector Policing,* 26.

87. Mbeki, "Address to the First Joint Sitting of the Third Democratic Parliament." Mbeki's emphasis on economic and social development also colored his 2004 inauguration speech. He said, "None of great social problems we have to solve is capable of resolution outside the context of the creation of jobs and the alleviation and eradication of poverty. This relates to everything, from the improvement of the health of our people, to reducing the levels of crime, raising the levels of literacy and numeracy, and opening the doors of learning and culture to all." Mbeki, "Address by the President of South Africa Thabo Mbeki on the Occasion of His Inauguration."

88. *Business Day,* August 28, 2002. NGOs opposing the law include the Freedom of Expression Institute, the Media Institute of Southern Africa, and the South African National NGO Coalition.

89. The final legislation is the Protection of Constitutional Democracy Against Terrorist and Related Activities Act.

90. South African Law Commission, "Anti-terrorism Draft Bill," summary, par. 5.

91. See Kimani, "Bill Finds a Terrorist."

92. Beckett, *Making Crime Pay,* 10.

Chapter 10

1. Baluma is a Cape Town journalist, quoted in Hootnick, "Improvised Justice," 56.

2. Christie, "Conflicts as Property," 7.

3. Dahl, "Problem of Civic Competence," 45.

4. Neild, "New Face of Impunity."

5. Friedman, "Not Just Order."

6. Afrobarometer survey figures are from Mattes et al., "Democratic Governance," 7; the approval rating comes from Mattes, "South Africa," 32.

7. Mistry, "Falling Crime, Rising Fear," 19. It should be noted that 52 percent

of respondents in the victimization survey said that the police were doing a good job in their localities.

8. Ibid.
9. Shaw, *Crime and Policing,* 156.
10. Minaar and Mistry, "Outsourcing."
11. By the end of 2002 national conviction rates for the magistrates' courts were 83 percent (district courts) and 74 percent (regional courts); for the high courts they were 82 percent. National Prosecuting Authority, Annual Report, 11.
12. Ibid., 13.
13. Ibid., 31.
14. Redpath, *The Scorpions,* 56. This researcher notes, at 62, that while the Directorate of Special Operations (Scorpions) "appears to have an excellent record of success in obtaining convictions in matters it chooses to prosecute, and does not waste resources with frivolous arrests or searches," it may be selecting only "big" cases and neglecting lesser ones that cumulatively have as great or greater impact on public safety.
15. See Johnston and Shearing, *Governing Security,* chap. 8.
16. Friedman, "The State, Civil Society and Social Policy."
17. Dixon, "Exclusive Societies," 217.
18. *Carmichele v. Minister of Safety and Security.*
19. Buur, "Crime and Punishment."
20. See Hootnick, "Improvised Justice."
21. Buur, "Crime and Punishment," 29.
22. Ibid., 38.
23. Dixon and Johns, "Gangs, Pagad and the State."
24. *Patterns of Global Terrorism, 2000.* United States Department of State, April 2001, http://library.nps.navy.mil/home/tgp/pagad.htm.
25. *Sunday Times,* February 22, 2004, http://www.sundaytimes.co.za/specialreports/budget2004/.
26. Mbeki, "State of the Nation Address," February 6, 2004; "ANC Today," October 22–28, 2004, http://www.anc.org.za/ancdocs/anctoday/2004/at42.htm.
27. Mbeki, "Address to the First Joint Sitting of the Third Democratic Parliament."
28. Mbeki, "Address at the Launch of the Expanded Public Works Program."
29. "National Crime Prevention Strategy," 12.
30. Cartwright, Jenneker, and Shearing, "Local Capacity Governance."
31. For a description of the Zwelethemba model and its theoretical underpinnings, see Johnston and Shearing, *Governing Security,* 138–60.
32. The Code of Good Practice includes these "guidelines":

We help to secure a safe and secure environment in our community.
We respect the South African Constitution.
We work within the law.
We do not use force or violence.
We do not take sides in disputes.
We work in the community as a co-operative team, not as individuals.

We follow procedures which are open for the community to see.
We do not gossip about our work or about other people.
We are committed to what we do.
Our aim is to heal, not hurt.
> (Cartwright, Jenneker, and Shearing, "Local Capacity Governance," 9–10.)

33. Cartwright, Jenneker, and Shearing, "Local Capacity Governance," 12.

34. See Held, *Models of Democracy,* chap. 9, and Hirst, *Associative Democracy,* 167–75.

35. John Cartwright, e-mail message to author, February 25, 2004.

36. Cartwright, Jenneker, and Shearing, "Local Capacity Governance," 15.

Bibliography

Note: A listing of South African and international legal references follows the bibliography.

Ackerman, Bruce, and James S. Fishkin. "Deliberation Day." In *Debating Deliberative Democracy,* ed. James S. Fishkin and Peter Laslett. Oxford: Blackwell, 2003.
Ackermann, Laurie. "Human Rights in an Emergency Oriented Society." In *Democracy and the Judiciary,* ed. Hugh Corder. Cape Town: Institute for a Democratic Alternative in South Africa, 1989.
African Law Today. American Bar Association, Section of International Law and Practice. http://www.abanet.org/intlaw/divisions/comparative/africanewsletter.html.
African National Congress. "Ready to Govern: ANC Policy Guidelines for a Democratic South Africa Adopted at the National Conference, 28–31 May, 1992." http://www.anc.org.za/ancdocs/history/readyto.html.
"Afrobarometer, Round 1: Compendium of Comparative Date from a Twelve-Nation Survey." March 2002. Afrobarometer Network. www.afrobarometer.org.
Agostinho, Zacarias. *Security and the State in Southern Africa.* New York: Tauris, 1999.
Altbeker, Anthony. *Solving Crime: The State of the SAPS Detective Service.* Monograph 31. Pretoria: Institute for Security Studies, 1998. http://www.iss.org.za/Pubs/Monographs/No31/Contents.html#Anchor-44249.
Amann, Diane Marie. "Harmonic Convergence? Constitutional Criminal Procedure in an International Context." *Indiana Law Journal* 75 (2000): 809–73.
Amnesty International. *South Africa: State of Fear.* New York: Amnesty International, 1992.
Annual Report of the National Commissioner for 2002–3, South African Police Service. http://www.saps.gov.za/saps_profile/strategic_framework/annual_report/2002-2003/pdf/SAPS_Annual_Report_Apr02–31Mar03.pdf
Applegate, Brandon K., Francis T. Cullen, Michael G. Turner, and Jody L. Sundt. "Assessing Public Support for Three-Strikes-and-You're-Out Laws: Global versus Specific Attitudes." *Crime and Delinquency* 42, no. 4 (1996): 517–34.
Barber, Benjamin. *Strong Democracy.* Berkeley and Los Angeles: University of California Press, 1984.

Bator, Paul M. "The Constitution as Architecture: Legislative and Administrative Courts under Article III." *Indiana Law Journal* 68 (1990): 233–75.

Bayley, David H. "Community Policing: A Report from the Devil's Advocate." In *Community Policing: Rhetoric or Reality,* ed. Jack R. Greene and Stephen D. Mastrofski. New York: Praeger, 1991.

———. "The Contemporary Practices of Policing: A Comparative View." In *Civilian Police and Multinational Peacekeeping—a Workshop Series: A Role for Democratic Policing,* ed. James Burack, William Lewis, Edward Marks, and Workshop Directors. Washington, D.C.: Office of Justice Programs, U.S. Department of Justice, 1999.

———. "Democratizing the Police Abroad: What to Do and How to Do It." U.S. Department of Justice, Office of Justice Programs, 2001.

———. *Patterns of Policing: A Comparative International Analysis.* New Brunswick, N.J.: Rutgers University Press, 1985.

———. *Police for the Future.* New York: Oxford University Press, 1994.

———. *Social Control and Political Change.* Research Monograph M. 49. Princeton: Center for International Studies, Woodrow Wilson School of Public Affairs, Princeton University, 1985.

Bayley, David, and Clifford Shearing. "The Future of Policing." *Law and Society Review* 30 (1996): 585–606.

Bazemore, Gordon, and Mark S. Umbreit. "Rethinking the Sanctioning Function in Juvenile Court: Retributive or Restorative Responses to Youth Crime." *Crime and Delinquency* 41 (1995): 296–316.

Beckett, Katherine. *Making Crime Pay: Law and Order in Contemporary American Politics.* New York: Oxford University Press, 1997.

Beinart, William. "Political and Collective Violence in Southern African Historiography." *Journal of Southern African Studies* 18 (1992): 455–86.

Beinart, William, and Saul Dubow, eds. *Segregation and Apartheid in Twentieth-Century South Africa.* New York: Routledge, 1999.

Bittner, Egon. *Aspects of Police Work.* Boston: Northeastern University Press, 1990.

Boister, Neil. "Transnational Penal Norm Transfer: The Transfer of Civil Forfeiture from the United States to South Africa as a Case in Point." *South African Journal of Criminal Justice* 16 (2003): 271–94.

Bond, Patrick. "From Racial to Class Apartheid: South Africa's Frustrating Decade of Freedom." *Monthly Review* 55, no. 10 (2004): 45–59.

Bouckaert, Peter Norbert. "Shutting Down the Death Factory: The Abolition of Capital Punishment in South Africa." *Stanford Journal of International Law* 32 (1996): 287–325.

Braithwaite, John. "Restorative Justice: Assessing Positive and Negative Accounts." In *Crime and Justice: A Review of Research,* vol. 25, ed. Michael Tonry. Chicago: University of Chicago Press, 1999.

Brewer, John D. *Black and Blue: Policing in South Africa.* New York: Oxford University Press, 1994.

———. "The Police in South African Politics." In *South Africa: No Turning Back,* ed. Shaun Johnson. London: Macmillan, 1998.

Brodeur, Jean Paul. "High Policing and Low Policing: Remarks about the Policing of Political Activities." *Social Problems* 30 (1983): 507–20.

Brogden, Mike. "The Indigenisation of Policing in South Africa." In *Policing Change, Changing Police: International Perspectives,* ed. Otwin Marenin. New York: Garland, 1996.

Brogden, Mike, and Clifford Shearing. *Policing for a New South Africa.* London: Routledge, 1993.

Bruce, David. "Gripes or Grievances: What the Independent Complaints Directorate Statistics Tell Us (or Not)." *SA Crime Quarterly,* no. 4 (2003). http://www.iss.co.za/Pubs/CrimeQ/No.4/Contents.html.

———. "Police Brutality in South Africa." Centre for the Study of Violence and Reconciliation, 2002. http://www.csvr.org.za/papers/papbruc5.htm.

Bruce, David, and Gabriel O'Malley. "In the Line of Duty? Shooting Incident Reports and Other Indicators of the Use and Abuse of Force by Members of the SAPS." Centre for the Study of Violence and Reconciliation, 2001. http://www.csvr.org.za/papers/papdb&go.htm.

Bruce, David, Kate Savage, and Johan de Waal. "A Duty to Answer Questions? The Police, the Independent Complaints Directorate and the Right to Remain Silent." *South African Journal on Human Rights* 16 (2000): 71–96.

Bunting, Brian. "The Origins of Apartheid." In *Apartheid: A Collection of Writings on South African Racism by South Africans,* ed. Alex La Guma. New York: International Publishers, 1971.

Burbank, Stephen B. "The Architecture of Judicial Independence." *Southern California Law Review* 72 (1999): 315–51.

Burbank, Stephen B., and Barry Friedman. "Reconsidering Judicial Independence." In *Judicial Independence at the Crossroads: An Interdisciplinary Approach,* ed. Stephen B. Burbank and Barry Friedman. Thousand Oaks, Calif.: Sage, 2002.

Burman, Sandra, and Wilfried Schärf. "Creating People's Justice: Street Committees and People's Courts in a South African City." *Law and Society Review* 24 (1990): 693–744.

Burton, Patrick, Anton du Plessis, Ted Leggett, Antoinette Louw, Duxita Mistry, and Hennie van Vuuren. *National Victims of Crime Survey, 2003.* Monograph No. 101. Pretoria: Institute for Security Studies, 2004.

Butterfield, Fox. "With Longer Sentences, Cost of Fighting Crime Is Higher." *New York Times,* May 3, 2004.

Buur, Lars. "Crime and Punishment on the Margins of the Post-apartheid State." *Anthropology and Humanism* 28, no. 1 (2003): 23–42.

Caldeira, Teresa P. R. "Building Up Walls: The New Pattern of Spatial Segregation in São Paolo." *International Social Science Journal* 48 (1996): 55–66.

———. *City of Walls: Crime, Segregation, and Citizenship in São Paolo.* Berkeley and Los Angeles: University of California Press, 2000.

Callinicos, Alex, and John Rogers. *Southern Africa after Soweto.* London: Pluto Press, 1977.

Cameron, Edwin. "Judicial Accountability in South Africa." *South African Journal of Human Rights* 6 (1990): 257–65.

Campbell, Catherine. "Learning to Kill? Masculinity, the Family and Violence in Natal." *Journal of Southern African Studies* 18 (1992): 614–28.

———. "Social Identity and Violence in the Domestic and Political Spheres: A Gendered Common Denominator?" In *Violence and Family Life in Contemporary South Africa: Research and Policy Issues,* ed. Lorraine E. Glanz and Andrew D. Spiegel. Pretoria: Human Sciences Research Council, 1996.

Cardozo, Benjamin N. *The Nature of the Judicial Process.* New Haven: Yale University Press, 1921.

Cartwright, John, Madeleine Jenneker, and Clifford Shearing. "Local Capacity Governance in South Africa: A Model for Peaceful Coexistence." Unpublished paper, University of the Western Cape, 2003, updated March 2004.

Cavallaro, James. *Police Brutality in Urban Brazil.* New York: Human Rights Watch, 1997.

Cawthra, Gavin. *Policing South Africa: The SAP and the Transition from Apartheid.* London: Zed Books, 1993.

Charney, Craig. "From Resistance to Reconstruction: Towards a New Research Agenda on South African Politics." *Journal of Southern African Studies* 16 (1990): 761–70.

Chaskalson, Arthur. "Bram Fischer Memorial Lecture." *South African Journal on Human Rights* 16, no. 2 (2000): 193–205.

Chaskalson, A., I. Mahomed, P. Langa, H. J. O. van Heerden, and M. M. Corbett. "The Legal System in South Africa, 1960–1994: Representations to the Truth and Reconciliation Commission." *South African Law Journal* 115 (part 1) (1998): 21–36.

Chazan, Naomi. "The New Politics of Participation in Tropical Africa." *Comparative Politics* 14 (1982): 169–90.

Chevigny, Paul. *Edge of the Knife: Police Violence in the Americas.* New York: New Press, 1995.

———. "The Populism of Fear: Politics of Crime in the Americas." *Punishment and Society* 5 (2003): 77–96.

Chikane, F. "Children in Turmoil: The Effects of the Unrest on Township Children." In *Growing Up in a Divided Society: The Contexts of Childhood in South Africa,* ed. Sandra Burman and Pamela Reynolds. Johannesburg: Ravan Press, 1986.

Chodosh, Hiram. "Emergence from the Dilemmas of Justice Reform." *Texas International Law Journal* 38 (2003): 586–620.

Christie, Nils. "Conflicts as Property." *British Journal of Criminology* 17 (1977): 1–15.

Cilliers, Jakkie. "Peace, Security and Democracy in Africa? A Summary of Outcomes from 2002 OAU/AU Summits in Durban." Paper 60, Institute for Security Studies, Pretoria, 2002. http://www.iss.co.za/PUBS/PAPERS/60/Paper60.html.

Clarke, Ronald V. "Situational Crime Prevention: Its Theoretical Basis and Practical Scope." In *Crime and Justice: An Annual Review of Research,* vol. 4, ed. Michael Tonry and Norval Morris. Chicago: University of Chicago Press, 1983.

———, ed. *Situational Crime Prevention: Successful Case Studies.* Guilderland, N.Y.: Harrow and Heston, 1997.

Clear, Todd R., and David R. Karp. *The Community Justice Ideal: Preventing Crime and Achieving Justice.* Boulder, Colo.: Westview Press, 1999.

Cock, J. "Political Violence." In *People and Violence in South Africa,* ed. Brian McKendrick and William Hoffmann. Cape Town: Oxford University Press, 1990.

Cohen, Lawrence E., and Marcus Felson. "Social Change and Crime Rate Trends: A Routine Activity Approach." *American Sociological Review* 44 (1979): 588–608.

Bibliography

Cole, Josette. *Crossroads: The Politics of Reform and Repression, 1976–1986*. Johannesburg: Ravan Press, 1987.

Corder, Hugh, ed. *Democracy and the Judiciary*. Cape Town: Institute for a Democratic Alternative for South Africa, 1989.

———. *Judges at Work: The Role and Attitudes of the South African Appellate Judiciary, 1910–1950*. Cape Town: Juta, 1984.

Cordner, Gary W. "Community Policing: Elements and Effects." In *Community Policing: Contemporary Readings*, ed. Geoffrey P. Alpert and Alex R. Piquero. 2nd ed. Prospect Heights, Ill.: Waveland Press, 2000.

Corradi, Juan E., Patricia Weiss Fagen, and Manuel Antonio Garreton, eds. *Fear at the Edge: State Terror and Resistance in Latin America*. Berkeley and Los Angeles: University of California Press, 1992.

Crawford, Adam. *Public Matters: Reviving Public Participation in Criminal Justice*. London: Institute for Public Policy Research, 2001.

"Crime Statistics as Released on 2003–09–22." South African Police Service, Crime Information Analysis Centre, 2003. http://www.saps.gov.za/8%5Fcrimeinfo/bulletin/index.htm. Retrieved November 2003.

Currie, Elliott. *Crime and Punishment in America*. New York: Henry Holt, 1998.

Dahl, Robert A. *Democracy and Its Critics*. New Haven: Yale University Press, 1989.

———. *Polyarchy: Participation and Opposition*. New Haven: Yale University Press, 1971.

———. *A Preface to Economic Democracy*. Berkeley and Los Angeles: University of California Press, 1985.

———. "The Problem of Civic Competence." *Journal of Democracy* 3, no. 4 (1992): 45–59.

———. "Why Free Markets Are Not Enough." *Journal of Democracy* 3, no. 3 (1992): 82–89.

Daly, Kathleen. "Conferencing in Australia and New Zealand: Variations, Research Findings and Prospects." In *Restorative Justice for Juveniles*, ed. Allison Morris and Gabrielle Maxwell. Portland, Ore.: Hart, 2001.

———. "Restorative Justice: The Real Story." *Punishment and Society* 4 (2002): 55–79.

Dapper, O. "Kaffraria or Land of the Kaffirs, Otherwise Named Hottentots." In *The Early Cape Hottentots*, ed. Isaac Schapera. Westport, Conn.: Negro Universities Press, 1970.

Davenport, Rodney, and Christopher Saunders, eds. *South Africa: A Modern History*. 5th ed. New York: St. Martin's Press, 2000.

Davis, Dennis. "Criminal Justice—State and Direction of Research in South Africa." In *Criminal Justice in South Africa: Selected Aspects of Discretion*, ed. M. C. J. Olmesdahl and N. C. Steytler. Cape Town: Juta, 1983.

Davis, Stephen M. *Apartheid's Rebels: Inside South Africa's Hidden War*. New Haven: Yale University Press, 1987.

de Kiewiet, C. W. *A History of South Africa*. London: Oxford University Press, 1941.

de Villiers, René. "Afrikaner Nationalism." In *The Oxford History of South Africa*, vol. 2, ed. Monica Wilson and Leonard Thompson. New York: Oxford University Press, 1969.

Diamond, Larry. *Developing Democracy: Toward Consolidation*. Baltimore: Johns Hopkins University Press, 1992.

Dinan, B. Ann, George J. McCall, and Diana Gibson. "Community Violence and PTSD in Selected South African Townships." *Journal of Interpersonal Violence* 19 (2004): 727–42.

Dixon, Bill. "Exclusive Societies: Towards a Critical Criminology of Post-apartheid South Africa." *Society in Transition* 32 (2001): 205–27.

Dixon, Bill, and Lisa-Marie Johns. "Gangs, Pagad and the State: Vigilantism and Revenge Violence in the Western Cape." Centre for the Study of Violence and Reconciliation, Violence and Transition series, vol. 2, May 2001. http://www.csvr.org.za/res/pubsvtp.htm.

Dixon, Bill, and Janine Rauch. *Sector Policing: Origins and Prospects.* Monograph No. 97. Pretoria: Institute for Security Studies, 2004.

"Documented Migration, 2003." Statistics South Africa. http://www.statssa.gov.za/publications/Report-03-51-03/Report-03-51-032003.pdf.

Downes, David. "The Macho Penal Economy: Mass Incarceration in the United States—a European Perspective." In *Punishment and Society* 3 (2001): 61–80.

Dugard, John. *Human Rights and the South African Legal Order.* Princeton: Princeton University Press, 1978.

———. "Should Judges Resign? (and Lawyers Participate?)." In *Democracy and the Judiciary,* ed. Hugh Corder. Cape Town: Institute for a Democratic Alternative for South Africa, 1989.

Edelman, Murray. *Constructing the Political Spectacle.* Chicago: University of Chicago Press, 1988.

———. *The Symbolic Uses of Politics.* Urbana: University of Illinois Press, 1964.

Ellmann, Stephen. *In a Time of Trouble: Law and Liberty in South Africa's State of Emergency.* New York: Oxford University Press, 1992.

———. "Law and Legitimacy in South Africa." *Law and Social Inquiry* 20 (1995): 407–79.

Elphick, Richard, and Hermann Giliomee. "European Dominance at the Cape, 1652–c.1840." In *The Shaping of South African Society, 1652–1840,* ed. Richard Elphick and Hermann Giliomee. Middletown, Conn.: Wesleyan University Press, 1988.

Eybers, G. W., ed. *Select Constitutional Documents Illustrating South African History, 1795–1910.* New York: Negro Universities Press, 1969.

FBI Uniform Crime Reports. "Crime in the United States, 2001." http://www.fbi.gov/ucr/ucr.htm.

FBI Uniform Crime Reports. "Crime in the United States, 2003." http://www.fbi.gov/ucr/cius_03/xl/03tbl01.xls.

Feeley, Malcolm, and Jonathan Simon, "The New Penology: Notes on the Emerging Strategy of Corrections and Its Implications." *Criminology* 30 (1992): 449–74.

Fisher, John. *The Afrikaners.* London: Cassell, 1969.

Fishkin, James S. *Democracy and Deliberation.* New Haven: Yale University Press, 1991.

Forst, Brian. "The Privatization and Civilianization of Policing." In *Boundary Changes in Criminal Justice Organizations,* vol. 2 of *Criminal Justice 2000.* Washington, D.C.: U.S. Department of Justice, Office of Justice Programs, 2000.

Foster, Don, and Diane Sandler. "A Study of Detention and Torture in South Africa."

Institute of Criminology, University of Cape Town, 1985. Summarized in South African Institute of Race Relations, *Race Relations Survey, 1985.*

Foucault, Michel. *Power/Knowledge: Selected Interviews and Other Writings, 1972–1977.* New York: Pantheon, 1980.

Frank, Jerome. *Law and the Modern Mind.* New York: Tudor, 1930.

Frankel, Philip. *An Ordinary Atrocity: Sharpeville and Its Massacre.* New Haven: Yale University Press, 2001.

———. *Pretoria's Praetorians: Civil-Military Relations in South Africa.* New York: Cambridge University Press, 1984.

Friedman, Steven. "Agreeing to Differ: African Democracy, Its Obstacles and Prospects." *Social Research* 66 (1999): 825–58.

———. "Diversity the Antidote to Biased Judges." *Business Day,* May 4, 1998

———. "Not Just Order but Democracy Threatened." *Business Day,* January 26, 1998.

———. "South African Citizens Should Start Flexing Muscle." *Business Day,* May 17, 1999.

———. "The State, Civil Society and Social Policy: Setting a Research Agenda." *Politikon* 30, no. 1 (2003): 3–25.

Friedman, Steven, and Doreen Atkinson, eds. *The Small Miracle: South Africa's Negotiated Settlement.* Johannesburg: Ravan Press, 1995.

Garland, David. *The Culture of Control: Crime and Social Order in Contemporary Society.* Chicago: University of Chicago Press, 2001.

Garretón, Manuel Antonio. "Redemocratization in Chile." *Journal of Democracy* 6 (1995): 146–58.

Gastrow, Peter. *Organized Crime in South Africa: An Assessment of Its Nature and Origins.* Monograph No. 28. Pretoria: Institute for Security Studies, 1998. http://www.iss.co.za/Pubs/Monographs/No28/Contents.html.

Gerhart, Gail M. *Black Power in South Africa: The Evolution of an Ideology.* Berkeley and Los Angeles: University of California Press, 1979.

Glanz, Lorraine. "Crime in South Africa: Incidence, Trends and Projections." In *Managing Crime in the New South Africa: Selected Readings,* ed. Lorraine Glanz. Pretoria: Human Sciences Research Council, 1993.

Glanz, Lorraine E., and Andrew D. Spiegel, eds. *Violence and Family Life in Contemporary South Africa: Research and Policy Issues.* Pretoria: Human Sciences Research Council, 1996.

Glaser, Clive. *Bo-Tsotsi: The Youth Gangs of Soweto.* Portsmouth, N.H.: Heinemann, 2000.

Goldman, Tanya, Leslie Andrews, Matthew Smith, and Debbie Budlender. "Evaluation of the Western Cape Community Policing Project." Unpublished paper, Community Agency for Social Enquiry, 1998.

Goldstein, Herman. *Problem-Oriented Policing.* Philadelphia: Temple University Press, 1990.

———. "Toward Community-Oriented Policing: Potential, Basic Requirements, and Threshold Questions." In *Community Policing: Contemporary Readings,* ed. Geoffrey P. Alpert and Alex R. Piquero. 2nd ed. Prospect Heights, Ill.: Waveland Press, 2000.

Gordimer, Nadine. "April 27: The First Time." In *S. A. April 1994: An Authors' Diary,* comp. André Brink. Preteria: Queillerie, 1994.

Gordon, Diana R. "Democratic Consolidation and Community Policing: Conflicting Imperatives in South Africa." *Policing and Society* 11 (2001): 121–50.

———. "Side by Side: Neoliberalism and Crime Control in Post-apartheid South Africa." *Social Justice* 28, no. 3 (2001): 57–67.

Gready, Paul, and Lazarus Kgalena. "Magistrates under Apartheid: A Case Study of the Politicisation of Justice and Complicity in Human Rights Abuse." *South African Journal of Human Rights* 19 (2003): 141–88.

Grundling, Albert. "'Protectors and Friends of the People'? The South African Constabulary in the Transvaal and Orange River Colony, 1900–1908." In *Policing the Empire: Government, Authority, and Control, 1830–1940,* ed. David M. Anderson and David Killingray. Manchester: Manchester University Press, 1991.

Gutmann, Amy, and Dennis Thompson. "Deliberative Democracy Beyond Process." In *Debating Deliberative Democracy,* ed. James S. Fishkin and Peter Laslett. Oxford: Blackwell, 2003.

———. *Democracy and Disagreement.* Cambridge: Harvard University Press, 1996.

Hahlo, H. R., and I. A. Maisels. "The Rule of Law in South Africa." *Virginia Law Review* 52 (1966): 1–32.

Hamber, Brandon. "'Dr. Jekyll and Mr. Hyde': Problems of Violence Prevention and Reconciliation in South Africa's Transition to Democracy." In *Violence in South Africa: A Variety of Perspectives,* ed. Elirea Bornman, René van Eeden, and Marie Wentzel. Pretoria: Human Sciences Research Council, 1998.

———. "'Have No Doubt It Is Fear in the Land': An Exploration of the Continuing Cycles of Violence in South Africa." *South African Journal of Child and Adolescent Mental Health* 12 (1999): 5–19.

———. "Living with the Legacy of Impunity: Lessons for South Africa about Truth, Justice and Crime in Brazil." *Latin American Report* (University of South Africa Centre for Latin American Studies) 13 (1997): 4–16.

Hanson, Margaret, and James J. Hentz. "Neocolonialism and Neoliberalism in South Africa and Zambia." *Political Science Quarterly* 114 (1999): 479–502.

Hansson, Desirée. "Changes in Counter-revolutionary State Strategy in the Decade 1979 to 1989." In *Towards Justice? Crime and State Control in South Africa,* ed. Desirée Hansson and Dirk van Zyl Smit. Cape Town: Oxford University Press, 1990.

Harbeson, John W., Donald Rothchild, and Naomi Hazan, eds. *Civil Society and the State in Africa.* Boulder, Colo.: Lynne Reinner, 1996.

Harris, Geoff. "The Irrationality of South Africa's Military Expenditure." *African Security Review* 11, no. 2 (2002). http://www.iss.co.za/PUBS/ASR/11No2/Harris.html.

Haysom, Nicholas. "Licence to Kill." *South African Journal of Human Rights* 3 (1987): 3–27.

———. *Mabangalala: The Rise of Right-Wing Vigilantes in South Africa.* Johannesburg: Centre for Applied Legal Studies, 1986.

Held, David. *Models of Democracy.* 2nd ed. Stanford, Calif.: Stanford University Press, 1996.

Henderson, Bart. "The Heart Rejoices but the Head Says No." *Business Day,* July 29, 1999.

Hepple, Alexander. *Verwoerd.* Baltimore: Penguin, 1967.
Hills, Alice. *Policing Africa: Internal Security and the Limits of Liberalization.* Boulder, Colo.: Lynne Reinner, 2000.
Hindson, Doug. *Pass Controls and the Urban African Proletariat in South Africa.* Johannesburg: Raven Press, 1987.
Hirst, Paul. *Associative Democracy: New Forms of Economic and Social Governance.* Amherst: University of Massachusetts Press, 1994.
Hoernlé, A. Winifred. "Social Organization." In *The Bantu-Speaking Tribes of South Africa: An Ethnographical Survey,* ed. Isaac Schapera. London: Routledge, 1937.
Hootnick, Adam. "Improvised Justice: Constitution vs. Reality in South Africa." *American Scholar* (winter 2003): 53–66.
Horrell, Muriel. *Bantu Education to 1968.* Johannesburg: South African Institute of Race Relations, 1968.
Human Rights Watch. *Behind Bars in Brazil.* "IV. São Paulo and Minas Gerais: The Police Lockup as Prison." 1998. http://www.hrw.org/reports98/brazil/Brazil-05.htm.
———. *Deadly Delay: South Africa's Effort to Prevent HIV in Survivors of Sexual Violence.* 2004. http://hrw.org/reports/2004/southafrica0304/.
———. *Police Brutality in Urban Brazil.* 1997. http://www.hrw.org/reports/1997/brazil/.
———. *Scared at School: Sexual Violence against Girls in South African Schools.* 2001. http://www.hrw.org/reports/2001/safrica/.
———. *The Warri Crisis: Fueling Violence.* "V. Security Forces." 2003. http://hrw.org/reports/2003/nigeria1103/6.htm#_Toc56571911.
Human Sciences Research Council. *Public Opinion on National Priority Issues: Election '99.* Pretoria: HSRC Publishers, 1999.
Huntington, Samuel. *The Third Wave: Democratization in the Late Twentieth Century.* Norman: University of Oklahoma Press, 1991.
Immarigeon, Russ. "Restorative Justice, Juvenile Offenders and Crime Victims." In *Restorative Juvenile Justice: Repairing the Harm of Youth Crime,* ed. Gordon Bazemore and Lode Walgrave. Monsey, N.Y.: Criminal Justice Press, 1999.
Independent Complaints Directorate. Annual Report, 2001–2. http://www.icd.gov.za/reports/2002/anualreport.pdf.
———. Annual Report, 2002–3. http://www.icd.gov.za/reports/2003/annualreport03.pdf.
International Narcotics Control Board. "Annual Report of the International Narcotics Control Board for 2001." http://www.incb.org/pdf/e/ar/2001/incb_report_2001_3_africa.pdf.
Jackson, John D. *Justice in South Africa.* London: Secker and Warburg, 1980.
Johns, Sheridan, III. *Protest and Hope, 1882–1934.* Vol. 1 of *From Protest to Challenge: A Documentary History of African Politics in South Africa, 1882–1964,* ed. Thomas Karis and Gwendolyn M. Carter. Stanford, Calif.: Hoover Institution Press, 1972.
Johnston, Les, and Clifford D. Shearing. *Governing Security: Explorations in Policing and Justice.* London: Routledge, 2003.
Joseph, Richard. "Democratization in Africa after 1989: Comparative and Theoretical

Perspectives." In *Transitions to Democracy,* ed. Lisa Anderson. New York: Columbia University Press, 1999.

Kahn, Ellison. "Restore the Jury? Or 'Reform? Reform? Aren't Things Bad Enough Already?'" *South African Law Journal* (vols. 1–5) 108–10 (1991, 1992, 1993).

Karis, Thomas, and Gail Gerhart. *Challenge and Violence, 1953–1964.* Vol. 3 of *From Protest to Challenge: A Documentary History of African Politics in South Africa, 1882–1964,* ed. Thomas Karis and Gwendolyn M. Carter. Stanford, Calif.: Hoover Institution Press, 1977.

Karmen, Andrew. *New York Murder Mystery: The True Story behind the Crime Crash of the 1990s.* New York: New York University Press, 2000.

Katzen, M. F. "White Settlers and the Origin of a New Society." In *The Oxford History of South Africa,* vol. 1, ed. Monica Wilson and Leonard Thompson. New York: Oxford University Press, 1969.

Kelling, George L., Tony Pate, Duane Diekman, and Charles E. Brown. *The Kansas City Prevention Patrol Experiment: A Summary Report.* Washington, D.C.: Police Foundation, 1974.

Keppel-Jones, Arthur. *South Africa: A Short History.* London: Hutchinson University Library, 1963.

"Key Findings about Public Opinion in Africa." Afrobarometer Briefing Paper No. 1. April 2002. http://www.afrobarometer.org/papers/AfrobriefNo1.pdf.

Kimani, Simon. "Bill Finds a Terrorist under Every Bed." *Mail and Guardian,* April 25, 2003.

Kinnes, Irvin. *From Urban Street Gangs to Criminal Empires: The Changing Face of Gangs in the Western Cape.* Monograph No. 48. Pretoria: Institute for Security Studies, 2000. http://www.iss.co.za/Pubs/Monographs/No48/Contents.html.

Klug, Heinz. *Constituting Democracy: Law, Globalism and South Africa's Political Reconstruction.* Cambridge: Cambridge University Press, 2000.

Kolb, Peter. *The Present State of the Cape of Good-Hope.* New York: Johnson Reprint Corporation, 1966.

Kurki, Leena. "Restorative and Community Justice." In *Crime and Justice: A Review of Research,* vol. 27, ed. Michael Tony. Chicago: University of Chicago Press, 2000.

Lane, Roger. "Urban Police and Crime in the Nineteenth-Century America." In *Modern Policing,* ed. Michael Tonry and Norval Morris. Chicago: University of Chicago Press, 1992.

Laurence, Patrick. "A Critical Moment in Our Political History." *Focus* (Helen Suzman Foundation), March 2004. http://www.hsf.org.za/focus33/focus33laurence.html.

Lee, Rebekah, and Jeremy Seekings. "Vigilantism and Popular Justice after Apartheid." In *Informal Criminal Justice,* ed. Dermot Feenan. London: Ashgate, 2002.

Leggett, Ted. "Improved Crime Reporting: Is South Africa's Crime Wave a Statistical Illusion?" *SA Crime Quarterly* 1 (2002). http://www.iss.co.za/.

———. "New Crime Bill a Powerful Weapon." *Mail and Guardian,* February 12, 1999.

———. "Performance Measures for the South African Police Service: Setting the Benchmarks for Service Delivery." *Transformation* 49 (2002): 55–85.

———. "The Sieve Effect: South Africa's Convictions Rates in Perspective." *Criminal Justice Monitor,* September 2003. http://www.iss.co.za/CJM/pdf/sieve.pdf.

———. "What Do the Police Do? Performance Measurement and the SAPS." Institute for Security Studies, Occasional Paper No. 66, February 2003.

Leggett, Ted, Antoinette Louw, Martin Schönteich, and Makubetse Sekhonyane. *Criminal Justice in Review: 2001/2002.* Monograph No. 88. Pretoria: Institute for Security Studies, 2003. http://www.iss.co.za/CJM/cjreview.html.

Le May, G. H. L. *The Afrikaners: An Historical Interpretation.* Oxford: Blackwell, 1995.

Lempert, Richard. "A Jury for Japan?" *American Journal of Comparative Law* 40 (1992): 37–71.

Linz, Juan, and Alfred Stepan. *Problems of Democratic Transition and Consolidation: Southern Europe, South America and Post-Communist Europe.* Baltimore: Johns Hopkins University Press, 1996.

Louw, Antoinette, and Mark Shaw. *Stolen Opportunities: The Impact of Crime on South Africa's Poor.* Monograph No. 14. Halfway House, S.A.: Institute for Security Studies, 1997. http://www.iss.co.za/Pubs/Monographs/No14/Contents.html.

Louw, Antoinette, Mark Shaw, Lila Camerer, and Rory Robertshaw. *Crime in Johannesburg: Results of a City Victim Survey.* Monograph No. 18. Pretoria: Institute for Security Studies, 1998. http://www.iss.co.za/Pubs/Monographs/No18/Contents.html.

Lucas, Pat. "Adolescence and Youth: Challenges in Post-conflict SA." *HSRC Review* 1 (2003): 7–8. www.hsrc.ac.za/about/HSRCReview.

Lyons, William. *The Politics of Community Policing: Rearranging the Power to Punish.* Ann Arbor: University of Michigan Press, 2002.

Macpherson, C. B. *Democratic Theory.* Oxford: Clarendon Press, 1973.

Magubane, Bernard M. *The Making of a Racist State: British Imperialism and the Union of South Africa, 1875–1910.* Trenton, N.J.: Africa World Press, 1996.

Mahomed, Ismail. "Address by Chief Justice I. Mahomed to the Second Annual General Conference of the Judicial Officers' Association of South Africa in Pretoria on 26 June 1998." *Judicial Officer* 1, no. 2 (1998): 45–50.

Mainwaring, Scott, Guillermo O'Donnell, and J. Samuel Valenzuela. *Issues in Democratic Consolidation: The New South American Democracies in Comparative Perspective.* Notre Dame, Ind.: University of Notre Dame Press, 1992.

Mamdani, Mahmood. *Citizen and Subject: Contemporary Africa and the Legacy of Late Colonialism.* Princeton: Princeton University Press, 1996.

———. "Social Movements and Constitutionalism: The African Context." In *Constitutionalism and Democracy,* ed. Douglas Greenberg, Stanley N. Katz, Melanie Beth Oliviero, and Steven C. Wheatley. New York: Oxford University Press, 1993.

Manby, Bronwen. *Unequal Protection: The State Response to Violent Crime on South African Farms.* New York: Human Rights Watch, 2001.

Mandela, Nelson. *Long Walk to Freedom.* Boston: Little, Brown, 1994.

———. "State of the Nation Address by the President of South Africa, Nelson Mandela." Cape Town, May 24, 1994. www.anc.org.za/ancdocs/history/mandela/1994/sp940524.html.

Manning, Peter K. "Community Policing as a Drama of Control." In *Community Policing: Rhetoric or Reality,* ed. Jack R. Greene and Stephen D. Mastrofski. New York: Praeger, 1991.

Mansbridge, Jane. *Beyond Adversary Democracy.* Chicago: University of Chicago Press, 1983.

Marais, Etienne, and Janine Rauch. "Policing South Africa: Reform and Prospects." Centre for the Study of Violence and Reconciliation, 1992. http://www.csvr.org.za/papers/papemjr.htm.

Marenin, Otwin. "Democracy, Democratization, Democratic Policing." In *Challenges of Policing Democracies: A World Perspective,* ed. Dilip K. Das and Otwin Marenin. Amsterdam: Gordon and Breach, 2000.

Marks, Monique. "Changing Police, Policing Change: The Case of Kwazulu Natal." *Society in Transition* 28 (1997): 54–70.

———. "Shifting Gears or Slamming the Brakes? A Review of Police Behavioural Change in a Post-apartheid Police Unit." *Policing and Society* 13 (2003): 235–58.

Marks, Shula. *Reluctant Rebellion: The 1906–1908 Disturbances in Natal.* Oxford: Clarendon Press, 1970.

Marks, Shula, and Neil Andersson. "The Epidemiology and Culture of Violence." In *Political Violence and the Struggle in South Africa,* ed. N. Chabani Manganyi and André du Toit. New York: St. Martin's Press, 1990.

Masuku, Sibusiso. "For Better and for Worse: South African Crime Trends in 2002." *SA Crime Quarterly* 3 (2003). http://www.iss.co.za/Pubs/CrimeQ/No.3/4Masuk.html.

———. "Policing the Police: SAPS Members Charged and Convicted of Crime." Nedbank ISS *Crime Index* 2 (2001). http://www.iss.co.za/pubs/crimeindex/01vol5no2/policing.html.

———. "Prevention Is Better Than Cure: Addressing Violent Crime in South Africa." *SA Crime Quarterly* 2 (2002). http://www.iss.co.za/Pubs/CrimeQ/No.2/2Masuku.html.

Mathews, A. S., and R. C. Albino. "The Permanence of the Temporary—an Examination of the 90- and 180-Day Detention Laws." *South African Law Journal* 83 (1966): 16–43.

Mattes, Robert. "South Africa: Democracy without the People." *Journal of Democracy* 13 (2002): 22–36.

Mattes, Robert, Christiaan Keulder, Annie B. Chikwana, Cherrel Africa, and Yull Derek Davids. "Democratic Governance in South Africa: The People's View." Afrobarometer Working Paper No. 24, 2003. http://www.afrobarometer.org/abseries.html.

Mbeki, Thabo. "Address at the Launch of the Expanded Public Works Programme." Sekhunyani Village, Giyani, Limpopo, May 18, 2004. http://www.anc.org.za/ancdocs/history/mbeki/2004/tm0518.html.

———. "Address by the President of South Africa Thabo Mbeki on the Occasion of His Inauguration and the 10th Anniversary of Freedom." Pretoria, April 27, 2004. http://www.anc.org.za/ancdocs/history/mbeki/2004/tm0427.html.

———. "Address of the President of the Republic of South Africa, Thabo Mbeki, at the Opening of Parliament: National Assembly, Cape Town, June 25, 1999." http://www.info.gov.za/speeches/1999/9906281018a1006.htm.

———. "Address to the First Joint Sitting of the Third Democratic Parliament." Cape

Town, May 21, 2004. http://www.anc.org.za/ancdocs/history/mbeki/2004/tm0521.html.

———. "State of the Nation Address." Cape Town, February 6, 2004. http://www.anc.org.za/ancdocs/history/mbeki/2004/tm0206.html.

———. "State of the Nation Address to the Joint Sitting of the Houses of Parliament." Cape Town, February 8, 2002. http://www.anc.org.za/ancdocs/history/mbeki/2002/tm0208.html.

McBarnet, Doreen J. *Conviction: Law, the State and the Construction of Justice.* London: Macmillan, 1981.

Medical Research Council. "'Every Six Hours a Woman Is Killed by Her Intimate Partner': A National Study of Female Homicide in South Africa." MRC Policy Brief, June 2004.

Meredith, Martin. *In the Name of Apartheid.* London: Hamish Hamilton, 1988.

Merton, Robert K. *Social Theory and Social Structure.* New York: Free Press, 1968.

Miller, David. "Deliberative Democracy and Social Choice." In *Debating Deliberative Democracy,* ed. James S. Fishkin and Peter Laslett. Oxford: Blackwell, 2003.

Minaar, Anthony, and Duxita Mistry. "Outsourcing and the South African Police Service." In *Private Muscle: Outsourcing the Provision of Criminal Justice Services,* ed. Martin Schönteich, Anthony Minaar, Duxita Mistry, and K. C. Goyer. Monograph No. 93. Pretoria: Institute for Security Studies, 2004.

Minaar, Anthony, Sam Pretorius, and Marie Wentzel. "Political Conflict and Other Manifestations of Violence in South Africa." In *Violence in South Africa: A Variety of Perspectives,* ed. Elirea Bornman, René van Eeden, and Marie Wentzel. Pretoria: Human Sciences Research Council, 1998.

Mistry, Duxita. "Falling Crime, Rising Fear." *SA Crime Quarterly* 8 (2004): 17–24.

Mistry, Duxita, Rika Snyman, and Marielize van Zyl. "Social Fabric Crime in the Northern Cape." Unpublished paper, Institute for Human Rights and Criminal Justice Studies, Technikon, S.A., September 2001.

Modisane, Bloke. *Blame Me on History.* New York: Simon and Schuster, 1986.

Monaghan, Rachel. "The Return of 'Captain Moonlight': Informal Justice in Northern Ireland." *Studies in Conflict and Terrorism* 25 (2002): 41–56.

Monkkonen, Eric. "History of Urban Police." In *Modern Policing,* ed. Michael Tonry and Norval Morris. Chicago: University of Chicago Press, 1992.

Moodie, Donald, ed. *The Record, or A Series of Official Papers Relative to the Condition and Treatment of the Native Tribes of South Africa.* Amsterdam: A. A. Balkema, 1960.

Moodie, T. Dunbar. *The Rise of Afrikanerdom: Power, Apartheid, and the Afrikaner Civil Religion.* Berkeley and Los Angeles: University of California Press, 1975.

Moore, Mark Harrison. "Problem-Solving and Community Policing." In *Modern Policing,* ed. Michael Tonry and Norval Morris. Chicago: University of Chicago Press, 1992.

Nasson, Bill. "Bobbies to Boers: Police, People and Social Control in Cape Town." In *Policing the Empire: Government Authority and Control, 1830–1940,* ed. David M. Anderson and David Killingray. New York: Manchester University Press, 1991.

Nathan, Laurie. "From a Police Force to a Police Service: The New Namibian Police." In *Policing and Conflict in South Africa,* ed. M. L. Mathews, Philip B. Heymann, and A. S. Mathews. Gainesville: University Press of Florida, 1993.

"National Crime Prevention Strategy." Department of Safety and Security, Pretoria, 1996.
National Prosecuting Authority. Annual Report, 2002–3. http://www.ndpp.gov.za/.
Nattrass, Nicoli. "The State of the Economy: Employment Crisis." In *The State of the Nation, 2002/03,* ed. John Daniel, Adam Habib, and Roger Southall. Pretoria: Human Sciences Research Council Press, 2003.
———. "Unemployment and AIDS: The Social-Democratic Challenge for South Africa." *Development Southern Africa* 21 (2004): 87–108.
Nedbank ISS. *Crime Index* 4 (2000). http://www.iss.co.za/pubs/crimeindex/00vol4no4/contents.html.
Nedbank ISS. *Crime Index* 5 (2001). http://www.iss.co.za/pubs/crimeindex/01vol5no1/contents.html.
Neild, Rachel. "Confronting a Culture of Impunity: The Promise and Pitfalls of Civilian Review of Police in Latin America." In *Civilian Oversight of Policing: Governance, Democracy and Human Rights,* ed. Andrew J. Goldsmith and Colleen Lewis. Portland, Ore.: Hart, 2000.
———. "From National Security to Citizen Security: Civil Society and the Evolution of Public Order Debates." International Centre for Human Rights and Democratic Development, Montreal. http://www.dd-rd.ca/frame2.iphtml?langue=0.
———. "The New Face of Impunity." *Human Rights Dialogue* 2, no. 8 (fall 2002). http://www.carnegiecouncil.org/viewMedia.php/prmTemplateID/8/prmID/799.
Newburn, Tim. "Atlantic Crossings: 'Policy Transfer' and Crime Control in the USA and Britain." *Punishment and Society* 4 (2002): 165–94.
Newham, Gareth. "Tackling Police Corruption in South Africa." Centre for the Study of Violence and Reconciliation, 2002. http://www.csvr.org.za/papers/papoli14.htm.
Newman, Graeme, ed. *Global Report on Crime and Justice.* New York: Oxford University Press, 1999.
News 24. http://www.news24.com.
Nina, Daniel. *Re-thinking Popular Justice.* Cape Town: Community Peace Foundation, 1999.
Nino, Carlos Santiago. *The Constitution of Deliberative Democracy.* New Haven: Yale University Press, 1996.
Nisbet, Robert A. *The Sociological Tradition.* New York: Basic Books, 1966.
Njoku, Felix Machi. "Nigeria at 40: Putting Africa's Giant Back on Its Feet." *Africa News,* September 30, 2000.
Nomoyi, Ntuthu, and Willem Schurink. "*Ukunxityiswa kwempimpi itayari njengotshaba lomzabalazo:* An Exploratory Study of Insider Accounts of Necklacing in Three Port Elizabeth Townships." (1998). In *Violence in South Africa: A Variety of Perspectives,* ed. Elirea Bornman, René van Eeden, and Marie Wentzel. Pretoria: Human Sciences Research Council, 1998.
O'Donnell, Guillermo. "Illusions about Consolidation." *Journal of Democracy* 7, no. 2 (1996): 34–51.
Oko, Okechukwu. "Subverting the Scourge of Corruption in Nigeria: A Reform Prospectus." *New York University School of Law Journal of International Law and Politics* 34 (2002): 397–472.
Omar, Dullah. "An Overview of State Lawlessness." In *Towards Justice? Crime and State*

Control in South Africa, ed. Desirée Hansson and Dirk van Zyl Smit. Cape Town: Oxford University Press, 1990.

O'Meara, Dan. *Forty Lost Years: The Apartheid State and the Politics of the National Party, 1948–1994.* Athens: Ohio University Press, 1996.

———. "The 1946 Mineworkers' Strike and the Political Economy of South Africa." *Journal of Commonwealth and Comparative Politics* 13 (1975): 146–73.

"Opinion '99: The Public Agenda." Cape Town: IDASA, 1999. http://www.idasa.org .za/pos/op99/op99_n034.htm. Retrieved June 2000.

Orogun, Paul. "'Blood Diamonds' and Africa's Armed Conflicts in the Post–Cold War Era." *World Affairs* 166 (2004): 151–62.

Palmary, Ingrid. "Shifting Safety Agendas: Crime Prevention in the Major Cities." In *Crime Prevention Partnerships: Lessons from Practice,* ed. Eric Pelser. Pretoria: Institute for Security Studies, 2002.

Pate, Anthony, and Penny Shtull. "Community Policing Grows in Brooklyn: An Inside View of the New York City Police Department's Model Precinct." *Crime and Delinquency* 40 (1994): 384–410.

Paton, Alan. *Cry the Beloved Country: A Story of Comfort in Desolation.* New York: Scribner's, 1950.

Patten Commission. *The Report of the Independent Commission on Policing for Northern Ireland.* 2000. http://www.belfast.org.uk/report.htm.

Pauw, Jacques. *Into the Heart of Darkness: Confessions of Apartheid's Assassins.* Johannesburg: Jonathan Ball, 1997.

Pavlich, George. "People's Courts, Postmodern Difference, and Socialist Justice in South Africa." *Social Justice* 19, no. 3 (1992): 29–45.

Pearce, Jenny. "From Civil War to 'Civil Society': Has the End of the Cold War Brought Peace to Central America?" *International Affairs* 74 (1998): 587–615.

Pelser, Eric. "The Challenges of Community Policing in South Africa." Occasional Paper No. 42, Institute for Security Studies, 1999.

Pelser, Eric, Antoinette Louw, and Sipho Ntuli. *Poor Safety: Crime and Policing in South Africa's Rural Areas.* Monograph No. 47. Pretoria: Institute for Security Studies, 2000. http://www.iss.co.za/Pubs/Monographs/No47/Contents.html.

Pelser, Eric, Johann Schneffler, and Antoinette Louw. *Not Everybody's Business: Community Policing in the SAPS' Priority Areas.* Monograph 71. Pretoria: Institute for Security Studies, 2002. http://www.iss.co.za/pubs/monographs/no71/chap3.html.

Pieres, J. B. "The British and the Cape, 1814–1834." In *The Shaping of South African Society, 1652–1840,* ed. Richard Elphick and Hermann Giliomee. Middletown, Conn.: Wesleyan University Press, 1988.

Pigou, Piers. "Monitoring Police Violence and Torture in South Africa." Paper presented at the International Seminar on Indicators and Diagnosis on Human Rights: The Case of Torture in Mexico, convened by the Mexican National Commission for Human Rights, April 2002. http://www.csvr.org.za/papers/papigou1.htm.

Plywaczewski, Emil W. "The Challenges of Policing Democracy in Poland." In *Challenges of Policing Democracies: A World Perspective,* ed. Dilip K. Das and Otwin Marenin. Amsterdam: Gordon and Breach, 2000.

Policy Coordinating and Advisory Services, The Presidency. "Towards a Ten Year

Review: Synthesis Report of Programme Implementations." 2003. http://www.10years.gov.za/review/documents.htm.

"Popular Participation in the Administration of Justice." Position paper (unsigned), South African Ministry of Justice, May 1997.

Posel, Deborah. *The Making of Apartheid, 1948–1961: Conflict and Compromise.* New York: Oxford University Press, 1991.

Potholm, Christian. "The Multiple Roles of the Police as Seen in the African Context." *Journal of Developing Areas* 3 (1969): 139–58.

Pound, Roscoe. "Discretion, Dispensation, and Mitigation: The Problem of the Individual Special Case." *New York University Law Review* 35 (1960): 925–37.

"Prison Brief for South Africa." International Centre for Prison Studies, 2003. http://www.prisonstudies.org/.

"Proceedings of the Civilian Oversight of the Police Mini-conference." Open Society Foundation South Africa, June 2003.

"Protecting Children against Violence in Schools." *HSRC Review* 1 (2003): 4–5.

Pye, Lucian. *Asian Power and Politics: The Cultural Dimensions of Authority.* Cambridge: Harvard University Press, 1985.

Ramaphosa, Cyril. "Negotiating a New Nation: Reflections on the Development of South Africa's Constitution." In *Post-apartheid Constitutions: Perspectives on South Africa's Basic Law,* ed. Penelope Andrews and Stephen Ellmann. Athens: Ohio University Press, 2001.

Rauch, Janine. "Changing Step: Crime Prevention Policy in South Africa." In *Crime Prevention Partnerships Lessons from Practice,* ed. Eric Pelser. Pretoria: Institute for Security Studies, 2002.

———. "Police Reform and South Africa's Transition." Centre for the Study of Violence and Reconciliation, 2000. http://www.csvr.org.za/papers/papsaiia.htm.

Rauch, Janine, Mark Shaw, and Antoinette Louw. *Municipal Policing in South Africa: Development and Challenges.* Monograph 67. Pretoria: Institute for Security Studies, 2001. http://www.iss.co.za/Pubs/Monographs/No67/Content.html.

Rawls, John. *Political Liberalism.* New York: Columbia University Press, 1993.

Redpath, Jean. "The Gang Landscape in the Western Cape." *Indicator SA* 18 (2001): 34–40.

———. *The Scorpions: Analysing the Directorate of Special Operations.* Monograph No. 96. Pretoria: Institute for Security Studies, 2004.

Reiner, Robert. *The Politics of the Police.* 2nd ed. Toronto: University of Toronto Press, 1992.

Rotberg, Robert. *The Founder: Cecil Rhodes and the Pursuit of Power.* New York: Oxford University Press, 1988.

Roux, Edward. *Time Longer Than Rope.* Madison: University of Wisconsin Press, 1964.

Rule, Stephen P., ed. *Public Opinion on National Priority Issues: Election '99.* Pretoria: Human Sciences Research Council, 1999.

Russell, Peter H. "Toward a General Theory of Judicial Independence." In *Judicial Independence in the Age of Democracy: Critical Perspectives from around the World,* ed. Peter H. Russell and David M. O'Brien. Charlottesville: University Press of Virginia, 2001.

SA 27 April 1994: An Authors' Diary. Comp. André Brink. Pretoria: Queillerie, 1994.

Sachs, Albie. *Justice in South Africa.* Berkeley and Los Angeles: University of California Press, 1973.

Sampson, Anthony. *Mandela: The Authorized Biography.* New York: Knopf, 1999.

Sayed, Taleh, and David Bruce. "Inside and Outside the Boundaries of Police Corruption." *African Security Review* 7, no. 2 (1998): http://www.iss.co.za/Pubs/ASR/7No2/SayedAndBruce.html.

Schapera, Isaac. "Law and Justice." In *The Bantu-Speaking Tribes of South Africa: An Ethnographical Survey,* ed. Isaac Schapera. London: Routledge, 1937.

———. "Political Institutions." In *The Bantu-Speaking Tribes of South Africa: An Ethnographical Survey,* ed. Isaac Schapera. London: Routledge, 1937.

Schärf, Wilfried. "Community Justice and Community Policing in Post-apartheid South Africa." Unpublished paper, Institute of Criminology, University of Cape Town, 2000.

———. "Non-state Justice Systems in Southern Africa: How Should Governments Respond?" Unpublished report, Institute of Criminology, University of Cape Town, 2003.

———. "Specialist Courts and Community Courts." Position paper prepared for the Ministry of Justice, May 1997.

———. "Transforming Community Policing in Black Townships in the New South Africa." Unpublished paper, Institute of Criminology, University of Cape Town, 1991.

Schärf, Wilfried, and Daniel Nina. *The Other Law: Non-state Ordering in South Africa.* Cape Town: Juta, 2001.

Schatz, Sayre P. "Pirate Capitalism and the Inert Economy of Nigeria." *Journal of Modern African Studies* 22 (1984): 45–57.

Scheppele, Kim Lane. "Declarations of Independence: Judicial Reactions to Political Pressure." In *Judicial Independence at the Crossroads: An Interdisciplinary Approach,* ed. Stephen B. Burbank and Barry Friedman. Thousand Oaks, Calif.: Sage, 2002.

Schiff, Mara. "The Impact of Restorative Interventions on Juvenile Offenders." In *Restorative Juvenile Justice: Repairing the Harm of Youth Crime,* ed. Gordon Bazemore and Lode Walgrave. Monsey, N.Y.: Criminal Justice Press, 1999.

Schmitter, Philippe, and Terry Lynn Karl. "What Democracy Is . . . and Is Not." *Journal of Democracy* 2 (1991): 75–88.

Schönteich, Martin. "Back to the Future? New South African Anti-terror Law." *Terrorism and Political Violence* 14 (2002): 1–22.

———. "Compulsory Lay Assessors: Popular (In)justice?" *Judicial Officer* (South Africa) 1, no. 2 (1998): 30–36.

———. "Does Capital Punishment Deter?" *African Security Review* 11, no. 2 (2002). http://www.iss.co.za/pubs/asr/11no2/schonteich.html.

———. *Lawyers for the People: The South African Prosecution Service.* Monograph No. 53. Pretoria: Institute for Security Studies, 2001.

Schönteich, Martin, and Henri Boshoff. *"Volk," Faith and Fatherland.* Pretoria: Institute for Security Studies, 2003.

Schönteich, Martin, Duxita Mistry, and Johan Struwig. "Qualitative Research Report on Sentencing." Unpublished paper commissioned by the German Technical Cooperation for the South African Law Commission, April 2000.

Schönteich, Martin, and Jonny Steinberg. *Attacks on Farms and Smallholdings: An Eval-*

uation of the Rural Protection Plan. Pretoria: Institute for Security Studies, 2000. http://www.iss.co.za/Pubs/Other/Farm%20attacks/1Contents.html.

Schumpeter, Joseph A. *Capitalism, Socialism, and Democracy*. 2nd ed. New York: Harper, 1947.

Seekings, Jeremy. *The UDF: A History of the United Democratic Front in South Africa, 1983–1991*. Athens: Ohio University Press, 2000.

Seekings, Jeremy, with Christina Murray. *Lay Assessors in South Africa's Magistrates' Courts*. Cape Town: University of Cape Town, Law, Race and Gender Research Unit, 1998.

Segal, Lauren, Joy Pelo, and Pule Rampa. "Into the Heart of Darkness: Journeys of the *Amagents* in Crime, Violence and Death." In *Crime Wave: The South African Underworld and Its Foes*, ed. Jonny Steinberg. Johannesburg: Jonathan Ball, 2001.

Sekhonyane, Makubetse, and Antoinette Louw. *Violent Justice: Vigilantism and the State's Response*. Monograph No. 72. Pretoria: Institute for Security Studies, 2002. http://www.iss.co.za/pubs/monographs/no72/content.html.

Sen, Amartya. *Development as Freedom*. New York: Knopf, 1999.

Shaw, Mark. *Crime and Policing in Post-apartheid South Africa: Transforming under Fire*. Bloomington: Indiana University Press, 2002.

———. "Crime, Police and Public in Transitional Societies." *Transformation* 49 (2002): 1–24.

Shearing, Clifford. "'A New Beginning' for Policing." *Journal of Law and Society* 27 (2000): 386–93.

———. "Punishment and the Changing Face of the Governance." *Punishment and Society* 3 (2001): 203–20.

Sherman, Lawrence, Denise Gottfredson, Doris MacKenzie, John Eck, Peter Reuter, and Shawn Bushaway. *Preventing Crime: What Works, What Doesn't, What's Promising: A Report to the United States Congress*. Washington, D.C.: U.S. Dept. of Justice, Office of Justice Programs, National Institute of Justice, 1998. http://www.ncjrs.org/works/.

Silverman, Eli B. *NYPD Battles Crime*. Boston: Northeastern University Press, 1999.

Simons, Harold Jack. *African Women: Their Legal Status in South Africa*. Evanston, Ill.: Northwestern University Press, 1968.

Simpson, Graeme. "Reconstruction and Reconciliation: Emerging from Transition." Centre for the Study of Violence and Reconciliation, 1997. http://www.csvr.org.za/papers/paprrgs.htm.

———. "Shock Troops and Bandits: Youth, Crime and Politics." In *Crime Wave: The South African Underworld and Its Foes*. Johannesburg: Witwatersrand University Press, 2001.

———. "'A Snake Gives Birth to a Snake.'" In *Justice Gained? Crime and Crime Control in South Africa's Transition*, ed. Bill Dixon and Elrena van der Spuy. Cape Town: Juta, 2004.

Simpson, Graeme, and Janine Rauch. "Political Violence, 1991." In *Human Rights Yearbook*, ed. Neil Boister and K. Ferguson-Brown. Cape Town: Oxford University Press, 1991.

Skogan, Wesley G. "Community Policing in Chicago." In *Community Policing: Contem-*

porary Readings, ed. Geoffrey P. Alpert and Alex R. Piquero. 2nd ed. Prospect Heights, Ill.: Waveland Press, 2000.

———. *Disorder and Decline: Crime and the Spiral of Decay in American Neighborhoods.* Berkeley and Los Angeles: University of California Press, 1990.

Skogan, Wesley G., and Susan M. Hartnett. *Community Policing, Chicago Style.* New York: Oxford University Press, 1997.

Skolnick, Jerome H., and David H. Bayley. *The New Blue Line: Police Innovation in Six American Cities.* New York: Free Press, 1986.

South African Department of Correctional Services. Annual Report, 2002. http://www-dcs.pwv.gov.za/annual_report/Annual_Report2002/Default.htm.

South African Department of Defence. Strategic Plan for 2002/3–2004/5. January 2002. http://www.mil.za/Articles%26Papers/StrategicPlan/Strategicplan2003/StratPlan0306.pdf.

South Africa Department of Safety and Security. "In Service of Safety, 1999–2004." http://www.gov.za/whitepaper/1998/safety.htm.

South Africa Human Rights Commission. *Enquiry into Racism and Racial Discrimination in the Department of Justice and Constitutional Development.* Johannesburg, 2002. http://www.sahrc.org.za/main_frameset.htm.

South African Institute of Race Relations. *Race Relations Survey,* 1982, 1985, 1987–88, 1994–95.

———. *South Africa Survey,* 1995–96, 1996–97, 1999–2000 (millennium edition), 2000–2001, 2001.

South African Law Commission. "Community Dispute Resolution Structures." Discussion Paper 87, Project 94, 1999.

South African Law Commission. "Anti-terrorism Draft Bill." Discussion Paper 92, Project 105, 2000.

South African Police. Annual Report, 1988.

South African Police Service. Annual Report, 2002–3. http://www.saps.gov.za/saps_profile/strategic_framework/annual_report/index.htm.

———. Crime Information Analysis Centre. http://www.saps.gov.za/statistics/reports/crimestats/2004/_pdf/crimes/rsa_ totals03_ 04_new.pdf.

———. "The South African Crime Profile, January–September 2001." http://www.saps.org.za/8_crimeinfo/200112/scrime_files/frame.htm. Retrieved May 2002.

Sparks, Allister. *Beyond the Miracle: Inside the New South Africa.* Chicago: University of Chicago Press, 2003.

———. *The Mind of South Africa.* New York: Ballantine, 1990.

Spelman, William, and Dale K. Brown. *Calling the Police: Citizen Reporting of Serious Crime.* Washington, D.C.: U.S. Department of Justice, National Institute of Justice, 1984.

Stack, Louise. "Understanding Policy Implementation: The Justice Sector." Unpublished paper, Centre for Policy Studies, February 2001.

Steinberg, Jonny. "Clumsy Foray into Pop Criminology." *Business Day,* June 4, 1999.

———. "Community Courts—Can They Work?" *Business Day,* November 9, 1998.

———. *Midlands.* Johannesburg: Jonathan Ball, 2002.

———. "Selebi Talks, but Will Police Listen?" *Business Day,* March 28, 2000.

Stenson, Kevin. "Rethinking Crime Control in Advanced Liberal Government: The 'Third Way' and the Return to the Local." In *Crime, Risk and Justice: The Politics of Crime Control in Liberal Democracies,* ed. Kevin Stenson and Robert R. Sullivan. Portland, Ore.: Willan, 2001.

Steytler, Nico. "Policing Political Opponents: Death Squads and Cop Culture." In *Towards Justice? Crime and State Control in South Africa,* ed. Desirée Hansson and Dirk van Zyl Smit. Cape Town: Oxford University Press, 1990.

Sunstein, Cass. *Designing Democracy: What Constitutions Do.* New York: Oxford University Press, 2001.

———. "The Law of Group Polarization." *Journal of Political Philosophy* 10 (2002): 175–95.

———. *The Partial Constitution.* Cambridge: Harvard University Press, 1993.

Tanner, Murray Scot. "Will the State Bring *You* Back In? Policing and Democratization." *Comparative Politics* 33 (2000): 101–24.

Taylor, Helen, and Robert Mattes. "Public Demands on Government: The People's Agenda." IDASA Public Opinion Service, July 1998.

Theal, G. McCall. *History of the Boers in South Africa.* Cape Town: C. Struik, 1973.

Thomas, Adèle. "Violence and Child Detainees." In *People and Violence in South Africa,* ed. Brian McKendrick and William Hoffmann. Cape Town: Oxford University Press, 1990.

Thomas, Vinod, Mansoor Dailami, Ashok Dhareshwar, Daniel Kaufman, Nalin Kishor, Ramón López, and Yan Wang. *The Quality of Growth.* New York: World Bank and Oxford University Press, 2000.

Thompson, E. P. *Writing by Candlelight.* London: Merlin, 1980.

Thompson, Leonard. *A History of South Africa.* New Haven: Yale University Press, 1990.

Tittle, Charles R. *Sanctions and Social Deviance.* New York: Praeger, 1980.

Tocqueville, Alexis de. *Democracy in America.* Vol. 1. New York: Knopf, 1946.

Tonry, Michael. *Malign Neglect: Race, Crime and Punishment in America.* New York: Oxford University Press, 1995.

Transparency International. "Global Corruption Barometer Survey." 2003. http://www.transparency.org/surveys/barometer/dnld/barometer2003_release.en .pdf.

United Nations Development Programme. "Human Development Report 1999." http://hdr.undp.org/reports/global/1999/en/.

United Nations Office on Drugs and Crime. "The Eighth United Nations Survey on Crime Trends and the Operations of Criminal Justice Systems (2001–2002)." http://www.unodc.org/unodc/en/crime_cicp_survey_eighth.html.

———. "The Seventh United Nations Survey on Crime Trends and the Operations of Criminal Justice Systems (1998–2000)." http://www.unodc.org/unodc/en/crime_cicp_survey_seventh.html.

———. "South Africa: Country Profile on Drugs and Crime, 2002." http://www.unodc.org/pdf/southafrica/country_profile_southafrica.pdf.

U.S. Department of Justice, Bureau of Justice Statistics. *Criminal Victimization in the United States, 1997.* Washington, D.C.: U.S. Department of Justice, 2000.

———. *Criminal Victimization in the United States, 2002.* http://www.ojp.usdoj.gov/bjs/abstract/cvus/reported_to607.htm.

———. *Sourcebook of Criminal Justice Statistics, 2002.* Washington, D.C.: U.S. Department of Justice, 2003.

U.S. Department of State. Human Rights Country Reports. "Sierra Leone Country Report on Human Rights Practices for 1996." February 1997.

van de Meeberg, Dann, and Alexis A. Aronowitz. "Challenges of Policing Democracies: The Dutch Experience." In *Challenges of Policing Democracies: A World Perspective,* ed. Dilip K. Das and Otwin Marenin. Amsterdam: Gordon and Breach, 2002.

van der Berg, Servaas, and Megan Louw. "Changing Patterns of South African Income Distribution: Towards Time Series Estimates of Distribution and Poverty." Bureau of Economic Research, University of Stellenbosch. Stellenbosch Economic Working Papers: 2/2003.

van der Spuy, Elrena. "Foreign Donor Assistance and Policing Reform in South Africa." *Policing and Society* 10 (2000): 343–66.

———. "Political Discourse and the History of the South African Police." In *Towards Justice? Crime and State Control in South Africa,* ed. Desirée Hansson and Dirk van Zyl Smit. Cape Town: Oxford University Press, 1990.

van Niekerk, Gardiol. "The Plurality of Legal Domains in South Africa: The State's Historical Legislative Intrusion into the Field of Urban Popular Justice and Customary Law." In *The Other Law: Non-state Ordering in South Africa,* ed. Wilfried Schärf and Daniel Nina. Cape Town: Juta, 2001.

van Zyl Smit, Dirk. "Contextualizing Criminology in Contemporary South Africa." In *Towards Justice? Crime and State Control in South Africa,* ed. Desirée Hansson and Dirk van Zyl Smit. Cape Town: Oxford University Press, 1990.

———. "Criminological Ideas and the South African Transition." *British Journal of Criminology* 39 (1999): 198–215.

van Zyl Smit, Dirk, and Elrena van der Spuy. "Importing Criminological Ideas in a New Democracy: Recent South African Experiences." In *Criminal Justice and Political Cultures,* ed. Tim Newburn and Richard Sparks. Devon: Willan, 2004.

Vindex [pseudonym for John Verschoyle]. *Cecil Rhodes—His Political Life and Speeches.* London: Chapman Hall, 1900.

Vold, George, and Thomas J. Bernard. *Theoretical Criminology.* 3rd ed. New York: Oxford University Press, 1986.

Volkov, Vadim. *Violent Entrepreneurs: The Use of Force in the Making of Russian Capitalism.* Ithaca: Cornell University Press, 2000.

Wacquant, Loïc. "'Suitable Enemies': Foreigners and Immigrants in the Prisons of Europe." *Punishment and Society* 1 (1999): 215–22.

Waldmeir, Patti. *Anatomy of a Miracle: The End of Apartheid and the Birth of the New South Africa.* New York: Norton, 1997.

Walker, Eric. *A History of Southern Africa.* London: Longmans, 1957.

Wallerstein, James S., and Clement J. Wylie. "Our Law-Abiding Law-breakers." *Probation* 25 (1947): 107–12.

Welsh, David. "The Growth of Towns." In *The Oxford History of South Africa,* vol. 1, ed.

Monica Wilson and Leonard Thompson. New York: Oxford University Press, 1969.

———. "An Outline of South African Reform Politics since February 1990." In *Policing the Conflict in South Africa,* ed. M. L. Mathews, Philip B. Heymann, and A. S. Mathews. Gainesville: University Press of Florida, 1993.

———. *The Roots of Segregation: Native Policy in Colonial Natal, 1845–1910.* Cape Town: Oxford University Press, 1971.

Wilson, James Q., and Allan Abrahamse. "Does Crime Pay?" *Justice Quarterly* 9 (1992): 359–77.

Wilson, Monica. "The Hunters and Herders." In *The Oxford History of South Africa,* vol. 1, ed. Monica Wilson and Leonard Thompson. New York: Oxford University Press, 1969.

———. "The Nguni People." In *The Oxford History of South Africa,* vol. 1, ed. Monica Wilson and Leonard Thompson. New York: Oxford University Press, 1969.

———. "The Sotho, Venda, and Tsonga." In *The Oxford History of South Africa,* vol. 1, ed. Monica Wilson and Leonard Thompson. New York: Oxford University Press, 1969.

Wilson, Monica, and Leonard Thompson, eds. *The Oxford History of South Africa.* Vols. 1 and 2. New York: Oxford University Press, 1969.

World Economic Forum. *Global Competitiveness Report, 2000.* New York: Oxford University Press, 2000.

Young, Iris Marion. "Activist Challenges to Deliberative Democracy." In *Debating Deliberative Democracy,* ed. James S. Fishkin and Peter Laslett. Oxford: Blackwell, 2003.

Young, Jock. *The Exclusive Society.* Thousand Oaks, Calif.: Sage, 1999.

Zulu, Paulus. "Political Violence and the 'Third Force.'" *Southern Africa Report* 8, no. 2 (1992): 8–12.

South African (and International) Legal References

Abolition of Juries Act 34 of 1969.
Anti-Terrorism Bill B12–2003. http://www.polity.org.za/pdf/Anti-Terrorism-Bill12.pdf.
August v. Electoral Commission, 1999 (3) SA 1 (CC).
Boesak v. State, 2000 SA 105/99 (SCA).
Carmichele v. Minister of Safety and Security, 2001 (4) SA 938 (CC).
Certification of the Constitution of the Republic of South Africa, 1996 (4) SA 744 (CC).
Child Justice Bill, B49–2002. http://www.polity.org.za/pdf/ChildJustB49.pdf.
Constitution of the Republic of South Africa, 1996.
Criminal Law Amendment Act 8 of 1953.
Criminal Law Amendment Act 105 of 1997.
Criminal Procedure Act 51 of 1977, Sections 49, 112, 217, and 218.
Criminal Procedure Second Amendment Act 75 of 1995.
Criminal Procedure Second Amendment Act 85 of 1997.
Dodo v. State, 2001 (3) SA 382 (CC).
European Code of Police Ethics, IV (A) (13). http://www.coe.int/T/E/Legal_Affairs/Legal_co-operation/Police_and_internal_security/Confer-

ences/2002_Vilnius/Rec(2001)10%20European%20Code%20of%20Police%20Ethics.asp.
Ferreira v. State, 2004 (SCA) 245/03.
General Law Amendment Act of 1962, Section 21.
Harris v. Minister of the Interior, 1952 (2) SA 428 (AD).
Interim Constitution of the Republic of South Africa, 1993.
Internal Security Act 74 of 1982, Section 29.
Judicial Matters Second Amendment Act 122 of 1998.
Magistrates Act 90 of 1993, as amended, Sections 13 (2), (3) and (4); Regulation 26 (1), (2) and (3).
Magistrates Amendment Act 66 of 1998.
Magistrates' Courts Amendment Act 118 of 1991.
Malgas v. State, 2001 SCA 117/00.
Mello v. State, 1998 (3) SA 712 (CC).
Minister of Health v. Treatment Action Campaign, 2002 (5) SA 721 (CC).
Minister of the Interior v. Harris, 1952 (4) SA 769 (AD).
Minister of the Interior v. Lockhat, 1961 (2) SA 587 (AD).
Minister of Justice v. Alexander, 1975 (4) SA 530 (AD).
Minister of Law and Order and Another v. Dempsey, 1988 (3) SA 19 (AD).
Minister of Law and Order and Others v. Hurley and Another, 1986 (3) SA 568 (AD).
Mohamed v. President of the Republic of South Africa, 2001 (3) SA 893 (CC).
Momonial and Naidoo v. Minister of Law and Order, 1986 (2) SA 264 (WL).
National Director of Public Prosecutions v. Mohamed NO and others, 2002 (4) SA 843 (CC).
National Director of Public Prosecutions v. R O Cook Properties (Pty) Ltd, 2004 (SCA) 260/03.
Omar and Others v. Minister of Law and Order and Others, 1987 (3) SA 859 (AD).
Premier, Mpumalanga, v. Association of State-Aided Schools: Eastern Transvaal, 1999 (2) SA 91 (CC).
President of the Republic of South Africa and Others v. South Africa Rugby Football Union and Others, 1999 (4) SA 147 (CC).
President of the Republic of South Africa and Others v. South Africa Rugby Football Union and Others, 2000 (1) SA 1 (CC).
Prevention of Organized Crime Act 121 of 1998.
Proceeds of Crime Act 76 of 1996.
Protection of Constitutional Democracy Against Terrorist and Related Activities Act 33 of 2004.
Public Safety Act 3 of 1953.
R. v. Radsha, 1923 A.D. 281.
R. v. Sisulu and others, 1953 (3) SA 276 (AD).
Raloso v. Wilson, 1998 (4) SA 369 (NCD).
Regulation of Gatherings Act 205 of 1993.
Republic of South Africa v. Grootboom, 2001(1) SA 46 (CC).
Rossouw v. Sachs, 1964 (2) SA 551 (AD).
Scagell v. Attorney General, Western Cape, 1996 CCT42/95.
Schermbrucker v. Klindt N.O., 1965 (4) SA 606 (AD).
Security Emergency Regulations, Proc. R. 97, Section 3 (1), June 1988.

Sigaba v. Minister of Defence and Police, 1980 (3) SA 536 (Tk SC).
South Africa Act, 1909.
South African Amendment Act 9 of 1956.
South African Law Commission Act 19 of 1973.
South African Police Service Act 68 of 1995.
State v. Abrahams, 2001 SA 88/00 (SCA)
State v. Bhulwana, 1996 (1) SA 388 (CC).
State v. Basson, 2003 SCA 404/02.
State v. Basson, 2004 (1) SA 246 (CC).
State v Dlamini, 1999 (4) 623 (CC).
State v. Gambushe, 1997 (1) SACR 638 (N).
State v. Makwanyane and Another, 1995 (3) SA 391 (CC).
State v. Ntuli, 1995 CCT/17/95.
State v. Salzwedel, 1999 SCA 273/98.
State v. Walters, 2002 (4) SA 613 (CC).
State v. Williams, 1995 (3) SA 632 (CC).
State v. Wood, 1976 (1) SA 703 (AD).
State v. Zuma, 1995 (2) SA 642 (CC).
Steyn v. State, 2000 CCT 19/00.
Suppression of Communism Act 44 of 1950, Section 1.
Thebus v. State, 2003 CCT 36/02.
Trop v. Dulles, 356 U.S. 86 (1958).
United Nations Code of Conduct for Law Enforcement Officials, Article 1 (b). http://www.coe.int/T/E/human_rights/Police/5._Reference_Documents/p._Code_of_Conduct_for_Law_Enforcement_Officials.asp#TopOfPage.
United Nations International Covenant on Civil and Political Rights, Article 9. http://www.hrweb.org/legal/cpr.html.
United Nations Universal Declaration of Human Rights, Article 11. http://www.un.org/Overview/rights.html.
Van Biljon v. Minister of Correctional Services, 1997 (4) SA 441 (CPD).
Van der Westhuizen NO v. United Democratic Front, 1989 (2) SA 242 (AD).
Van Rooyen v. State, 2000 CCT 19/00.

Index

Abolition of Passes and Coordination of Documents Act (1952), 56
accountability: balancing judicial independence and, 126–30, 148–58, 305n42; civilian oversight of police and, 12; constitutional democracy and, 116; criminal justice institutions as instruments of self-governance and, 123–24; judicial, at end of apartheid, 308n40; lay assessors program and, 236; for nonstate justice structures, 240–41; openness in criminal justice proceedings and, 121; of police, CPFs and, 219, 221–22, 223–24; of police, Independent Complaints Directorate and, 225; in post-apartheid South Africa, 152; public-empowering justice and, 197; reciprocal, citizens, criminal justice systems and, 213; regime change and, 250; state sponsorship and regulation of nonstate justice structures for, 240; transparency in democratizing countries and, 132
Africanists, tensions with antiapartheid activists, 67
African law/tradition: conflict resolution among Nguni-speaking groups, 33–34; on crime control, European authority over, 46; Langalibalele affair and legal representation under, 38; outcomes of Western approach to criminal incident intervention versus outcomes of, 216; Shepstone's usurpation through indirect rule of, 37–38. *See also* chiefs' courts
African National Congress (ANC): commitment to public role in policing before liberation, 243, 320n90; crime as 1995 campaign slogan of, 250; Defiance Campaign, emergency law and, 59; democratic transformation and, 3, 4; implied changes in justice system with voting for, 7; SAP discussions during National Peace Accord with, 8; Sharpeville massacre and banning of leaders of, 57–58; on use of sabotage, 103; Vaal uprising (1984) and, 68; violence in clashes with Inkatha, 71, 104–5; Zulu massacre assisted by police in Boipatong and, 72. *See also* ANC government
African Union, 131
Afrikaners: appointments as magistrates and judges, 75; under British colonial rule, 31; divine agent of civil faith of, 293–94n4; Great Trek eastward, 33–34; ideology of violence and, 103; resentment of English-speakers, National Party and, 52; slavery's role in nationalism of, 24; social attitudes, subjugation of blacks and, 50; tensions between British and, 25; use of term, xiii. *See also* National Party

351

Afrobarometer Network survey: on corruption among public servants in South Africa, 161; on corruption of judiciary in South Africa, 159; on crime and confidence in criminal justice system, 203; on distrust of police and courts and disapproval of government's handling of crime, 273

AIDS: exhaustion of reformers from social chaos of democratic transition and, 243; police arrests of groups protesting South African policy on, 257; rape and spread of, 97–98, 301n66; South African response to unemployment and, 17–18. *See also* HIV

alcohol: crime in communities and, 97, 239; problems among magistrates, 159; tot system for, 88. *See also* liquor laws

Alexander, Neville, 83

Amadlozi, radically democratic service ethic of, 280

Amnesty International, 70, 71

amputation, as traditional punishment, 135

ANC government: commitment to public-empowering justice, 216–17; criticism of judicial accountability by, 149; criticism on crime control by, 85; death penalty and, 139, 164, 252; ideals of public protection, individual rights under, 139; on minimum sentences legislation, 254; neoliberal policymaking and, 267; police investigation into criticism of Mbeki, 143; political consequences of AIDS management by, 18; preparation for crime control by, 262–63; reluctance to invest in public-empowering policies, 242–43; understanding of regime change and violent crime, 250. *See also* state; voting day in 1994

Andean Trade Promotion and Drug Eradication Act (U.S.), 183

antiapartheid activists: tensions with Africanists, 67. *See also specific groups*

Anti-Privatization Campaign, 270, 285

apartheid: Botha era of reform and repression, 64–70; challenges in development of, 50–51; as "colossal social experiment," Appellate Division on, 76; crime and, 88–89, 95, 300n24, 301n53; crime rates as reminders of, 274; high policing and enforcement of, 59–62; as ideology of violence, 103–4; law of, 54–59; as National Party campaign slogan, 53; National Party's 1948 electoral victory and, 25; separate but unequal philosophy of, 55, 294n23; sources for, 52–54; Supreme Court and human rights under, 73–82; turbulent transition from, 70–72; unconstrained police enforcement of, 62–64

apartheid courts: defending government policies, 76–79; judging by, 72–73, 148–49, 308n39; penalizing ordinary and political crimes, 79–82; public attitudes toward, 5; repressive regulations and, 6; resistance to repression in, 74–75. *See also* Supreme Court

appellate courts: Afrikaner composition of, 54; for review of lower court decisions, 127; segregation policy and, 45–46

Appellate Division: during apartheid era, 73; on arrests under Internal Security Act, 79; on banning orders as political punishment, 77–78, 298n119; competence and fairness of, 46, 48; detention laws interpretation by, 76–77, 298n117; executive branch priorities during apartheid and, 151; franchise for black South Africans under apartheid and, 75; on Group Areas Act, 55; parliamentary sovereignty and, 47. *See also* Supreme Court of Appeal

Arendse, Jeffrey, 83

Argentina, police brutality and torture in, 114
Aristotle, on judicial participation by ideal citizen, 209
Arms and Ammunition Act (1969), Constitutional Court's interpretation of, 165
arms trafficking, replacement of repression with individual liberty and, 121
army: transformation and immediate reforms to, 5. *See also* military
arrests: humane conditions for, 133, 134; in Japan, ostracism of, 135; for pass law violations (1980s), 65, 299n139; under security law, Supreme Court on, 79; without warrant, indefinite detention and, 5–6, 58
askaris, police use of, 64, 296n72
asset forfeiture, post-apartheid program on, 255–56
association, freedom of, Regulation of Gatherings Act and, 270
authoritarian regimes: democratic transition from, crime patterns and, 93–94, 202; democratic transition from, dignity of the person and, 5; democratic transition from, public- empowering justice and, 201; public-empowering justice for countries in transition from, 180–81, 201
AWB (Afrikaner resistance movement), 159

bail reform, 252–53, 263
Baluma, Vuyo, 273
Bambatha rebellion, Natal (1906), 48, 293n109
bans/banning orders: Appellate Division on extension of, 77–78, 298n119; of meetings and outdoor funerals, 69; of organizations and individuals under apartheid, 51, 58, 63, 297n88
Bantu Administration and Development (BAD), Division of, 73. *See also* Native Affairs, Department of
Bantu commissioners' courts, 55, 73, 81–82, 295n36. *See also* chiefs' courts; traditional courts; tribal courts
Bantu (Urban Areas) Consolidation Act (1952), 55
Bantu Education Act (1953), 55, 105, 294n26
Bantu-speaking people, xiii, 296n64
Barber, Benjamin, 179, 181
Bartleman, James, 87
Basson (Wouter) case, 171, 237, 319n73. *See also* "Doctor Death" case
Bator, Paul, 128
Bayley, David: on community policing, 191, 202, 218; on police reform in democracies, 122; on responsibility for policing, 187; on state formation impact on police structure and operations, 6
Biko, Steve, 54, 64, 103
Black Administration Act (1927), 214
black consciousness movement, 62, 64, 102, 103
black police: institutional thinking by, 69; killing blacks in the name of apartheid, 63; post-apartheid, as part of SAPS, 142; pre-apartheid, 45; separate development policy and, 62; violence against black political rivals by, 71. *See also* police
blacks: apartheid law and, 54–59; apartheid-spawned tensions among, 67–68; Boers' labor needs and views of crime by, 290n42, 290n43; constitutional rights in Union of South Africa for, 43; criminalization during apartheid of, 82; divisions among, 276–78; hunchback beaten to death by right-wing whites, 159, 170; judicial appointments of, 149, 307n36, 308n47; as lay assessors, 230; Natal Code of Native Law and segregation of, 37; post-apartheid average income of, 288n37; in post-apartheid criminal justice system, 172–75; property-owning Cape Colony, 35; property-owning Cape Colony, democratic

blacks (*continued*)
transformation and, 3; racial repression by colonists of, 30–31; on single, state-structured justice system, 240; students, higher education opportunities for, 17; use of term, xiii, 287n5; as vigilantes and *kitskonstabels*, 64. *See also* urban migration
Blackstone, William, 228
Boeremag (far-right white group), 144, 145, 169, 307n23
Boer rebellion of 1815, executions after, 25
Boer republics, 46, 47. *See also* Orange Free State; Transvaal
Boers: antivagrancy concerns among, 32–33, 290n42, 290n43; use of term, xiii. *See also* Afrikaners
Boesak, Allan, 157, 169, 309n79
Boister, Neil, 256
Bolivia: military involvement in drug enforcement in, 126; police brutality against labor protesters in, 114
Booysen, Judge, 154, 155
Bophuthatswana, Sharpeville Day violence in, 71
Botha, P. W., 52, 64–65
Botswana, incarceration rates in, 322n49
Braithwaite, John, 194
Bratton, William, 196
Brazil: awards for journalists from, 133; censorship in, 132, 306n59; corruption as threat to democracy in, 130; democratization and police brutality, 182–83; military police and urban violence in, 182; police brutality and torture in, 114, 304n7; revelations of corruption and political accountability in, 131
Brewer, John D.: on Afrikanerization of police, 45; on character of Afrikaner police, 30; on emergency regulations of mid-1980s, 59; on police in black townships, 60–61, 66; on SAP recruitment of blacks for keeping order and repressing resistance, 63

Britain. *See* United Kingdom
British colonialists: criminal justice under, 31–42; domination of blacks, 34–35, 291n53; freedom of press, judicial system of, 290n33; liberalism of, 31–33; on native self-regulation through customary law applied by chiefs' courts, 214; tensions between Afrikaners and, 25; use of term, xiii
British criminal law: adoption of, 290n39; African exclusion in Natal from, 37; judicial interpretations of 1980s states of emergency and, 78; parliamentary sovereignty and, 47; as reminders of imperial authority, 290n34; social attitudes and, 32
British imperialism, slavery's role in, 24
Broederbond, 53, 154
Brogden, Mike, 53
Bruce, David, 147
budgets. *See* resources
Bushmen, arrival of Europeans and, 27
Buthelezi, Mangosuthu, 72
Buur, Lars, 279–80

Campbell, Catherine, 108
Cape Colony: competence of judiciary in, 46; criminal justice in, 26–31; democratic transformation and property-owning blacks of, 3; eastern expansion during Great Trek, 33; masters and servants legislation in, 39; parliamentary sovereignty in, 47; segregation in, 42
Cape Mounted Rifles, 42
Cape of Good Hope Punishment Act (1835), 36
Cape Town: Dutch requirements for passes for Khoikhoi in, 138; forced removals during apartheid from, 65; gangs in, 95; liberal social atmosphere of nineteenth-century, 35, 49; nineteenth-century British-run, 25, 32; police enforcement of apartheid in, 62; police resistance to segregation enforcement in, 45, 293n101; police

sweeps in, 257; policing in early twentieth-century, 293n100; poor citizens as police patrol auxiliaries in, 282; post-apartheid violence in, 87–88, 99, 160, 270; race of convicted criminals in, 290n43; taxi wars in, 102; violence by Pagad in, 144, 280–81
capitalism: democratic, 18–19; inefficiency of democracy and, 120–21; segregation and development of, 44, 293n93
capital punishment: under apartheid, 253, 320n19; blacks in Transvaal before union and, 292n72; under British colonists, 31; citizen support for reinstatement of, 251; colonizers versus Africans on, 38; Constitutional Court on, 164, 320n11; as hypothetical subject for democratic discussion, 209; increased use after 1958 of, 80–81, 299n136; juries' reluctance for use of, 210; *Makwanyane, State v.*, 288n23; post-apartheid prohibitions against, 8–9, 135, 155, 163; for rape, race of the offender and, 80; as slave punishment by Dutch settlers, 29. *See also* punishments
carceral societies, Foucault's description of, 20
Cardozo, Benjamin, 129
Carmichele, Alix, 279
Cartwright, John, 283–84
Catholic bishops, on police role in townships, 66
cattle rustling. *See* stock thefts
Cawthra, Gavin, 63
censorship, transparency in democratizing countries and, 132, 306n59
Centre for the Study of Violence and Reconciliation (CSVR), 140, 166, 219
Chaskalson, Arthur: as chief justice, 300n27, 307n37; on Constitution and democratic transformation, 1; on legal support for apartheid, 148; on office resources for judiciary, 152; retirement of, 174–75; support for judicial independence in Zimbabwe, 309n76; violent crime and, 89
Chevigny, Paul, 101
chiefs' courts: during apartheid, 72; British authority superseding authority of, 46; under British colonialism, 214; post-apartheid, 238; of twenty-first century, 215. *See also* Bantu commissioners' courts; traditional courts; tribal courts
Chikane, F., on apartheid society, 50
Child Justice Bill, 241–42, 268, 277, 323n79
children, African: abuse of, 98; apartheid and crimes against, 108; capture of, as apprentices or servants, 39; caught in dragnets, 66; detention in solitary confinement of, 58; lengthy prison terms for, 81; police restructuring and reductions in violence against, 275; sexual assaults of, 91, 97–98
child support, aggressive pursuit of, 275
Christianity, apartheid's use of, 53, 293–94n4
Christie, Nils, 273, 314n51
citizens/citizenry: democratization and competence of, 273; as lay participants in criminal trials, 236–37; legitimacy of criminal justice institutions and, 118–19; participation in maintenance of public order and, 190–93. *See also* lay assessors; nonstate justice; vigilantes/vigilante groups
citizenship: competent, Zwelethemba model and enhancement of, 284; as novelty, 275–76. *See also* participatory citizenship
Civil Cooperation Bureau, 104
civilian authority: for police and courts, 11–12. *See also* civil society; demilitarization
civil liberties: democratic governance and expectation of, 120. *See also* culture of rights; group rights; human rights; individual rights; voting rights

civil order: state use of police in maintenance of, 140–41. *See also* public order
civil servants, pre- and post-apartheid authority of, 138
civil service, negotiated settlement, police reforms and, 142
civil society: public-empowering justice and, 197–98; as vehicle for citizen participation in public life, 278
Clear, Todd, 180, 192–93, 197
Cock, J., 83
Code of Good Practice, of Peace Committees, 282–83, 324–25n32
Coetzee, Johan, 69, 70
coloured, use of term, xiii
Commission of Inquiry, British colonial, 31
Commission of Inquiry into Public Violence and Intimidation, 143
communists/Communism: act on suppression of (1950), 57, 298n114; Afrikaners' on threat of, 52; ANC leaders of Defiance Campaign charged as, 76; Botha's total strategy and, 65; detention of, 58; high policing and, 61; National Party on ANC Freedom Charter and, 4; police defense against African nationalism and threats of, 63, 69; suppression of individual liberties and perceived threats of, 51
community building: political consciousness-raising and, 284–85; public-empowering justice and, 276–78; Zwelethemba model and enhancement of, 284
community/communities: apartheid violence and violence within, 105; drugs and alcohol abuse and, 97; gangs and, 96–97; geographic variation of serious crimes in, 98; rape and, 97–98; use of term, 180; vigilantism and crime in, 98–99
community courts, use of term, 319n80
community justice: during apartheid, 68, 214–15, 317n5; Clear and Karp on, 192–93; consensual traditions among, 243; of 1990s, 215; plans for regulating courts used during liberation struggle for, 217; post-apartheid courts, 238. *See also* community police forums; community policing
Community Justice Center (Clear and Karp), 193
community leadership, revealed and fostered by CPFs, 224
Community Peace Programme (CPP), 282–84
community police forums (CPFs), 218–26; consequences of demise of, 225–26; as crime prevention instrument, 222–23; divergent visions for, 218–19; early attempts to influence SAPS by, 222; foreign support for, 318n35; intelligence gathering for police by, 237; interim constitution (1993) on, 221–22; organizational characteristics, 220–21, 317n22; plan for, 216–17; police opinion of, 244; Police Service Act (1995) on role of, 222; positive consequences for, 224–25; provincial department support for, 242; transition planners for, 317n17
community policing: benefits of, 197, 200; crime control and, 196–97; economic and training factors in, 202; as function at some remove from state, 197–98; funding and training as evidence of state commitment to self-government, 203; lay participation in, 12; literature on, 314n48; meanings for, and criticisms of, 191; mutual distrust between officials and citizens on, 202; post-apartheid planners on, 8, 10; post-apartheid reality of, 217; resources for, 218; SAPS commitment to crime prevention and, 269–70; state dominance of, 237; strengthened community voice and, 199; theory, constitutional design in South Africa and, 218–19; use of term, 180. *See also* public-empowering justice

"Community Policing Policy Framework and Guidelines" (1997), 222
community safety forums (CSF), 225, 242, 282
confessions: complexity of building cases without coerced, 243; criminal procedure law revisions and involuntary, 80, 298n131; post-apartheid procedures for, 164–65, 168, 311n112
conflict resolution. *See* dispute resolution
Congo, Democratic Republic of, dangers of police and military in, 138
consent to be governed: democracy and, 117–18; lay assessors program and, 236; personal freedoms, civil liberties and, 121
constituency shifting: democratic transition and, 118–19; integrity of criminal justice operatives and, 158–59; as military goal, 146; paradigm description, 122–24, 304n32; for police and courts, 11–12, 119
constitution, South African: bail reform under, 252–53; bill of rights on criminal procedure, 163; bill of rights scope in, 304–5n33; on crime prevention as police job, 217; failure to educate public about public-empowering policies with, 279; ideals in preamble of, 148; on judiciary, 149; public concerns about "too many rights" in, 172; on right to dignity, minimum sentences legislation and, 254–55; transformative nature of, 137. *See also* constitutions
Constitutional Assembly (1996), 4, 155
Constitutional Court: on asset forfeiture law, 255–56; on bail reform legislation, 253; on capital punishment, 8–9, 155, 320n11; chief justice of, 308n50; commitment to independence of, 155; demographic composition, 175; on duty to develop common law to reflect the Constitution, 164; inclusion of blacks and women on, 249; independence of, 155–56; on Magistrates' Act, 153, 308n59; on minimum sentences legislation, 254–55; on prior legislative decisions that did not meet human rights standards of new government, 168; transformation of judiciary, magistracy and, 149–50; on use of force against fleeing criminal suspects, 167
constitutional democracy: constituency shifting during development of, 124; contradictions to protection of law-abiding majority in, 184–85; criminal justice transformation and complexity of, 6–7; South African development of, 14; yearning for public order and, 115
constitutional transformation, 2–3. *See also* transformation
constitutions: impeachment of judges under, 127; judicial autonomy under, 129
convictions: of ANC leaders of Defiance Campaign by Appellate Division, 76; in cases prosecuted by Scorpions, 275, 324n14; in magistrates' courts, 275, 324n11; for pass law offenses, 56, 57, 299n139; racial disparities in, 80, 298n132; rates in South Africa, research on, 167, 311n128; sieve effect of, 258; for unlicensed weapons, 165
Corbett, Michael, 8
Corder, Hugh, 47–48, 293n104
Correctional Services, Department of, 259
corruption: confidence in the state and, 273–74; perceived, in South Africa, 159; police, post-apartheid, 160–61, 162, 250; police, under apartheid, 61; police restructuring and reductions in, 275; state, versus corruption of police and courts, 182; transparency as hedge against, 132; various definitions of, 130–31
Council of Policy, of Dutch settlers, 28–29

counsel, right to: failure to educate public about, 279. *See also* representation, legal
courts: Afrikaner composition of, 54; British colonial, 32; crime control during apartheid by, 90; delays in moving cases through, 259, 322n53; documentation and research on, 167–68; enforcement of laws enacted by democratic means, 124–26; improvements in, 275; under National Party government, 51; post-apartheid race-based sentencing, 250–51; professionalism as goal for, 217; public opinion on effectiveness of, 171–72; racial subjugation under British and Afrikaner governments by, 26, 49, 293n110; reform difficulties, 6; as regime enforcers, 113–15; segregation policy and, 44, 45–46; shifting constituencies for, 11–12, 119. *See also* judges; juries; lay assessors; magistrates; Supreme Court; *specific courts*
crack cocaine, 97; labs for, 96
Crawford, Adam, 211
crime: apartheid and, 88–89, 95, 300n24, 301n53; definitions of, 186, 313n19; democratization of, 89, 202; foreign press on South African, 86–87; hidden, revealed as increased, 262; historical precedents for South African, 88; independence from criminal justice system, 183–84, 312n15; intensified patrols for hot spots, 274; international availability of data on, 185–86, 313n28, 313n29; labeling shift and incidence of South African, 93; outcomes of African tradition versus Western interventions for, 216; patterns, democratic transitions and, 93–95, 202, 301n46; as post-apartheid political issue, 250–52; as recent South African phenomenon, 87–88; reporting and data on South African, 91–92, 301n46; reporting on, 184, 313n21; responsibility for prevention of, community policing and, 197, 205; South African, drop in recent years of, 101–2, 258; in South African communities, 96–99, 301n67; on South African farms, 99–100, 302n83; South African government data on, 89–92, 300n30; by South African police, 100–101; South African police and courts' control of, 121; South African politics and issue of, 84–86; South African public opinion on, 84, 86; taxi wars, 102, 107–8, 145, 160, 239. *See also* corruption; crime prevention; rape; transnational crime; violent crime

crime, ordinary: criminal procedure law revisions and penalties for, 80; increases during apartheid of 1960s and 1970s in, 62–63; as justification for delaying promised improvements to living conditions, 67; police neglect during apartheid of, 141–42; political struggle as screen for, 68; post-apartheid definitions of, 93; South African procedural difficulties in handling, 9; use of term, 313n19

crime prevention: democratic justice and, 122; environmental or situational, 181–82, 189–90; liquor laws as, 44; Mbeki's focus on social roots of crime and, 269; pass laws as, 44, 48–49; post-apartheid plan for public involvement in, 217; as private responsibility, 277–78; responsibility for, community policing and, 197, 205; SAPS attention to community problems and, 269–70; South Africa's choice for get-tough programs versus, 266–67; violent, and management of, 9–10

Criminal Assets Recovery Account, 255
criminal courts: security laws and, 79–80. *See also* courts
criminal justice: balancing judicial accountability and judicial indepen-

dence, 126–30, 148–58; consent to be governed and, 117–18; in a democracy, 122–34; fundamental fairness and, 133–34; indigenous traditions, Western standards for rule of law and, 250; integrity of police and judges, 130–31; post-apartheid planners on communitarian policing, 8, 10; public confidence in, 85; regime performance under democracy and, 121–22; repoliticization and demilitarization of law enforcement, 124–26; repressive nature of, 113; taxation metaphor for control and liberty with, 119; transformation and, 4–11; transparency and, 131–33; watershed period for, 181–87; watershed policy responses, 187–95; what is not, 134–36. *See also* apartheid courts; courts; police; pre-apartheid justice
criminal law: regime enforcement and, 113–15; use of to establish or maintain power relations, 51
Criminal Procedure Act (1977), 168
Criminal Procedures and Evidence Act (1917), 229
criminal suspects, fleeing, use of force against, 166–67
criminologists: CPFs planning and, 219; on narrowed function of CPFs, 223–24
Crossroads (squatter community), 67
crowd control. *See* public order
culture, acceptance of deliberative democracy and, 212
culture of rights: as alien to South Africans, Hofmeyr on, 261; building South African, 162; South African failure to encourage, 278–79; transformation and development of, 2–3, 250. *See also* civil liberties; group rights; human rights; individual rights
culture of violence: during 1950s and 1960s, 88; criminal pathology of past regimes and, 94, 301n53; criticism of ANC government about, 84; as influence of past on present, 102. *See also* domestic violence; political violence; structural violence; violent crime
customary courts. *See* chiefs' courts

dagga (marijuana) sales, 96, 97
Dahl, Robert, 19, 120–21, 273, 304n12
death penalty. *See* capital punishment
death squads, secret SAP, 69–71, 104–5
defendants awaiting trials, 169–70
de Klerk, F. W.: announcement of police reform, 142; demilitarization under, 144; restriction of police from political policing by, 71, 249, 297n97; testimony on death squads by, 69
de Kock, Eugene, 162
de Lange, Jonny, 263
deliberative democracy: criminal justice issues and, 208–9; global issues and, 210; negative aspects of, 211; public-empowering justice and, 207; punitive program of criminal justice policy and, 209–10; rights as preconditions for, 210–11, 316n99; socially transforming logic of participation in, 211–12; theory of, 207–8, 316n86, 316n90
deliberative opinion poll, 208
demilitarization: of police, 125–26; progress toward, 144. *See also* civilian authority; military
democracy: criminal justice in, 122–34; definitions of, 116–17; deliberative, public-empowering justice and, 207–12, 316n86, 316n90, 316n99; democratization versus, 117; linking coercion and, 116–22; strong, Barber on, 179, 181; transparency and, 131–33. *See also* constitutional democracy
democratic autonomy, principle of, 13
democratic consolidation, 304n18; concerns about increased crime after, 188–89; shifting constituency for police, courts and, 119

democratic justice: crime prevention and, 122; paths to, 11–16; public-empowering justice and, 197–98
Democratic Party, 85, 250
democratization/democratic transition: community policing as reconciliation measure after, 205; CPF goals by planners of, 219; crime control breakdown and, 182; crime patterns, postauthoritarian policing and, 93–94; as crimogenic time, 186; definition of, 117; double reforms of state and civil society with, 135–36, 198; institutional development, public-empowered justice and, 202; legitimacy of new regime with new tasks for old operatives and, 109–10; public-empowering justice and, 200–207; relevance of failed innovations to, 245; repoliticization of public policing and, 143; requirements for law enforcement, 124–26; shifting constituency of institutions from state to citizenry and, 118–19; as South African miracle, 1–2; in sub-Saharan Africa, 288n20
detention laws: Appellate Division interpretation of, 76–77, 298n117; post-apartheid bail reform, 252–53; Supreme Court opinions on, 79; warrantless arrests under apartheid and, 5–6, 58
developing countries: behavior of criminal justice systems in, 188; public-empowering justice factors for, 201
Development Bank of Southern Africa, 266
de Villiers, J. H., 47–48
Diamond, Larry, 121
diamond industry, 42. *See also* mines/mining
dignity of the person: abuse of, during apartheid, 82; competitive markets and, 18–19; death penalty and, 135; democratization and, 117, 118, 133; judicial accountability for, 148; public empowerment and, 12, 14; South African constitution on, 1, 2, 7, 9, 137, 163; South African women and children and, 157; transformation from authoritarian to democratic government and, 5
Dingane (Zulu king), 35
dispute resolution: alternative, assumptions about responsibility for social ordering and, 190–91; community-based, participation options for, 199; community-based, sponsorship for, 242; funding and training as evidence of state commitment to self-government, 203; Johnston and Shearing's peacemaking model for, 193; lay participation in, 10, 12; mutual distrust between officials and citizens on, 202; among Nguni-speaking people, 33–34; nonstate centers in townships for, 72; police on crime control and potential increase of unregulated, 239; post-apartheid projects for, 217; in public forum, fundamental fairness of, 133; by regulated nonstate justice structures, 241; Zwelethemba model for, 282–83
distrust: between Inkatha and ANC, 276; between officials and citizens, community policing, dispute resolution and, 202, 277; between police and citizens, CPFs' failure as mechanisms of police accountability and, 223–24; of police and judges in democratizing countries, 182; of police in African nations, 203; post-apartheid culture of, 244. *See also* trust
"Doctor Death" case, 171, 237, 255, 319n73
domestic violence: children as objects of, 98; consideration of context of and sentencing for, 269; criticism of post-apartheid justice system's response to, 250; Hofmeyr on investigative work and reduction in, 261; in townships, 251; widespread poverty, alcohol use

and, 239; women on justice systems' indifference to, 182
Domestic Violence Act, 91
double democratization: factors for development of, 245; of state and civil society with, 135–36, 198
Drugs and Drug Trafficking Act, 168
drug trafficking and manufacture, 96, 301n60; lack of advancement opportunities for blacks and, 239; military involvement in controlling, 126; Operation Crackdown and, 257; police restructuring and reductions in, 275; post-apartheid prosecutions for, 165; replacement of repression with individual liberty and, 121
due process: adoption in South Africa, 140; asset forfeiture law and, 256; failure to educate South African public about, 279; fundamental fairness in, 134; in post-apartheid South Africa, 162–72; research on, anxiety about general lawlessness and, 167. *See also* get-tough programs
Dugard, John, 47, 51, 54–55
Dutch East India Company, 25, 26–27
Dutch Reformed Church, National Party and, 53
Dutch settlement to British occupation era, 25
Dutch settlers: adjudication of social order by, 28–29; rural justice and, 214; use of term, xiii. *See also* Afrikaners

East Germany, Stasi surveillance for regime policing in, 119
economy: democratic capitalism and, 18–19; Diamond on regime legitimacy and performance of, 121; post-apartheid data on, 288n40; postauthoritarian regimes, resources for public-empowering justice and, 202, 205–6; restorative justice and, 202–3
education: of citizens on rewards of system guaranteeing dignity of the person, 163, 164; on democracy, deliberative activity and, 212; on democracy, encouragement of rights culture and, 278–79; segregation in, damage to society as a whole and, 295n27; state-provided, 17; state-provided, under apartheid, 55, 294n26
Egypt: political repression in, 114, 303–4n6; regime enforcement by State Security Court, 119
Electronic Mail & Guardian, 84
elites: American, on get-tough programs, 267; black, proletariat black needs versus, 18; criminal law as benefit for, 115; deepening democracy in criminal justice as risk for, 13; inefficiency of democracy for, 120; of legal profession, 174; mechanisms of social order in democratizing country and, 226; post-1996 government, "back to basics" policing and, 226; of post-apartheid government, preparation for crime control by, 262–63; public-empowering justice and, 196; responses to post-apartheid crime by, 251, 274; shifting constituencies initiated by, 11, 123; South African, pride in creating institutions that respect rule of law by, 285; transformation by, 6; white judges during apartheid, 47, 73, 150
Ellmann, Stephen, 59, 78
Eloff, Louis, 218, 219–20
emergency, states of: during 1980s, judicial capitulation to apartheid and, 78–79; ANC consideration of, 86; under apartheid, 58–59, 307n38; appellate judges on apartheid ideology and, 119; license to kill for security police under, 68–69, 296–97n85
emigration: due to crime, 84; reasons for, 299n7; of technical and managerial professionals, 265
employment concerns. *See* unemployment

employment discrimination, influence on current societal violence, 105
England. *See* United Kingdom
English, use of term, xiii
environmental crime prevention, 181–82. *See also* situational crime prevention
equality, transformation and commitment to definitions of, 2–3
ethnic rivalries, criminal justice under democracy and, 7
Europe, Americanization of crime control in, 185, 313n26
European Code of Police Ethics, 126
European Parliament, on AIDS and crime policies, 87
executive power: courts' deference to, 77–78; interference in judicial decision-making and, 128; judicial nominations as function of, 127; parliament as rubber stamp during 1980s of, 78
exile, as traditional punishment, 135
Extension of University Education Act (1959), 55

fairness, fundamental, 133–34; judicial independence and, 127–28, 305n44; lack of understanding about role of crime investigation in, 279; in post-apartheid South Africa, 162–72; research on, anxiety about general lawlessness and, 167
family group conferences, as restorative justice, 192, 197
Family Justice Act, 276
farm crime, 99–100, 302n83
financial resources. *See* resources
Firearms Control Bill, 275
(The) Firm (Western Cape gang), 96
Fishkin, James, 208
Fivaz, George, 256
flogging: of American youth in Singapore, 184; colonial courts on, 29; de Villiers' opposition to, 47–48; exemption of whites in Transvaal from, 292n72; of juveniles, Constitutional Court nullification of, 168; among Khoikhoi, 28; for political protests, 56; post-apartheid era and, 30; public empowerment and degradation of, 12; as punishment by people's courts, 215; as traditional punishment, 135; vigilante organizations' use of, 99; for violating masters and servants legislation in Natal, 39; white subjugation of blacks using, 48. *See also* thrashings
forced removals: under Botha to homelands, 65; from Crossroads to Khayelitsha, murders during, 67; gang membership and, 106; stresses from, 277
foreign aid: financial coercion for neoliberal macroeconomic strategies and, 267; perception of crime in South Africa and, 266–67
foreign investment in South Africa, crime control and, 261, 274
foreign press, on crime in post-apartheid South Africa, 86–87, 101
Forst, Brian, 200
Foucault, Michel, 20
Foundation for Peace and Justice, Boesak's, 157
Foxcroft, Judge, 158
France: criminal justice as regime enforcement in, 114–15; police with military functions in, 126
freedom. *See* personal freedom
Freedom Charter (ANC, 1955), 3–4, 243
Freedom Front, 144
Friedman, Steven, 273, 278
funding. *See* resources

gacaca court system, 205, 316n84
Gambling Act, 168
Gandhi, Mahatma, 41
gangs: boys' dreams of joining, 83; communities controlled by, 96–99; criminal justice under democracy and, 189; lack of advancement opportunities for

blacks and, 239; persistence and transformation of, 105–6; police and, 100; police participation in, 160; political and criminal violence of, 106–7, 303n114; taxi warlords and, 102. *See also* vigilantes/vigilante groups
Garland, David, 183, 185, 249, 313n23
GEAR (growth, employment, and redistribution) economic policy, 18–19
Gerhart, Gail, 103
German business leaders, as crime victims, 87
get-tough programs: asset forfeiture, 255–56; bail reform, 252–53; criminal justice crisis and, 187; impact of, 258–61; minimum sentences, 253–55; police crackdowns, 256–58, 321n38; post-apartheid, 10, 16, 19, 251–52; in South Africa versus United States, 270–72; in United States, as example for other governments, 266. *See also* due process; human rights
Giuliani, Rudolph, 10, 188, 196
Glaser, Clive, 106
globalization: effects on crime, 183, 186; of ideas about governance, 116; investment in South Africa, perception of crime and, 266
global versus local issues: deliberative democracy and, 210; transformation and, 3
gold mining. *See* mines/mining
Goldstone, Richard, 71, 143
Goldstone Commission, 71, 143
Gordimer, Nadine, 2
governance deficit, Community Peace Program and, 283–84
governance through voluntary associations, principle of, 13
government. *See* ANC government; state
Group Areas Act (1950), 55, 76, 173
group polarization, deliberative democracy and, 211
group rights: as brake on state authority in criminal matters, 7. *See also* civil liberties; culture of rights; human rights; individual rights; voting rights
Guatemala, postauthoritarian collaborations between police and military in, 126
Gutmann, Amy, 208

Hahlo, H. R., 50
Hanson, Margaret, 267
Harms Commission, 70–71
Haysom, Nicholas, 141
Health, Department of, on Constitutional Court ruling on prevention of mother-to-child transmission of HIV, 156
health care issues, 17
Held, David, 113, 135–36, 198
Hentz, James, 267
Hertzog, J. B. M., 43
High Court: selection of judges for, 150; separation of powers and, 156–57
high policing: predominance under apartheid, 60–61; redefinitions in post-apartheid era, 142–43; use of term, 59
Hills, Alice, 140–41, 288n20, 305n37
Hindus, restorative justice among, 194
historically disadvantaged tertiary educational institutions, improvements to, 17
HIV: Constitutional Court on prevention of mother-to-child transmission of, 156; South African response to unemployment and, 17–18. *See also* AIDS
Hofmeyr, Willie, 89, 260–61, 263, 264
Holiday, Anthony, 137
Holtzman, Zelda, 224
homelands: forced removals under Botha to, 65; laws trapping Africans in, 54; police brutality in, during demise of apartheid, 71; post-apartheid police as part of SAPS, 142; "separate development" policy and, 51, 62; Verwoerd and establishment of, 73. *See also* townships

homelessness. *See* squatter communities
Hottentots: arrival of Europeans and, 27; use of term, xiii
housing construction, 17
human rights: under apartheid, Supreme Court and, 73–82; constitutional, viewed as threat to personal safety, 279; criminal justice and, 133–34; get-tough program versus, 263–64; objections to bail reform on basis of, 253; ordinary citizens on state's respect for, 171–72; under post-apartheid South African constitution, 163; as protection for victim rather than due process, 170; South African understanding of, 162–63; training for post-apartheid police, 143. *See also* civil liberties; culture of rights; group rights; individual rights
Human Rights Commission, 140
Human Rights Watch, 182
Human Sciences Research Council, 85, 98
Hungary: democratic transition and increased crime in, 93–94; incarceration rates in, 188
Huntington, Samuel, 117, 120
Hurley decision (1986), 79

Ibrahim, Saad Eddin, 119, 303–4n6
immigrants/immigration: chiefs courts treatment of, 241; indigenous values, community decision-making, and oppression of, 200; Operation Crackdown and, 257; police dog attacks (1998) on Mozambican, 9, 165; prohibitions against nonwhite Asian, 75; right to legal representation for, 311n137
impartiality toward policy solutions, deliberative process and, 212
income gap: CPF program and gulf in, 223–24; intraracial, 17. *See also* poverty
Indemnity Act (1977), 68
independence, judicial: balancing accountability and, 148–58; behavioral standards for, 127; Boesak trial and, 157; of Constitutional Court, 155–56; early twentieth-century, 46; of Judicial Service Commission, 153–54; of Magistrates' Commission, 152–53; in post-apartheid South Africa, 150–51; sentences for rape and, 157–58; separation of powers and, 127–28
Independent (London), on crime statistics, 87
Independent Advisory Team, 317n18
Independent Board of Inquiry into Informal Repression (1989), 70
Independent Complaints Directorate (ICD): on complaints for police performance, 310n103; on deaths as result of police action, 101; on deaths during police custody or action, 165; investigations of misconduct by SAPS under, 160; judge, magistrate accountability and, 140; limits on efficacy of, 306n7; police accountability and, 225, 275; on torture by police, 165–66; trust in, 161
India, corruption in, 131
indigent defendants, post-apartheid legal aid for, 169
indirect rule, Natal Code of Native Law and, 37, 291n60
individual rights: as brake on state authority in criminal matters, 7; criminal justice institutions as instruments of self-governance and, 123; new constitutions on scope of, 304–5n33; restorative justice and, 194–95; South African constitutional obligations and, 14. *See also* civil liberties; culture of rights; group rights; human rights
industrialized nations, behavior of criminal justice systems in, 188
influx control laws: under apartheid, 25; brutal enforcement of, 60; delays and compromises in imposition of, 73;

democratization of crime and repeal of, 89; "separate development" policy and, 62; use as juvenile delinquency strategy, 106. *See also* pass laws
informal justice, use of term, 319n76
Inkatha Freedom Party: battles with UDF supporters, 67; criticism on crime control by ANC government, 85; Malan's "total onslaught" strategy and, 171; police participation in attacks on ANC and UDF with, 141; violence in ANC clashes with, 71; Vlakplaas and violent conflicts with ANC, 104–5
inland expansion and colonization from early nineteenth century to end of South African War, 25
insistence legitimacy, criminal justice institutions and, 118–19
Institute for Democracy in South Africa (IDASA), 219
Institute for Security Studies, 100, 161–62, 165
Institute of Criminology, University of Cape Town, 78–79
integrity of criminal justice operatives, 130–31; in post-apartheid South Africa, 158–62
Inter American Press Association awards, 133
interest groups, judicial independence and bribery by, 128
Internal Security Act (1982), 65, 68, 79. *See also* security laws
Internal Security Unit, dismantling of, 249
Internal Stability Division, SAP, public order policing by, 147
International Covenant on Civil and Political Rights (1966), 134, 306n62
International Crime Victim Survey (U.N.), 185
International Monetary Fund (IMF), 266, 267
international political culture, late twentieth-century political reconstruction and, 115

Interpol data on crime, 97, 301n64
Islamic law, constitutional democracy and, 115–16

Jackson, Jesse, 297n88
Jameson raid on the Transvaal (1895), criminal "justice" after, 25–26
Japan: arrest as source of shame in, 135; juries thought unnecessary in, 228; low victimization rates in, 184; public-empowering justice in, 179–80
Johannesburg: crime in, 94–95, 96, 98; as frontier town, 41; police sweeps in, 257; safety of, 86–87, 300n18
Johnston, Les, 179, 193, 284
Joseph, Richard, 123
judges: accountability of, 305n42; Afrikaners appointed as, 75; blacks and women as, 307n36, 308n47; constitutional standards for, 123–24; delivery of democracy and, 121; early twentieth-century, 46, 47, 293n104; historical versus current selection of, 150–51; integrity of, 130–31, 158–60; on minimum sentences legislation, 254; post-apartheid training and diversity, 174; role under British colonialists of, 290n38; shifting constituencies for, 139–40. *See also* apartheid courts; courts; independence, judicial; pre-apartheid justice
judicial review: judicial independence and, 127–28, 129; in South Africa, 149
Judicial Service Commission (JSC): on candidates for deputy judge president in KwaZulu-Natal, 154–55; composition, 308n50, 308n51; judicial independence and accountability conveyed by, 153–54, 308–9n61; scope and purpose, 152
juries: benefits of, 228; criticisms of, 228–29; historical use in South Africa, 229; South Africa's reasons for not using, 229–30. *See also* lay assessors

justice, pre-apartheid. *See* pre-apartheid justice
Justice/Justice and Constitutional Development, Department of: abandonment of lay assessors by, 235; contradictory conceptions of lay assessors' role, 235; draft procedures for behavior problems in judiciary by, 152; guidelines for lay assessors by, 230; magistrates as employees during apartheid of, 150; priorities for, 317n9; on resources for incorporating nonstate justice bodies into state system, 240

"Kaffir wars" (1779–1878), 34, 35, 291n53
Kahn, Ellison, 228–29
Kahn, Gadijah, 244–45
Karl, Terry Lynn, 134
Karp, David, 180, 192–93, 197
Keppel-Jones, Arthur, 32, 40–41, 292n73, 292n74
Khoikhoi: adjudication of social disorder among, 27–28, 289n17; arrival of Europeans and, 27; Boers and right to sue masters under British colonial rule by, 32; colonial legal system and, 29–30; forced to work for Dutch, 40, 292n74; use of term, xiii; white subjugation of, 48
Khoisan: arrival of Europeans and, 27; colonial legal system and, 29–30; extermination of, 48
kitskonstabels ("instant constables"), 64, 141–42, 146–47
Kolb, Peter, 27–28, 30, 289n17
Koornhof, Piet, 52
Kruger, Jimmy, 60
KwaMashu, criminals as police in, 160
KwaZulu-Natal: candidates for deputy judge president, 154–55; community safety forums in, 225; gangs in, 99; Inkatha and ANC clashes in, 276; police and post-apartheid interparty fratricide in, 143; political enforcement by police in, 71; on post-apartheid representation of, 72; violence in, 102

labor: black, apartheid and, 51, 56; black, exploitation of, 48, 49; black, Natives Urban Areas Act on, 42; black, regulatory controls over, 40; black, trade unionism and, 52; forced, British on inefficiency of, 31; forced, in Transvaal, 36; forced, Khoikhoi and slaves suits against, 32; forced, racial oppression and, 38–39; indigenous, Dutch use of, 29; organized, privatization concerns of, 18; protests as resistance to white rule, 45; racial domination and exploitation of, 24; slave, Dutch use of, 25, 26, 29; strikes, brutal punishments for, 42
labor market: criminal law as disciplinary tool, 48–49; macroeconomic policy and, 18–19; unemployment, AIDS and reform of, 17–18. *See also* capitalism
Landless People's Movement, 143–44, 257, 285
Landsdowne Commission, 53
Langa, Pius, 163, 174
Langalibalele affair (1874), 38
Latin America: criminal justice in, 12; oral trials in, USAID support for, 189; police and courts contribution to violence in, 182
law and order: apartheid police on Jesus Christ as king of, 53; Botha's total strategy for, 65–66; politics of, 188; post-apartheid planners on, 215; rule of, white South Africans on rule of law as, 276; segregation policy and brutality in, 44
law enforcement: discussion of alternative priorities for, 280–81; as maintenance of race relations in nineteenth century, 292n92; Mbeki on relationship between social service providers and, 270, 281–82, 323n87; repoliti-

cization and demilitarization, 124–26; repoliticization and demilitarization in South Africa, 140–48; vigilantes' view of assistance to, 279–80
Law Society for the Western Cape, 169
lawyers: British, appointed as colonial judges, 32; post-apartheid planning and, 4, 8; professional bodies of, judicial conduct standards and, 127; shortage of, 169; shortage of black and female, 173. *See also* legal profession; legal scholars; legal system
lay assessors: abandonment of, 234–35; characteristics and attitudes of, 231–32, 318n60; contradictory conceptions of role for, 235; enthusiasm for, 236; as familiar to government, 227–28; impact of, 237–38; lack of resources for, 218; late-apartheid introduction of, 226–27, 250, 318n43; magistrates' acceptance of, 234; magistrates' resistance to, 233–34, 277, 319n64; planners for, on demise of, 244–45; resources for, 234, 319n67; selection and use of, 230–31; in South African criminal trials, 217. *See also* juries; participatory citizenship
Legal Aid Board, 169
legal profession: English divisions in, 31–32; lay assessors and expertise of, 235–36; post-apartheid changes in, 8. *See also* lawyers
Legal Resources Centre, 169
legal scholars: CPFs planning and, 219. *See also* lawyers
legal system: apartheid, perceptions of legitimacy of, 5, 287n15; colonial, Khoikhoi and San interaction with, 29–30. *See also* lawyers
Leggett, Ted, 92, 262
legislation: on burden of proof in criminal cases, 253; creation and regulation of courts by, 127; interference in judicial decision-making through, 128; restrictions on jury trials through, 229
legislative supremacy. *See* parliamentary sovereignty
legitimacy: of criminal justice system, public-empowered justice programs and, 206–7; of judicial decisions, 127; lack of, for police, 66–67; of new regime, lay assessors and, 235–36; of new regime with new tasks for old operatives, 109; of police, 91; of post-apartheid courts, 154; of SAPS, CPFs and, 226; of violence by those liberating selves from violent state, 15
Le May, G. H. L., xiii
liberal democracy, deliberative democracy versus, 208, 213
liberation. *See* democratization/democratic transition
liquor laws: as crime prevention, 44; as formal restraint on blacks, 39, 292n69. *See also* alcohol
local divisions of Supreme Court: during apartheid era, 73; deference to security forces during 1980s by, 78–79
locations: for Africans in Natal, 37. *See also* homelands; townships
low policing: as screen for high policing under apartheid, 60; use of term, 59
Lula da Silva, Luiz Inacio, 131

macroeconomic policy: crime policy and, 267–68; labor market and, 18–19; market solutions for state problems with, 277–78; neoliberal, foreign financial coercion for, 267–68
Madison, James, 207
Madlanga, Mbuyiseli, 151
magistrates: acceptance of lay assessor program, 234; Afrikaners as, 75, 81; blacks and women as, 174, 307n36, 308n47; blacks appointed as, 73; British colonial, 32; historical versus current selection of, 150; on minimum sentences legislation, 254; on nonstate justice bodies, 239; post-

magistrates (*continued*)
  apartheid transformation in role of, 151; public opinion on crime control and decisions by, 88; resistance to lay assessor program by, 233–34, 244; on roles and functions during apartheid, 308n43; rule-making power under apartheid, 68; shifting constituencies for, 139–40. *See also* courts; independence, judicial
Magistrates' Act, 152–53
Magistrates' Commission, 152–53, 308n56
magistrates' courts: during apartheid, 73, 74; chaos in, due process and, 263; convictions in, 275, 324n11; demographic composition, 174, 175; difficulty in obtaining useful information from, 167; pace of cultural, institutional change in, 150; racial hostility in working environment of, 312n149; representation for defendants in, 169; segregation policy and, 45–46; service in high courts versus in, 151
Magistrates' Courts Amendment Act (1991), 227, 230
Mahomed, Ismail, 149, 174, 175
Mail and Guardian: rating of health minister for, 156; study on gangs in Cape Peninsula, 96–97
Maisels, I. A., 50
Malan, D. F., 53, 55
Malan, Magnus, 170–71
Mamdani, Mahmood, 134
Mandela, Nelson: Boesak trial and, 157; charges in Rivonia trial of 1963–64 against, 58; on consensual traditions of African communities, 243; on crime statistics, 87; on criminals and liberation, 109; criticism on crime control by, 85; on legal career, 173; on legal system legitimacy, 5; on properly controlled violence, 103; prosecution of, 4; Sharpeville massacre and, 57; South African Rugby Football Union investigation and, 155; on state respecting and enhancing freedom of others, 137; support for Malan case verdict and, 171; voting day in 1994 and, 2. *See also* ANC government
Mandela, Winnie, detention in 1969 of, 58, 295n42
Mandrax (methaqualone) sales, 96, 97
Maori, restorative justice among, 194
Mapogo a Mathamaga, 99, 279
Marenin, Otwin, 202
marijuana sales, 96, 97
Marks, Monique, 147–48
Mashele, Julia, 322n53
Mashiyane, Mduduzi, 220, 245
Masters and Servants Act, 24, 39, 40, 292n69, 292n73
maximum force, under Botha's total strategy, 65
Mazwai, Thami, 249
Mbeki, Thabo: on constitution of 1996, 4; crime control policies, 85, 257–58; on evolving act of self-definition, 10; focus on social roots of crime by, 270, 281–82, 323n87; law-and-order legislation under, 252; on need for "moral regeneration," 281; on reducing corruption and promoting democracy, 131; on sources of crime, 87, 88; on use of force against fleeing criminal suspects, 167. *See also* ANC government
MDMA (Ecstasy) labs, 96
Meadowlands-Diepkloof Taxi Association, 102
mediation: late-apartheid politics and introduction of, 226; as restorative justice, 192, 194; as social control in pre-European South Africa, 27; victim-offender, 196–97, 282; victim satisfaction with formal procedures versus, 210
mediation centers, use of term, 319n80
Meijer, Johannes, 159
men, African: apartheid and disempow-

erment of, 108; young, get-tough program effects on, 260, 271–72; young, late-apartheid educational vacuum, crime and, 109; young, vigilantes view of teaching moral definitions to, 280. *See also* domestic violence; gangs

Merton, Robert, 106

methamphetamine labs, 96

methaqualone sales, 96

Mexico, awards for journalists from, 133

migration. *See* emigration; forced removals; immigrants/immigration; urban migration

military: separation from police, 145–46, 307n29; shifting authority for policing power from, 124–26. *See also* army; demilitarization

Milner, Alfred, 24, 43

mines/mining: crime and migration to, 45; laws on Africans in, 43; Milner on natives in, 24; pass laws and, 41; police hired by, 63; strike of 1946, 52; whites' exploitation of blacks for, 48

moral community, vigilantes' re-creation of, 280

Moral Regeneration Summit, 88

Motshekga, Mathole, 240

Mozambique: police dog attacks (1998) on immigrants from, 9, 165; South African civil defense force and post-independence rebels in, 145

Mufamadi, Sidney, 222, 262

Mugabe, Robert, 114

murder: data on locations for, 97, 301n61; data since 1994 on, 91–92; by farm owners and managers, 100; lay assessors and trials for, 230; poverty, race, and incidence of, 98, 301–2n68. *See also* violent crime

Murray, Christina, 227, 245

Namibia, SAP units sent to, 63

Natal: African reserves in, 42; Bambatha rebellion (1906), 48, 293n109; black-on-black violence in, 67–68, 71; British annexation of, 35; British colonial merger with Cape Colony, 25; capitulation to racial repression in, 36–37; Code of Native Law, 37, 291n60; judicial appointments during apartheid in, 148; jury diversity in early twentieth-century, 229; masters and servants legislation in, 39; neglect of police response in, 61; parliamentary sovereignty in, 46–47; pass laws in, 40–41; self-regulation through chiefs courts in, 214; voting rights in, 43. *See also* KwaZulu-Natal

National Crime Combating Strategy, 257

National Crime Prevention Strategy (1996), 225, 269

national identity, nationalism versus, 7

National Management System, 144, 307n24

National Party: apartheid of, 3; electoral victory 1948 and start of apartheid era, 25, 294n9; on Freedom Charter, 4; police and courts under, 51. *See also* Afrikaners

National Peace Accord, SAP and ANC discussions as part of, 7–8

National Prosecuting Authority: asset forfeiture under, 255; blacks and women in, 173; as control of Scorpions, 261; economic crime, political corruption and, 258; professionalism as goal for, 217; sophisticated investigations under, 243

native(s), use of term, xiii

Native Administration Act (1927), 46

Native Affairs, Department of: English-speaking employees purged from, 54; other names for, 294n7; police hired by, 63

Native Affairs Commission, on racial separation, 42

Native Affairs Police, 42

Native law. *See* African law/tradition

Natives Land Act (1913), 43

Natives Urban Areas Act (1923), 42, 43, 45
Nattrass, Nicoli, 17–18
Navajos, restorative justice among, 194
Nazi organizations, Afrikaners and, 52–53
necklacing, as punishment by people's courts in townships, 68, 215
neighborhood watches, post-apartheid, 238, 319n79
Neild, Rachel, 94
Netherlands: crime statistics during 1990s in, 312n17; incarceration rates in, 322n49; police interrogations in, 182; private security in, 190
"(A) New Approach to Policing" (ANC), 219
New National Party, 85
Ngcuka, Bulelani, 143
NGOs (nongovernmental organizations): on benefits of planning for community policing, 225; CPFs planning and, 219; Egypt's limitations on, 114; on narrowed function of CPFs, 223–24; nonstate justice programs and, 241; observations of vigilante justice by, 280; on Regulation of Gatherings Act, 323n88
Nguni-speaking people, xiii; characteristics, 33–34; conflict resolution among, 33–34; cultural preservation among, 34–35
Nigeria: constitutional democracy and, 116; corruption as threat to democracy in, 130, 131; economy of, 19; Islamic law in, 115–16; military force and postauthoritarian chaos in, 126; organized crime syndicates in, 95; police as source of criminality in, 138; police brutality and torture in, 182, 312n10; rioting after press story on beauty contest in, 132–33; transformation of police in, 12
Nina, Daniel, 243
Nkosi, Lewis, 56–57

nonracial democracy, rejection of apartheid and, 1–2
nonstate justice: cooperation with state, 238–39; crime reduction as boost to foreign confidence through, 266; criminal justice operatives versus participant views of, 239–40; debates on state justice structures' relationship to, 240–41; post-apartheid structures for, police suspicion of, 217; proposals for state sponsorship and regulation of, 240; types of bodies, 238, 319n80; use of term, 319n76; Zwelethemba model of, 284
nonwhite(s), use of term, xiii
Northern Ireland: British response to community policing in, 201–2; Patten Commission on networks of policing nodes in, 204, 315–16n83
Nqakula, Charles, 269, 272
nullification, of court proceedings by juries, 228

Obansanjo, Olusegun, 130, 133
Omar, Dullah, 54, 148, 227, 262, 264
Omar case (1987), 79
Operation Crackdown: crime targets in, 259, 321–22n48; military involvement in, 145; police sweeps of, 226; SAPS' follow-up to, 269–70; under Selebi, 257; Tshwete's announcement of, 85
Operation Zealot, 144
opinion polls, deliberative, 208. *See also* public opinion
oral trials, USAID support for, 189
Orange Free State: juror requirements in, 229; masters and servants legislation in, 39; merger with British colonies, 25; parliamentary sovereignty of, 46–47; post–South African War black police in, 44; white domination in, 36; women's antipass campaign in, 41. *See also* Boer republics; Dutch settlers
Ordinance 50, 31, 40

organized crime, 19, 95–96; communities controlled by, 96–99; intelligence-led concentration on, 274; police participation in, 160; post-apartheid, 251; post-apartheid asset forfeiture and, 255–56
Ossewabrandweg, 52–53
"own areas" policy, 60; Africans policing own subordination under, 64

Pagad (People Against Gangs and Drugs), 98–99, 144, 280–81
Pan-Africanist Congress (PAC): as banned organization, 62; reconciliation with ANC, 145; Sharpeville massacre and antipass campaign by, 57; squatter struggles and, 67; Unlawful Organizations Act outlawing, 58; violent versus nonviolent tactics of, 103, 105
parliamentary sovereignty: apartheid and, 54; courts and, 74; judicial interpretations of 1980s states of emergency and, 78; ouster clauses and, 76; under South Africa Act, 46–47; vote case and, 75
parole boards, citizen participation in, 242, 282
participatory citizenship: community building and, 277–78; contributions in democratic countries by, 13; criminal justice paradigm assumptions and, 10, 190–93; divergent post-apartheid goals for, 216–17; future of, 242–45; group polarization and, 211; of police, 275; post-apartheid planners on, 8; public-empowering justice and, 197; regime change and, 250; responsibility for restorative justice and, 194; socially transforming logic of, 211–12; state role and responsibility in, 198; state's presumptions about budget savings from, 195, 205–6. *See also* citizens/citizenry; citizenship; community police forums; community policing; lay assessors

pass laws: under apartheid, 56–57; apartheid system of influx control and, 25; arrests in 1980s for violations of, 65, 299n139; as crime prevention, 44, 48–49; at end of South African War, 40–41, 292n74; as formal restraint on blacks, 39, 292n69; history of, 295n29, 295n32; irrelevance during nineteenth century of, 36; Ordinance 50 and, 40; requirements for women under, 73; resistance to, 41–42; sentencing for violations of, 81–82; under Union of South Africa, 43, 292n86. *See also* influx control laws
Paton, Alan, 88
Paton, Anne, 84
Patten Commission, 204, 315–16n83
Pauw, Jacques, 70
Peace Committees (Johnston and Shearing), 193; Code of Good Practice, 282–83, 324–25n32
PeaceMaking and PeaceBuilding, Zwelethemba model for, 282–83
Peel, Robert, 193–94
People Against Gangs and Drugs (Pagad), 98–99, 144, 280–81
people's courts. *See* community justice
performance legitimacy, criminal justice institutions and, 118
personal freedom: democratic governance and expectation of, 120; protection of expressions of, 121. *See also* civil liberties; individual rights
Peterson, Hector, 64
petty apartheid, judicial rejection of, 74
Pieres, J. B., 290n39
pigmentocracy: under apartheid, 75; use of term, 297–98n111
Pine, Benjamin, 38
plea bargaining: citizen responsibilities for deliberative participation and, 211. *See also* due process
Poland: democratic transition and increased crime in, 93–94; juries in, 228

police: Afrikaner composition of, 54; apartheid and judicial protection of, 79; apartheid and rights demanded by, 51; under British colonialists, 31; on citizen involvement in policing, 244; corruption, 61, 160–61, 162, 182, 250; crackdowns, as evidence of state strength, 265; crackdowns, post-1996, 256–58, 321n38; crime control during apartheid by, 90; crime prevention measures of, 217; as criminals, 100–101, 160, 310n90; cultural resistance to change by, 202; de Klerk's reforms of, 142; delivery of democracy and, 121; demise of CPFs and, 225–26; difficulties in reforming, 6; distancing effects of professionalism of, 274; effects on crime overall, 258–59; enforcement of laws enacted by democratic means, 124–26; integrity of, 130–31, 158–59; international assistance in training, 189; loss of legitimacy by, 66–67; national, development of, 44–45, 293n100; nonstate justice and, 238–39; "own areas" policy of, 60–61; Peace Committees and, 283; post-apartheid attitudes of, 147–48, 251; post-apartheid commitment to CPFs by, 219–20; post-apartheid deaths from shootings by, 165–66, 311n119; post-apartheid ineptitude of, 263; post-apartheid planners on communitarian methods for, 8; professionalism as goal for, 217, 226; public opinion on effectiveness of, 171–72; public opinion on incompetence or corruption of, 88; race of commissioned officers in, 9; racial subjugation under British and Afrikaner governments by, 26, 49; as regime enforcers, 113–15, 119; reluctance to invest in public-empowering policies, 242–43; separation from military, 145–46, 307n29; shifting constituencies for, 11–12, 119, 139; supplements to, 63–64; transformation and immediate reforms to, 5; violence against blacks under apartheid, 61–62. *See also* black police; public order; security police; South African Police; South African Police Service; vigilantes/vigilante groups

police-community relations: development of national police force and, 45; SAP commitment to, 218

Police Service Act (1995), 164, 222, 225–26

policing: as barometer for political development in sub-Saharan Africa, 140–41; high versus low, 59; private providers of, 181; redefinitions in post-apartheid era, 142–43; in sub-Saharan Africa, 288n20, 305n37. *See also* community policing

political institutions, access to and opportunity for representation in, 121

political parties: crime control issue and, 85–86; interracial, banning under apartheid of, 56. *See also specific parties*

political violence: criminal violence and, 89; decline in, 101–2, 302n92; transformation into social violence, 102–3. *See also* culture of violence

poll tax, 39, 292n69, 293n109. *See also* voting rights

popular justice: incorporation into formal South African justice system, 216; retributive justice and, 199; use of term, 319n76. *See also* vigilantes/vigilante groups

Population Registration Act (1950), 54–55

poverty: exhaustion of reformers from social chaos of democratic transition and, 243; legal aid and, 169; Mbeki's commitment to ending, 270; post-apartheid data on, 288n37. *See also* income gap; unemployment pre-apartheid justice, 23–49, 290n31; by British colonists, 31–42; segregation and, 42–48; by settlers, 26–31; slavery and, 24–25

press: concern for crime victims by, 170; foreign, on crime in post-apartheid South Africa, 86–87, 101; freedom of, transparency in democratizing countries and, 132; freedom of, under British colonialists, 290n33; Judicial Service Commission meetings and, 309n61; post-apartheid crime reports, 251; scrutiny of behavior by magistrates and police by, 140

Prevention of Organized Crime Act (1999), 255, 265

prisons: crime reduction and, 184; incarceration rates in various world regions, 188; overcrowding in South African, 259, 322n49; as preferred sanction for serious crime, 185, 313–14n31; transformation and immediate reforms to, 5

privacy: asset forfeiture and, 256; pluralizing responsibility and authority for, 14. *See also* civil liberties; human rights; individual rights

private security companies: for the affluent, 15, 274, 279; crime watches by, 101; criminal justice crisis and, 187; evictions of squatters on private property by, 257; informal justice versus, 319n76; for maintenance of public order, 114; participatory justice and, 193; post-apartheid, 238; as situational crime prevention, 190; state's reliance on, 273

privatization: of criminal justice system, as commodity, 14; of criminal justice system, participatory citizenship and, 195, 278; get-tough programs and, 266; as macroeconomic strategy, 18

problem-centered policing, 274

Proceeds of Crime Act, 255

Promotion of Bantu Self-government Act, 296n64

proportionality principle, use of force against fleeing criminal suspects and, 167

protests/protesters: labor, as resistance to white rule, 45; labor, in Bolivia, police brutality against, 114; Landless Movement, armed resistance of police against, 143–44; political, flogging for, 56; political, Operation Crackdown and, 257; Regulation of Gatherings Act and arrests of, 270; of women required to abide by pass laws, 292n90

provincial divisions of Supreme Court: during apartheid era, 73; deference to security forces during 1980s by, 78–79

public-empowering justice, 12, 179–213; for countries in transition from authoritarian regimes, 180–81; criminal justice crisis and, 181–87; deliberative democracy and, 207–12; democratic transition and, 200–207; directions for, 195–98; expectations of broader popular authority and, 285; experiments in, 179–80; limitations of, 198; lost opportunities from failure to implement, 276–81; policy shifts toward, 187–95; in South Africa, divergent goals for, 215–16, 288n27; South African constitutional development and, 14; top-down government and, 13; unintended consequences of, 199–200. *See also* participatory citizenship; *under* community building

public goods, democratic governance and expectation of benefits from, 120–21

public opinion: absolutist, on punishment and protection, 185, 313n23; Constitutional Court on need for constitutional adjudication and, 320n11; on law enforcement services and procedures, 209–10; South African, on core authority of state to regulate

public opinion (*continued*)
   behavior, 140, 306n8; South African, on crime, 84, 203, 299n8; South African, on crime, demographics of, 86; South African, on crime victims, 170
public order: citizen participation in maintenance of, 190–93; Dutch settlers' adjudication of, 28–29; Khoikhoi adjudication of, 27–28, 30; policing, at end of apartheid, 71; policing, citizen participation in vigilante groups and, 15; policing, SAP recruitment of township blacks for, 63; political complexity of crowd control and, 146–48; private security companies for maintenance of, 114; public yearning for mechanisms of, 115; state use of police in maintenance of, 140–41. *See also* police; social order
Public Safety Act (1953), 59, 68
punishments: increased severity of as evidence of state strength, 265; by Khoikhoi, 27, 28; by lay assessors versus magistrates, 232–33; public-empowered justice and retributive, 199; sieve effect of convictions, 258; symbolic effect of, 259–60; transformations in types of, 12. *See also* capital punishment
punitive populism, symbolic power of, 209

Rabie, Pieter, 8
racial minorities, political influence of, 13
rape: alcohol abuse and, 97; data since 1994 on, 91; judicial independence and post-apartheid sentencing for, 157–58; spread of AIDS and, 97–98
Rauch, Janine, 225, 244
"Ready to Govern" (ANC), 219, 320n90
reciprocity, in deliberative democracy, 208
Regulation of Gatherings Act, 147, 270

Reiner, Robert, 125–26
repoliticization, democratic, 143
representation, legal: Constitutional Court on right to a fair trial and, 168; constitution and Constitutional Court on, 164; constitution on substantial injustice and, 168–69, 311n137; regime change and, 250. *See also* counsel, right to
Representation of Natives Act (1936), 43
repugnancy clause, application under colonial and apartheid rule, 37, 214, 291n63
Reservation of Separate Amenities Act (1953), 55
reserves, for Africans in Natal, 37, 42. *See also* homelands; townships
resources: asset forfeiture to fund crime-fighting, 255–56; for constitutional protections of human rights, 164; for CPFs, 223–24; for crime prevention as private responsibility, 278; for judiciary, 152; for lay assessors program, 234, 319n67; for prison building and aggressive policing, 252; prospects for change and shortage of, 281; strain from public-empowering policies on, 243; for training and equipment for SAPS officers, 275
respect: for the community, CPF program and, 225; for general population, constituency shifting of democratization and, 118; group identity for African men and, 108; for judicial independence, 156–57; for justice system, by citizens, 131; by justice system for individual autonomy and rights, 115; for offenders, victim-offender mediation and, 191; for police, police corruption and, 162; by police of citizens, 137; public empowerment and, 12; state's, for citizens, 133; state's, for citizens, lay assessors and, 235; state's, for human rights, 120, 122, 143; state's, for human

rights, ordinary citizens on, 171–72; state's, for individual dignity, 213; state's, for rule of law, 285; state's, Mandela on freedom of others and, 137

restorative justice: commitment to constitutional norms of liberty and equality and, 12; economic factors in, 202–3; historical precedents for, 193–94; international spread of, 15; for juvenile offenders, 268; marginalization of, 241; post-apartheid projects for, 217; public involvement in social ordering and, 191–92, 314n51; responsibilities with, 194; sponsorship of, 242; state role and responsibility in, 198; strengthened community voice and, 199; as tradition of African communities, 7. *See also* public-empowering justice

"Restore the Jury? Or 'Reform? Reform? Aren't Things Bad Enough Already?'" (Kahn), 228

Retief, Piet, 33, 291n45

retributive justice: crime prevention as alternative to, 189; long sentences as, 170; nonstate justice versus, 239–40; against people reporting police abuses, 160; as political enforcement, 60; popular justice and, 199; public-empowering justice as alternative to, 194, 198; public-empowering justice as supplement to, 193; restorative justice as alternative to, 191–92; social chaos of postauthoritarian societies and, 202

Rhodes, Cecil John, 23

Rhodesia: SAP units sent to, 63; South African civil defense force and counterinsurgency in, 145. *See also* Zimbabwe

rights. *See* civil liberties; culture of rights; group rights; human rights; individual rights; voting rights

riot control, as civil war, 66

Riot Unit, during apartheid, 146–47

Robben Island, 31, 81

robbery, data since 1994 on, 90–91, 300n32

Roman-Dutch law, 29, 32, 37, 78

Romania, demilitarization and reduction of corruption in, 126

rule of law: as beacon for oppressed people, 116; as force for general emancipation or constraint on popular sovereignty, 285; among Nguni-speakers, 34; Sachs on market liberalization and, 266; Western standards for, indigenous traditions and, 250; white South Africans on rule of law and order as, 276

Russia: incarceration rates in, 188, 314n35, 322n49; juries in, 228; safety concerns in, 203

Rwanda, criminal justice system after civil war in, 204–5

Sabotage Act, detention laws and, 58

Sachs, Albie: on adjudication of social order by Dutch East India Company, 29; on apartheid justice, 58; on competence of Cape Colony judiciary, 46; on convictions for pass law offenses, 57; on execution of black man for rape of white woman, 80; on participation of tribesmen, 214; on potential public disruption of bail for violent defendant, 263; on relationships and attitudes formed under slavery, 289n3; in solitary confinement, 76–77

Sachs, Jeffrey, 266

Safety and Security Secretariat, 160, 275, 310n80

sanctioning sources, variations in authoritative, 135

San people: arrival of Europeans and, 27; colonial legal system and, 29–30; extermination of, 48

Sauer Commission, on African urbanization, 56

Schapera, Isaac, 34

Schärf, Wilfried: on community safety forums, 225; on incorporation of nonstate justice structures into state justice system, 241; on justice systems and needs of citizens, 214; on regime legitimacy and integration of nonstate structures into formal system, 213; on vigilantism and law enforcement response, 99, 319n78
Scheppele, Kim Lane, 129–30
Schmitter, Philippe, 134
Schönteich, Martin, 165
Schreiner, Olive, 44
Schumpeter, Joseph, 116
Scorpions (Directorate of Special Operations): blacks and women in, 173; convictions in cases prosecuted by, 275, 324n14; creation of, 257–58, 321n43; creation of versus other reforms, 263; Hofmeyr endorsement of, 261; sophisticated investigations and, 243
Section 29, on detention in solitary confinement, 58
Section 49, on use of force against fleeing criminal suspects, 166–67
sector policing, 269–70
security laws: Appellate Division interpretation of, 76–77; dissent and delinquency under, 58; Sharpeville massacre and, 57–58; states of emergency and, 295n43; summary of, 295n47. *See also* Internal Security Act
security police: court rulings during 1960s for, 77; de Klerk's dissolution of, 142; license to kill under states of emergency for, 68–69; political violence and, 71, 297n101. *See also* police
Seekings, Jeremy, 227, 229, 231–33, 234
segregation: development of, 42–49, 293n110; influence on current societal violence, 105; Natal Code of Native Law and, 37; of schools, judiciary on, 75. *See also* apartheid
Selebi, Jackie, 256–57, 260, 267

self-governance: citizen access to political institutions and, 121; criminal justice institutions as instruments of, 123; Dahl's advocacy for, 304n12; democratic governance and expectation for future of, 120
self-help, as tradition of African communities, 7
sentences/sentencing: under apartheid, race of the offender and, 80, 298n132; gentler approach to, 268–69; longer, for minor crimes, 181, 185, 188, 195, 314n37; magistrates and judges on mandatory minimum, 321n24; mandatory minimums, criticism of, 263; mandatory minimums, legislation on, 253–55; post-apartheid race-based, 250–51; procedural fairness in, 275
sentencing circles, 192, 204, 209
separate development policy: black magistrates under, 73; homelands and, 51, 62; homelands police forces and, 64; influence on current societal violence, 105; Verwoerd commitment to, 57
Separate Representation of Voters Act (1951), 75
separation of powers: degree of, in democratic countries, 305n46; judicial independence and, 127–28
sexual offenses courts, 275
Shaka (Zulu king), 35
Sharpeville massacre (1960), 51, 57, 62, 83, 141
Shearing, Clifford, 53, 179, 187, 193, 284
Shepstone, Theophilus, 36–37
shifting constituencies. *See* constituency shifting
Sierra Leone: repression by police and military in, 114, 303n4; rights and justice after war and violence in, 120
Simpson, Graeme, 82, 89, 107
situational crime prevention, 181–82, 189–90, 274, 314n45
slavery: British colonialism and end of,

31, 48; relationships and attitudes formed under, 289n3; seventeenth century, 24. *See also* Masters and Servants Act
slaves: Boers and right to sue masters under British colonial rule by, 32; Cape Colony treatment of crime by, 29
small claims court, late-apartheid introduction of, 226
Smuts, Jan, 43–44
social order: antiapartheid activists goals for citizen regulation of, 66; under apartheid, 52; democratic transformation and, 3; organization around, as community building, 277; post-apartheid capacity for regulation of, 106; post-apartheid planners on community participation in creation and maintenance of, 10; public-empowering justice and, 14, 276; regime enforcement versus regulation of, 113–14; self-government paradigm and Western models for, 123; South African, as criminogenic, 101. *See also* public order
South Africa Act (1909): parliamentary sovereignty under, 46–47, 293n103
South Africa Constitution Act (1951), 75
South African Act Amendment Act (1956), 76, 298n113
South African Constabulary, 44
South African Defence Force (SADF), 63, 65, 104, 145
South African Institute of Race Relations, 62–63
South African Law Commission (now South African Law Reform Commission): on antiterrorism bill, 86; enabling legislation, 306n6; planning for new constitution and, 138; proposal for "community forums," 241; on second tier of dispute resolution forums, 240; on terrorism legislation, 270; on Zwelethemba model, 284

South African Mounted Policemen, 293n94
South African National Defence Force (SANDF), 145–46, 307n29
South African Police (SAP), 293n94; adaptation from colonial to civil policing models and, 293n100; ANC discussions during National Peace Accord with, 8; black-on-black violence and, 71–72; civil defense force and, 145; counterinsurgency units sent to guard Namibia and Rhodesia, 63; development of, 44–45; political enforcement by, 61, 62–64, 296n63; reform challenges for transformation of, 141–42; SADF as supplement to, 65; secret death squads within, 69–70; separation of high and low policing by, 60; strategic plan on police-community relations, 218. *See also* police
South African Police Service (SAPS): blacks and women in, 173; choice of CPFs for community policing by, 220; community police forums and, 217; crime data of, 90–92, 300n32, 300n34, 300n39; demilitarization of, 144; dual commitment to sector policing and community problems by, 269–70; on fatalities as result of police action, 101; handling of white, right-wing extremism by, 144; legislation and official rhetoric on integrity of, 160; legitimacy of, CPFs and, 226; members convicted of crimes, 100; post-apartheid changes in, 8; priorities for, 317n9; professionalization challenges, 142; racial integration of, 143; reorganization (2000–2003), 257; repression of legitimate dissent by, 143–44, 307n19; role models for, 162; on use of force against fleeing criminal suspects, 166–67. *See also* police
South African Races Congress, 42
South African Republic. *See* Transvaal

South African Reserve Bank, 85
South African Rugby Football Union investigation, 155
South African War (1899–1902), 3, 25, 40–41
Soviet states, former: telephone justice in, 128, 150. *See also* Russia
Soweto: community police forums in, 318n38; ordinary crime increases under apartheid in, 62–63
Soweto Electricity Crisis Committee, 285
Soweto uprising: black resistance and, 64; black vigilante groups and, 51; riot squads of police divisions after, 146–47; SAP and, 141
Sparks, Allister, 3, 65, 148, 291n53
squatter communities: Operation Crackdown and, 257; police harassment and violence against, 67
state: ambivalence about nonstate justice, 239; central control as choice of, 244; contradiction of democratic principles by, 274; democratic justice function with public-empowered justice and, 122; nonstate cooperation with, 238–39; nonstate justice bodies and, 238; participatory justice initiatives and, 237–38; role in restorative justice programs of, 194–95; weaknesses in exercising power with and over society, 264. *See also* ANC government
State Security Council: Botha on, 65; National Security Management System, 66; states of emergency during 1980s and, 78
statutory laws, as formal restraints on blacks, 38–39, 292n69
Steytler, Nico, 69
stock thefts: by early settlers, 30, 88; execution by Dutch settlers for, 28; from farms in 1990s, 99; by indigenous people, 30, 33, 88; by Natal troops, 293n109; punishment for, race regulations and, 24; in twenty-first century, 289n6
street committees, 238, 239–40, 319n80
structural violence, democratic transformation and, 109
Sunstein, Cass, 210, 211
Suppression of Communism Act (1950), 57, 61
Supreme Court: during apartheid, 73, 150–51; British colonial, 32; human rights under apartheid and, 73–82; resistance to repression by, 74–75; for Union of South Africa, 46. *See also* High Court
Supreme Court of Appeal: on asset forfeiture law, 256; on Basson acquittal, 237; black chief justice for, 149; Boesak trial and independence of, 157, 158; demographic composition, 174, 175; integration of, 9; on minimum sentences legislation, 254; president of, 308n50; on sentence in rape case, 158. *See also* Appellate Division
Swazis: Afrikaner migration eastward and, 33–34; conflict resolution among, 34
symbolism: of crime in Western societies undermining faith in institutions of welfare state, 183; of get-tough programs, 259–61, 264, 271–72, 322n66
Tambo, Oliver, 173
taxi wars, 102, 107–8, 145, 160, 239
telephone justice, in former Soviet states, 128, 150
terrorism: proposed legislation on, 270, 323n90; urban violence viewed as, 86; U.S. State Department labels of, 281
Terrorism Act (1967), 58; conviction for criticism of, 299n136
Thompson, Dennis, 208
Thompson, Leonard, 35
thrashings: as private and summary justice by Afrikaners, 50; by vigilante groups, 279. *See also* flogging
Till, Emmett, 64

Tocqueville, Alexis de, 228
torture: Afrikaner objections to British abolition of, 31; of detainees during 1980s, 78–79; of farm tenants, 100; parents of political detainees in 1982 on, 65–66; by SAP, 69, 70; by SAPS, 165–66; as slave punishment by Dutch settlers, 29; validity of involuntary confessions and, 80
"total strategy," Botha's, 65
tot system, alcohol-induced crime and, 88, 97
tough on crime legislation. *See* get-tough programs
townships: under apartheid, 54; "own areas" policing in, 60; people's courts in, 215; residents on policing during apartheid in, 61; urban, zero-tolerance policing in, 10. *See also* homelands
trade, international, violent crime as deterrent to, 87
trade unions: black, 52. *See also* labor
traditional courts: use of term, 319n80. *See also* chiefs' courts; tribal courts
transformation: criminal justice and, 4–11; democratic euphoria of early 1990s and, 249; planning for, 3–4; punitive criminal justice program and, 271–72; structural violence and, 109; use of term, 2
Transkei, separate development and black magistrates in, 73
transnational crime: globalization and, 183, 186; police restructuring and reductions in, 275; South Africa's link to international law enforcement and, 183
transparency: comprehensibility of police procedures and, 274; constitutional democracy and, 116; criminal justice institutions as instruments of self-governance and, 123–24; democracy and, 131–33; in judicial appointments and discipline, 153–54; of judicial proceedings in democratizing countries, 127; lay assessors program

and, 236; public-empowering justice and, 197; regime change and, 250
Transparency International, 132, 161, 309–10n84
Transvaal: black crime concerns in, 44; blacks caught digging for gold in, 41; British annexation of, 35; convictions for pass law violations in, 56; Jameson raid on, 25–26; juries in, 229; masters and servants legislation in, 39; parliamentary sovereignty effects on courts in, 47; pass laws in, 40, 41; racial disparity in pre-union punishments in, 292n72; stability of courts in post–South African War turbulence in, 46; state-building and white domination in, 36; union with British colonies, 25; white takeovers of black property in, 292n73. *See also* Boer republics; Dutch settlers
travel industry, crime in South Africa and, 261, 274
Treatment Action Campaign, 156
Trengove, Wim, 237
trial courts. *See* magistrates' courts
tribal courts: under apartheid, 215; British authority superseding authority of, 46. *See also* chiefs' courts
tribes, use of term, xiii
trust: as challenge for police and CPFs, 224; in democratic process, deliberation and, 212; in Independent Complaints Directorate, 161; of natives, Europeans on, 23; nonstate adjudication of breaches of, 239; between police and citizens, 226, 273; of provincial officials, 162, 244; in South African political institutions, 273. *See also* distrust
Truth and Reconciliation Commission: apartheid victims testimony on torture and atrocities before, 66; judicial independence and accountability before, 124; magistrates and judges testimony on judiciary role in perpetuating apartheid, 167; restorative

Truth and Reconciliation Commission (*continued*)
justice tradition and, 15; sins of apartheid and, 10; testimony about death squads during, 69, 297n91; on voices of ordinary people shaping the future, 243
Tshabalala, Vuka, 154, 155
Tshwete, Steve, 85, 256, 260, 264, 281
Tutu, Desmond, 104, 157

Umkonto We Sizwe (Spear of the Nation), 103
unemployment: crime in communities and, 239; exhaustion of reformers from social chaos of democratic transition and, 243; gang recruitment and, 258; HIV/AIDS and, 17–18; post-apartheid data on, 288n40; public opinion and statistics about, 84–85. *See also* poverty
Union of South Africa: political color bar in constitution of, 43; unification of (1910), 25, 39
United Democratic Front (UDF): activities curbed by minister of law and order, 78; battles with Inkatha supporters, 67; Boesak and, 157; Botha's proposal for new constitution and creation of, 66; meetings banned for, 69; Vaal uprising (1984) and, 68
United Kingdom: community-oriented policing in North Ireland and, 201–2; crime prevention methods in, 190; pressure on South Africa as link in international law enforcement chain by, 265; restorative justice in, 192. *See also* British colonialists; British criminal law; British imperialism
United Nations: Code of Conduct for Law Enforcement Officials, on separation of police and military, 126; International Crime Victim Survey, 185; Office on Drugs and Crime, on drug trade in South Africa, 96; on organized crime, 95; pressure on South Africa as link in international law enforcement chain by, 265; Security Council's Universal Declaration of Human Rights, 134; surveys on behavior of criminal justice systems, 187–88, 314n34; World Summit on Sustainable Development, 257
United Party: Afrikaners on policies of, 52; election of 1948 and, 294n9
United States: Agency for International Development on crime effects on investment in South Africa, 266, 267–68; asset forfeiture problems in, 256; community policing in, 191; constitutional framers on public deliberation in politics in, 207–8; crime data in South Africa versus, 90, 300n31, 300n32, 301n46; crime in, 184, 313n18, 313n20, 313n21; crime prevention methods in, 190; criminal justice system in, 181; Drug Enforcement Administration's worldwide field offices, 188; get-tough programs as social policy reconstruction, 271; incarceration rates in, 322n49; independence of crime from criminal justice system in, 183, 312n15; justification of criminal charges to deport immigrants from, 115; police brutality in, 182; pressure on South Africa as link in international law enforcement chain by, 265; public opinion on poor people and criminal offenders, 183; restorative justice in, 192; sentencing in, 314n37; Terrorist Group Profiles, 281
Universal Declaration of Human Rights, 134
University of Cape Town, 55, 78–79
University of the Western Cape, Community Peace Programme of, 282
University of the Witwatersrand, 17, 55
Unlawful Organizations Act, 58
urban migration: apartheid policies and, 51, 52; legal limitations for Africans on, 55; Natives Urban Areas Act and,

42–43; Sauer Commission on, 56. *See also* pass laws
urban petty crime, recast as urban renewal, 269
urban terrorism, 86; terrorism legislation and, 270, 323n90. *See also* terrorism
Uys, Pieter-Dirk, 163

Vaal uprising (1984), 68
vagrancy laws: blacks caught digging for gold in Transvaal and, 41; Boers' justification for, 290n42, 290n43; British abolition of, 31, 32; migration deterrence and, 24
van der Spuy, Elrena, 224
van Niekerk, Barend, 299n136
van Riebeeck, Jan, 23, 29, 289n1
van Zyl Smit, Dirk, xi
Verwoerd, Hendrik, 50, 56, 57, 73, 296n64
victimization studies: by countries and UN, 185; on feeling safe, 85; increased feelings of crime and being unsafe in neighborhood, 273, 323–24n7; on recent decline in crime, 101; unreported crimes and, 91
victims/victimization: of apartheid, anger and suspicion of criminal justice institutions by, 216; constitutional acknowledgment of suffering from, 163; of crime, misunderstandings of criminal justice system operations by, 279; reluctance to participate in civic life and, 274; restorative justice and, 192; social divisions reinforced by, 110; worldwide crime policy variations and, 183–84, 312n17
vigilantes/vigilante groups: bail reform legislation and, 253; black, deputized by police, 63–64; citizen participation in maintaining neighborhood order and, 15, 319n78; corruption in police, judiciary and, 182; CPFs as defense mechanism for, 245; crime patterns, postauthoritarian policing and, 94; "criminal-friendly" South African constitution and, 172; criminal justice under democracy and, 7, 189; get-tough programs and symbolic approval of, 260; as impediment or benefit to public-empowering justice, 204–5; Mapogo a Mathamaga, 99, 279; Pagad, 98–99, 144, 280–81; police on crime control and potential increase of, 239; police participation in, 160; police use of, 64, 296n72, 314n39; population cynical about government's protective abilities and, 114, 263; post-apartheid, 238; post-apartheid, citizen support for, 251; prevention, 279–81; public opinion on, 185; radically democratic service ethic of, 280; taxi owners and, 107–8; use of term, 315n82; violence in poor communities and, 98–99; Zwelethemba model as alternative to, 284
violent crime: apartheid and, 88–89; in context of ideology and structure, 102–8; data since voting day in 1994 on, 90–92, 300n30; drop in recent years of, 101–2; historical patterns of, 83–84; against journalists in democratizing countries, 132–33; as national problem, 19; normalization of, 83, 98; post-apartheid data on, 93, 94–95; prevention and management of, 9–10; as public relations problem, 261–68. *See also* crime; culture of violence; rape; terrorism
violent state model, 15
Vlakplaas (death squad), 70, 71, 104–5, 162, 297n94
Voortrekkers, 40. *See also* Natal
voting day in 1994: data on violent crime since, 90–92; Gordimer and Mandela on, 2; political violence among African groups after, 72. *See also* ANC government

voting rights: under apartheid, 55; for black South Africans under apartheid, Appellate Division and, 75; for property-owning blacks under British colonial rule, 35, 291n54; in Union of South Africa, 43; whites' denial for blacks of, 48. *See also* civil liberties; poll tax

Walker, Eric, 28–29, 290n33
warrants: arrests without, detention laws under apartheid and, 5–6, 58; searches without, under apartheid, 62
watershed, use of term, 312n6
Welsh, David, 37
Wessels, Johannes Wilhelmus, 48
Western criminal justice: adherence in South Africa to model of, 218; foreign government funding for CPF model and, 220; outcome of African tradition of criminal incident intervention versus outcome of, 216; rule of law, indigenous traditions and, 250
Western liberal traditions, constituency shifting paradigm and, 123
Westminster, Statute of, legislative supremacy of British Parliament over South African courts and, 75
whipping. *See* flogging
"White Paper on Safety and Security" (1998), 222–23
witches/witchcraft: British prohibition on ritual killings and punishment for, 46; colonizers versus Africans on punishments for, 38; nonstate justice on, 319n80; repugnancy laws on, 214; traditional law on, 7, 28
women: apartheid and violence by intimate partners against, 108, 303n120; chiefs courts treatment of, 239, 241; on criminal justice system indifference to rape and domestic violence, 182; enforcement of pass laws applied to, 292n90; indigenous values, community decision-making, and oppression of, 200; judicial appointments of, 149, 307n36, 308n47; police restructuring and reductions in violence against, 275; political influence of, 13; in post-apartheid criminal justice system, 172–75. *See also* rape
workers: political influence of, 13. *See also* labor
World Bank, 266, 267
World Economic Forum's Global Competitiveness Report, 266
World Summit on Sustainable Development (2002), 143–44, 270
World War II: Afrikaners and, 52–53; Afrikaners incarcerated during, National Party's 1948 election and, 54

Xhosa: Afrikaner migration eastward and, 33–34; conflict resolution among, 34; missionary influences on, 35; pass laws and, 40

yard committees, use of term, 319n80
Yizo, Yizo (television program), 280
young people: African communities on autonomy for, 7; chiefs courts treatment of, 241; male, get-tough program effects on, 260, 271–72; male, late-apartheid educational vacuum, crime and, 109; male, vigilantes view of teaching moral definitions to, 280. *See also* gangs

zero-tolerance policing, 10, 187, 188, 199. *See also* get-tough programs
Zimbabwe: judicial harassment in, 128, 156, 309n76; political repression in, 114. *See also* Rhodesia
Zulu: Afrikaner migration eastward and, 33–34; conflict resolution among, 34; drought and brutal rulers of, 35–36; massacre assisted by police in Boipatong, 72
Zwelethemba model, for PeaceMaking and PeaceBuilding, 282–83